European Community Social Policy
Its Impact on the UK

Dr Chris Brewster is Senior Lecturer in Industrial Relations and Personnel at the Cranfield School of Management which he joined in January 1985. Prior to this he worked for a major trade union, for the Commission on Industrial Relations, a specialist Industrial Relations magazine and Industrial Relations Law Reports. He has also worked in personnel in the construction and air-transport industries.

Dr Brewster has acted as a consultant to UK and international organisations, mainly in the areas of personnel policies and management training. His written work includes *Understanding Industrial Relations* (1984), *Cost Effective Strategies in Industrial Relations* (1985) and numerous articles on personnel policy.

Dr Paul Teague studied Economics at the University of East Anglia and Queens University, Belfast, and Industrial Relations at the London School of Economics. He is the author of several publications on labour and employment affairs in the European Community.

He is currently a Fulbright Scholar at the Southeastern Massachusetts University, teaching about European employment policies.

European Community Social Policy

Its Impact on the UK

Chris Brewster and Paul Teague

Institute of Personnel Management

First published 1989

Phototypeset by Paragon Photoset, Aylesbury
and printed in Great Britain by
Dotesios Printers Ltd, Bradford-on-Avon, Wiltshire

British Library Cataloguing in Publication Data

Brewster, Chris
European Community social policy: its impact on the UK.
1. Great Britain. Social services. Government policies. Implications of policies of European Community
I. Title II. Teague, Paul
361'1'0941

ISBN 0-85292-408-9

Contents

Foreword

As 1992 approaches, and with it the Single European Market, the European Community is becoming ever more important for British industry and commerce. Managers have a clear and growing need for information and guidance about the challenges and opportunities that Europe offers. In particular, members of the personnel profession – and many other people – require an authoritative understanding of how EC social policy has developed, the impact it has already had in the UK, and the likely prospects for the future.

It was with this in mind that the Institute of Personnel Management's International Committee selected the Cranfield School of Management to conduct the research for this book. Since it is a joint project, the authors were guided by a Steering Committee composed of representatives of both bodies. We hope that the result will prove useful for all British companies doing business in Europe, and required reading for all conscientious and forward-looking personnel managers.

W H Robbins
Chairman of the Project Steering Group
IPM Vice President – International, 1983–8

Acknowledgements

The book would not have been possible without the help of many people. Bill Robbins, in particular, originated the project on which the book is based, obtained funding and was a continual source of expertise and advice. He was ably backed by a Steering Committee drawn from the IPM International Committee and representatives of all the Institute's other national committees. (Although they made a significant contribution to guiding the project and commenting on research, however, the views and conclusions expressed in this book are the authors' alone and do not necessarily coincide with those of every Steering Committee member.)

Information, support and help were generously provided by a large number of people, whom we cannot mention by name, in the Commission of the European Community, in several British Government departments and in a wide range of pressure groups, employers' organisations and academic institutions. Although nameless here, we are grateful to them all.

We would also like to thank the twelve major companies and organisations – the Beecham Group, British Gas, British Telecom, Grand Metropolitan, IBM, Marks & Spencer, the Post Office, Rio Tinto Zinc, Shell UK, Tate & Lyle, the Wellcome Foundation and a company which wished to remain anonymous – for their help in financing the project.

Finally, we owe a special debt to Sarah Atterbury, Michele Sheehan and other colleagues at Cranfield School of Management who undertook the difficult task of creating something legible from our script.

This text was prepared in 1988. In a fast-moving area, references to such bodies as the Manpower Services Commission (which became first the Training Commission and then the Training Agency) may be outdated. Nevertheless, these are peripheral matters and do not alter the substantive analysis in the text.

Chris Brewster and Paul Teague

Chapter I

Introduction

The purpose of this book is to detail the nature and extent of European Community influences on the British employment environment. This study was considered important for several reasons. In the first place, although many references are made to the fact that the Community appears to have a significant influence on the employment environment in individual member states, no detailed study has so far been undertaken to assess whether this is actually the case and, if it is, the importance of these influences. Furthermore, this study is particularly interesting in relation to Britain, for not only is its employment environment highly distinctive in comparison with those of other member states, but also the question of the extent to which the EC should be allowed to influence British economic and political practice has been highly controversial. Finally, as the Community is making a major effort to complete the internal market by 1992 to revitalise the European ideal, some insight will be gained into what role EC social policy may play in this project.

It is necessary to start by placing the study in its proper context, namely the growing influence of international factors on national employment policies and practices. This is the theme of this introductory chapter. International influences take many forms and are mediated through different processes and mechanisms. The chapter identifies and assesses different sorts of international influence on employment policies and practices in Britain: spontaneous market-driven influences, technological influences, horizontal influences and vertical influences. It argues that these are all important and in some way interconnected.

Market-driven Influences

The first way international issues can affect the national employment environment is through spontaneous market-driven influences. As commercial and business activities have become more integrated on a world scale company managers are increasingly facing similar commercial pressures. The need to restructure in the face of saturated markets or the need to innovate to avoid falling behind competitors is as great in France, Italy, the USA and Japan as it is in Britain. This convergence of market pressures has given rise to similar corporate strategies – including personnel policies – across frontiers.

Take, for instance, the crisis in the European steel industry during the late seventies/early eighties.[1] No western European country was spared the impact of this crisis in chronic over-capacity and the personnel policies devised to deal with the problem bore a striking resemblance across national boundaries. They included: (i) major redundancy programmes: the result of which was the reduction of the European steel workforce by two fifths – in the United Kingdom between 1974 and the summer of 1983 steel industry employment fell from 194,500 to 67,400; in West Germany from 232,000 to 168,000; France 157,800 to 92,400; Belgium 63,700 to 40,000; and Luxembourg 23,500 to 11,700; (ii) wage cuts (in 1981 at the Dalmine, Logne and Piombino plants in Italy and in Belgium in 1983) or wage freezes (as in West Germany in 1983 and the United Kingdom in 1982 and 1983) or increases below the national average or the current inflation rate (almost everywhere after 1979); (iii) decentralised wage bargaining to plant or regional level (as in the United Kingdom, West Germany and Italy); (iv) more flexible work practices and the progressive elimination of demarcation lines; (v) greater discipline on the shopfloor and measures to reduce absenteeism.

The automobile industry serves as another example. Until the early seventies, the world car industry enjoyed a virtuous circle of growth. Markets grew steadily, allowing for even longer production runs which enabled manufacturers to introduce new, more efficient product-specific machinery. The resulting reductions in production costs encouraged further expansion of the market. However, the oil price shocks in 1973 and 1979, and increasing international competition as domestic markets became saturated, led to pressure to cut production and to increase the quality of the standard models. Although the degree of subsequent car import penetration has at times been overestimated, the new international competitive climate did lead to market segmentation. This segmentation coupled with increased price competition has meant that car companies, irrespective of their national location, have been under pressure to introduce new flexible forms of work, particularly with the widespread introduction of new manufacturing technologies. As a result, labour strategies within the international automobile industry have been converging around a fixed set of issues, commonly referred to as the 'co-operative model' of industrial relations.[2]

The Technological Factor

A second factor opening up national employment environments to international influences is the large-scale diffusion of new technology in a variety of economic sectors. It has long been understood that technological change, through its impact on the economics of production and distribution, and on the flow of information, is a principal factor determining the structure of industry on a national scale. This has now become true on a global scale. Long-term technological trends and recent advances are reconfiguring the location, ownership and management of various types of productive activity among countries and regions. The increasing ease with which technical and market knowledge, capital, physical artifacts, and managerial control can be extended around the globe has made feasible the integration of economic activity in many separated locations.[3]

This trend, and new forms of international investment, is probably most pronounced in the distributive trades. A good example is the Italian clothing firm Benetton. Their clothes are made by 11,000 workers in Northern Italy, only 1,800 of whom work directly for Benetton. The rest are employed by sub-contractors in factories of 30-50 workers each. The clothes are sold through 2,000 tied retail outlets, all of them franchised. Benetton provide the designs, control material stocks, and orchestrate what is produced according to the computerised daily sales returns which flow back to their Italian headquarters from all parts of Europe. Similar systems are at the heart of the success in the UK of the 'new wave' clothiers, such as Next and Richards shops.

Central to this system of production is the use of new technologies. New flexible all-purpose machinery is used to produce a variety of products. Computers have been applied to design, cutting down waste and stock control. Distribution has been revolutionised, as has the link between sales, production and innovation. This establishment of single integrated systems of production and distribution has permitted the break up of large factory complexes and the creation of a new employment system. At its extreme, it is argued that this divides the workforce into a central core, with the related corporate welfare systems, high skill levels and jobs for life; and a peripheral workforce employed for the most part by sub-contractors or on a casual or part-time basis. This is but one example of how new technologies are having a direct impact on national and international employment environments. If anything, the effect of technological advances on company employment and industrial relations systems is still in its infancy.[4]

Horizontal Influences

The third way national employment environments can be affected by international factors is through horizontal influences. To a large extent, horizontal influences refer to the role played by multinational corporations (MNCs) in the world economy. Multinationals may influence national employment environments through their labour utilisation strategies. One common way is to establish international forms of labour-market segmentation by pursuing a variety of stratification policies. Thus, British publishing companies, for example, often have the physical printing process carried out in the cheap labour conditions of the Far East, whilst retaining the more specialised editorial work in the UK. It has been argued that MNCs have been at the forefront of creating a new international class structure comprised of a transnational managerial class, an established labour class and social marginals.[5] A related but perhaps a more convincing thesis is reflected in the publishing example. It is argued that MNCs centralise control and innovatory functions within the advanced (core) nations and assign production and assembly operations to less developed (peripheral) economies.[6]

The type of investment made by a multinational in a host country also has a significant bearing on the national employment environment. If an MNC opens a plant with considerable research and development potential as well as extensive production capabilities, then the impact will be more favourable in terms of generating a demand for skilled labour than if it only establishes an assembly operation which will require a relatively non-skilled workforce. Furthermore, the extent of the wider internal employment benefits arising from an international investment project largely depends on whether the MNC pursues a cross-border or national sub-contracting strategy. Obviously, if an MNC obtains its intermediate goods and services from local suppliers then more employment will be generated than if these were imported.[7]

Finally, MNCs can affect national employment environments by influencing the industrial relations policies of indigenous companies. Although by no means automatic, a multinational investing abroad may decide to export its existing employment policies and industrial relations practices. At the outset these policies and practices may well be 'foreign' to indigenous businesses but after some time, if the merits of these practices become apparent, local companies may begin to replicate them. For example, Taylorist and 'Fordist' production techniques were introduced into less developed countries by MNCs.[8] An example from Britain is the so called 'Japanisation' of British industrial relations. Japanese subsidiaries in Britain have widely varying personnel practices and tend not to introduce a fully-fledged Japanese system of employee relations. Nevertheless, the personnel policies and arrangements of these subsidiaries are different in several important respects from those which generally prevail in indigenous British factories. In particular, much more emphasis is placed on establishing job flexibility, promoting corporate culture through a variety of welfare schemes, and avoiding extensive formal bargaining with trade unions. It has been found that the majority of Japanese subsidiaries in Britain had been visited by managers of British companies to see if they could learn from so-called Japanese managerial techniques and procedures.[9]

Another potential source of international influence on national employment environments is the trade union movement. During the late sixties/early seventies the unions anticipated that international forms of collective bargaining would develop inside multinational corporations, and possibly other extra-national institutions (e.g. the EC).[10] Subsequent history has shown that this has not happened. Obviously the deep economic crisis in the world during the seventies was a major reason for the fact that few significant developments occurred on this front. The international trade union action that did take place was often disjointed and ineffectual. Thus it would be a mistake to overestimate the influence trade unions have at the international level. At the same time, it would be wrong to conclude that they have no influence whatsoever. In recent years, signs have emerged that a type of international trade union transmission mechanism has opened up in which developments in one country can affect developments in another. Thus the strike of the German trade union, I G Metall, in 1984 in support of its claim for a 35-hour week, undoubtedly contributed to similar pressures to reduce working time in Spain, France and Italy.[11] If the economic situation gets better within Western Europe, then this mechanism could come more to the fore.

Vertical Influences

The phrase 'vertical influences' refers to the impact of international organisations on national employment environment. Several such bodies exist; the discussion here will be restricted to the most directly relevant bodies. These are:

- the International Labour Organisation (ILO)
- the Organisation for Economic Cooperation and Development (OECD)
- the European Social Charter
- the European Community

The International Labour Organisation

Formed in 1919 within the framework of the Versailles Treaty, the ILO was recognised in 1946 as the first specialised body of the United Nations.[12] Since that time, its membership has grown from 58 to over 150. The main work of the ILO relates to the establishment of international labour standards which it defines as 'standards concerning employment and working conditions found acceptable by labour and management through collective bargaining and by the legislator through labour laws and regulations.' They comprise (a) Conventions, which not only set standards of achievement but also, when ratified, create binding international obligations for the countries concerned (in relation to Britain, however, conventions which are signed by a government carry no force in law as international treaties do not enter British statutes unless an Act of Parliament stipulates otherwise): and (b) Recommendations, which are not binding. Since 1919, the ILO conference has adopted 159 conventions and 168 recommendations. Most of the conventions adopted relate to matters of universal interest, such as freedom of association, forced labour, the protection of women and young workers, the search for employment, safety and hygiene at work, hours of work and paid vacations. Recent statistics indicate the average number of ratifications per state in the various regions – Europe: 57 (Western Europe: 60, Eastern Europe: 50); Americas: 38; Africa: 28; Asia and the Pacific: 20. Of particular interest here is the record of EC member states in ratifying and complying with international labour standards. Although the record of the EC member states compares very favourably with that of the other member countries of the ILO, there are considerable variations. Table Ii shows ratifications by member states.

It can be seen from the table that since 1970 Spain has been the most active supporter of ILO conventions, catching up and then overtaking other member states. On the other hand, Luxembourg ratified few conventions. Furthermore, since the early 1980s, only a select few member states have ratified conventions. This appears to be the most significant trend in recent years. For instance, whereas 21 ILO conventions were concluded between 1970 and 1978 and were the subject of 125 ratifications by the member states of the Community, only ten conventions were concluded between 1979 and 1985 and were the subject of 13 ratifications by the member states, including 7 by Spain.

Since 1980, seven conventions have been denounced by the member states; these are shown in Table Iii. Luxembourg, for instance, denounced two conventions in 1980: Nos 4 and 89 concerning night work (women); Ireland also denounced two conventions in 1980, No 20 on nightwork bakeries and No 89 on night work (women). Lastly, the United Kingdom denounced three conventions: in 1982, No 94 on labour clauses (public contracts), providing protection for low-grade employees; in 1983, No 95 on the protection of wages, which provides basic guarantees as regards remuneration; and in 1985, No 26 on minimum wage fixing machinery. The three conventions denounced by the United Kingdom had not been ratified by every other member state. Thus, convention No 26 on minimum wage fixing machinery has not been ratified by either

Table Ii ILO Conventions Ratified by Member States of the EC between 1970 and 1985

MS	Total Ratif 1970 1985	Total Ratif pre 1970	131	132	133	134	135	136	137	138	139	140	141	142	143	144	145	146	147	148	149	150	151	152	153	154	155	156	157	158	159	160	161
B	2	7														X			X														
D	14	12		X	X	X	X	X		X	X	X	X	X		X			X			X		X									
DK	11	11				X	X				X		X	X		X			X		X	X	X								X		
E	24	36	X	X		X	X	X	X	X		X	X	X		X	X	X	X	X		X	X	X	X	X	X	X	X	X			
F	16	14	X		X	X	X	X	X			X	X	X		X	X	X	X	X	X			X									
GB	10	4			X		X					X	X	X		X			X	X		X	X										
GR	6	13				X		X								X			X			X									X		
IRL	4	7		X						X				X		X																	
I	19	15		X	X	X	X	X	X	X	X		X	X	X	X	X	X	X	X	X	X	X										
L	3	2		X			X			X																							
NL	13	7	X		X		X		X	X		X	X	X		X	X	X	X			X											
P	16	20	X	X			X		X					X	X	X	X	X	X	X	X	X	X				X	X					

54th Session (1970)
131 Minimum Wage Fixing
132 Holidays with Pay (rev)

55th Session (1970)
133 Accommodation of Crews (Supplementary provs.)
134 Prevention of Accidents (Seafarers)

56th Session (1971)
135 Workers' Reps.
136 Benzene

58th Session (1973)
137 Dock Work
138 Minimum Wage

59th Session (1974)
139 Occupational Cancer
140 Paid Educational Leave

60th Session (1975)
141 Rural Workers' Orgs.
142 Human Resources Devmnt.
143 Migrant Workers (supplementary provs.)

61st Session (1976)
144 Tripartite consultation (Intern. Labour Standards)

62nd Session (1976)
145 Continuity of Employment (Seafarers)
146 Seafarers' Annual Leave with pay
147 Merchant Shipping (minimum standards)

63rd Session
148 Working Environment (Air pollution, noise, vibration)
149 Nursing Personnel

64th Session (1978)
150 Labour Administration
151 Labour Relations (Public service)

65th Session (1979)
152 Occupational Safety and Health (Dock work)
153 Hours of Work and Rest Periods (Road Transport)

67th Session (1981)
154 Collective Bargaining
155 Occupational Health and Safety
156 Workers with family responsibilities

68th Session (1982)
157 Maintenance Social Sec. rights
158 Termination of Employment

69th Session (1983)
159 Voc. Rehabilitation and Employment (Disabled)

71st Session (1985)
160 Labour Statistics
161 Occupational Health Services

Table Iii International Labour Standards ratified by several Member States of the EEC but subsequently denounced by one or more of them

Convention no	Subject and year of adoption	Ratification by MS indicating year in which ratification took place											
		B	D	DK	E	F	GB	GR	IRL	I	L	NL	P
6	Night work of young persons (industry) 1919	1924		1923	1932	1925	1921*	1920	1925	1923	1928	1924^{+}	1932
90	Night work of young persons (industry) revised, 1948				1971	1985		1962		1952	1958	1954	
4	Night work (women) 1919	1924^{+}			1932	1925^{+}	1921^{+}	1920^{+}	1925^{+}	1923	1928^{+}	1922^{+}	1932
41	Night work (women) revised 1934	1937^{+}				1938^{+}	1937*	1936^{+}	1937^{+}			1934^{+}	
89	Night work (women) revised 1948	1952			1958	1953		1959	1952^{+}	1952	1958^{+}	1954^{+}	1964
20	Night work (breweries) 1925				1932				1937*		1928		
26	Minimum wage fixing machinery 1928	1937	1929		1930	1930	1929*		1930	1930	1958	1936	1959
43	Sheet glass workers 1934	1937				1938	1937*		1939				
88	Employment Service 1948	1953	1954	1972	1960	1952	1949*	1955	1969	1952*	1958	1950	1972
94	Labour clauses (public contracts) 1949	1952		1955	1971	1951	1950*			1952		1952	
95	Protection of wages 1948	1970			1958	1952	1951*	1955		1952		1952	1983

+ – denunciation as a result of the ratification of subsequent revising conventions and thus merely involving a substitution of obligations
* – 'genuine' denunciation leading to the termination of obligations

Denmark or Greece; convention No 94 on labour clauses (public contracts) has not been ratified by Ireland, Luxembourg, West Germany, Greece or Portugal and convention No 95 on the protection of wages has not been ratified by Ireland, Luxembourg, West Germany or Denmark. The pattern of denunciation by member-states is shown in Table Iii.

The OECD Multinational Guidelines

The Organisation for Economic Cooperation and Development is another international institution which has a role in employment and labour affairs. This role was established when the Council of Ministers of that body adopted the OECD guidelines for multinational enterprises in 1976. These guidelines were established as a result of the publicity given to alleged malpractices on the part of some MNCs in the early seventies, and the continual trade union lobbying and pressure for such a code of practice.[13] The guidelines cover seven areas: general policies, disclosure of information, competition, finance taxation, science and technology, employment and industrial relations. The last section is the most relevant here, and is included as Appendix 9.

Although the guidelines were conceived as only voluntary, the trade union organisation inside the OECD – the Trade Union Advisory Committee (TUAC) – lost no time in testing their effectiveness. For example in 1977, TUAC brought the celebrated 'Badger Case' to the OECD's International Investment and Multinational Enterprise Committee. They wanted that Committee to examine alleged infractions by individual companies and give an interpretation of the guidelines so that precedents could be established. After strong protests from the employers' Business and Industry Advisory Group (BIAC) the Committee refused to give such an interpretation. This ruling meant that the guidelines were not enforceable and a body of test-case precedents could not be established. In the eyes of the trade unions, this significantly diluted the guidelines. The TUAC stated 'those who argue that the voluntary guidelines work well, and that thus there is no need for more binding rules . . . have not recognised the extent of the infringements of the guidelines by the enterprises'.[14]

Since they were first introduced, the guidelines have undergone several reviews. For example, as a result of a review conducted in 1979, National Contact Points were established by all member countries, to disseminate, explain and promote the guidelines, as well as collect information relating to their operation. In 1984, another review took place. The main outcome of this review was the clarification of some individual clauses in the guidelines. For instance, important clarifications were made to the use of a national language when dealing with employees, and it was especially stated for the first time that employees are entitled to more specific information than the public at large. Overall, the guidelines have not had a major impact on the conduct and behaviour of multinationals in the empoyee relations field. One commentator concludes 'although enforcement procedures were not used and are non-existent, the guidelines have had a net, if limited, impact on international industrial relations'.[15] MNCs, however, argue that the guidelines merely incorporated the prevailing good practice of most multinationals and that the instances of infraction, much quoted by the unions, are isolated exceptions.

The European Social Charter

In current discussion about the future direction of EC social policy, one proposal is for the clauses of the European Social Charter to form the basis of a new European Social Constitution. Thus it may be worthwhile to examine the charter in detail.

The European Social Charter was signed by thirteen of the member states of the Council of Europe in Turin on October 18th 1961.[16] It is conceived as the counterpart to the 1950 European Convention on Human Rights. While the convention protects civil rights, the charter deals with social rights, nineteen in total. Rights:

- to work
- to just conditions of work
- to safe and healthy working conditions
- to a fair remuneration
- to organise
- to bargain collectively
- to the protection of children and young persons
- of employed women to protection
- to vocational guidance
- to vocational training
- to protection of health
- to social security
- to social and medical assistance
- to benefit from social welfare services
- to vocational training, rehabilitation and social resettlement for phsyically disabled persons
- an equivalent right for the mentally disabled
- of the family to social, legal and economic protection
- to engage in a gainful occupation in the territory of other contracting parties
- of migrant workers and their families to protection and assistance.

The rights are first listed in brief and general terms in Part 1 of the charter. Then each right is taken separately, in the order indicated above, in one of the nineteen articles of Part II and made the subject of a number of legal undertakings.

As many of the rights only paralleled standards set by the conventions and recommendations of the ILO, the charter was not regarded at the time as a far-reaching document. The charter does not guarantee rights directly. Instead, the contracting member states give undertakings which are expected to lead to the 'effective exercise' of the right concerned. This approach is significantly different from that adopted in the 1950 Human Rights Convention, where the contracting parties undertake directly to 'secure to everyone within their jurisdiction the rights and freedoms defined' (in the convention) (Article 1 1950). The reason for the distinction appears to be that a number of social rights cannot be made the subject of an absolute guarantee.

Although the charter laid down only two basic undertakings, these are somewhat complicated. In the first place, a contracting member state must 'undertake to consider Part 1 of the Charter as a declaration which it will pursue by all appropriate means' (Article 20 (i) (a)). Secondly, it must undertake to consider itself bound in their entirety by at least ten of the nineteen articles which made up Part II of the charter. In addition, a contracting party must accept in their entirety at least five out of seven specified articles. The result of this complicated scheme is that a member state need accept only between half and two-thirds of the substantive undertakings of the charter.

The system devised to supervise the operation of the charter is based upon the submission of reports by the contracting parties. Two kinds of reports are required. First, the contracting parties must make a report every two years concerning the application of the substantive undertakings they have accepted as binding. Second, they must send, at appropriate intervals, as requested by the Committee of Ministers of the Council of Europe, reports relating to some or all of those undertakings which have not been accepted. These reports are examined first by a Committee of Experts. After examining the reports, this committee draws up its conclusions which are submitted, together with the reports of the member states, to a sub-committee of the Government Social Committee of the Council of Europe. This sub-committee, composed of one representative of each member state, examines and drafts its own conclusions which are sent, in company with the conclusions of the Committee of Experts, to the Committee of Ministers for its consideration. This is the final stage and the Committee of Ministers can make 'any necessary recommendations' to the relevant member states.

This is not a judicial system of supervision. The recommendations of the Committee of Ministers are not binding upon the member state. In addition, there are no sanctions which are binding on a member state if it refuses to conform to the recommendation. The worst that can theoretically happen to a member state if it persistently and openly flouts the articles of the charter is expulsion from the Council.

It has been argued that the Social Charter has impinged on British labour legislation in a number of ways.[17] For instance Article 8 (1) of the charter on paid leave for women employees before and after child-birth is the source for Articles 33–5 of the Employment Protection (Consolidation) Act, 1978. And as a result of pressure from the Committee of Experts, Britain dissolved arrangements with Denmark, the Federal Republic of Germany and the Netherlands and Greece for the surrender of merchant seamen deserters – a specialised form of extradition. On a number of occasions Britain has been found to be in breach of a number of charter obligations. In 1981 it was found guilty of failing to provide adequate minimum periods of notice for workers dismissed with under two years' employment. Overall, however, the charter's impact on British labour legislation has been small; its impact limited to a few select cases. Nevertheless, its existence has acted as an important legal benchmark for British labour law.

The European Community

By far the most important institution in this category of vertical influences is the European Community (EC). Although it has not the full range of powers and competencies of national government institutions, it has more extensive authority than any other international organisation. In one sense, the EC is best described as an extranational institution, as it constitutes a half-way house between organisations at the national and international levels. As a result of membership, the various member states have opened up a wide range of their domestic policy areas and rule-making activity to Community influences. The most obvious example is the agricultural sector where the member states have transferred substantial authority to the Community level. No such clear-cut supranational Community regime exists in any other policy area. Nevertheless, in many instances the EC has developed policies and programmes which overlap, even compete with, activities of national authorities. As a result, a dense network of policy-making and implementation processes has been created between the member states which have impacted to varying degrees on national policy-making processes.[18]

Member states' employment environments have not remained immune from these dynamics of European integration. Traditionally, the boundaries of a recognisably distinct employment environment were regarded as identical to the boundaries of the nation state. In other words, the basic character of an employment environment has traditionally been seen as being determined by national political, economic and social environments as well as the peculiarities of the industry structure, employing organisations and industrial interest groups within the nation state. The existence of the European Community is widely regarded as undermining this traditional stereotype, or at least as opening up a new dimension to a national employment environment. In relation to the industrial relations system which constitutes a large part of an employment environment, one commentator suggested: 'It is my thesis that we shall see gradually develop a European pattern of industrial relations. There will, of course, remain a considerable element of national difference. This means that we are moving into a two-tier system of industrial systems which will create difficulties of the type familiar to federal states'.[19] Paradoxically, while the EC has more potential to influence national employment environment than any other international organisation, much more has been written about the role of the ILO and OECD in this area. Hopefully, however, this book will go some way towards filling this gap in the existing literature.

Assessing the influence of the European Community on the employment environment in Britain is a complex task. The most immediate problem is defining what is actually meant by the term 'EC influence'. For instance, limiting the definition to formal Community policies in the field of social and labour affairs would be inappropriate, as other initiatives, although not reaching the Community's statute-book, clearly have had some impact on UK business behaviour: the draft Vredeling Directive is an obvious case in point. Moreover, adopting a narrow legalistic approach would exclude from the study important issues such as whether Britain's membership of the Community has affected the behaviour of interest groups like the CBI and TUC or employment policy makers in national organisations like the MSC or the Department of Employment. Thus, we interpreted the notion of 'EC influence' fairly broadly so as to incorporate adopted and proposed Community legislation, as well as other more informal, less precise connections between the UK employment environment and the Community.

Similar definitional problems arise when the concept of employment environment is considered. This notion suffers from being an open-ended and catch-all term. Faced with this difficulty, we thought the best way forward was to divide the 'employment environment' into several self-contained policy areas, the sum of which make up that environment. This disaggregation had the methodological merit of allowing a thorough investigation into the nature and extent of EC influences and linkages in relatively discrete policy areas. Adopting this methodology was soon vindicated as it quickly became apparent that EC influences differed considerably across the employment environment. Overall, it is felt that this broad yet structured approach (which is detailed in more depth in Appendix 3) has made possible a comprehensive identification and explanation of EC influences operating on employment policies and practices in the UK.

Outline

The chapters in the rest of the book follow on from this approach. Chapter II covers the main institutions established at the origin of the Community and explains the complex and often changing nature of the relationships between them. It charts the development of additional institutions throughout the history of the EC, up to and including the Single European Act.

Chapters III and IV look in detail at the development of social policy within the European Community. The first of these two chapters analyses progress up to 1973, by which time the EC had tested its ability to pursue policies in a strictly limited and experimental fashion, concentrating largely on establishing the free movement of labour. 1974 saw the adoption of the Social Action Programme which mapped out the second phase of the development of social policy: a phase which explicitly aimed at being more comprehensive, and more interventionist. The playing out of this phase is the subject of Chapter IV. That chapter also shows how the second phase broke down into an uncertain and controversial third phase, the current phase, where the Commission attempted to come to terms with its inability to push through a more interventionist approach.

Chapters V, VI and VII cover three specific aspects of the employment environment: namely the administrative, political and legal dimensions. Chapter V examines the way in which national government and quasi-governmental bodies in the employment arena have adapted themselves to relate to the EC decision making system. Chapter VI is concerned both with national politics in relation to the EC and with the policies towards and links with the Community developed by the more partial lobbying groups (unions, employers and single-interest groups). Chapter VII examines the legal dimension: looking at the role and status of European law generally and then at the relationship of specific social policy legislation to the national UK law.

The following three chapters present unique data from our empirical research. They assess the impact of the European Community's social policy on employing institutions in Britain. Chapter VIII provides a detailed analysis of the way local authorities deal with European Community issues. It explores what is happening in the local authorities in terms of their links with Brussels, their lobbying, their adaptation to handle relevant issues arising in the EC and the relationship of personnel practices in those areas to EC policies. Chapter IX covers the same ground for the public enterprises. Chapter X undertakes a similar analysis for the private sector, drawing on a wide range of different private sector organisations in the manufacturing and service sectors.

The foundations for the future development of a harmonised social policy are examined in Chapter XI. The analysis here is undertaken on the basis of a precise and detailed examination of the wide variety of labour-market trends in the various member states of the Community.

The concluding chapter provides, in effect, an executive summary of the book and goes on to an assessment of the future.

Notes and References

1 HENRY, Y and WRIGHT, V (ed). *The Politics of Steel: Western Europe and the Steel Industry in the Crisis Years* (1974-1984); W de Gruyter, Berlin 1980

2 KATZ, H and SABEL, C. Industrial Relations and Industrial Adjustment in the Car Industry, *Industrial Relations Journal*, Vol 24, Fall 1985, pp 295-315

3 See National Academy of Engineering. *Technology and Global Industry*, National Academy Research, New York 1987

4 BRUSCO, S. 'The Emilian Model: Productive Decentralisation and Social Integration,' *Cambridge Journal of Economics* No 2 1982 pp 167–85

5 COX, R. *Production, Power and World Order: Social Forces in the making of history*, Columbia University Press, New York 1987

6 See Chapter 4 of STRANGE S, *States and Markets*, Frances Pinter, London 1988

7 ENDERWICK, P. *Multinational Business and Labour*, Croom Helm, London 1985

8 LIPIETZ, A. *Mirages and Miracles: The Crisis of Global Fordism*, London, Verso 1987

9 DUNNING, J H. *Japanese Participation in British Industry*, Croom Helm, London 1987. See also the special edition of *Industrial Relations Journal*, Spring 1988 on the Japanisation of British Industrial Relations

10 See WINDMILLER, J. European labour and Politics: A Symposium (i) (ii) *Industrial and Labour Relations Review*, Vol 28 No 1 October

1974 pp 3–88. GUNTER, K. 'Union Responses in Continental Europe', in Flanagan and Weber (ed) *Bargaining without Boundaries*, University of Chicago Press, Chicago 1974. HONTHYS, S. 'Aspects Européens et Internationaux du syndicalisme', *Chronique de Politiqué Etrangère* Vol 38 July 1974

11 ETUI, *Trends in Collective Bargaining in Western Europe*, Brussels 1983

12 FOGGON, G. 'The Origin and Development of the ILO and International Labour Organisations', TAYLOR, P. and GROOM, A J R (eds) *International Institutions at Work*, Frances Pinter, London 1988

13 BLANPAIN, R. *The OECD Guidelines*, Kluwer Deventer, The Netherlands 1982

14 Op cit. p 136

15 ROJOT, J. The 1984 Revision of the OECD Guidelines for Multinational Enterprises, *British Journal of Industrial Relations* No 42 1985 p 381

16 See HARRIS, D. *The European Social Charter*, University Press of Virginia, Charlottesville 1982

17 O'HIGGINS, M. 'International Standards and British Labour Law' in LEWIS, R (ed). *Labour Law in Britain*, Basil Blackwell, Oxford 1986

18 WALLACE, H, WALLACE, W, WEBB, C (eds). *Policy Making in the European Community*, Macmillan, London 1978

19 ROBERTS, B. 'Industrial Relations and the EEC', *Labour Law Journal* Vol 24, August 1973, p 480.

Chapter II

The Institutions and Decision-making Processes of the European Community

Introduction

To many people, and not only the layman, the European Community is a remote and distant institution. As a result, only a few 'experts' have a detailed knowledge of the Community's decision-making structure and how it operates. To assist those without a detailed knowledge of the workings of the Community, this chapter gives an overview of the political and institutional developments since the signing of the Treaty of Rome in 1957 which set up the Common Market. This chapter provides the necessary background information for the subsequent discussion of EC social policy.

The first part of the chapter aims to provide a straightforward guide to the main institutions established at the origin of the Community – the Commission, the Council of Ministers and the Committee of Permanent Representatives, the European Court of Justice, the European Assembly (subsequently renamed the European Parliament) and the Economic and Social Committee. The next part discusses the fluctuating relationships between these bodies from the inception of the Community to 1974. Then, the chapter outlines subsequent institutional developments – the creation of the European Council, the expansion in importance of the Presidency and the introduction of direct elections to the European Parliament in 1979. The penultimate section charts the debate which gave rise to the Single European Act and examines the potential effects this may have on the operation of the Community. The final part outlines the specific institutional framework set up at the European level to deal with social policy matters.

European Integration – The Formative Years

After the end of the Second World War, a European Movement with widespread support both at elite and popular levels, emerged almost spontaneously within war-ravaged mainland Europe. Although this movement was divided between federalists, those who wanted to see immediate steps taken towards full European union, and functionalists, those who took a more pragmatic and gradual approach towards European integration, the common motivating goal was to bring to an end historic national antagonisms, primarily between France and Germany. This political objective was paramount; economic considerations played only a small part in the motivations of people concerned to obtain greater European integration. At this stage, it should be pointed out that Britain remained for the most part immune from this European integrationist fervour. Speeches were made by leading British figures in support of European union, but the practice of successive British governments was to remain at arms' length from such developments.[1]

From about the late forties Continental governments, with the active support of the USA, started translating the sentiment for new European-wide integration into reality. In 1947 General Marshall, a leading member of the Allied command staff, proposed in a speech at Harvard University that American money should be made available to stimulate European recovery. As a result, a European Payments Union was established and dollars were distributed across Europe to facilitate investment and economic growth. Whether or not this recovery programme, known as the Marshall Plan, was actually needed is the matter of a heated academic debate.[2] However, the Union did have a lasting effect, in that in 1948 it gave rise to the Organisation for European Economic Co-operation, now called OECD.

Other regional organisations rapidly started to appear on the European political landscape: Benelux, the economic union of Belgium, the Netherlands and Luxembourg was created in 1947; and in 1949, the Council of Europe was established, involving 15 European nations. The purpose of this body was to bring together parliamentarians from European countries to launch and promote initiatives on co-operation. However, this European institution was not endowed with any substantive political or economic powers, largely as a result of Britain's reluctance to participate in an extra-national body with supranational authority.[3]

The first pan-European institution with genuine authority was the European Coal and Steel Community (ECSC), established when France, West Germany, Italy and the Benelux countries signed the Paris Treaty in 1951. This Treaty placed the coal and steel industries of these countries under the control of a common European body.[4] Although it was thought that such an arrangement would bring considerable economic benefits, the underlying objective of the Paris Treaty was political: it was to remove from the nation states sole control of the key industries which sustain war. The ECSC was given substantial formal powers of its own and the right to raise its own financial resources. At the time, it was widely acknowledged that the first step had been taken towards a 'United States of Europe'.[5]

However, the drive towards a federated Europe experienced a major setback when a proposal for a European Defence Community ran aground. Like the ECSC, the idea for a European defence community was conceived by the French Government. René Pleven, the French Defence Minister, had presented a plan suggesting the creation of a West European security arrangement to the Foreign Ministers of the member countries of the ECSC. The main proposal was to create a European Army made up of national units each consisting of about 15,000 men. Germany would be allowed to contribute to the defence of Western Europe without being permitted to re-militarise. The Foreign Ministers of all the ECSC member states supported the plan and indeed signed an agreement to establish a European Army, but when the plan came before the French Parliament in 1954 it was defeated. The effect was to defeat the entire proposal.[6] In response to the collapse of the European Defence Community, an organisation called the Western European Union, with limited powers, was established by the six states.[7]

The Emergence of the European Economic Community

The failure of the European Defence Community proposal had the effect of quelling the federalist tendencies of some European enthusiasts, but leading politicians in the six member countries of the ECSC continued to work actively for greater European cooperation. At a conference in Messina in 1955 the Foreign Ministers of these countries set up a committee, under the chairmanship of Paul Henri Spaak, to study ways in which a fresh advance toward the concept of a United States of Europe could be achieved. The prevailing view in all European capitals was that to avoid another failure, any new initiative to further integration should build on the success of the ECSC and should be in the economic rather than the political field. Thus, when the Spaak Committee produced its report in the following year, the main proposal was for the construction of a customs union between the six ECSC countries.

The report was approved by the Foreign Ministers of the six, and the negotiations immediately commenced on drafting a treaty based on the Spaak Committee's recommendations. These negotiations led to the signing of the Treaty of Rome in March 1957, establishing the European Economic Community and Euratom (the European Atomic Agency).

A key feature of the Treaty of Rome is that with the exception of specific obligations spelled out in regard to the establishment of a customs union, it amounts to a general statement of goals with a set of institutions and a procedure for their attainment. For instance, no explicit clauses relating to political objectives were contained in the treaty. Article 2 only referred to the shared determination of the member countries to establish the foundations of an ever-closer union among European states. Thus it is useful to distinguish between the narrow and broad objectives of the Treaty of Rome. The narrow objective was the creation of a customs union: the elimination of all tariff barriers between the participating member states, and the construction of a common external tariff over a twelve-year timespan. The broader, but unwritten, objective was the development of common economic policies and the gradual convergence of national economies.[8] Agriculture and transport were the only two named economic sectors for which the Community was given legal obligations to devise active policies. Nevertheless, it was widely recognised among the member states that over time the Community would bring about an advance in most aspects of economic policy.

The Institutional System of the European Community

The institutional system established by the Treaty of Rome is outlined in diagram form in figure IIi. Before describing the nature and extent of the interactions, it may be useful to outline the powers invested in each body.

The Commission

The Commission is a collegiate body appointed by the governments of the member states. Each member country has the right to at least one commissioner, appointed for a renewable term of four years. The treaty provides that the members of the Commission should be chosen for their general competence and they take an oath of independence from their Government. The President of the Commission is appointed through the combined decision of the member states, and the normal practice is for this position to rotate between countries every four years. However, rotation is not a hard-and-fast rule, and the opportunity exists for the incumbent President to be appointed to further terms of office.[9] The Commission has five main functions: administrative; initiating; brokerage; guardian and representative.

Administrative Function

The Commission, with an envisaged staff of about 11,000, was set up as the Community's civil service, carrying out for the most part routine secretarial and organisational tasks to ensure the smooth running of the institutional system. In addition to these duties the Commission was also charged with the management and implementation of certain Community programmes: these included the European Social Fund and a

Figure Iii The community's decision-making process

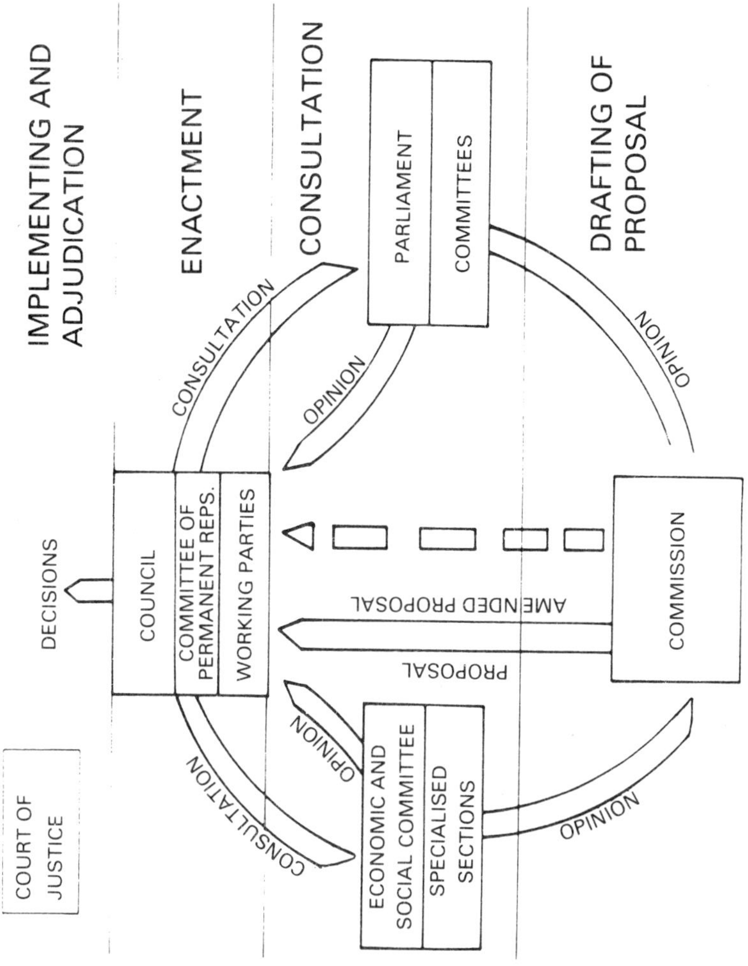

variety of agricultural schemes. This managerial role gave the Commission considerable discretionary powers to take decisions regarding the implementation of Community policies. To give but one example, it would have the authority to introduce levies on certain imported agricultural products.

Initiating Function
The founding fathers of the Community, however, did not want the Commission's authority limited to administrative tasks; they wanted the Commission to have explicit supranational powers. But this ambition was frustrated by the original six members states, which were reluctant to cede any significant elements of sovereignty to a supranational institution. Nevertheless, a modicum of direct political authority was delegated to the Commission by virtue of the initiatory role laid down by the Treaty of Rome. The intention was that, with a few exceptions, Community policies would be based on proposals made by the Commission. This initiating role potentially gave the Commission considerable power to shape the direction of Community policies.

Brokerage Function
The Commission was given responsibility to mediate in the event of disagreement among member-states or between parts of the Community's decision-making machinery. In particular the Commission was given the authority to amend its proposals so as to ease the process of obtaining compromise agreements when appropriate.

Guardian Function
The 'guardian function' of the Commission is established by Article 155 of the treaty. This article gave the Commission the duty of 'monitoring the application of the Treaty and of the provisions adopted by the institutions of the Community in parallel thereof'. If the Commission finds that a government, firm or even an individual of any member state has breached Community law, it has power to bring them before the Court of Justice. By virtue of being the 'Guardian' of the Treaty of Rome, the Commission was to be the body above national interest, performing the role of Community conscience.

Representative Function
Being a major new extra-national actor, maintaining contact with other international organisations was obviously going to be a major function of the Community. This task was explicitly given to the Commission by the treaty. In addition, it was also given the right to negotiate commercial treaties in liaison with a sub-committee of the Council of Ministers and within limits laid down by the Council.

The Council of Ministers

The Rome Treaty designated the Council of Ministers as the main decision-making body of the Community, consisting of ministers from the member states, with the Commission present in a non-voting capacity. The Council was given the authority to issue Regulations and Directives, make Decisions and formulate Recommendations or Opinions. *Regulations* have general application and are binding in every respect and directly applicable in each member state. This is a real 'European' power, for the Community is here granted the right to legislate directly on the populations of member countries without passing through national Parliaments or other organs of national government. *Directives* are binding on any member-state to which they are addressed with regard to the result to be achieved. They leave to domestic agencies the determination of form and means. *Decisions* are binding in their entirety and can be addressed to Government, or to an enterprise or to a private individual. *Recommendations* and *Opinions* have no binding force although they do carry some informal influence.

Under the conditions set by the treaty, the Council in the early years was to operate under the unanimity voting arrangement. Thereafter, particularly when acting on proposals put forward by the Commission, the treaty stipulated that the Council should move to a qualified majority voting system. Under this voting system, the votes of the member states would be weighted: four each for Germany, France and Italy, two each for Belgium and the Netherlands, and one for Luxembourg.

By laying down a transitional period in which Community action would require the support of every member state, the treaty was clearly adopting a gradual approach to European integration. The consensus view of the member states must have been that it would take time before they could fully adjust to Community membership. But equally they must also have assumed that after becoming familiar with Community procedures and so on, they would be able to move to a supranational majority voting system.

The Council of Ministers in carrying out its legislative functions was to be assisted by the Permanent Representatives Committee (COREPER). These representatives are civil servants from each of the member states, some with the rank and role of ambassadors. Part of their duties was envisaged as communicating to the various Community institutions, particularly the Commission, the views and interests of their respective countries, but their most important role was to ensure that any proposal being prepared by the Council could be approved by their Government. If any disagreements emerged within the Permanent Representatives Committee or between it and the Commission then the two bodies were expected to make the necessary efforts to reach a compromise. Thus the basic purpose of COREPER was to ensure that any opposition or reservations about particular proposals were resolved before the proposals reached the Council of Ministers. Many of the architects of the Community regarded this type of preparatory work committee as indispensable to the development of the Community.[10]

The European Court of Justice

The Court of Justice is charged with the principal task of ensuring compliance with the Rome Treaty, and with Community legislation. The Treaty of Rome laid down a number of different situations in which the Court was to act. In some cases it was to act on a complaint from the Commission or from a member state against another member, or from a firm or an individual claiming that Community legislation had been violated. In other instances it was assigned the task of giving 'Preliminary Ruling' on an aspect of Community law to a judge from a member state presiding over a case which involves that law. The Court was also given the power to deal with disputes between Community institutions. Finally, it was also able to adjudicate between the institutions and their employees over such matters as wrongful dismissal or refusal of promotion opportunities. Thus the Court was to operate at many different levels: it was to act as a constitutional court, as a labour tribunal, as a court of appeal from community decisions and as a court of interpretation for the assistance of national courts. This wide range of functions ensured the Court would be a key actor in the Community's decision-making process.

The Court was established with seven judges (now 13), one from each of the six member states and an additional one to ensure that in all cases it would be able to reach a verdict. Despite this precautionary arrangement, it was generally expected that the Court would aim for consensus judgments and would avoid taking formal votes to decide the result of any cases.[11] The Treaty of Rome decreed that every judge 'shall be chosen from persons whose independence is beyond doubt and who possess the qualification required for appointment to the highest judicial offices in their respective countries or who are jurisconsults of recognised competence'. Each judge is appointed for six years by common accord of the member states. Like other Community institutions, the Court has its own permanent staff to assist in its work.

General Assembly (European Parliament)

A General Assembly, subsequently renamed the European Parliament, was established by articles 137-144 of the Rome Treaty. The main power assigned to the Assembly by the treaty is its formal control of the

Commission. It was laid down that if the Assembly passes a vote of no-confidence by a two-thirds majority against the Commission, then that body is required to resign. Other functions, such as the right to review and to be consulted before action is taken by the Council or Commission, were also established. But none of the Opinions or Resolutions formulated by the Assembly were given any formal status. Thus at the outset the General Assembly was viewed as a consultative body. However, further extensions of its power were left open by the Treaty of Rome. For instance, Article 138 stipulated that direct elections in accordance with a uniform procedure in all member states should be established at some undefined future stage.

Economic and Social Committee

The Economic and Social Committee was established to act as the main forum for consumer, labour and employer interest groups to make their views known to the Community on political and general topics. Like the General Assembly, it was given the right to be consulted by the Council or Commission before decisions were made in certain policy areas, and the treaty obliged the main Community institutions (Commission and Council) to give full consideration to the views expressed by the Economic and Social Committee.

Relationships

From this description of the role and functions of the different institutions established by the Treaty of Rome, it should be fairly clear how the founding fathers wanted the Community's decision-making system to work. The Commission after consultation with recognised legal and policy experts would draft policy proposals. This would go to the Parliament, Economic and Social Committee and COREPER for consideration. Although the view of the former two bodies would be taken into account, the Commission would be mainly interested in the reaction of COREPER: in essence a proposal would only progress if that organisation signalled its support. If COREPER or any specific member states opposed the proposal then an intensive round of negotiations would follow to see if a compromise could be reached which would command general support. If COREPER supported the initiative or if a compromise deal occurred then the proposal would go before the Council of Ministers for a decision.

Clearly the relationship between the Commission and the Council of Ministers is at the heart of the decision-making process. However, there is some disagreement about how this relationship should be interpreted. One view is that the institutional framework established by the treaty amounted to the Commission being a European government in embryo: it would act as a motor of integration by generating new ideas, by defending the interests of the Community as a whole and by putting constant pressure on the member states to reach compromises on common policies.[12] An alternative view was that the Treaty of Rome created an institutional and political balance between the promotion of the European idea by the Commission and the safeguarding of national interests by allowing member states a continuous and close role in the decision-making process.[13]

Irrespective of one's view about the constitutional objectives of the founding fathers of the Community, the general consensus is that between 1958–62 the development of the Community system was an unqualified success. The Commission, reviewing the results of these years, observed 'it can now be claimed with certainty that the Common Market can no longer be called into question and that there will be no going back; it may also be affirmed that this economic unification is part of an advance towards political unification which is being pursued on parallel lines'.[14]

So smooth was the development of the Community that it was assumed that the conditions existed for a new higher level of European integration, involving the member states introducing majority-voting inside the Council of Ministers and making the requisite changes to transform the Commission into a genuinely supranational body. In fact by this stage senior members of the Commission were confident enough to claim that in de facto terms it had become the lynch-pin of the Community's decision-making structure. Thus Emile Noel, the Commission's General Secretary, stated that 'the Council can only come to a decision on the proposal of the Commission . . . If the Commission does not submit any proposals, the Council is paralysed and the Community's progress halted.'[15]

These federalist sentiments were shared by some of the member states, for at Bonn in July 1961 they agreed to establish a treaty-drafting committee, known as the Fouchet Committee after its French chairman, on the creation of a Union of the Peoples of Europe. The idea was to establish a Political Community to operate in parallel to the Economic Community. The first draft Treaty of the Committee was rejected as it was regarded as deficient on a number of accounts. Widely regarded as acting on the instruction of the French President, General de Gaulle, Fouchet quickly tabled a second draft (the Fouchet Plan Mark II) proposing a framework which was highly intergovernmental in character. This institutional form was vigorously opposed by the rest of the Six since they wanted an arrangement which was more supranational in character. But the French refused to compromise on the contents of the Fouchet

Plan Mark II, plunging the drafting committee into deadlock. The net result was that the idea of creating a 'Union of the Peoples of Europe' had to be abandoned.[16]

This clash between the French administration's minimalist view of European integration and the maximalist perspective of the Commission and some of the other members states, particularly the smaller ones, came to a head in 1965. The cause was ostensibly a set of proposals produced by the Commission to change the financial regulations of the Common Agricultural Policy. But it has been suggested that the uncomfortably proximity of 1st January 1966 – the date laid down by the Rome Treaty when majority voting in the Council of Ministers was due to come into force – was the real factor which triggered the crisis.[17] As the episode is a landmark in Community affairs, it is worth describing it in some detail. Part of the Common Agricultural Policy was a complicated financial support mechanism known as the European Agricultural Guidance and Guarantee Fund. The arrangement up to 1965 was that all member states made direct weighted contributions to a common fund which was then dispensed amongst qualifying applicants. The Commission wanted to do away with this common fund and make the necessary changes so that direct Community revenues could be raised, from which financial support to farmers would be paid. The idea of direct Community revenue not subject to the control of national parliaments or governments had long been a contentious issue. The Commission tried to placate such fears by including in their proposal an arrangement to strengthen the budgetary powers of the European Parliament.

Without informing member states of the proposals, the Commission presented its plan to the European Parliament. This outraged the French who thought that the Commission was not only acting audaciously but also overstepping its powers. Elsewhere within the Community, the response to the proposal was generally favourable. This difference in opinion produced a political clash within the Council of Ministers, resulting in France withdrawing its permanent representatives from Brussels and announcing that it was boycotting Community institutions. The French grievance was in two parts – an unwillingness to accept transition to majority voting in the Council of Ministers and a list of ten complaints against the behaviour of the Commission. Because of the boycott, key parts of the Community's decision-making process could not function and proposals tabled for ratification simply piled up. After six months (in January 1966) the French agreed to meet with their Community partners to negotiate a resolution to the boycott. With only minimal concessions being made by the other five member states about the conduct of the Community's information policy, the French agreed to take their seat once again. No move towards majority voting was made – 1st January 1966, which should have seen the introduction of this practice, passed unnoticed. But as none of the member states wanted a repeat of the boycott, no one was prepared to press for the introduction of this voting practice.[18]

The Luxembourg Compromise, as the resolution of the French boycott is known, has had a lasting effect on the direction and nature of the European Community. The failure of the Community to progress to majority voting was a major blow to the cause of European supranationalism. Having to conduct its business on the basis of consent and consensus meant that the Community in effect took the form of a confederal organisation. Under the confederal model the idea that the Commission should be an independent institution 'above' the member states is effectively renounced: member states take a greater role in the formation of policy.[19] In practice this meant elevating the status of the Committee of Permanent Representatives so that it was closely involved in all stages of the decision-making process.

At the time, some commentators argued that the Luxembourg Compromise and subsequent developments effectively emasculated all the Commission's discretionary powers, reducing its role to a technocratic body at the service of the Council.[20] As following chapters will show, this assessment is not totally accurate as the Commission retained important powers to formulate and initiate policy proposals. Certainly, the boycott episode weakened the Commission but it did not make it impotent. However, such was the state of Community affairs in the late sixties it is easy to see why commentators were drawn to this conclusion. The prevailing climate inside the Community at that time was unpropitious, as member states, particularly the French, were lacking in enthusiasm for promoting the European integrationist project. Some straightforward and relatively uncontentious proposals made by the Commission failed to enlist their support.[21] What compounded these difficulties was the implementation of the Merger Treaty in 1967. This treaty brought together most of the executive bodies of the European Coal and Steel Community (ECSC), the European Atomic Energy Community (Euratom) and the European Community into a new unified administrative system. In the future there was to be only one Commission, European Parliament and Court of Justice to oversee the work of the Community.

The hope of many Commission officials was that the merger would restore many of its powers weakened by the Luxembourg Compromise. The opposite turned out to be the case. Instead of the Merger Treaty creating a window of opportunity to strengthen the powers of the Commission, it placed enormous strains on the Community's institutional system. In addition to the political problems which had been created by the French boycott, the new institutional structure had to contend with the crises in the European coal industry, which for years the ECSC had struggled against without success, and the paralysis that had crept into the work of Euratom. As well as these operational problems, the task of co-ordinating and integrating staff and departments proved to be an organisational and administrative nightmare.[22] Unquestionably, the late sixties was one of the most difficult periods in EC history. On all fronts – policy implementation, administrative and organisational co-ordination, the negotiations of the entry of new members (United Kingdom, Denmark and Ireland) – progress was virtually non-existent. During this difficult period, the Commission, under the control of President Rey, astutely avoided raising any policies which could generate further controversy. The main focus of the Commission's work was on completing the transnational period so that a customs union could be pronounced established. The strategy of the Commission was to stabilise and consolidate developments inside the Community.

This unfavourable climate for Community action, however, did not last long. The resignation of General de Gaulle and the election of Georges Pompidou to the Presidency of France in 1969, almost spontaneously ushered in a more positive and optimistic environment. For many, the nationalistic outlook of de Gaulle was the main reason why France had been so opposed to any increase in the scope and depth of European integration. With de Gaulle out of the picture, there was an immediate increase in the work and activity of Community institutions. The Commission reported 'from the month of June, work was intensified in all institutions. The Commission had to work without pause in order to be ready with its proposals . . . The Council multiplied the number of its sessions . . . The European Parliament met several times in extraordinary sessions'.[23]

This upsurge in activity gave rise to renewed co-operation between the member states, which was reflected in the Hague Summit in December 1969. At that summit, the member countries re-affirmed their commitment to the political objective of a United States of Europe, and amongst other things, agreed to work gradually towards an economic and monetary union, to investigate the most feasible path towards political union, and to support the enlargement of the Community. The problems of the late sixties now appeared to be firmly left behind and the motors of integration started once again. Developments in the early seventies appeared to endorse this view. An important summit was held in Paris in 1972, where the member states signed a declaration which affirmed their intention of transforming their relations as a whole into a European Union by 31 December 1980 at the latest. In addition, they instructed the Commission and other Community bodies to start immediate work on the construction of monetary union, and the development of a range of policies in the social field. Finally, in 1972,

Britain, Denmark and Ireland had signed accession treaties in Brussels and were busily engaged in preparing the way for their formal entry into the Community the following year. Thus on the face of things all appeared well inside the Community.

But on closer examination adverse developments could be detected. One expert commentator suggested, for instance, that the growth of the Commission as an organisation after the Merger Treaty, coupled with the departure of some of the original committed and campaigning Europeans from its leadership, caused it to become more and more bureaucratic in approach.[24] Looking at the evidence there appears to be a good deal of substance to this thesis. The Merger Treaty made a fundamental impact on the size and shape of the Commission. For example, between 1967-68, the number of Directorates General increased from 10 to 20, the number of Directorates increased from 36 to 66, the number of Divisions in Specialized Services increased from 124 to 238. The number of people employed by the Commission rose by about 90 per cent in that year, from 2,738 to 5,149. As a result of this rapid increase in the size of the Commission, it ceased to be a fairly small, administratively tight organisation and became a large body with complex structures.

The multiplication in the number of Directorates General had the effect of undermining the homogeneity and cohesiveness of the Commission's policy-making process. Because of the growth of these Directorates General and their differentiation into relatively self-contained policy areas, the work of Commission officials became almost entirely dictated by the specific field in which they operated. The outcome of this 'compartmentalisation' process, was that it became more and more misleading to talk about the Commission as a fully-integrated body trying to progress European integration along a single path. One analysis drew the conclusion 'that collaboration with the Commission among the various Directorates General is rather slight. The development trend has been towards an increasing diversification of positions and strategies. One could even go so far as to say that we are witnessing the breakdown of the organisation internally into separate subsystems, each acting for its own account, defending its own interests, having recourse to its own policies, and co-existing rather than interacting with the others'.[25]

The fragmentation of policy-making inside the Commission was noted by several important studies, most notably the Ortoli and Spiekenberg Reports, as a matter of genuine concern. These reports concluded that fragmentation undermined the Commission's role as initiator and planner of Community affairs. To restore a higher degree of co-ordination and coherence in its policy-making, the reports concluded that the political role of the Commission should once again be strengthened. But two developments vitiated the practicality of this proposal. First, as mentioned earlier, a new more technocratic personnel, relatively untouched by the Europeanization fervour of the late fifties, now dominated the leadership of the Commission. These people were most reluctant to take up an overtly political role similar to that adopted by Hallstein and other predecessors. More importantly, by the early seventies the member states were playing a central role in setting the Community's policy agenda.

Development of the European Council

In fact, probably the key development inside the Community during the seventies was the institutionalisation of this central role of the member states. This institutionalisation was achieved through the creation of the European Council and by upgrading the role of Presidency of the Council of Ministers. Part of the communiqué from the Paris Summit of 1974 announced that the member countries had agreed to establish regular summit meetings to be held two times a year. These summits were given the title of European Councils. The constitutional status of this entirely new Community body was not spelt out in any detail.

The rationale for establishing the European Council appears threefold. First, the experiences of earlier ad hoc summit meetings (in 1961, 1967, 1972 and 1973) indicated that these occasions could be used to resolve conflicts on certain issues and as a launching pad for further integration projects. Secondly, the highly unstable international economic environment that emerged in the wake of the oil price shocks in 1973/74 influenced the member states to increase their cohesion at the EC level so that clear policy signals could be sent to the outside world. Thirdly, the European Council was regarded as necessary to co-ordinate the dense network of relations which had grown up between the member states and Community institutions over the years. In the absence of such co-ordination it was considered that the Community's potential to achieve policy goals would be seriously undermined.

Since its inception, the role of the European Council has grown considerably. The functions of the body have been classified into nine categories which are listed overleaf.

1. informal exchanges amongst the European Community heads of government
2. a strategic function relating to the overall direction of European unification
3. setting more detailed guidelines for specific policy areas
4. launching new policy areas for co-operation/integration through 'scope enlargement'
5. policy co-ordination both within and between EC sectors
6. issuing important declarations of foreign policy
7. decision-making as a special session of the Council of Ministers
8. problem-solving concerning issues deadlocked at lower levels of the EC decision-making hierarchies.
9. policy control and implementation.[26]

During the first decade or so the Council has been grafted on to the pre-existing Community institutional framework without any major disruption. The main body it appears to have impinged upon is the Council of Ministers. Although there is no clear-cut division of labour between the two organisations, it is generally accepted that the European Council is now the highest level of authority responsible for setting policy objectives, while the Council of Ministers is primarily concerned with the technical and administrative aspects of policy implementation.[27]

The consensus appears to be that the performance of the European Council has been somewhat mixed. On the positive side, its biggest success has been the creation of the European Monetary System. In addition, the Council has created worthwhile policy initiatives on such issues as security, terrorism, and cultural co-operation. On the negative side, the Council has been unable to execute its problem-solving function to any great effect. On numerous occasions, it has remained impotent in the face of major disputes over the EC budget and the Common Agricultural Policy. Furthermore, initiatives by the Council which can be regarded as a success are not apparent in the spheres of strategic integration, formulating new policy guidelines and policy monitoring.

Expansion of the Presidency

In addition to the emergence of the European Council as a major new Community institution, the Presidency of the Council of Ministers also grew in importance. During the early years of the Community this was a relatively unimportant office, as the agenda of the Council of Ministers was more or less pre-ordained by treaty commitments and as outlined the Community was progressing smoothly in all areas. But towards the end of the 1960s, the Presidency came to occupy a more pivotal role. It is suggested that this resulted from a combination of a number of factors: 'a more explicit discussion with the Council over how most appropriately to manage business; the rapid proliferation of Councils at ministerial level and of working groups; the vesting in the Community Council of the problems of inter-ministerial co-ordination in national capitals; changes in the political and economic environment of the EC; the burgeoning of Community action in the broader international stage; and the decrease in the power and effectiveness of the Commission'.[28]

Although the Presidency continued to grow in importance during the seventies, formal recognition of this position was not agreed to by the Council of Ministers until 1979. Then several distinct formal functions were allocated to the Presidency: planning the calendar and convening of meetings; formulating provisional agendas of the Council; signing the minutes of meetings drawn up by the General Secretariat of the Council; signing acts adopted by the Council; ensuring that acts are properly published; chairing COREPER and other working groups; and acting as a collective point of contact for third parties. These were narrow, mainly administrative, functions which in no way reflected the wide range of activities undertaken by the President during the seventies and eighties.

By the turn of the eighties, the Presidency had developed five distinct functions: the management of the Council; the promotion of political initiatives; the construction of package deals; liaison with other Community institutions; and spokesman on foreign affairs. These new functions transformed the Presidency into one of the key posts in the Community decision-making process.

Direct Elections to the European Parliament

The only other institutional change of any significance which took place in the seventies was the first direct elections to the European Parliament in 1979. Although the Treaty of Rome stipulated that the member states should work towards a democratically elected European parliamentary body, it took twenty years of continuous lobbying by ardent federalists such as Spinelli, an Italian MEP, to see that clause put into practice. The hope of Spinelli and others with a similar outlook was that European elections would help correct the tilting of the institutional balance towards the member states inside the Community. Before 1979 the European Parliament consisted of nominees from national parliaments in each member state. The general consensus, however, was that few of the brighter or more senior members of these institutions were attracted to the European Parliament. It was hoped that a new independent

European Parliament would attract young, able politicians willing to fight for a new identity and role for that body. In short, the anticipation was that with direct elections a new European political elite would emerge. But things did not turn out as expected. Direct elections have not significantly increased the legitimacy of the Parliament amongst Community citizens. Moreover, a series of bad press reports about its apparent inefficiency has added to its problems in obtaining credibility.[29]

Despite these drawbacks, the Parliament has managed to gate-crash a role in European affairs. In the process for negotiating the budget, for example, Parliament has grown in importance. It has become embroiled in many of the controversies which rage from time to time over particular Community policies: for instance, it took an active part in the debate over the so-called Vredeling Directive. What is more, as shall be seen below, through the assiduous work of a group of MEPs it forced the pace of institutional change in the eighties. By and large, therefore, it can be said that direct elections elevated Parliament's status within the Community's institutional system, if not perhaps amongst the European public.

A New Treaty?

Bogged down by an ineffective decision-making process, a lack of common outlook amongst the member states, and an increasingly economically divergent Community, the EC by the early eighties was in a state of near paralysis. Several initiatives were launched to give a face-lift to what was becoming a haggard and wind-swept structure. One proposal originated from the European Parliament and was known as the Draft Treaty establishing the European Union. In June 1980 Altiero Spinelli circulated a letter to all his fellow parliamentarians, setting out the idea for a European Parliament initiative to resolve the political crisis inside the Community. Only eight MEPs responded and at a subsequent dinner at the Crocodile Restaurant in Strasbourg Spinelli along with these people formed the Crocodile Club. This club immediately became active, holding monthly meetings and publishing newsletters. By the end of the year this group had attracted over 80 MEPs. In early 1981, the club tabled a motion known as the Crocodile Resolution at a Parliamentary session, calling for the establishment of a working party representing the different currents of thought inside the Parliament to prepare a range of options about the future of the EC to be debated by the MEPs.[30] This working group, called the Ad Hoc Committee on Institutional Affairs, sat for over two years thrashing out the details of a revamped Community framework to which all MEPs could agree. What finally emerged was the Draft Treaty establishing the European Union.

In essence the draft treaty sought to: 1) broaden the economic and political competence of the present Community, and introduce procedures which would allow successive developments as necessary; 2) make the present Commission into a true government within the competences of the Union; 3) give Parliament real power of co-decision in matters of control of the executive, legislation, taxation and budget; 4) reduce the present powers of the Council of Ministers, require a different composition of the Council, and abolish unanimous voting; 5) foresee the coming into force of the Union even if not all member states of the Community wish to become members of the Union.

Against a background of continuous political infighting between the member-states, it appeared a highly optimistic if not naïve venture to propose a new reconstruction of the Community's institutional structure along federalist lines. Yet within three months of the Parliament approving the draft treaty, it received the endorsement, in principle at least, of President Mitterrand of France.

In what was clearly a response to the European Parliament's initiative, the Council of Ministers established its own working party known as the Dooge Committee 'to make suggestions for the improvement of the operation of European co-operation in both the Community field and that of political, or any other co-operation'.[31] A central part of the Dooge Committee Report was the idea of 'a genuine leap forward': in the words of the report 'we must now make a qualitative leap and present the various proposals in a global manner, thus demonstrating the common political will of the Member States. At the end that will must be expressed by the formulation of a genuine political entity among European states, ie a European Union'.[32] The rest of the report focused on the institutional changes required to satisfy this goal. The Dooge Report differed from the European Parliament's draft treaty in several important respects. Probably the most important were the caveats relating to the envisaged decision-making process entered by the British, Danish and Greek Governments which insisted that when a state considered it had important national interests at stake, discussions should continue until unanimous agreement was reached. The main conclusion of the report when published in March 1985 was that an intergovernmental conference should be convened to negotiate a new treaty.

The Single European Act

The Single European Act is what emerged from the intergovernmental conference.[33] As the Act is a complicated and subtly worded legal document it is worthwhile breaking down the contents and placing these under different headings: namely functional provisions; institutional reform; and other procedural and lesser changes.

Functional Provisions

The central functional provision of the Single European Act is the establishment of a completely liberalised internal market. Article 3A calls for this process to be completed by the end of 1992, and Article 100a (which replaces Article 100 of the Treaty of Rome which urges the approximation of national laws which affect the functioning of the Common Market) is the principal instrument for the accomplishment of this task. The Act outlines in considerable detail the actions that have to be taken for the establishment of a true internal market. These are summarised below. One of the central tasks is to achieve the harmonisation of indirect taxes in so far as is necessary to ensure the establishment and functioning of the internal market. (Decisions of the Council of Ministers on this issue have to be taken on the basis of unanimity after consulting the European Parliament.)

The Act also allows the Council to adopt measures which 'approximate' national provisions in other areas. In particular, the Act permits the Council to introduce measures which allow for a high level of protection in the fields of health, safety, environmental protection and consumer protection. Controls and restrictions are also imposed on member states unilaterally introducing measures which affect imports. To assist this liberalisation of the internal market, the Council, taking account of the differences between economies, has to determine guidelines and conditions necessary to secure balanced progress. After 1992 the Commission has to forward proposals for future action in the internal market.

Another key aspect of the Act is the strengthening of economic and social cohesion inside the Community by reducing regional disparities. To this end, the various sub-parts of Article 130 detail the methods to be used to reduce the backwardness of less favoured regions, and instruct the Council within a year to revise and realign the rules of the various structural funds to meet the objectives.

A further functional area covered by the Act is Technology Policy and the Environment. In the area of technology policy the Act instructs the Council to establish multi-annual framework programmes, and in relation to the environment it sets out a series of objectives and defines what action needs to be taken to meet them.

The only other significant part of the Act is that which gives formal recognition to the European Council and provides for European co-operation in the sphere of Foreign Policy.

Institutional Reform

One important aspect of the Single European Act concerns the institutional revisions it introduces into the Community's decision-making process. The objectives of these revisions, known as the co-operation procedure, are to give the European Parliament an enlarged and more formalised role (although it does not give it any further rights or powers) and to introduce qualified majority voting into some areas of the Community. The new co-operation procedure will work as follows. The Council, acting by a qualified majority on a proposal from the Commission and after obtaining the opinion of the European Parliament, adopts a common position. Then the Council communicates that common position to the European Parliament (with a statement of reasons and of the Commission's position). If within three months, the European Parliament approves the common position or takes no decision the Council can act on the basis of that policy. Alternatively, the European Parliament may propose amendments to the Council's common position or reject that common position (in which case, the Council must act unanimously on a second reading). Then the Commission shall, within a month, re-examine its original proposals and forward to the Council its re-examined proposals (stating its opinion on any unaccepted amendments proposed by the European Parliament: these the Council may adopt unanimously). After this stage Council shall, by qualified majority, adopt the re-examined proposal (unanimity is required for any amendment). If the Council does not act within three months, the Commission proposals are deemed to be rejected. Figure IIii outlines these new decision-making procedures.

It is important to recognise that this new procedure only applies where the Council is operating by the principle of qualified majority voting. The specific articles where this applies are outlined below.

Article 49:	measures to bring about freedom of movement for workers.
Article 54(2):	directives for abolishing restrictions on freedom of establishment.
Article 56(2):	(*second sentence*) directives for co-ordination of national measures providing for special treatment of foreign nationals on grounds of public policy, security or health.
Article 57:	directives for mutual recognition of formal qualifications; directives for co-ordination of national measures concerning the taking up and pursuit of activities as self-employed persons; (*but excluding*) directives relating to training for and conditions of

Figure IIIii Flow-chart illustrating legislative process in the community

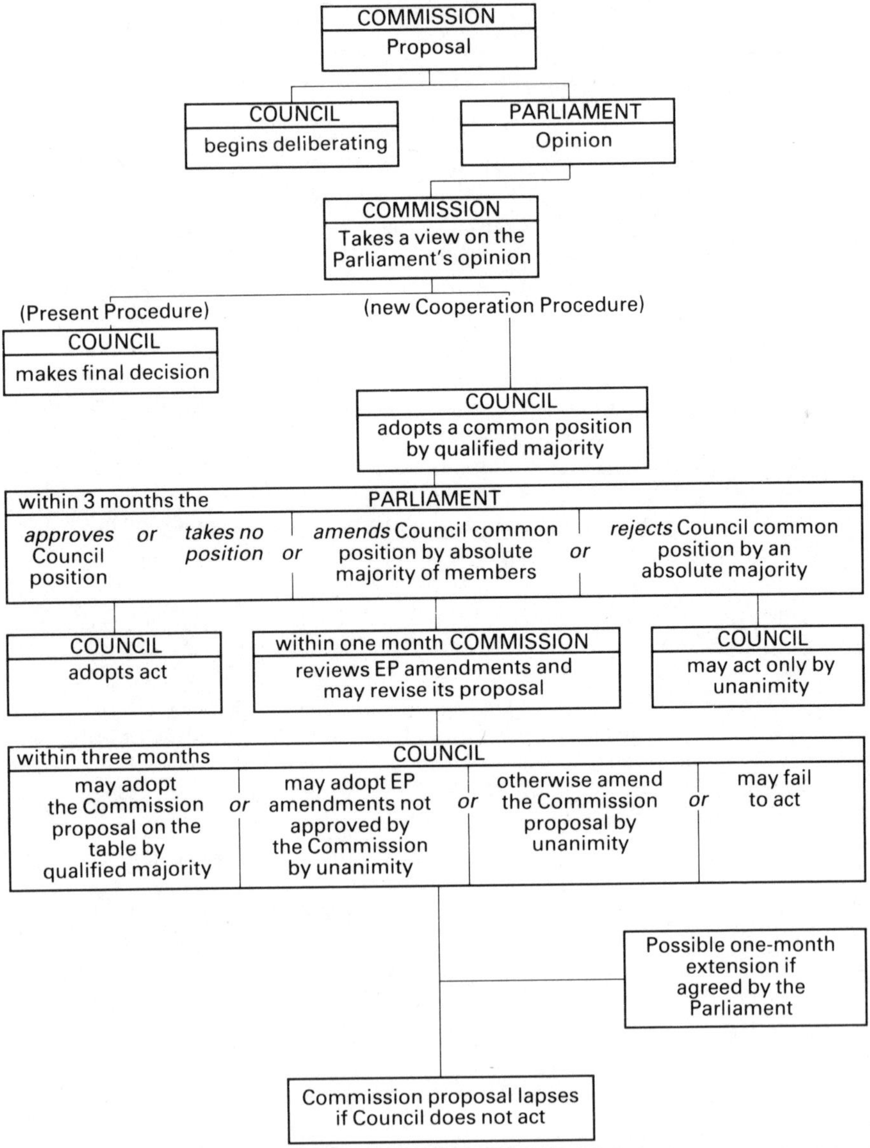

	access to the professions (where unanimity is required).
Article 100A:	measures for approximation of national provisions as to the internal market.
Article 100B:	proposals for mopping up national measures not harmonised by the end of 1992.
Article 118A:	adoption to minimum requirements for gradual implementation of improvements as regards health and safety of workers.
Article 130E:	implementation of decisions relating to the ERDF.
Article 130Q(2):	adoption of supplementary programmes in field of regional development.

Other procedural changes are introduced, but these are of a lesser scale. One new provision makes minor changes to the Court of Justice so that it can hear 'certain classes of action brought by national or legal persons'. Under another revision the assent of the European Parliament becomes necessary for the admission of new member states and for the conclusion of certain international agreements.

Considerable confusion exists as to whether the Single European Act is a supranational or intergovernmental document. For instance, Mrs Thatcher has told the House of Commons that the Act does not undermine the Luxembourg Compromise to any great extent. Yet in Ireland the Supreme Court ruled that a referendum had to be held on the subject because the Act undermined national decision-making in the area of foreign affairs, thereby jeopardising Irish neutrality. To some extent both views are right; the Act entrenches the principle of unanimity in some areas, but opens up others to qualified majority. In this sense it cannot be seen as either a supranational or an intergovernmental Treaty. Probably it is best viewed as making a number of statements of intent and objectives in various areas, some of which will involve majority voting. Thus, in the short term, the Act should not be interpreted as obliging any significant transfer of political authority from the national to European sphere. But the changes it introduces will in all probability remove some of the legal and decision-making bottlenecks that have tied up the Community in recent years. As a result, the immediate impact of the Act will be the speeding up of the Community decision-making process. Beyond that it is too early to make any other predictions.

The Institutional Framework for Social Policy

Beneath the Community's main decision-making process, there exists in each policy area, whether it is the Common Agricultural Policy, the

European Monetary System, or Social Policy, a separate institutional framework to undertake the necessary tasks to make EC policies operational. The institutional framework for social policy is outlined in Figure IIiii. This shows the various committees and bodies involved in the formulation and administration of social policies.

Standing Committee on Employment

The Standing Committee on Employment was established by a Council decision of May 1970. This committee was to be a consultative forum where the trade unions and employers could exchange and express views on employment matters. However, the Committee immediately ran into problems over the number of representatives both management and labour were to have. As a result of this dispute, the Committee did not actually meet. But, in the mid-seventies, it was resurrected as a result of pressure from the trade unions. The trade unions wanted the Committee to act as the catalyst for Community action on the increasing problem of European unemployment. On several occasions, the unions tried to get the Committee to adopt a Community employment plan, but these failed partly because the trade union proposals were not significantly clear, and partly because the employers' representatives were reluctant to agree to a 'tripartite' initiative at Community level. Thus, the Committee has not lived up to trade union expectations. At the moment, the employers are the harshest critics of the Committee. They see the Committee as serving no worthwhile purpose, for it is simply used by both sides of industry to express in public their views on employment matters. In fact, there is a strong view amongst the employers that the Committee should be abolished.

Sector Committees

In the fifties, the High Authority of the ECSC established two committees – one relating to coal and the other to steel – involving the social partners, to undertake the detailed groundwork necessary to harmonise working conditions in both industries. The general view, after a period of time, was that these committees carried out useful work, particularly as regards the collection of statistics on working conditions within each member state. As a result, the Commission decided during the sixties to establish similar committees for other economic sectors. The list below shows the number of committees set up as well as the establishment date of each.

Figure IIiii The social policy institutional framework

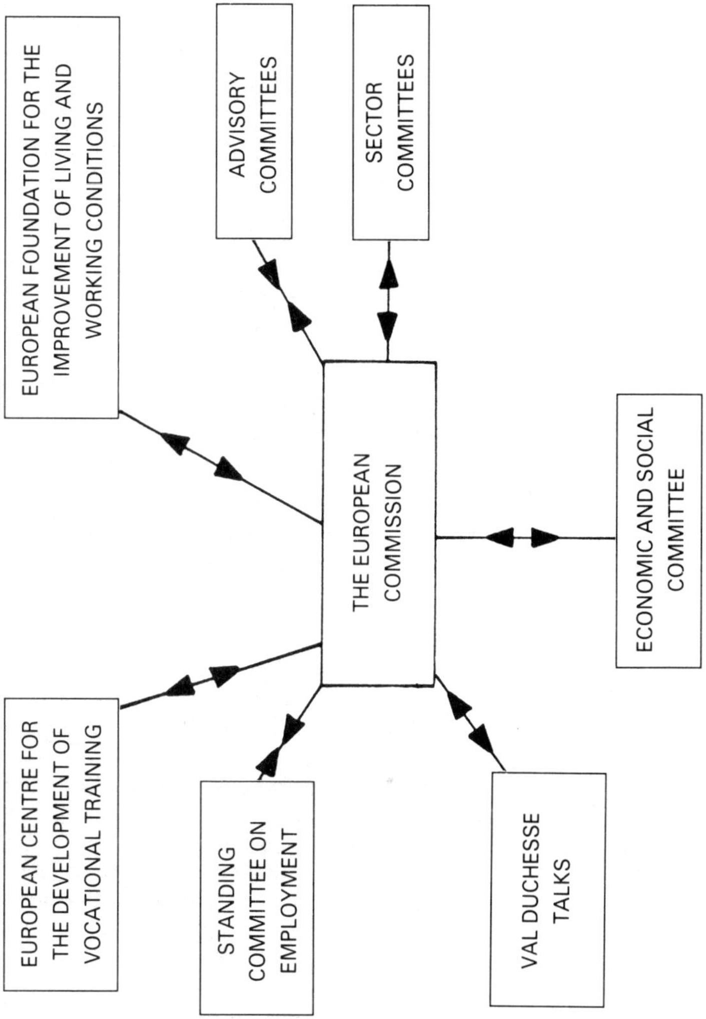

1. Joint Committee for the Harmonisation of Working Conditions in the Coal Industry (1955)
2. Joint Committee for the Harmonisation of Working Conditions in the Iron and Steel Industry (1955)
3. Joint Committee on Social Problems of Agricultural Workers (1963)
4. Joint Advisory Committee for Social Problems in Road Transport (1965)
5. Joint Advisory Committe for Social Problems in Inland Navigation (1967)
6. Joint Committee on Social Problems in Sea Fishing (1968)
7. Joint Advisory Committee on Social Questions in the Railways (1971)
8. Joint Committee for the Footwear Industry (set up in 1971, but suspended in 1982)

Each Committee was to be composed of equal numbers of management and labour representatives appointed by the Commission on the recommendation of European employers' associations and trade unions. Thus the UK representatives on the committees are selected either by the relevant European trade union organisation or the relevant European employers' organisation. There was to be no direct contact between the committees and national labour or management groups. The Commission was to take on the associated administrative and organisational tasks. In 1973, Mr Altons, the Chairman of the Economic and Social Committee, described the purpose of the sector committees as to 'keep a watch on economic and social developments in their sectors, seek to conclude model collective agreements and submit proposals for Community action to institutions'.[34] Thus the goals of the committee were ambitious – to contribute to the construction of a European system of collective agreements. However, the committees have failed to live up to this early expectation. Only the Agricultural Workers Committee succeeded in concluding a 'Community Agreement'. This agreement stipulated that the hours worked by agricultural workers across the Community should be set at 44 hours. As agreements at the national level went much further than this stipulation, the general verdict is that it was not that important.

There are several reasons why the joint sector committees have not lived up to early expectations. For a start, during the seventies, the committees were operating within a very different economic context to the one which prevailed in the sixties. Economic prosperity and growth had given way to economic recession, resulting in the social partners becoming more concerned with developments at the national rather than European level. Furthermore, the employers' organisations had serious misgivings about entering into Community-level agreements with trade unions. Their argument was that the social partners (trade unions and employers) at the European level had no mandate to enter into formal agreements on behalf of their constituent members, nor the necessary authority to oblige members to implement any agreement that they may have reached. Lastly, many of the committees, it is fair to say, suffered from a lack of clarity and direction, as the social partners were uncertain about the status of discussions in committees and the scope of any conclusions arising.

Despite the disappointing performance of these committee during the seventies, they are currently enjoying a revival, or at least the Commission is doing its upmost to transform them into more purposeful institutions. Learning from the seventies' experience, the Commission is not pushing for these committees to conclude 'Community collective agreements, but for them to engage in an "informal" social dialogue'. Under this new approach, the deliberations of the sector committees would be based more on a frank exchange of views than negotiations in the strict sense. It is too early to say if this informal social dialogue will be a success.

The Related Advisory Committees

i) Advisory Committee on Vocational Training
ii) Advisory Committee on Safety, Hygiene and Health Protection at Work
iii) Mines Health and Safety Committee
iv) General Committee for Health and Safety
v) European Social Fund
vi) Social Security – Migrant Workers
vii) Free Movement of Workers

The Advisory Committees were established for a variety of reasons. One was to advise on the implementation of particular policies. Thus, for example, the Mines Health and Safety Committee, consisting of mining engineers from the member states, provides the Commission with crucial information both on the drawbacks and potential of certain policies. Another reason was to further the structural policies of the Community. This category more or less refers to the work of the European Social Fund. Thirdly, some of the committees – for instance the Advisory Committee on Safety, Hygiene and Health Protection at Work – deal primarily with the approximation of laws. Lastly, more generally, the committees are expected to contribute to the development of EC Social Policy.

European Foundation for the Improvement of Living and Working Conditions

The Foundation is primarily a research and policy centre. Its charter states that 'the aim of the Foundation is to contribute to the planning and establishment of better living and working through action designed to increase and disseminate knowledge likely to assist this development'. The work of the Foundation is overseen by a management committee made up of employer, trade union and Commission representatives.

For the most part, the Foundation fosters the exchange of information and experience in a wide range of fields. Thus, its main work is facilitating contact between universities in different EC member states, setting up working groups on particular policy issues, providing (financial) assistance for pilot projects and organising courses, conferences and seminars. Recent examples of research are the impact of new technology on employment practices in specific economic sectors and policies to protect the environment against pollution.

European Centre for the Development of Vocational Training

In February 1975, the Council of Ministers approved a Resolution establishing the European Centre for the Development of Vocational Training. The role of this centre, CEDEFOP, which is located in Berlin, is to: i) assist the Commission in encouraging, at Community level, the promotion and development of vocational training and continuing education; ii) compile documentation on recent research studies in relevant fields; iii) contribute to the further development and coordination of research in relevant fields; iv) further the exchange of information and experience; v) disseminate information and documentation. The centre is directed by a management committee consisting of 10 representatives of employers' organisations, 10 representatives of trade unions, 10 representatives of Government and three representatives of the Commission. This 'quadri-partite' organisation meets three times a year to supervise the direction of the Centre's research activities.

In recent years, a considerable amount of the Centre's research activities has been focused on identifying the obstacles, and suggesting solutions, to the mutual recognition of training qualifications among the various member states. Special research projects have also been undertaken in relation to strategies to upgrade the skill base of Spain and Portugal. In addition to these research studies, the Centre has a number of 'permanent activities'. It publishes three periodicals: the main one being *Vocational Training* which comes out quarterly, the bulletin *Cedefop News*, and *Cedefop Flash*. In 1986, it began work on an ambitious programme to establish a comprehensive documentary co-operation network which is still continuing.

The Social Policy Framework in Practice

Although there are no hard and fast rules, the policy framework normally works along the lines detailed in figure IIiv. The example used in the figure is a health and safety initiative, but it could be any number of issues. The Commission normally triggers the policy process by producing a proposal. This proposal is immediately sent to the Council, who publishes it in the Community's *Official Journal*, the European Parliament, and the social partners. Consultation about the proposals goes on both at the national and European levels, and the results of these discussions are all chanelled into a Council working group. If there is a general agreement on the proposal, then it will fairly quickly go to COREPER which formally ensures that there is no opposition to it from any of the member states. After this stage, the Council of Ministers ratifies the proposals and it is implemented in national legislation in each member state. More often than not, however, especially as regards social policy, a proposal remains at the Council working group stage for considerable periods of time. As a result, endless rounds of negotiations have to take place to establish compromise agreements. Until these agreements are reached, the proposal tends to remain with COREPER.

One author has suggested that the development of this social policy framework, along with other attempts to incorporate interest groups within the Community's decision-making process, can be interpreted as an attempt at creating a corporatist system at the EC level.[35] Certainly, the consultative role of the social partners grew significantly during the seventies, and there are very few policy initiatives about which they are not now consulted. However, it is somewhat inaccurate to suggest that the Community's decision-making process has evolved into a corporatist system.

Corporatism normally implies that the nation state takes a directive and influential role in economic and social affairs, especially in cases where the expectations and aspirations of independent groups overload the ability of the government and economy to gratify those demands. The term should not be taken simply to mean interest intermediation between different interest groups. Used in its proper sense, corporatism is inappropriate to explain the development of the Community's decision-making process during the seventies simply because the EC has not the capacity to intervene directly and fully in economic and social matters. Even if this problem is overlooked, the corporatist thesis would still be inaccurate because crucial to the success of such a system is the

Figure IIiv Formulation of Directive

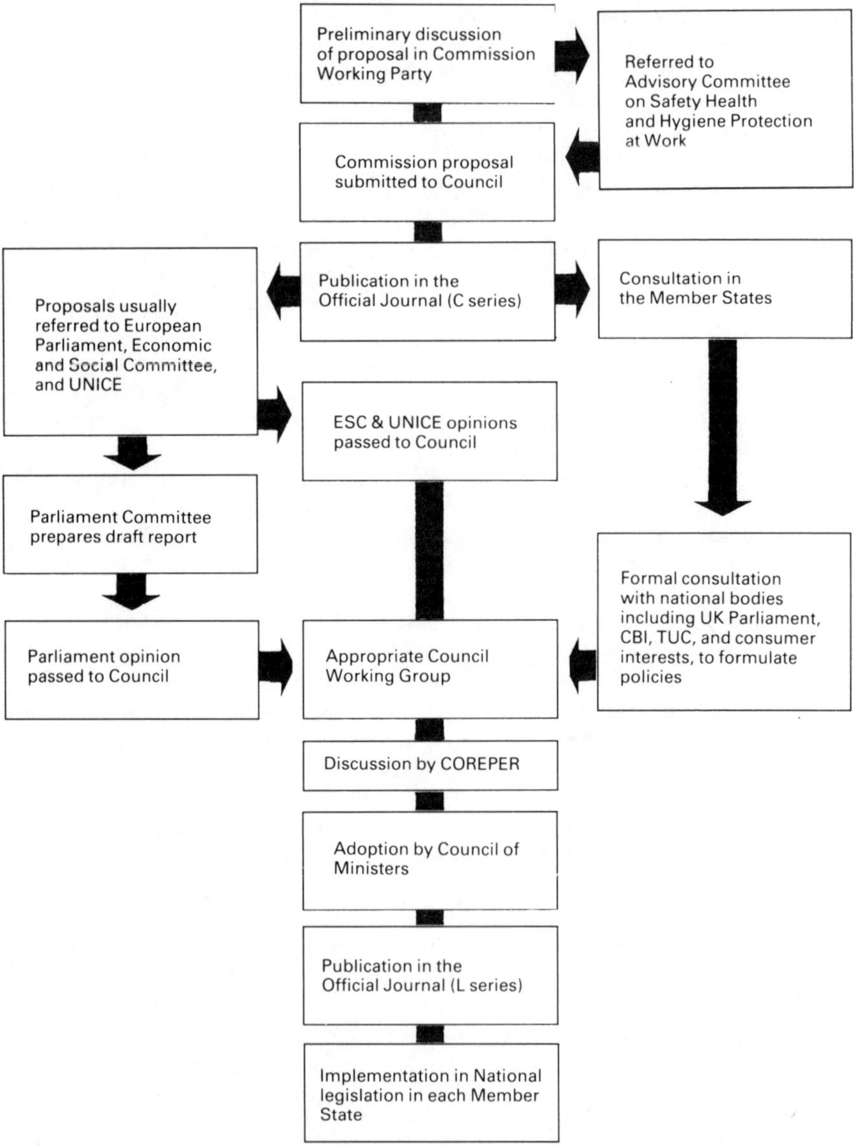

willingness of interest groups to participate within it, and the capacity of groups to discipline their members to accept the decisions made inside the corporatist framework. These preconditions do not exist inside the Community social-policy framework: the employers are not willing to enter into European-level agreements, nor do any of the interest groups have the capacity to bind their members to any decisions emanating from EC committees or institutions.

The development of the EC social-policy institutional framework is best understood from the standpoint of the dynamics of European integration. Once it has been established that a greater EC presence is required in a particular policy area, the first action normally taken by the Commission is to develop a policy framework so that the Community initiatives gain a degree of legitimacy.[36] Thus, once the Commission decided that an active social policy should be pursued, no time was lost in building a framework involving the member states and the social partners. In other words the establishment of the social-policy framework was a legitimation process intended to facilitate interventions in that area.

Notes and References

1 For a good account of Britain's lukewarm approach to European integration see the early chapters of COOK, C. and SKED, A. *Postwar Britain – A political history*, Penguin, Harmondsworth 1983, and BARKER, E. *Britain in a Divided Europe 1948-1970*, Weidenfeld, London 1971

2 For conflicting interpretations about the role of the Marshall Plan *see* KINDLEBERGER, C P. *Marshall Plan Days*, Allen and Unwin, London 1987, for a positive assessment and MILWARD, A. *The Reconstruction of Western European 1945–51*, Methuen, London 1984, for a sceptical view

3 *See the chapter on the Council of Europe in LAMBERT, J and PALMER, M. European Unity, A Survey of European Organisations*, Allen and Unwin, London, 1968

4 The central coordinating body of the ECSC was the High Authority. This body was given the power to make binding decisions in relation to the member countries' coal and steel industries. This power made the High Authority a genuinely supranational organisation. The main supranational clauses of the Treaty were Articles 58, 61 and 74 which allowed the ECSC to impose production quotas, introduce minimum prices, and set import ceilings when either the

coal or steel industry was in a state of manifest crisis. A 'manifest crisis' could only be declared when extremely bad economic circumstances prevailed in either industry. The initial structure of the ECSC was revised by the Merger Treaty of 1966. This treaty integrated the different EC organisations into one single body. The high Authority and other ECSC bodies were abolished and their responsibilities transferred to the European Commission. The Treaty of Paris was left intact, however, which meant that the Commission had still the authority to act in a supranational manner

5 See HAAS, E B. *The Uniting of Europe: Political, Social and Economic forces*, Stanford University Press, California 1968

6 See Chapters one and two in IONESCU, G *The New Politics of European Intregration*, Allen and Unwin, London 1973

7 Currently the West European Union is enjoying a revival as the British, German and French Governments appear to be in agreement that this is the ideal body through which distinctly European policies and approaches can be established on security matters

8 LINDBERG, L W. *The Political Dynamics of European Economic Integration*, Stanford University Press, California 1963

9 At the time of writing (early 1988) it is widely expected that the current President, Jacques Delors, will seek re-appointment

10 HALLSTEIN, W. *Europe in the Making*, Allen and Unwin, London 1972 p 77

11 For a detailed account of the work of the Court of Justice see USHER, M. *European Court of Justice Practice*, Sweet and Maxwell, London 1983

12 WALLACE, H. 'Institutions in a Decentralized Community', *New Europe* No. 3, Summer 1977 pp 21–34

13 See HENIG, S. *Power and Delusion in Europe: the political institutions of the European Community*, Europotentials, London 1980

14 European Commission, *First Stage*, Brussels 1962 p 12

15 NOEL, E. *Memorandum de la Commission sur la Programme d'action pendant la deuxième stage*, European Commission, Brussels 1962 p 27

16 For more on the Fouchet Plan proposals, see the editor's introduction in HILL, C. (ed) *National Foreign Policies and European Political Cooperation* Allen and Unwin, London 1983

17 See HOLT, S. *The Common Market: The Conflict of Theory and Practice*, Hamish Hamilton, London 1971

18 See HEATHCOTE, N. 'The Crisis of European Supranationality', *Journal of Common Market Studies* Vol V No 2 Dec 1966 pp 140–71

19 See TAYLOR, P. 'Politics of the European Communities', *World Politics* Vol. 27, 3 April 1975 pp 336–60

20 See CAMPS, M. *European Unification in the Sixties*, Praegar, New York 1977

21 PUCHALA, D. 'Of Blind Men, Elephants and International Integration', *Journal of Common Market Studies*, Volume 10 No 1 p 267

22 The institutional problems arising from the Merger Treaty are comprehensively described in PRYCE, R. *The Politics of the European Community*, Butterworth, London 1973

23 EC Commision, *Third General Report 1969*, Brussels, p 16

24 COOMBES, D. *Politics and Bureaucracy*, Allen and Unwin, London 1970

25 POULLET, E and DEPREY, G. 'The Place of the Commission within the Institutional system', in SASSE, C (ed), *Decision-making in the European Community*, Praegar, New York 1977 p 157

26 See BULMER, S and WESSELS, W. *The European Council decision-making in European Politics*, Macmillan, London 1987

27 See O'NUALLAIN, C (ed). *The Presidency of the European Council of Ministers*, Croom Helm, London 1985

28 EDMUNDS G and WALLACE, H. *The Council of Ministers of the European Community and its President in Office*, Federal Trust, London 1977

29 For a good account of the work of the European Parliament until the late seventies see FITZMAURICE, J. *The European Parliament*, Saxon House, Farnborough, Hants 1978. For a more recent exposition on the problems this institution faces in the Community decision-making machinery see ROBINSON, A. *The European Parliament in the EC policy process*, Policy Studies Institute, London 1984, and BOURGUIGNON, R. *et al* 'Five years of the directly elected European Parliament', *Journal of Common Market Studies*, Vol. XXIV 1. September 1985 pp 39–60

30 See CORDOZO, R and CORBETT, R. 'The Crocodile Group' in Lodge, J. (ed) *European Union: the European Community in search of a future*, Macmillan, London, 1987 pp 15–47

31 House of Lords Sub-Committee on the European Community: European Union Report No.11 1984 p 11

32 *op. cit.* p 12

33 For further information on the Single European Act see LODGE, J. 'The Single European Act: towards a new Euro Dynamism?' *Journal of Common Market Studies* XXIV no 3 March 1986 pp 203–24; European Commission, 'Single European Act', *European Community Bulletin,* Supplement 2/1986; and CORBETT, R. 'The 1985 Intergovernmental conference and the Single European Act' in PRYCE, R. (ed), *The Dynamics of European Union,* Croom Helm, London 1987 pp 238–271

34 CRIPPS, L. 'The Social Policy of the European Community', *Social Europe,* January No 1 Brussels p 53

35 SARGANT, J. 'British Finance and Industrial Capital and the European Communities', *West European Politics,* Volume 6 No 2 April pp 14–36

36 TUGENDHAT, C. *Making Sense of the Europe* Viking, London 1986

Chapter III

Social Policy: The First Phase

This chapter and the next examine Community social policies. It is argued that social policy at the Community level has evolved in three phases, although each phase has added a new range of policies rather than replacing those already in operation. In the first phase, which lasted from the formation of the EC in 1957 until 1972, the main focus was on increasing labour mobility inside the Common Market. This goal restricted Community action to a series of essentially legalistic measures to reduce barriers and other rigidities hindering the free movement of workers between member states.

The second phase which lasted from 1973–1983 is the subject of the next chapter. Community social policy initiatives in those years were more positive and interventionist than the first phase. The widespread feeling within member states for a more equitable and socially just European society, and the desire on the part of the Commission to increase integration in the social arena were the two key factors which led to this new departure. The objective of Community social policy in this period became the harmonisation and the progressive upgrading of standards in employment practices and in the labour market more generally amongst the member states. For a variety of reasons, analysed in chapter IV, this phase ended in the early eighties. Since then, several initiatives have been taken, as yet without success, to launch a new third phase. As a result, the future direction and scope of Community social policy has yet to emerge.

This chapter focuses on the first phase of Community social policy. The first part examines the debate about the need for a social policy before the establishment of the Common Market. Then an appraisal is made of the social policy clauses of the Treaty of Rome. The next section, which is the main body of the chapter, outlines the developments that took place during the sixties. Finally, we look at the pressures which led to the Community changing direction in the social field, and formulating the Social Action Programme in 1974.

To Introduce a Social Policy? The debate outlined

In the years leading up to the establishment of the Common Market, it was hotly debated whether or not a new economic arrangement in

Europe needed a social dimension. To examine this issue in detail, the ILO set up a group of experts. It is worth detailing the conclusions of their report in some depth, particularly as they range over some of the current controversies about whether or not the completion of the internal market project should have a social dimension. The extent to which closer economic integration between a number of countries may lead to 'unfair' competition from countries with lower labour standards had been a matter of some dispute for a considerable period of time. In addressing this issue, the 'group of experts' distinguished between the general level of labour costs on the one hand and differences in the inter-industrial pattern of labour costs on the other.

The report of the experts argued that differences in the general level of wages and social charges between different countries broadly reflect differences in productivity. Where productivity is high because a country has rich natural resources, abundant capital, efficient entrepreneurs and skilled labour, the general level of wages as well as of other incomes will be high. But the workings of the exchange-rate mechanism ensure that differences in levels of wages and other incomes in the various countries remain in line with international differences in productivity. If a country finds that its costs of production for most commodities are too high to enable it to pay its way, equilibrium could be restored by letting the price level fall as productivity increases, by fresh investment in export industries, or by revision of the rate of exchange. The conclusion of this line of argument is that differences in the general level of labour costs between countries do not create lasting disparities and, as a result, there is no need for active interventionist policies to encourage a broad equivalence of such overheads in a pan-European economic area.

The experts go on to say, however, that the case is different if the foreign competition to which a particular group of enterprises in one country is exposed arises not because the general level of labour costs in the competing country is low, but because foreign producers in the same business sector pay wages or have to bear social charges (national insurance charges, etc) that are exceptionally low in comparison with the general level of wages and social changes in the same country. In this case, it is justifiable for a country to forbid or reduce imports of such products until labour costs in the industry in question have been brought into line with those in other industries in their country of origin. Equally, the experts regarded it as justifiable for the authority overseeing or administering economic integration to have powers to bring about such social harmonisation.

As well as examining the possible distortions which differences in labour costs could have on international trade, the experts analysed some particular instances of differences in social policy which, it may be argued, ought to be reduced or eliminated before, during or after the establishment of freer markets in Europe. The instances included wages, methods of financing social security and welfare schemes, hours of work and overtime premium rates. As regards wages, the report was clear: 'an attempt to establish identical patterns of relative wage rates and labour conditions in different industries in each of a number of countries would certainly represent an unduly rigid approach'.[1] In relation to questions of equal pay for equal value, the report recommended an ILO European Regional Conference or something similar to design regulations for the European Community based on existing international labour conventions. There was a recommendation that if any regulations on wages were to be established by a European economic organisation they should be 'minimalist' in character.

Another matter addressed by the group of experts was whether producers in certain countries who paid directly for social security and welfare schemes would be put at a disadvantage against countries where such programmes were financed out of general tax revenue. The experts were of the view that it would be neither desirable nor feasible to undertake the harmonising of social security schemes. They argued that a uniformly applied method of financing social security programmes may have an unequal impact on different industries even within one country. This is because producers will compensate for social charges by raising their prices to consumers, or by not reducing these prices by the full amount which productivity improvements would have permitted, or by increasing wages more slowly than otherwise would have been the case. Moreover, they went on to state that if it could be shown that a particular system of financing social security affected one industry more than another, this might compensate, and might have been deliberately designed to compensate, for the unequal effects of other taxes (e.g. freight taxes).

The committee also rejected the idea that hours of work and overtime rates should be standardised within a European integrated area. The length of the working week and related topics were regarded as matters to be determined by each country or industry. The experts were strongly of the view that there was no economic case for harmonisation in this field, for a country's or industry's preference to work longer or shorter hours would be reflected in its international trade and production specialisation. (Through the workings of international trade those countries preferring to work longer hours would be dominated by labour-intensive industries, those choosing to work shorter hours would be made up with capital-intensive industries.)

Thus for the most part, the group of experts thought that an active interventionist social policy was not a necessary part of a new economic arrangement in Europe. At the same time, however, they were of a view that certain measures were necessary in this field to ensure that 'unfair competition' did not occur between countries belonging to such an arrangement. In addition, the committee also thought that standards laid down in international labour conventions relating to such matters as labour inspection service, and health and safety at the work-place, could be applied to a group of countries, as well as to a single country. Finally, the experts considered that the establishment of a fund designed specifically to assist the disadvantaged countries in such matters as training was also appropriate. As the next section shows, the Treaty of Rome adopts a 'minimalist approach' to social policy, very similar to that recommended by the group of experts.[2]

Social Policy and the Treaty of Rome

There is a virtual consensus that the Treaty of Rome (1958) is a highly non-interventionist and market-orientated document. The direction and ethos of the treaty is captured well in Article 3 of Part One which outlines the principles of the Common Market. The article has eleven separate clauses, the vast majority of which talk about the abolition or removal of barriers to trade and the construction of a customs union. Only one sub-clause (sub-clause i) explicitly relates to social policy, committing the Common Market to establishing a Social Fund and to work towards the general improvement of living standards of workers. One commentator suggests that this sub-clause should not be read as any commitment to an interventionist philosophy on the part of the founding fathers of the Community.[3] Instead it should be interpreted as being subsidiary to the market orientation of the treaty: the Social Fund was conceived in order to facilitate the free movement of workers, while the improvement of living standards of workers was regarded as a by-product of the dynamic gains brought about by the creation of a Common Market.

The specific social policy clauses of the treaty are Articles 117–128 and come in the third part of the treaty; 'Economic Policy' of the Community. These are reproduced in Appendix 1. Articles 117 and 118 oblige the member states to work towards the harmonisation of their social systems, while at the same time making continuous improvements to their living standards. As the wording of these articles is general and inexact it has been hard to interpret what practical obligations they imposed on the member states. Indeed, a legal controversy exists about the extent to which these clauses of the Treaty of Rome provide the basis for the standardisation of social policies and provisions across the Community. Article 119, on the application of the principle that 'men and women should receive equal pay for equal work', was only inserted on the insistence of French employers who were concerned that their high manufacturing costs would lead to the other member states obtaining a competitive advantage. The architects of the Treaty of Rome were lukewarm about including such a specific clause. Moreover, the article's wording was for a long time interpreted as putting the onus on member states to achieve the principle, and it was not until a Court of Justice ruling in the 1970s that it was established that the article gave individuals direct rights.[4]

Article 120 states that 'Member-States shall endeavour to maintain the existing equivalence between paid holiday schemes'. Again there is no general agreement about the exact legal standing of this clause. One possibility is that it was intended to ensure that no downward pressure was imposed on holiday rates inside the Community. Whatever its meaning, little in the way of concrete action has been launched on the basis of this clause. Articles 121-122 commit the Commission to produce a separate chapter on social developments in its annual report, and gives the European Parliament the authority to request from the Commission a report 'on any particular problem concerning social conditions'. Over the years this 'chapter' has developed into a separate annual report containing a wealth of information on trends and new developments in the member states' social policies. Articles 123–8 relate to the operation of the Social Fund, the main function of which was 'to improve employment opportunities for workers'. The Social Fund was a weaker version of the training and retraining schemes established by the European Coal and Steel Community.

The Free Movement of Labour

The free movement of labour was the cornerstone of the social provisions of the Treaty of Rome. The first Community legislation concerning this subject was passed in 1961, and is known as Regulation 15. This Regulation only *authorised* (rather than granted the right to) Community workers to hold salaried employment in another member state if there were no workers available in the national labour markets. Moreover, it did not apply to seasonal or frontier workers or to non-salaried staff. Nonetheless, the regulation was regarded as important because it established a basic framework for handling some complex questions associated with promoting the free movement of labour.[5] Articles 1 and 3 of the regulation covered the problem of the extent to which national priority over other member states and Community priority over non-member countries was to be established. On the first issue the legal provision was clear: jobs in those regions and professions where a scarcity of labour existed were immediately available to outside workers; in those regions and professions having labour surpluses, a three-week period was set down in which priority would be given to national applicants for job vacancies; after that this national priority would be removed.

The question of whether or not Community workers should obtain priority over those from third countries was a matter of considerable dispute. The Italian Government, no doubt recognising that the regional unemployment problem in Southern Italy was being ameliorated by emigration, lobbied strongly for Community workers to be given priority in employment inside the Common Market. On the other hand, West Germany, and to a lesser extent France, who were using workers from Turkey and other non-member third countries to ease their labour-scarcity problems, were unwilling to accept this principle. This issue was dealt with very untidily by the Regulation. In particular, the Regulation did not clearly establish whether Community nationals should receive preferential treatment over migrants from third countries. Thus confusion reigns over the state of play in this area, leading one commentator to conclude 'the claim that it was accepted from the start that one aim of the community was to absorb its labour surpluses seems somewhat excessive'.[6]

The changes made by Regulation 15 to the existing national regulations and restrictions on the type and length of employment for workers from other member states were extremely modest. Article 6 gave each Community worker the right to have his/her work permit renewed after a year of regular employment in another member state. After three years of regular employment, any worker was eligible to move to a different profession (provided he/she were suitably qualified). Finally, after four years of regular employment such workers would be eligible to work in any salaried profession under the same conditions as national workers. The Regulation also dealt with the position of the families of Community workers. Article 11 permitted the spouse and young children of a Community worker to accompany him, provided he/she had been admitted to work in another member state and had acquired 'normal' housing for his family. In addition, Article 15 guaranteed children of Community workers attendance in vocational training courses and allowed them to apprentice themselves under the same conditions as the children of nationals.

To oversee the implementation of the Regulation, and to advise the Community on matters relating to the free movement of workers, a Consultative Committee was established, consisting of two government officials from each member state and two trade union and management representatives. A Technical Committee was also established as a sub-organ of the Consultative Committee to deal with the details of promoting co-ordination of the labour ministries in the six member countries.

A series of administrative and technical problems delayed the implementation of the framework set up by the Regulation. But this did not cause any particular problems, partly because of the modest objectives contained in the Regulation and partly because some of the issues identified as problem-areas were not proving to be so. For instance, there were no recorded problems with the 'national priorities' issue. Housing shortages in Germany, France and Holland led to the most serious difficulties in relation to implementing the Regulation fully. As a result, few families were able immediately to accompany workers.

Overall, it can be concluded that the importance of Regulation 15 lies not in its goals, which by any standard were modest, but in the fact that it marked the first step towards establishing rules and regulations governing the free movement of workers inside the Community. For this reason the Commission was content with Regulation 15: having established a bridgehead in this area it regarded the major task ahead as one of extending, over a period of time, a body of related legislation. However, developing the next stage proved to be an unexpectedly long and complicated process.

The programme proposed by the Commission to further liberalise and encourage labour mobility included two proposals which proved to be highly controversial: (i) that Community workers should be eligible for election to works councils (under Regulation 15 they had only the right to vote in works council elections); and (ii) that the system of national priorities allowed for in Regulation 15 should be abolished. The strongest opposition to the first proposal came from the Germans and it was based on thinly disguised xenophobia. Both German trade unions and management feared that if Community workers were eligible for election to works councils instances would arise where such employees, with the help of other foreign workers (Turks and Greeks), would take control of these bodies. In relation to the proposals to discontinue the system of national priorities, a head-on clash developed between Germany and France, who were against the proposals, and the Italians, who were strongly in favour.[7]

Protracted, and at times acrimonious, negotiations took place. After eighteen months of hard bargaining, compromises were reached on the two points of controversy. Concerning the eligibility of Community workers to serve on works councils, it was agreed by all parties that the worker would have to have three years' experience in the same enterprise before this could occur. The agreement relating to the system of national priorities was elaborate, involving several different clauses and subsequent counter-clauses. The net result was that the period of national priorities was reduced from three to two years. With these compromises secured, the Council of Ministers was able in 1964 to ratify Regulation 38 on the free movement of labour. As well as including clauses covering these compromises, Regulation 38 contained other important provisions. It granted each Community worker the *right* to salaried employment in another member state, rather than the authorisation that was granted under Regulation 15. The definition of 'family' was expanded to include not only the spouse and young children, but all children, parents and grandparents dependent on the worker. Several new categories of worker were included in the new regulation, particularly frontier and seasonal workers. Agreement was reached on a new directive (Directive 64/221/EEC) to specify that reasons of 'public order, safety, and health' cannot be used to resist the entry of workers from other member-states and that any proceedings to deny, revoke or refuse renewal of residence permits must be conducted strictly on an individual basis. Finally, another Directive passed in 1964 (Directive 64/240/EEC) liberalised the system by which documents are administered.

The final steps towards abolishing all legal discrimination against migrant workers were taken by the Council of Ministers in 1968, when it approved Regulation 16/2/66, and the accompanying Directive 68/360/EEC. This Regulation laid down that all wage and salary earners in the Community may apply for job vacancies in any member state whatever their nationality, reside in another state for that purpose, settle there in order to take up employment and be joined there by their families; they are also eligible for the same rights as nationals as regards working conditions and terms of employment. However, a few restrictions are maintained on the grounds of public policy, public security or public health, particularly as regards employment in the public service. Overall, this regulation was widely considered to remove all the legal barriers to the free movement of labour.[8]

The European Social Fund

Although explicitly mentioned in the treaty, the European Social Fund did not become operational until 1962. But by the end of the Transitional Period in 1968 almost one million people had benefited from Social Fund interventions – subsidies amounting to 10 per cent of project costs and representing an equal financing share to defray costs incurred by sponsoring public bodies. On the face of it, this seems a fairly impressive record, but a closer examination reveals certain drawbacks.

Table IIIi outlines the number of applications presented by the member states, how many of these were approved and how many workers were assisted. It shows that about 95 per cent of all applications reviewed were approved, costing cumulatively about $80.3 million. A detailed break-down of the contributions and receipts is made in Table IIIii.

Table IIIi Summary of member applications and disposition period: September 20 1960–December 31 1968

Member	Applications presented	Applications reviewed	Applications approved	Workers assisted
Germany	37,414,153	23,166,430	21,902,430	284,404
Belgium	5,005,981	4,044,889	3,954,951	7,849
France	23,910,986	20,758,897	20,506,928	109,090
Italy	48,462,896	28,549,137	27,212,328	543,347
Luxembourg	34,660	12,896	12,896	96
Netherlands	8,120,093	7,217,769	6,669,362	11,427

Table IIIii shows that Italian project sponsors realised about 53 per cent of total project reimbursements while providing 20 per cent of all fund transfers. France and Germany contributed 65 per cent in return for 52 per cent in Social Fund repayments. Thus, the contributions received by Italy were in effect significantly subsidised by surplus French-German fund transfers. These two countries provided about $9 million more than they received – an amount which substantially accounts for the $11.2 million received by Italy in excess of regular Italian contributions.

Table IIIii Contributions and receipts by member state, 1962-68 (dollars)

Member State	Contributions	Receipts	Difference	(*)
Germany	25,682,846.63	21,902,430.37	3,780,416.26	(−)
Belgium	7,062,782.81	3,954,951.10	3,107,831.71	(−)
France	25,682,846.63	20,506,927.66	5,175,918.97	(−)
Italy	16,051,327.84	27,212,327.84	11,160,548.70	(+)
Luxembourg	160,517.80	12,896.44	147,621.36	(−)
Netherlands	5,618,122.71	6,669,362.31	1,051,239.60	(+)

Many of the Social Fund interventions aimed at solving the unemployment problem of labour surplus areas by reskilling redundant workers and encouraging them to migrate to some other part of the Community. The experience of Italy is indicative. By the end of 1968, 543,000 Italian workers had received some form of skills training; from this 340,000 were resettled in France and Germany. Although about

150,000 were still available in 1968 for inter-Community migration, it can be concluded that the Social Fund played a positive role in reducing the labour surplus problem inside one part of the Community.[9] The Social Fund was also used to help upgrade the skill base of the existing workforce of the Northern European member states. But relative to what the member states were doing themselves on this subject, Social Fund payments contributed only modestly to this task.

Although the Social Fund facilitated labour migration between the member states, it did not come near to resolving the persistent problem of community labour dislocations: during 1968, for instance, a monthly average of 423,000 skilled job openings were available while at the same time unemployment exceeded one million. What also puts the operation of the Social Fund into context is that the labour inputs from non-member states outnumbered Community sources during the sixties by wide margins. In 1962, six of ten 'outside' workers obtaining employment in the member states were from countries external to the Community. From 1963 to 1967, the rate varied between 66 per cent and 72 per cent. In 1966, for example, of 593,000 non-national workers in the six member states, 382,600 were from non-EC countries.[10] These figures suggest that despite the large number of grants given to intra-Community resettlements, the Social Fund was really of minimal importance.

Moreover, towards the end of the sixties, it began to be questioned whether the Social Fund should focus primarily on encouraging the free movement of workers across the Community. The criticism was voiced by the European Parliament amongst others that encouraging labour migration indiscriminately drained depressed regions of skilled workers and facilitated the clustering of these workers in urban concentrations. It was argued that the Fund should be used to facilitate the more difficult task of assisting indigenous industrial restructuring through the provision of retraining and wage-support grants. These comments gave rise to calls that the Social Fund should be transformed into a more effective employment policy instrument. Thus in 1969 the European Parliament passed a resolution urging the member states 'to promote a common social policy and in particular to reform the European Social Fund, which should become a genuine common tool for a policy of full employment and for raising living standards in the Community'[11]

Opinion varies about whether or not the operation of the Social Fund was a success during the sixties. On the positive side one author concluded 'Phase I emerges as a period of successful experimental testing . . . For the results have provided valuable experience identifying pitfalls, areas of both weakness and strength and need for redirection of effort. Thus the basis was created in Phase I for informed oversight, critical assessments and restructuring'.[12] Less favourable assessments have also been made: 'when we bear in mind the cash amounts that were available the overall conclusion would indeed seem to be that the fund was confined to a limited, and largely passive role, in which initiatory or experimental activities were impossible'.[13] Probably the more acccurate of these two views is the second interpretation. Although there was evidence to suggest a certain amount of experimenting, this was not done in the context of a fully developed Community employment programme.

Wages and Working Conditions

Although the Treaty of Rome said nothing about the wages policies of the member states, and gave the Community no rights to interfere in them, it became apparent early on that for the Commission to have a detailed knowledge of the economic and social conditions inside the Community (an obligation which was laid down by the treaty) it needed more comprehensive data on salaries and incomes in Europe. Thus in 1960 the Council approved a regulation (Regulation 10) allowing the Commission to commence work on devising uniform definitions and methods of collecting materials on wages and labour costs. In the following three years several major investigations were conducted into differences in industrial labour costs between the member states, compulsory and voluntary charges in all firms employing more than 50 people, manpower costs and real wages in the Community. A further Regulation in 1964 enabled the Commission to organise other surveys into differences in wages structures resulting from factors such as the age and sex pattern of the Community labour force and the size of firms. These studies formed the basis of the labour force surveys now carried out on a regular basis by the Community which are held in high regard in policy-making and academic circles.

Equal Pay

One of the few explicit social policy clauses in the Treaty of Rome related to equal pay (Article 119). Yet one report claimed that 'no country can point to a practical initiative taken by it prior to 30th June 1961 by virtue of the recommendation'.[14] The year 1961 was important, for it marked the end of the first stage of the Common Market, and theoretically, if not legally, the member states should have taken some action on the subject of equal pay. At the end of the year the Council, to save any embarrassment which may have been caused, established a special working party to collect and analyse information on the position of equal pay in each member state and to study possible measures to ensure effective implementation. But it soon was apparent that this working party was only a means to defer meaningful action on this issue. In 1962 the Commission drew the attention of members to the continuing failure of some states to apply the principle of equal pay, and commented on the general lack of enthusiasm shown both by the member countries and the social partners. This exhortation made some contribution to heightening awareness of the issue amongst employers and trade unions in the member states, but in terms of the actual implementation of Article 119 little headway was made in the sixties.

Health and Safety

It was not until 1962 that an Industrial Health and Safety Division was established inside the Commission, and it took another two years before any proposals were forwarded for Community action. During 1964-1965 the Commission submitted three Directives to the Council of Ministers. One was a specific technical directive relating to the introduction of standardised control of the manufacture and use of cartridge-operated stud drivers. Another 'outline' directive concerned the classification of dangerous substances, the use of symbols to denote danger and the nature of the risk involved in the use of particular substances. The last directive related to the classification, labelling and packaging of certain dangerous substances aimed at eliminating discrepancies between national rules. Only the last directive was approved by the Council, in June 1967. In addition to preparing these draft directives, the Commission also worked on a programme of Recommendations designed to establish minimum standards in various fields of health and safety, including the protection of young people at work, industrial medicine facilities, and the payments for industrial disease. All the Recommendations on these topics were approved by the Council.

Training and Occupational Training

As far back as the early sixties academic writers were observing that the Treaty of Rome contained no consideration of the close relationship between occupational training and broader economic goals.[15] While that may be the case, the Commission, from a fairly early stage, attempted to establish a role for itself in training matters within the member states. In 1961 it produced a proposal which would have given it the responsibility amongst other things for encouraging the exchange of information amongst the member states and the collection of material concerning national training systems. The objective was to help the Commission to formulate European policies, involving the funding and administering of training projects. But the text which was passed by the Council in 1963 represented a considerable watering down of the original proposals. The member states were not prepared to sanction an increase in the Commission's authority in this area. As the final Council document stated, 'When speaking of a common training policy area, we do not have the intention of creating a uniform system of training in the members states.'[16] The actions detailed in the final policy were vague and obscure. One of the few immediate actions taken on the basis of the policy was the establishment of an Advisory Committee comprising of representatives from trade unions, employers and governments to assist in the formulation of training policy and schemes. Other than the establishment of this committee, virtually no action was taken on occupational training during the sixties. The only exception was an action programme for agricultural workers, but this was a low-key initiative with the emphasis placed on exchange schemes and obtaining greater uniformity in training standards.

Youth Exchanges

Article 50 of the Treaty of Rome obliged the Community to develop young workers' exchange schemes. Such exchanges were regarded as necessary to instill a European consciousness amongst the young as well as contributing towards the concentration of member states' training for this group of workers. Accordingly, the Commission submitted to the Council on February 1962 a proposal for a Community programme on exchanges which would aim to improve the quality and quantity of existing schemes. The member states agreed to establish national advisory committees, with the Commission playing a co-ordinating and facilitating role in the exchange arrangements. But at the same time they were at pains to keep the exchanges as a form of orthodox international collaboration rather than transform them into fully-fledged Community initiatives. The general impression is that the exchanges had practical value: in the three years after the first programmes were started in 1965 some 5,501 young people had participated in the exchange arrangements.

Overall, though, the conclusion must be that during the sixties, despite a considerable amount of paperwork and the production of proposals, Community initiatives relating to training were fairly modest. In the words of one commentator, 'In retrospect the achievements of the Community in the field of occupational training appear surprisingly limited for a period in which there was both widespread interest and belief in it as a cause as well as a consequence of economic and social developments'.[17]

Social Security

It was a common practice long before the Common Market was established for different countries to conclude agreements on social security. For example, between 1946-1958 there were nearly 80 bilateral social security agreements between the original six member states. Thus it should be of no surprise that the Treaty of Rome made direct reference to the co-ordination of social security between the member states. The most important Article concerning social security in the Treaty of Rome was Article 51, which charged the member states with adopting 'such measures in the field of social security as are necessary to provide for the freedom of movement of workers'. The wording of the rest of the Article clearly implies that complete social security harmonisation might be a long-term goal, but that in the short term the imperative of economic growth necessitated a degree of co-ordination in this policy area.

The implementation of Article 51 was achieved rapidly by the adoption of Regulations Three and Four in September and December 1958. The fundamental principles established by these Regulations were: 1) equal treatment for all workers while in another country; 2) aggregation of benefits acquired by any migrant worker working in more than one EC country; and 3) benefits were exportable to other countries in the EC (and thus families of migrant workers living in another country had to be taken into account when the benefits were being worked out).

By no means can Regulations Three and Four be regarded as comprehensive, for many complex and difficult issues were left unaddressed. For a start, the wide disparities in the actual definition of social security between the six member states were not tackled. These definitional differences posed considerable difficulties for co-ordinating social security programmes. For example, in France high family allowances were paid during the sixties and seventies as part of a population policy designed to increase the number of young people. Self-evidently it would have been totally inappropriate to have transferred that system to Italy, where there existed a chronic labour surplus problem. Other examples in the areas of taxation allowance, means test benefits, maternity leave and so on could be cited to show the difficulties in exporting social security systems across national boundaries.

Regulation Three established an Administrative Committee with the power 'to settle by binding decisions all questions of administration or interpretation arising from the regulation', in the hope that the complexities which would inevitably arise in the future would be resolved smoothly. While the committee, made up of representatives from each member state, the Commission and the ILO, worked admirably to resolve some of the complexities which did arise, it could not prevent cases relating to social security for migrant workers being brought before the Court of Justice for its ruling.[18] As well as overseeing the implementation of the regulations, the Administrative Committee throughout the sixties initiated discussions on how to simplify existing law and to obtain closer co-ordination in the social security field. As a result of these efforts, the 1963 and 1968 Regulations on the free movement of workers contained clauses which made it easier for migrant workers to obtain a wider range of social security benefits. And in 1970 the Council of Ministers ratified a series of revisions to Regulations Three and Four leading to quicker calculations and prompter payment of benefits for migrant workers.[19] Overall, then, it can be concluded that gradual progress was made in social security matters, particularly in regard to the area of migrant workers.

Towards an Active Social Policy

By the end of the sixties, all the indications were that the Community was ready to develop a much more active and interventionist social policy. In 1968, the Commission produced a report which stressed that social policy should be linked to, and developed simultaneously with, wider economic policies. In addition, the report stressed that the Social Fund needed to be revamped, as it was only having a limited impact on the Community's labour market. Similar considerations were reflected in a memorandum on social policy submitted to the Hague Summit of 1969 by Willi Brandt, then the Chancellor of West Germany. Brandt argued that advances in economic integration necessitated corresponding progress in social matters, and his memorandum recommended that at a minimum, the social policies of the member states should be harmonised. Considerable support was expressed for these ideas by other member states at the summit: the final communiqué spoke of the need for greater concertation on social policy matters.

What motivated the member states to want to change the nature and direction of EC social policy is a matter of some dispute. One observer suggested, 'Worsening economic conditions in the community, monetary upheavals, persistence of imbalances and unemployment problems undoubtedly contributed to the decision by national elites to promote an active EEC social policy'.[20] Others, however, emphasised a different set of factors.[21] It was argued that by the end of the 1960s the principle of 'economic growth at any price' was being increasingly called into question and that the ideals of equity and redistribution were coming more to the fore: people expected that the fruits of economic growth could be shared with under-privileged regions and under-privileged sections of the population. Leaders like Willi Brandt were becoming very conscious of the need to give the Community a 'human face' if the European integration project was going to progress during the seventies.

On balance, this latter account is the most convincing. Although economic growth was slowing by the end of the sixties, there were no generally perceived unemployment or social problems, at least by today's standards. The general feeling within European society was of wealth abundance and not wealth shortage. The student and trade union unrests which swept Europe at this time took place against the backdrop of almost full employment and the expansion of higher education, not at a time of mass unemployment or education contraction. Values of peace and environmentalism were widespread amongst the young. In a sense, the late sixties was a unique period, and it would be naïve to believe that governments or the Community could remain immune from the emerging ideas and attitudes.

During the early seventies pressure increased for a more integrated and wide-ranging social policy. As a result of this pressure, the final communiqué of the 1972 Paris Summit stated that the Heads of Government of the member states 'attached as much importance to vigorous action in the social field as to achievement of economic union . . . (and considered) it essential to ensure the increasing involvement of labour and management in the economic and social decisions of the Community'. In the following year the Council of Ministers adopted a resolution supporting the introduction of a Social Action Programme for 1974-1976. The Commission welcomed this quick action as 'the first attempt by the Community to draw up a coherent policy setting out in a purposeful way the initial practical steps on the road towards the ultimate goal of European Social Union'.[22]

The Social Action Programme set out three broad principles which should guide future Community action in the social field: full and better employment; the improvement of living and working conditions; and greater participation in the economic and social decisions of the Community. Under these three headings, 36 separate proposals were made for Community action, each of which had to be argued separately through the Council. The priority items listed in the programme were as follows.

Full and Better Employment

i) The establishment of appropriate consultation between member states in their employment policies and the promotion of better co-operation by national employment services.
ii) The establishment of an action programme for migrant workers who are nationals of member states or third countries.
iii) The implementation of a common vocational training policy and the setting up of a European Vocational Training Centre.

iv) The undertaking of action to achieve equality between men and women as regards access to employment and vocational training and advancement and as regards working conditions including pay.

Improvement of Living and Working Conditions

i) The establishment of appropriate consultations between member states on their social protection policies.
ii) The establishment of an initial action programme, relating to health and safety at work, the health of workers and improved organisations of tasks, beginning in those sectors where working conditions appear to be the most difficult.
iii) The implementation in co-operation with the member states of specific measures to combat poverty by drawing up pilot schemes.

Participation

i) The progressive involvement of workers and their representatives in the life of undertakings in the Community.
ii) The promotion of the involvement of management and labour in the economic and social decisions of the Community.

In addition to the above nine priority items, the Commission quickly prepared a supplementary list of other priority objectives. These were:

i) Assistance from the European Social Fund for migrant workers and for handicapped workers.
ii) An action programme for handicapped workers.
iii) The establishment of a European General Industrial Safety committee.
iv) A Directive on the approximation of member states' legislation on collective dismissals.
v) A Directive on the harmonisation of laws with regard to the retention of workers' rights and advantages in the event of changes in collective dismissals.
vi) A Directive on the harmonisation of laws with regard to the protection of workers' rights in the event of changes in the ownership of undertakings, in particular in the event of mergers.
vii) The designation as an immediate objective of the overall application of the principle of the standard 40-hour working week by 1975, and the principle of four weeks' annual paid leave by 1976.
viii) The setting up of a European Foundation for the improvement of the environment and of living and working conditions.

As mentioned earlier, there is some disagreement over whether or not the legal basis exists in the Treaty of Rome for the Community to legislate extensively in the social field. One authority suggests that the legal basis did exist,[23] but Michael Shanks, who was head of the Social Affairs Directorate General for most of the seventies, takes a different view. In his book he suggests that 'the priorities in the programme thus reflected a political judgement of what was thought to be both desirable and possible, rather than a judicial judgement of what were thought to be the social policy implications of the Treaty of Rome'.[24] In other words the legal principles of the Treaty of Rome were of secondary importance to the political desire of the Commission to establish a fully-fledged Community Social Policy. In fact, a reading of Shanks' book gives a clear insight into the extent to which the member states and the Commission were determined to construct a social dimension to the Community at the turn of the seventies. The extent to which these ambitions were fulfilled is the subject of the next chapter.

Notes and References

1 *Social Aspects of European Economic Cooperation:* Report by a Group of Experts, Studies and Reports, New Series No 46 Geneva ILO 1956 p 131

2 See HEILPEKIN, M. *Freer Trade and Social Welfare: Some marginal comments on the Ohlin Report*, International Labour Review vol No 3 1957, pp 173–193

3 VAN MEERHAEGHE, M. *International Economic Institutions*, Martinus Nighoff, The Hague, 4th Revised edition 1986

4 REED, B. *Social Security and Health Care in the Context of the European Community*, Chatham House, London (PEP European series No 23) 1975, p 49

5 LEVIN, K. 'The Free Movement of Workers', *Common Market Law Review*, Vol 2, No 3 1964, pp 300–5

6 COLLINS, D. *The European Communities, the Social Policy of the First Phase*, Vol II, Martin Robertson, London 1975, p 104

7 See DAHLBERY, K. 'EEC Commission and the Politics of the Free Movement of Workers', *Journal of Common Market Studies*, Vol VI No 4, 1968, pp 310–333

8 See BALFOUR, C. *Industrial Relations in the Common Market*, Routledge and Kegan Paul, London 1972

9 See O'GRADA, C. 'The Vocational Training Policy of the EEC and the Free Movement of Skilled Labour', *Journal of Common Market Studies*, Vol VIII 1969, pp 11–109.

10 See KINDLEBERGER, C. *Europe's Postwar Growth: The Role of Labour Supply*, Harvard University Press, Cambridge, Mass. 1967

11 European Parliament, 'Fundamental Problems of European Community Policy', 3rd Nov 1969, Para 2C

12 PETTACIO, V. 'The European Social Fund, Phase 1 in Positive Retrospect', *Journal of Common Market Studies* Vol X No 3 March 1972, p 249–267

13 COLLINS, D. *(op. cit)*

14 Parliament Doc 18 Para 18, 1961–62

15 KAHN-FREUND, O. 'Social Policy and the Common Market', *Political Quarterly* Vol 32 No 4 1961 pp 341–52

16 NEIRINCK, J. 'Social Policy of the EC Commission: A General Survey', Mineo 1967 p 14

17 COLLINS, D. *op. cit.* p 56

18 The ILO representatives were co-opted on to the Committee, as a significant part of its work since 1948 involved encouraging international comparability of national social security systems and it was considered that ILO experience would substantially assist the EC's Committee in its deliberations

19 European Commission, *Report on the Development of the Social Situation in the Community in 1972*, Brussels 1973 p 14

20 LODGE, J. 'Towards a Human union: EEC Social Policy and European Integration', *British Review of International Studies*, 4 1978, p 120

21 SHANKS, M. *European Social Policy, Today and Tomorrow*, Pergamon Press, Oxford 1977

22 cited in LODGE, J. *op cit* p 123

23 PIPKORN, J. 'Comparative Labour Law in the Harmonisation of Social Standards' in the European Community Comparative Labour Law 1977

24 SHANKS, M. *op cit* p 13

Chapter IV

Social Policy: The Second Phase

EC Social Policy Initiatives

The social policies of the Community developed since the early seventies have impinged on a wide range of areas. For the purpose of clarity and structure, the initiatives are assessed under the following headings: equal opportunities; company organisation and employee involvement; collective and individual rights; health and safety at work; the reorganisation of working time; employment generation schemes; and general labour-market initiatives. There is also a brief consideration of education policy and social security before an assessment is made of the whole of the second phase of the EC social policy and where the Community now stands.

Equal Opportunities Policies

Perhaps the most successful area of Community action has been that relating to the position of women in the Community. As already mentioned, the principle of 'equal pay for equal work' was actually included in the Treaty of Rome under Article 119. In the words of the article, 'each member state shall during the first stage ensure and subsequently maintain the application of the principle that men and women should receive equal pay for equal work'.

However, it was subsequent legislation which gave substance to the Community's equal opportunities policy. The first piece of legislation was the Equal Pay Directive of 1975 which obliged member states to abolish all discrimination between the pay of men and women arising from their laws, regulations and administrative provisions and to take the measures necessary to ensure that the principle of equal pay for work of equal value is applied. It also required them to introduce legal mechanisms through which people can challenge what they regard as discriminatory practices or decisions.

This was bolstered by the Equal Treatment Directive of the following year. Equal treatment was defined in Article 2 as 'the absence of all discrimination whatsoever on grounds of sex either directly or indirectly by reference in particular to marital and family status'. The Directive was particularly concerned with promoting equal treatment for women as regards access to employment, vocational training, promotion and working conditions. Under the Directive member states are required to ensure that all formal types of discrimination in these areas are abolished, including those embodied in collective agreements, individual contracts, staff regulations or rules governing independent occupations and professions. Moreover, the Directive also stipulates that member states must introduce into their legal systems such measures as are necessary to enable all persons who consider themselves wronged by failure to implement the principle of equal treatment to pursue their claims by judicial means. The member states are required to take the necessary measures to protect employees against dismissal by employers, either as a reaction to complaints or to legal proceedings arising out of enforcement of the principle of equal treatment. And they are obliged to ensure that the provisions of the Directive and other related EC and national legislation are brought to the attention of employers by 'all appropriate means'.

In 1978 the Social Security Directive extended the list of equal opportunity policies to include statutory social security schemes. This Directive is designed to eliminate from social security schemes all discrimination based on sex, either directly or indirectly by reference in particular to marital or family status. The discrimination to be eliminated mainly concerns the scope of schemes and the conditions of access, the obligation to contribute and calculation of contributions, the calculation of benefits, including increases in respect of a spouse and for dependents, and the conditions governing the duration and continuance of entitlement to benefits. In 1986 the Council of Ministers adopted a similar Directive, covering private-sector social security provisions. This Directive established for the first time international social security standards for private-sector occupational schemes.

In 1983 the Commission also proposed in this equal opportunity category a draft Directive relating to parental leave for family reasons. On parental leave, the draft Directive would entitle an employed parent (father or mother) taking principal charge of a child after the end of maternity leave, on giving no more than two months' notice, to take at least three months' leave for that purpose before the child is two years' old. More generous provisions are granted where the child is handicapped, or there is only one parent. On leave for family reasons, the proposal is that each state should specify a minimum number of paid leave days a year which an employee could take for pressing reasons – illness of spouse; death of a near relative; wedding of a child; illness of a child or the person taking care of it. Single-parent families or families with three or more children could be given a larger entitlement. Both Directives have yet to be ratified by the Council, as a result of opposition from some governments, including the UK.

The Court of Justice has played a key role in maintaining, and indeed furthering, EC equal opportunities legislation. The Court's first ruling in this area came in 1976 when Madame Defrenne, who worked for Belgium's Sabena Airlines, brought before it an equal pay case. She successfully claimed equal pay with a male cabin steward under Article 119 of the Rome treaty, even though at that stage the Belgium Parliament had not itself legislated for equal pay. The Court in Luxembourg has dealt with more equal opportunities cases from Britain than from any other Community country. Three cases particularly stand out, as they had wide implications for women. Smith, a manager in a pharmaceutical company, won her case on the grounds that, though she took up her post four months after her predecessor who was a man, a woman can legitimately compare her pay with that of a man previously doing the same job. Two women employees at Lloyds Bank succeeded in their claim that the Bank's occupational pension scheme discriminated in favour of male workers, both as regards contributions and certain other benefits. Jenkins, a part-time worker, established that in certain circumstances part-time workers should not be paid pro-rata less than full-time ones.

On several different occasions Britain has been brought before the Court. A series of cases brought before the Court of Justice between 1979–1981 showed that Britain had failed to implement the Equal Pay Directive properly. In particular, Britain was found guilty of not giving a sufficiently clear right to women to claim equal pay for work of equal value. This decision forced the British Government to introduce a series of amendments to the 1970 Equal Pay Act, which allowed women from 1984 to make equal value claims. However, the Equal Opportunities Commission and others have criticized the changes made to the Equal Pay Act by the Government for not reflecting the Court's decision. Whether or not these criticisms are valid, the changes have facilitated equal value claims in Britain's industrial tribunals.

More recently, the Court of Justice ruled in two cases brought before it by British women that the UK Government was still presiding over unlawful and discriminatory practices. In the first ruling in February 1986, relating to the Marshall case, the Court declared that it was contrary to EC law to force women to retire before men. As a result, the British Government introduced legislation making it unlawful to set different retirement ages for men and women. The second case, brought by Drake with the backing of the Child Poverty Action Group, concerned social security payments. The Court ruled that it was discriminatory to exclude married women from a welfare benefit that was paid to men and single women. As a result the DHSS is now for the first time paying invalid care allowances to married women.

Complementing the various legal Directives on women's rights, the Commission introduced an action programme aimed at promoting equal opportunities for women. The programme was based on two principles: the reinforcement of individual liberties; and the achievement of equal opportunities in practice by means of 'positive action'. The Commission's motivation for introducing the programme was to prevent the issue of equal opportunities from slipping down the priority order due to the prevailing economic crisis. In the area of individual liberties, the programme covered the elimination of the adverse effect of certain taxations systems on the employment of women, and the revision of protective legislation. In the area of positive action, initiatives include training courses for women in the new technologies, the dissemination of information on opportunities for vocational choice for girls and the diversification of employment for women.

The impact of these non-legislative actions appears to have been limited, for in its assessment of the programme the Commission concluded that it was 'necessary to express certain reservations about the overall effectiveness of efforts taken towards the implementation of these actions'.[1] This was not taken to mean that such initiatives should be abandoned, but rather that the role of the Commission should increase in the area: in its own words 'it should be noted in this context that the Commission has become aware that women's groups and organisations within all member states increasingly tend to require action to be generated on a Community level rather than by national governments'.[2] As a result, a new, more substantial action programme has been drawn up and is currently being implemented. But it is too early to assess whether this has met with more success than the previous one.

Although the bulk of the Community's action in the field of equal opportunities has concentrated on women's rights, several action programmes have been implemented to improve the lot of other minority groups. One programme is concerned with promoting the economic and social integration of the disabled inside the Community by the harmonisation and progressive raising of the applicable standards in each member state. The action programme covers three particular issues. First, the standardisation of specific measures for the disabled across the Community: existing policies in the different member states are highly uneven and even contradictory. (For example, there are marked differences in the definitions of who qualifies as being disabled.) Secondly, the encouragement and sponsorship of innovative projects to promote the integration of disabled people, particularly in the sphere of vocational integration. To this end some novel and original schemes have been developed in the areas of rehabilitation programmes, placements and vocational training. Thirdly, a Disabled Bureau has been established to monitor developments and to examine potential new ways to improve the position of disabled people.[3]

Another action programme relates to migrants. The main focus of this programme is on member states in mainland Europe who have large groups of migrants. The Commission has been preoccupied with this area since the first action programme, introduced in 1974, which aimed at protecting the rights of migrants and promoting their assimilation into the indigenous population. A revised and up-dated version of this programme was implemented recently. The type of actions proposed by this programme includes the adoption of Community law which ensures that migrants are covered by member states' social security and pension schemes; promoting better information and training for the staff of public authorities in daily contact with migrants; improving the quality of legal assistance and representation; and the use of the Social Fund to sponsor training projects for migrants.[4]

Company Organisation and Employee Involvement

Company organisation and employee involvement have long been major issues in EC social policy. A 1975 Commission policy document outlined the rationale for EC action in this area: the document argued that 'if progress is to be made towards a European Community in the real sense of the words, a common market for companies is an essential part of the basic structure which must be created'.[5] The Commission has drawn up twelve separate proposals in this area.

The proposed Fifth Directive on the structure of public limited companies inside the Community is of most interest to the analysis here. It was first presented to the Council in 1972, but that body refused to take any decision on the issue. Since then there have been protracted consultations on the proposal. In its original form, the draft Fifth Directive proposed that all limited liability companies with at least 500 workers should establish a two-tier board structure; a supervisory board handling policy issues and another board dealing with day-to-day management functions.

To some extent, the proposal reflected statutory forms of workers' involvement already in place or developing in some Community countries. Yet the Directive met with strong opposition from the employers' organisation UNICE, and from some member states. The opposition forced the Commission to back-track on the proposal and to take the unusual step of issuing a Green Paper on the whole question of employee participation and company structure. In the Green Paper the Commission affirmed its belief in the two-tier board system with employee participation on the supervisory board. However, it recognised that existing company structures differ from one member state to another because of diverse economic, social and legal tradition. It therefore considered a transitional period to be desirable during which member states should be given the choice between a dual or a unitary board structure, and that employee representation should similarly be made compulsory only after a transitional period.

After years of seemingly endless discussions and negotiations on the contents of the Green Paper, the Commission produced an amended version of the initial draft. The revised proposals introduced a greater degree of flexibility into the envisaged participation structure, and generally watered down the clauses of the original version. In particular, the new proposals were to apply only to companies with 1000 workers or more; they enabled member states either to impose a two-tier system or to give companies the choice between a two-tier or single board structure; and they provided for four alternative forms of participation. They also allowed parent companies in large groups to apply participation provisions on behalf of their subsidiaries. This revised proposal was delivered to the Council of Ministers in October 1983.[6] However, the Directive has not so far been ratified, largely because the member states regard the proposal as too complex and too unwieldy to implement. A clear-cut decision has yet to be made on the proposal.

Closely connected with the draft Fifth Directive is the proposal for a Community Regulation for a European Company Statute. Its original form embodies all the traditional Community company law prescriptions – such as two-tier boards with employee participation. At present, like the Fifth Directive, it has been bogged down at the negotiation stage for some years. But there is a big difference between the proposed European Company Statute and the draft Fifth Directive, in that the former is a Resolution, which means that, if adopted, companies can take it up or ignore it as they choose. It is the Statute's voluntary character which is now being seized on by the Commission as a possible way out of the long-standing resistance it has faced from member states on the sensitive issue of company organisation and employee involvement. Whether it will be ratified by the Council is open to doubt, but it is figuring prominently in Community level discussions at the moment (1988).

The most controversial initiative by the Commission in the social policy sphere has been the proposed Directive on employee information and consultation procedures, popularly known as the draft 'Vredeling' Directive. When the Commission first produced this proposal informally to the social partners, it was only to apply to multinational corporations. But the employers' organisation (UNICE) pointed out that making a distinction between mulitnational and other enterprises was against community law. As a result, the first formal draft proposal which was published in 1980 fell into two parts: one applied to multinational corporations; and the other to companies which had several establishments and/or subsidiaries within a single country. Under the provisions of the draft, companies and subsidiaries employing at least

100 people would be required to give the work-force relevant information on their activities as a whole at least once every six months. In particular, the information should relate to structure and manning; economic and financial situation; position and probable development of the business and of production and sales; employment and probable future trends; production and investment programmes; rationalisation plans; manufacturing and working methods, especially the introduction of new working methods; and all procedures and plans likely to have a substantial effect on the employees' interests. Employees in subsidiaries who were refused information on the above issues would have the right to 'by-pass' local management and request the information from the company's head office.[7]

The draft Directive was full of technical blemishes. For example, the definition of an employer representative was quite different to the one used in the Fifth Directive, and some of the provisions were mutually conflicting, particularly the ones relating to the furnishing of information and the safeguarding of its confidentiality.[8]

The proposals were opposed by the employers' organisations inside the Community and indeed throughout the world,[9] and also by some member states, most notably the UK. Opposition from these quarters succeeded in getting the proposals amended and limited. The revised Directive would only apply to national corporations and multinationals with subsidiaries employing at least 1,000 workers, instead of the 100 workers originally proposed; the conditions affecting secrecy and confidentiality of information were tightened up; information would only have to be passed on annually rather than at six-monthly periods; and employees would no longer have the automatic right to open consultations with the parent organisation.[10] The view was that these revisions transformed the 'Vredeling' Directive into a relatively weak proposal. But as far as the UK Government was concerned, these revisions were still insufficiently flexible, and it used its right in the Council of Ministers to veto the revised draft in early 1983.

At this stage, the common view was that the draft 'Vredeling' Directive would not be raised again. However, during its Presidency, the Irish Government rescued the proposal from oblivion by convening a special working group known as the Redmond Committee to try and reformulate its clauses so that they were satisfactory to all member states. The working group's revisions recommended a shift away from the *obligation* to provide information and consult employers towards a system of positive rights of employees to be informed and consulted. (In practice this would have shifted the onus from the employers to the employees' side.) In addition, the group suggested amending Articles 3 and 4 of the proposed Directive so that they only related to 'employers' and not to parent and subsidiary companies. The recommendation went before the Council of Ministers in 1986, but again the UK Government expressed its opposition to the proposals, and as a result, it was decided that the issue should not be discussed until 1989.[11] Although the draft Directive is still on the negotiating table, there is virtual consensus amongst those closely involved in EC social policy questions both inside the Commission and in Whitehall that the proposal is now moribund.

Collective and Individual Workers' Rights

The question of collective and individual workers' rights is a third area in which the Commission attempted, particularly during the seventies, to obtain a degree of European harmonization. A number of Directives have been adopted, and initiatives undertaken in this area. The first initiative by the Commission, subsequently passed as a Directive by the Council, was on procedures to be applied in redundancy situations to protect the rights of workers. The main clause of the Directive obliged companies who were enacting redundancies to give the workers, and their representatives, at least 30 days' notice. This was intended to give workers the opportunity to negotiate on whether there was any alternative to closure, or on the exact terms and conditions of any redundancy packages.[12] Employers were required to notify in writing any projected collective redundancies to the appropriate national authority. Member states were allowed two years to pass the necessary legislation to implement the Directive.

Not long after this Directive was put on the Community statute book, the Commission produced another draft Directive which aimed at harmonising the legislative provisions and regulations of workers' rights and advantages in cases of company mergers, transfers of establishments and business concentrations. In their original form, the Commission's proposals would have introduced wide-ranging and stringent regulations.[13] These, however, were subsequently revised in the light of comments made by the Parliament and the Council. Nevertheless, the Directive that was eventually passed included the automatic transfer of workers' rights in instances of mergers and takeovers and the right of workers' representatives in companies employing more than 50 people to be informed in writing at least two months prior to the transfer.[14]

In 1980 a Directive which was passed by the Council in the area of collective rights concerned the protection of employees in the event of the insolvency of their employers. The key feature of the Directive was the creation of institutions at the member-state level to pay workers' outstanding claims which arose from their employment relationship before the employer ceased to meet his obligations. Another important feature of the Directive was that it was highly flexible, allowing the member states to implement the terms of the legislation within their existing industrial-relations framework.

Health and Safety at Work

Few health and safety initiatives were passed by the Council in the sixties. However, in the mid seventies the Council of Ministers, by agreeing to an action programme for safety, hygiene and health protection at work, signalled that the Community's involvement in the area was to be increased in the forthcoming years. As a result of this action programme, a number of Directives relating to health and safety were passed in the late seventies. The first Directive to be ratified was the harmonisation of safety signs used at the workplace. The primary aim of this piece of legislation is to help combat industrial accidents and disease. The safety signs prescribed in the Directive were made as simple and striking as possible and no words at all are used, so that everyone, in particular foreign workers, should be able to tell at a glance what must and must not be done. On the face of it the Directive was a straightforward piece of legislation, but it actually took considerable preparation, as there existed in the various Community countries wide differences in the shapes, colours and symbols of safety signs.

The second Directive to be passed in 1976 concerned the protection of workers exposed to vinyl chloride monomer. The basic substance of plastics, vinyl chloride monomer (VCM) is a toxic gas which can cause a variety of diseases. The Directive aims at reinforcing existing legislation in the member states for the protection of exposed workers by laying down: maximum permitted levels for the atmosphere concentration of VCM in the working areas; the measuring and monitoring techniques necessary for this purpose, as well as other preventive measures; and guidelines for medical surveillance. It was also laid down that a committee be set up to review the Directive at least every two years in the light of developments in technology and occupational medicine. This Directive followed another approved earlier in the year which restricted the marketing of certain dangerous substances and preparations, including the outlawing of vinyl chloride monomer as a propellant for aerosols, so as to protect workers and the general public from risks associated with the use of certain chemicals.

In 1979 the Council approved a Directive concerned with the prevention of major accidents in certain industrial activities, probably more widely known as the Seveso Directive. The objective of the Directive is to prevent such accidents, and to limit their effects on human beings (workers and adjacent population) and on the environment. The first part of the legislation takes the form of a framework Directive intended to cover any industrial activity, including certain storage conditions, which involves or may involve dangerous substances. It also requires a safety report to be made available to the competent authorities and provides for informing workers and the public in the surrounding area. The second part applies to industrial activities which involve or may involve particularly dangerous substances, defined by a set of criteria specified in the Directive, which are present or potentially present in the industrial activity in excess of a particular quantity. In this case the manufacturer will have to send the competent authorities a more detailed safety report on the substances, facilities and points where major accidents could occur. The report also has to contain, among other things, an analysis of the reliability of the facilities, a description of the hazards for people and the environment and an outline of the safety measures needed as a result.

In 1983 a Directive was adopted on the protection of workers from the risks due to exposure at work to asbestos. With only a few minor exceptions, the Directive applies to all activities in which workers are, or may be, exposed to asbestos. The Directive laid down a number of requirements: including the notification of work with asbestos; and that the level of asbestos be reduced to as low a level as is reasonably practicable. Specific provisions are also made on demolition work, together with general protective measures and a requirement on the provision of information to workers on the dangers of working with asbestos and on the precautions that must be taken. The Directive also contains provisions for medical surveillance and for the keeping of records.

After four years of extensive discussions and negotiations, the Council of Ministers finally adopted a Directive in May 1986 on the protection of workers from noise. The Directive applies to all workers (with the exception of those who work in maritime and air transport). It lays down a noise evaluation and measurement method for which the employer is responsible. Member states may choose between two measurement criteria laid down in the Directive: daily exposure of each worker to noise; or sound levels registered daily at the work-place over a period of at least eight hours. Where either criteria is used, the Directive requires certain measures to be taken when noise levels exceed 85 decibels, and other more binding measures when levels pass 90 decibels.

Other proposals for Directives on health and safety will shortly come before the Council. The first will probably be over the protection of workers from the risks related to exposure at work to benzene. In its present form, this proposed Directive requires a substitute for benzene to be used whenever technically possible and where no substitute exists, to reduce the exposure to a minimum. Finally it requires employers to keep records of all activities, irrespective of the level of exposure, and to provide specified information on request to national authorities. The outcome of this Directive could be highly significant, for it could establish the pattern by which future health and safety matters are dealt with under the new legal provisions of the Single European Act.

The third Community action programme on safety, hygiene and health at work adopted by the Council in mid 1987 gives some idea of the initiatives the Commission will put to the Council on the basis of the new legal arrangement. In the area of *safety and ergonomics at work,* the Commission intends to forward proposals for Directives on the following: creating safe working conditions through the organisation of safety measures; the selection and the use of suitable plant, equipment and machinery, and the adoption of rules for the use and selection of individual protective equipment; revising the 1977 Directive on the provision of safety signs at places at work; harmonising the composition of pharmacies on board ships; the protection of farm workers handling pesticides; safety in the building industry.

In *occupational health and hygiene* the Commission intends to draw up Directives concerning carcinogens, protection against biological agents, calcium compounds, and the protection of agricultural workers, who are in any circumstances exposed to certain pesticides. In addition the Commission also proposes to put forward amendments to the Directives on asbestos, lead, noise, and on the ban on dangerous substances, including limits relating to chemical agents absorbed through the skin. On *training*, the Commission plans to create a network for collaboration between training centres covering all aspects of safety and health protection; to continue to devise general training schemes for those employed in high-risk activities; to include proposals on health, hygiene and safety at work in its draft programme of in-service training for adults; and also to include such proposals in its draft Recommendation on vocational training for women.

For the first time, the Commission has included the particular health and safety problems relating to small and medium-sized businesses in its action programme. In this area, the Commission intends:

i) to review the extent to which the existing regulations are understood and applied in this field by studying a sample of small and medium-sized undertakings;
ii) to carry out a study of the special rules and exemptions applicable to small businesses in national health and safety legislation and to assess the need for action and for the harmonisation of legislation;
iii) to study the influence of new work layouts on health, hygiene and safety in small businesses;
iv) to study how health and safety regulations can be made more readily understandable to owners of small businesses;

v) to prepare information manuals containing advice for those setting up small businesses;
vi) to prepare safety training modules aimed at those setting up small businesses; and
vii) to develop a system to enable small businesses to have a rapid access to information on safety equipment and individual protective equipment.

This is a highly ambitious programme. If past experience is anything to go by, the Commission will be hard pressed to achieve all the objectives in the programme. For example, in 1978 the Commission put forward a 14 point action programme; however, by 1982, the date when the programme expired, not one of these points had been fully realised.

The Reorganisation of Working Time

As the seventies drew to a close, the Commission started to place greater emphasis on developing active labour-market policies, instead of promoting initiatives on the collective and individual rights of workers. Perhaps the most important initiatives here have been in the area of the reorganisation of working time. The Commission first signalled its interest in this area in 1979 by producing a document called Community Measures on Work Sharing. It was suggested in the document that action should be taken at the Community level as a matter of priority on certain issues: the conclusion of outline agreements by both sides of industry at the community level on the number of hours worked per year; the possibility of an EC Directive restricting systematic overtime; measures to regulate shiftwork in the Community; the encouragement of flexible retirement schemes in the member states; the regulation and protection of part-time workers and temporary workers.

The Commission lost little time in developing some of these issues further. In 1981 it put forward a draft Directive on voluntary part-time work and a proposal for a Council recommendation on flexible retirement. The aim of the Directive was to fill considerable gaps in national legislation as regards the social security and employment rights of part-time workers. In particular the draft Directive set out to ensure: the implementation of the principle of equal rights for part-time and full-time workers; proportional rights with regard to remuneration, holiday payments, redundancy and retirement payments; the provision of a written agreement between employer and worker; priority for workers in an establishment who wish to transfer from part-time to full-time or vice versa; that part-timers are taken into account in the total account of employees in an undertaking; and the application of procedures for informing and consulting workers' representatives regarding the introduction of part-time work. The flexible retirement proposal mainly urged member states to encourage the development of such schemes.

Both the part-time and flexible retirement proposals were discussed by the Council meeting in December 1982. Some disquiet was expressed about the draft Directive on part-time work. The main reservation was that the proposed areas to be regulated by the Directive were too extensive. The Commission revised the draft Directive and resubmitted it to the Council. But again it was not adopted, largely due to the opposition of the British Government. The proposal on flexible retirement fared somewhat better, probably because it had the status of a Recommendation and not a Directive. The Council adopted the proposal at its December 1982 meeting. It was also stipulated in the Council's decision that the member states had to submit progress reports by June 1985. But these progress reports did not appear until 1987. The Commission concluded from these reports that 'it can be said that real progress had been achieved, but not on the scale sufficient to be described as "substantial" '.[15]

In 1983 the Commission proposed another initiative: a Recommendation on the reduction and reorganisation of working-time. It was the Commission's first specific proposal aimed at improving the employment situation by reducing working time. The actions proposed were more detailed versions of the issues outlined by the Commission in its work-sharing document in 1979. The Recommendation had two specific aims: a reduction in individual working time, combined with its reorganisation, sufficiently substantial to support the positive development of employment; and stricter limitations on systematic paid overtime.[16]

When the proposal reached the Council, the UK Government once again used the veto to block its passage, despite the fact that it carried no binding authority. Tom King, the then Employment Minister, said that the proposal would go no way to help increase employment. The stance of the UK Government caused a serious clash with other member states, particularly with France, whose President had been committed to the proposal, as domestic pressures had already pushed France further down this route than other member states. The UK Government has continued to take a hard line on the issue: whenever it is brought up in the Council, the UK Government makes it very clear that it will use its veto.

The Commission has also made proposals on temporary work and fixed-duration contracts of employment. The Commission proposed that temporary workers and workers on fixed-duration contracts should be protected by guaranteeing them, as far as possible, the same rights as permanent workers. It also suggested that unjustified recourse to temporary work or fixed-duration contracts should be restricted so that permanent employees are protected. Finally, the Commission proposed action to ensure that temporary employment agencies are of good standing.[17] This draft Directive, although revised and modified on several different occasions, has not yet been ratified by the Council. Again the UK Government was at the forefront of the opposition.

Thus although the Commission designated the reduction and reorganisation of working time as a high priority for Community action during the eighties, not one significant piece of legislation on the subject has been passed by the Council of Ministers. The designs of the Commission were continually frustrated, mainly by the UK Government continually using its veto inside the Council of Ministers. This caused considerable dismay and frustration inside the Commission. In interviews with the authors, senior officials of the Commission were highly critical of what they saw as a negative and belligerent stance by the Thatcher Government. Whatever one's views of the UK actions on these issues, there can hardly be any disagreement about the effects. It has brought the Commission's initiatives in the area to a virtual standstill.

Employment Generation Schemes

At the same time as trying to establish a legislative dimension to Community social policy, substantial revisions were made to the Social Fund so that it would make a tangible contribution to the fight against unemployment in the member states. The next section examines the function and operation of the Social Fund.

The Function of the Social Fund

The Social Fund is a key aspect of the employment policy of the European Community, being established by Articles 123–27 of the Treaty of Rome. The architects of the Community saw it as a mechanism to increase geographical and occupational mobility of workers. As mentioned earlier, during the sixties the Fund was not much in use – the number of schemes sponsored were few and most of these were primarily concerned with encouraging labour-market mobility inside the Common Market.

Since the early seventies all this has changed. The Social Fund has undergone four separate revisions during the past decade or so. The net result is that it is now focused on helping member states combat the unemployment crisis by sponsoring employment and training schemes. Perhaps the main factor forcing this reorientation was the emerging unemployment crisis. But it should also be noted that the Commission was eager to increase its presence in this area so that the faltering dynamics of European integration could be rejuvenated.

At present the Fund has four main priorities:

1. tackling youth unemployment (not less than 75% of total available grants must be allocated to such projects);
2. improving employment opportunities in the Community's designated priority action regions (approximately 40% of the total allocations each year have to go to this objective, including some of the youth unemployment allocations);
3. funding employment-related initiatives in other depressed regions in the Community; and
4. encouraging the implementation of innovatory projects.

The emphasis is on making a contribution to the fight against structural unemployment, and easing the acute disadvantage of some special groups. Money is usually allocated to four types of initiatives – vocational training and guidance; recruitment and wage grants; resettlement and socio-vocational integration programmes in connection with geographical mobility; and services and technical advice concerned with job creation. Both public and private organisations can apply for a Social Fund grant. But the rules of the Fund require that no schemes can be financed wholly by money from Europe. For initiatives run by public bodies the Fund will give a grant up to 50% of the costs, while for schemes run by private organisations the Fund's grant will not be more than the grant from a national authority. The Fund has grown substantially in the past decade from about 170 million ECU in 1973 to 2,188,350 million ECU in 1985. But this should be placed in context – the Social Fund only represents about 6.8 per cent of the Community's total budget (the Common Agricultural Policy consumes approximately 72.5 per cent).

The Operation of the European Social Fund

A long-standing criticism of the Fund is that it is organised and operated in a bureaucratic way. A study of the Fund concludes that it 'is a complex of managerial, administrative and financial issues which together have created a system cumbersome to operate, slow to decide and pay out and which operational bodies find hard to understand.'[18] Attempts have been made in recent years to reduce some of these problems, but many deficiencies still remain. The main target for much of the criticism is the Fund's budgetary arrangements. There is some basis for such attacks. First, the total 'appropriation' of the Fund each year is dependent on the outcome of the annual negotiations for the entire Community budget. As is well known, these have been the scene of acrimonious and prolonged disputes in recent years. On occasions it has been well into the financial year before these disputes are resolved and money distributed to the various programmes of the Commission, including the Social Fund.

The result is that the administrators of the Fund in Brussels are constrained in the possible improvements they can make. For example, one suggestion for improvement is that a long-term strategic component should be introduced into the Fund, but this is well-nigh impossible at present. The administrators have no way of knowing the scale and nature of the Fund's budget from one year to the next. The situation also causes much uncertainty and difficulty for the national organisations which have made applications. In particular, they experience long delays before being told whether their application has been successful, and if so, the amount they will receive. In the majority of cases the national organisations have either to abandon the proposed project or to start it without knowing whether they will actually obtain a Social Fund grant.

This situation is compounded by other problems. The financial year of the Fund runs from January to December, while the financial year for most British organisations is April to March, which creates self-evident administrative and financial difficulties. Furthermore, applications for grants must only be for a specific calendar year. Thus if an organisation wants a grant to help fund a three-year scheme, it must make three separate applications. The only exception is the innovatory projects category for which grants for up to three years can be secured on the basis of a single application. This adds to the administrative burden that organisations have to carry if they decide to attract money from Europe. Finally, the procedure for actually allocating grants is less than straightforward. Theoretically, once a scheme gains approval, an initial contribution of 50 per cent should be made immediately, with the remainder of the money being given at the end of the scheme. In practice this procedure is rarely followed: many recipients of Social Fund grants complain that they have to wait upwards of two years before being paid any money from Brussels. In the meantime they have to meet all the expenses of the projects.

Clearly these budgetary and financial arrangements make the Fund excessively cumbersome. Some of these, like the mismatch between the Community's and the British financial years, could be smoothed out with specific internal changes. But it is hard to see how the more fundamental difficulties could be resolved without root-and-branch revisions of the entire Community budgetary framework. While these complexities are very real, it would be misleading to attach disproportionate importance to them, for every year the Fund is hugely oversubscribed. In fact it has got to the stage where the Commission has had to introduce a 'weighted reduction' system in which a certain amount (depending mainly on the geographical location of the applying body) is taken from successful applications in certain categories because there are insufficient funds to meet their requests in full. In other words, while the above complexities may frustrate and inconvenience national organisations, they do not deter them from applying.

Another much-maligned feature of the Social Fund is the administrative procedure for processing applications. Here the justification for such complaints is less clear-cut. It could be argued, on the surface at least, that as the division in the Commission which administers the Fund has only 20 staff who process 6,000 applications annually, the administrative procedure is efficient.

It is valuable, in addressing this criticism, to outline the procedure. The Social Fund is administered in Brussels by a division of the Directorate of Social Affairs, Employment and Education, DG v. The exact location of grants is worked out by the staff in the Division. The eligibility criteria and other guidelines by which staff assess applications are drawn up by the Social Fund Advisory Committee, made up of representatives from member states' governments, the European employers organisation (UNICE), and the corresponding trade union body (ETUC). The Committee also ratifies the final allocations of grants made by Commission staff.

Within each member state there is a government department responsible for coordinating the operation of the Fund within its territory; and for performing a preliminary gate-keeping function. In Britain this task is assigned to the Department of Employment. Organisations within each member state receive and return their applications for Social Fund grants to their respective national departments, which assess whether these conform to the rules and regulations governing the Fund. Only 'eligible' applications are sent to Brussels for consideration. The government departments do not make judgements about the merits of any application; this is the sole prerogative of the Commission. However, they do operate in a highly partisan fashion: each government department aims to send forward as many applications as possible. They give a lot of advice and guidance to organisations on how to make a valid application. Some promote the existence of the Fund, and encourage individual organisations to apply to the Fund, while others operate early deadline dates so that they have the time to examine applications and send them back for redrafting if necessary before they are sent to Brussels. No doubt there are countless other ways in which each government department seeks to improve the quantity and quality of applications from its country. The Department of Employment is considered by Commission officials to be the most efficient national body of all the member states at promoting and processing Social Fund applications.

This closer examination does not support the idea that there are glaring inadequacies in the administrative procedure of the Fund (as suggested by some of the critics). Certainly, there are particular aspects that could be made more efficient, and particular regulations could be made easier, but any significant qualitative improvement to the administration of the Fund would require quite marked increases in the administrative budget of the Fund, which is unrealistic in a period of financial stringency in the Community.

General labour market initiatives

In addition to the above programmes and schemes sponsored by the Social Fund, the Commission has launched several general labour-market initiatives. To some extent, this involved continuing the central activity of the first phase, namely promoting the free movement of labour inside the Community. Several other important initiatives were also embarked upon, the most significant of which was probably the proposal for the mutual recognition of diplomas. This principle was first adopted by the Council back in 1974, but it became evident early on that to attempt a complete harmonisation of qualifications inside the Community would be fraught with difficulties. As a result, the Commission changed tack, lowered its sights and became content with proposing Directives which listed each member state's diploma awards for specific professions so that they can be recognised in all other EC countries. This less ambitious approach has been easier to implement (though certain problems have been encountered).[19] There now exist five Directives, covering doctors, nurses, vets, dentists and midwives.

In addition to these Directives, the Council in 1985 gave the Commission the responsibility for bringing about the equivalence of vocational training qualifications between member states, starting with a priority group of sectors (which it left the Commission to select). The sectors identified by the Commission for priority action were the hotel and catering industry, the motor vehicle engineering industry, and the construction trades. These sectors were selected because it was thought that a broad consensus of agreement might be reached in them more easily than in other areas. Each national labour-market institution (e.g. in relation to the UK, it was the MSC) was charged with the responsibility of identifying the revisions that would be required to other member states' qualifications to make them broadly comparable with existing national qualifications. Work on these three sectors is close to completion and the Commission hopes to publish the results in the near future. In anticipation that the Council will support their Recommendations on these three sectors, the Commission has started work on three further sectors: agriculture, the electricity industry and the forestry industry.[20]

Other action in the field of promoting the free movement of labour includes SEDOC (the European system for the international clearing of vacancies and applications for employment) which was set up by Regulation No 1612/68, but did not come into effect until 1973. Its main task is to promote at the Community level the transfer of information about unfilled national vacancies and applications. The system is based on a register of occupations and professions especially designed for international exchange, and it works by unfilled vacancies and applications being telexed each month by the SEDOC service in each member state to the SEDOC services of the other member states. Where the initial exchange of general information concerning the existence of a particular vacancy or application reveals an opportunity for clearing, then the related SEDOC services pass more detailed information. In addition to exchanging vacancies and applications for employment, SEDOC also provides information for workers willing to work in another member state and for employers unable to find the workers they require on the national market.

The general opinion is that the results from SEDOC since its establishment have been fairly modest. A number of technical matters limit its effectiveness. For instance, the register for occupations was compiled at the beginning of the seventies, which means that it does not contain most of the new occupations created by recent technological developments. Despite this lacklustre performance, the Commission is revolutionising the system in the context of completing the internal market by 1992 when it is hoped that the free movement of labour will genuinely take place. Four changes will occur as a result of the Commission's revitalisation programme:

i) the system will be extended to the new member states – Spain and Portugal;
ii) the SEDOC register of occupations will be reclassified and updated;
iii) the exchange network will be computerised, allowing for the transfer of more frequent comprehensive information;
iv) information services on the system will be broadened;

These changes will obviously improve the system, but against a background of high European unemployment, the apparent reluctance of workers within the Community to cross frontiers for new jobs, and the widespread qualitative gap between vacancies and applications for employment in the member states, it would be shortsighted to hold out any hope for the SEDOC system being transformed into a truly effective Community agent.[21]

Another aspect of Community activity in the category of general labour-market policy concerns training. The Commission launched the first major initiative on training when it delivered a Recommendation to the member states on vocational preparation for young people under 25. In this document the Commission argued that member states should provide vocational preparation and guidance, practical basic training and work experience for this age group. This led the Council of Ministers to declare in 1979 that each member state should establish co-ordinated programmes for young people on training. By 1984 the Commission was satisfied that all member states met all the requirements laid down by the declaration. In 1982 the Commission produced a more comprehensive document on training inside the Community.

The Commission also attempted to get better co-operation between the various national employment services in this period. In 1980 the Council adopted a resolution which stipulated that the Community should increase its activity on labour market policy in the following three areas:

i) improvement of labour-market knowledge. In particular it was recommended that co-operation be strengthened between national and Community employment services in matters such as length of work, different forms of employment, unemployment flows and so on;
ii) development and co-operation of placement services. Provision was made for an action programme for the development of and co-operation between national placement services, particularly in areas such as staff training;
iii) concerted forward-looking management of the labour market. The aim here was to increase co-operation between the social partners and the employment services so as to achieve forward-looking manpower utilisation policies.

For the most part, these general labour-market policies promoted by the Commission were technical and administrative, and as a result none were controversial. At the same time, however, none can be classified as having a telling impact. This was partly because some of the issues being tackled were highly complex, and partly because many of the demands made by the Commission were low-priority tasks for national labour-market bodies already under pressure from the large rises in unemployment in their respective countries. Thus, it is probably fair to conclude that the benefits from these general labour-market policies will only be realised in the longer term.

Education Policy

In May 1987, the Education Ministers of the member states agreed to set up a European Community action scheme for the mobility of university students (known as *the ERASMUS Programme*), with a total budget of 85 million ecu until 1990. On the face of it, this programme appears non-controversial, but an agreement was actually hard to conclude. The Commission first proposed the scheme in early 1986, but certain member states objected to the proposed budget and to the legal base upon which the Commission's proposals rested. Later that year, the issue was once again discussed by the Council, but fearing that it might be adopted with a small budget and limited objectives, the Commission withdrew the proposals. After several months of top-level informal negotiations and lobbying, the Commission retabled unamended its proposal, and this time it got the approval of the member states.

The main objective of the programme is to encourage and facilitate student mobility within the Community by creating a major scheme of grants to students to enable them to spend a recognised period of study in another Community country. In addition to this student grant support, ERASMUS also seeks to facilitate exchanges of teaching staff between higher education institutions within the member states. In the initial phase of the programme, the academic year 1988/1989, it is envisaged that it will be possible to award some 20,000 mobility grants to students. At this stage, the potential for ERASMUS to trigger new forms of co-operation between higher education institutions in the member states appears considerable.

The European Community action programme for education and training for technology – *the Comett Programme* – was put into operation in 1987. Comett is primarily concerned with advanced-level training for technology, particularly focusing on technological management. Set up in the first instance for three years, its objectives are: (i) to bring a European dimension to university/enterprise cooperation in training related to new technologies; (ii) to promote joint university/enterprise development, both within and across member states, of training programmes at advanced level; (iii)to improve the supply and level of such training at local, regional and national levels. The programme focuses on four inter-related strands of action designed to support enterprises and universities. Strand A is the development of university/enterprise partnerships to meet training requirements for highly qualified manpower on a structured and co-ordinated basis. Strand B is transnational exchanges of students and personnel to reinforce or create the 'transnational' character of the person's training. Strand C covers the design and testing of joint university-enterprise in continuing education and new technology. D is concerned with mutli-media training systems for new technologies. Once again, the hope is that Comett will promote new linkages between higher-education on new technologies across the Community and also lead to a greater emphasis on University scientific and technological research.

Social Security

As noted in Chapter II, one of the first actions of the Community was to introduce two Regulations relating to social security. But as a result of the steadily accumulating amendments to these Regulations, the Community decided to adopt two new Regulations to incorporate all these revisions. These new Regulations are Nos 1408/71 and 574/72. The first Regulation deals with all the substantive provisions regarding the co-ordination of social security schemes. All persons who have been employed or self-employed are covered as well as their families. The Regulation, which only applies to state social security schemes, covers all social security legislation dealing with sickness and maternity benefits; invalidity benefits; benefits in respect of accidents at work and occupational diseases; death grants; unemployment benefits; and family benefits. The provisions of Regulation No 574/72 are intended to facilitate the administrative application of the substantive provisions.

It is important to stress that these Regulations did not create or impose a uniform social security scheme throughout the EC. National schemes remain more or less technically intact. What they did, however, was to lay down and update certain rights for migrant workers inside the Community. In fact, apart from the equality provisions outlined earlier, these Regulations have been the only pieces of legislation passed relating to social security during the seventies or eighties. This is because the social security systems of the member states are so diverse (see chapter XI) that it was virtually impossible to make harmonising proposals. To its credit, the Commission has realised that to harmonise social security inside the Community is unrealistic. What it is now proposing is policy concentration amongst the member states around common themes, namely, ways of containing growth in social expenditure, particularly spending in health care, ways of revising existing systems of social protection to ensure that the 'new poor' (e.g. one-parent families) are comprehensively covered, and reviewing methods of financing social security systems. While there has been continuing discussion on these points, no concrete proposals have yet emerged.

The above overview shows that the second phase of EC social policy has been in sharp contrast to the first, where the emphasis was on low-key technical initiatives. During the seventies, policies of a more active and far-reaching type were pursued. The Social Fund was substantially reformed so that it could play a more concrete role in the fight against growing unemployment experienced by all member states. The sponsorship and encouragement of employment generation and training schemes through the Social Fund and other EC structural funds enjoyed (and continues to enjoy) widespread support. Also, the Commission's initiatives on education, general labour-market schemes and social security were regarded as non-controversial. But as the above analysis shows, attempts by the Commission to develop a legislative dimension to the Community social policy was stoutly opposed in some quarters, with the result that its efforts met with mixed success.

Perhaps the Commission was most successful in the sphere of equal opportunities, as it was able to steer through several important Directives aimed at promoting and protecting the rights of women in employment and economic matters inside the Community.[22] The fact that the Republic of Ireland, after a major political battle, was forced to introduce the Equal Pay Directive, shows that this repertoire of equal opportunities legislation did more than mirror existing legal measures at member-state level. Moreover, EC law is presently attaining high visibility, as many national equal opportunities pressure groups are bringing cases to the European Court of Justice in an effort to undermine the labour-market deregulation policies being implemented by many national governments.[23] Clearly, EC Directives on equal opportunities are an important and meaningful set of instruments.

Several factors account for the success of the Commission in the equal opportunities area. One was the ability of the Commission to evoke a clause in the Treaty of Rome which explicitly stated that the promotion of equal pay should be an intrinsic aspect of the Common Market. The existence of that clause effectively rendered impotent any legal opposition which may have arisen from member states. Another was that the political composition of the Council (of the 'big three' member states, two, Britain and Germany, had social democratic Governments at the time) made it easier to get Directives ratified on the issue. But perhaps the most important reason for the Commission's success was that it was accepted almost everywhere in Europe that a legal framework was required to promote equal opportunities for women. In other words, the Commission's initiatives on equal opportunities formalised a widely-held social value. This highlights the particular 'policy style' of the Commission in the field of social policy, namely, its attempts to give concrete expression to developing pressures or values in wider European society. And the evidence tends to suggest that the Commission's most successful initiatives are on issues which command widespread social support.

The Commission was also relatively successful in the area of collective and individual rights. None of the Directives passed in this category encountered much opposition from the employers. This was mainly because the Commission was prepared to remove the clauses in its original proposals which the employers found objectionable. As a result many of the Directives ratified by the Council of Ministers only supplemented existing national legislation. For example, in Britain many of the rights conferred on workers by the redundancy and take-over Directives were already established by the Employment Protection Act. What is more, to a large extent, many of the actions which employers were obliged to undertake under the Directive were already being implemented by companies across the Community.

The various health and safety Directives proposed by the Commission, which are classified under individual workers' rights, have been adopted by the Council of Ministers and incorporated within national law without any real controversy. Essentially this is because Commission proposals in this area are fairly technical and are subject to considerable scrutiny and discussion from health and safety experts in all the member states. As a result, by the time draft Directives are sent to the Council for ratification, they have undergone numerous changes and revisions, and normally obtain automatic agreement.

The draft Fifth Directive on company organisation relating to employee participation structures has failed to be ratified by the Council of Ministers despite being on the agenda for fifteen years. Much of the blame for this must be placed at the door of the Commission. As seen earlier, its original draft proposal published in 1972 was an ill thought-out and overly ambitious document, triggering opposition from all quarters. Even the West Germans, firm supporters of the principle of employee representation, expressed reservations about the draft Directive. The result has been a seemingly endless round of consultations and revisions which has yet to product a formula agreeable to all member states.

Similar criticism can be levied against the Commission in relation to the proposed Vredeling Directive. This proposal was produced by the Commission with the minimum of prior consultations, contrary to the spirit if not the letter of the social policy dialogue inside the Community. No other proposal by the Commission in the social policy field has met with such opposition. The European employers' organisation, UNICE, launched a campaign of opposition unprecedented in scale. As a result, the Commission, the European Parliament (which sided with UNICE) the employers' organisations and trade unions became involved in a battle on the issue. The winners, at least to date, have unquestionably been the employers and the European Parliament, the losers the Commission and trade unions. But the battle has left its scars. For years, considerable suspicion and ill feeling existed between the social partners.[24]

Certainly from a labour-law perspective, the idea of transferring industrial relations policies across frontiers is considered fraught with problems. As one labour lawyer suggests 'we cannot take for granted that rules or institutions are transplantable . . . any attempt to use a pattern of law outside the environment of its origin continues to entail the risk of rejection. Labour law is a part of a system and the consequuences of change in one aspect of the system depends upon the relationship between all elements of the system. Since these relations may not be similar between the two societies, the effects of similar legislation may differ significantly as between the two settings'.[25] Thus, in this view, attempts at transplanting industrial relations practices across different national boundaries would more likely fail than succeed.

For the most part, however, the Commission approached the question of social policy during this second phase, not from a labour law perspective, but from the standpoint of European integration. This involved the Commission scanning member states to discover 'best practice' on particular employment-related issues and then making that the basis of a draft Directive. The ultimate goal was the gradual upward harmonisation of social provisions amongst the member states. As a result, the Commission remained insensitive to the problems which may arise from transplanting a practice from one member state to others. This naïve faith in the virtues and the dynamics of integration has led to several major Commission proposals ending up as embarrassing failures. The classic case in point is the Fifth Directive.

What stands out from the above analysis is that only those policies which correspond to widely-held social values, or which involve small-scale changes in the law of member states, or which mainly relate to technical matters, are readily conducive to harmonisation.[26] Conversely, those policies which entail far-reaching policies or which intervene too directly in the power relations between capital and labour in the member states are unlikely to be adopted as EC policy. This conclusion is different to the orthodox view held in Brussels that the tactics of the Thatcher Government are largely responsible for the lack of progress on Community social policy. The stalemate which developed on social policy in the early eighties cannot be laid solely at the door of the UK Government. As already mentioned, some Commission's proposals, such as the draft Fifth Directive, were not adopted by the Council of Ministers before the present Conservative administration came to office. To put it another way, it is by no means certain that the various Commission proposals would have been ratified if a non-Conservative Government was in power in Britain. It just may be the case that certain employment policies and practices are not amenable to European harmonisation.

L'Espace Sociale initiative

When Jacques Delors became President of the Commission in 1984 one of the main objectives he set was to resolve the stalemate on whether or not there should be a legal social policy. But the conundrum he faced was formidable: if the Commission continued to try to establish a social dimension to the Community via the legislative route it ran the risk of being accused of forcing change against national patterns; but if no Community legislation existed, the result could well be that EC social policy would be nothing more than a series of non-binding guidelines. As a way out of this dilemma Delors put forward the concept of *l'espace sociale* – one of those French terms which loses its full meaning when translated into English. A good deal of confusion exists about the policy implications of the idea of a European social area. Some perceived it as a new policy formulation, but it was actually first put forward by the French Government in 1981. At that stage the European Parliament took the idea to mean a European employment plan.

Part of the reason why so much confusion reigns about the notion is that nobody has spelt out clearly what it would mean in practice. From the evidence that exists, it appears that Delors linked the idea of *l'espace sociale* to the more central objective of completing the internal market by 1992. In particular, he envisaged *l'espace sociale* establishing some sort of equivalence of social standards inside the Community so as to avoid 'social dumping' – the situation whereby high-wage economies could lose out to low-wage economies or to those who effectively export their unemployment by cutting the benefits that employees have, when the remaining trade barriers are removed. However, it is far from clear how Delors intended to implement his notion. One element of his plan seems to have been the establishment, or perhaps more accurately the re-establishment, of a social dialogue between employers and trade unions, the so-called social partners, with the purpose of them establishing common agreements on various employment and work-related issues. Thus when presenting the Commission's programme for 1985 to the European Parliament Delors said that 'policies based on agreements and negotiation between management and labour are one of the cornerstones of this new social area'. Some interpreted this proposal as yet another attempt to establish some form of European collective bargaining. Although many in the Commission and in European trade unions still harbour that desire, the social dialogue idea appears to have more to do with reorganising the policy formation process on social matters. In particular, the intention appeared to be to base EC legislation on agreements emerging from the social dialogue between management and labour rather than relying on the Commission for ideas or proposals. In other words, the trade unions and employers would become the initiators of policy in the social field. It was such thinking that lay behind Delors' statement to UNICE and the ETUC in 1985 that if they entered into a social dialogue the Commission would refrain from developing any new social policy initiatives.

The practical significance of Delors' plan was that it represented a withdrawal from the 'monolithic harmonisation' approach adopted by the Commission in the seventies. Under this approach, the Commission not only laid down the social policy objectives of a Directive, but also the mechanism and methods by which these objectives were to be reached. Since it was up to the social partners to initiate social proposals, Delors was hoping that they would focus on policy principles and objectives and leave open the issue of how these were to be implemented so that member states would be free to introduce them within their existing industrial relations framework. In other words, Delors seems to be wanting a convergence in employment and labour policy goals rather than the standardisation of industrial relations institutions and processes. And as there is a growing convergence amongst the member states on industrial relations issues, this approach would, in theory, ensure that the policy agenda on social and employment affairs across the Community was similar at any one time.

As a first step towards creating a European social area, two working parties involving the social partners were set up, one relating to macro-economic policy and employment, and the other covering new technology and work. The precise status of these working groups, which became known as the 'Val Duchesse talks', was unclear. For UNICE the working parties were solely a forum through which the employers would discuss social and employment matters with the trade unions and the Commission. At the same time, however, it was made clear that they were unwilling to enter into any dialogue which sought to establish binding agreement. The view of the trade unions was that the Val Duchesse talks were preparing the groundwork for effective (legislative) action in selected social policy areas. For its part, the Commission appeared to be of the view that any agreement arising from the talks would map out the extent and nature of Community action, some of which would be legislative.

These differences of interpretation about the status of the Val Duchesse talks and the significance of any agreements which may arise from them surfaced when both working parties came to communicate their findings. The employers insisted that the final texts should be described as joint opinions and not as joint agreements, arguing that an agreement tied the partners to certain arrangements or actions, while an opinion was an open-ended expression or judgement on a particular matter. The working party on macro-economic policy and employment produced its joint opinion first. This was largely based on the economic programme proposed by the Commission in its Annual Economic Report 1986. It suggested three central objectives for Community and member-state economic policy: a mild form of reflation through public and infrastructural investment; moderation in wage settlements; and the control of inflation. The working party on new technology sat for much longer as it found considerable difficulty in concluding a joint opinion. Finally one was produced, but this was loosely worded, binding neither the trade unions nor the employers to any specific action.

Clearly, the experience of these two working parties dealt a major blow to Delors' objective that the social partners should be the initiators of Community policy in the employment and labour affairs field. In fact, before the employers would sign the final texts, he had to give them an undertaking that the Commission would not propose any legislation on the basis of the joint opinions. Thus the idea of a social dialogue between management and labour being a 'cornerstone' of *l'espace sociale* appears to be in ruins. One tangible benefit, however, of the Val Duchesse talks has been the restoration of good working relations between the social partners which were severely strained during the early eighties. And for this reason the talks are continuing (the social partners are now discussing flexibility and adaptability of the labour market), but their importance has diminished.

The failure of the Val Duchesse talks to live up to early expectations means that if the Commission wants a social dimension to the internal market then it may once again have to produce policy and legislative proposals. If the present Community decision-making arrangements were to stay the same, and as long as the present UK Conservative Government was in power, there would be little likelihood of Commission legislative proposals of any significance being adopted by the Council. But the Single European Act which came into force in 1987 changes the situation by allowing a measure of qualified majority voting on certain social policy matters. However, the clauses relating to social policies are a little confusing. Article 100 A (2) makes 'the rights and interests of employed persons' clearly a matter for decision by unanimous voting only, while Article 118A, which covers issues open to majority voting, lays down that 'member states shall pay particular attention to encouraging improvements, in the working environment, as regards health and safety of workers'. Thus it seems certain that health and safety will be a matter for qualified majority voting under the SEA. But it is uncertain whether the reference to the 'working environment' in the clause would allow the Commission to introduce proposals on other aspects of working conditions to be decided by qualified majority voting. In all likelihood, this legal uncertainty will only be resolved by a test case before the European Court of Justice.

Labour Market Flexibility

In what was widely regarded as an alternative to the Delors project, the UK Government in conjunction with the Italian and Irish Governments launched during its Presidency in the second half of 1986 a proposal for an Action Programme for Employment Growth. The origins of the proposal lie in the realisation on the part of Kenneth Clarke, a former Secretary of State for Employment, that it was bad politics to be seen in the negative light of continually blocking Commission proposals. The centrepiece of the Action Plan was that the removal of labour market rigidities inside the Community was required before a renewal of employment growth could take place. The Action Programme selected four fields for particular attention: the promotion of flexible employment patterns and conditions of work; concentration on the needs of the long-termed unemployed and training in the particular skills that were needed in the marketplace; encouraging teaching and training in management and entrepreneurial skills; a redirection of the European Social Fund to support small and medium-sized businesses.

To some extent, the specific proposals in the document overlapped with existing Commission policies and initiatives. For instance, the section on training made policy recommendations which the Commission had been pursuing for years. Similarly, the type of schemes which the UK Government wanted to see supported to encourage enterprise and employment were already receiving Social Fund sponsorship. Finally, the Commission, by establishing in 1986 a Task Force to study ways in which burdens could be reduced on businesses, had begun to focus on flexibility and deregulation issues. Thus individually the proposals and recommendations of the action for employment growth broke no new ground. But taken as a whole the UK Government initiative represented a clear departure from the previous direction of EC social policy. In particular, the UK initiative championed the cause of labour-market deregulation against the Commission's social protectionist approach. Thus while the Commission made much of the social dialogue idea, that term was not mentioned once in the papers accompanying the UK proposals.

After considerable behind-the-scene lobbying and persuasion the UK Government (along with the Italian and Irish administrations) felt confident enough to place the proposal on the agenda for the December 1986 European Council. At this meeting some member states expressed certain misgivings that there was no mention of the social dialogue or the cooperative growth strategy, but after some amendments which referred to these notions were inserted, the Action Programme was unanimously adopted.

On paper it appeared that the UK had pulled off a remarkable victory, for it is seldom that the European Council adopts an initiative in the Social Policy sphere from a group of member states which is opposed, or at least is not supported, by the Commission. Theoretically, the Commission should be developing a wide range of labour-market flexibility initiatives, but a reading of the Commission's follow-up report on the issue suggests this is not happening to any significant extent. It appears that the Commission is using its role as helmsman of policy development to frustrate the key objectives of the UK Government by identifying proposals in the Action Programme which correspond broadly with previous EC initiatives.

Certainly, the Commission has not given up on the idea of social protection. In its report on Social Developments 1986, published in April 1987, it was suggested that 'the Commission intends in the near future to devise new proposals and initiatives aimed at achieving the goal of social cohesion at Community level. These proposals will be drawn up following thorough consultations with the main organisations representing employers and workers and should contribute to correcting existing imbalances within the Community, the establishment of a safety net of protective social provisions and the strengthening of consultation at Community level'.[27] This outlook and its control over the policy implementation machinery gives the Commission a determining influence on the extent to which the UK Government's objectives of flexibility and deregulation are realised. At present, not surprisingly, the UK Government is dissatisfied with the progress being made.

The underlying philosophy and direction of the Action Programme for employment growth was also challenged by the Belgian Government when it occupied the Presidency during the first half of 1987. The Belgian Government proposed an initiative under the theme of adaptability. The basic thrust of this initiative was that flexibility should not be used as a device to obtain general social deregulation. Thus it proposed the establishment of a 'plinth' of fundamental Community social rights. These rights should include the following: trade union freedom and the right of organisation and collective bargaining; the right of every worker to be covered by a collective convention or professional agreement; the right of part-time workers to normal social security benefits; a freely negotiated work contract and the right to be represented in collective bargaining; a ban on excessive renewals of fixed term contracts; the right for workers in the various forms of atypical work to social security benefits and protection as regards working hours; the right of workers to protective measures for health and safety; and the right of every worker to fair pay and to enable him and his family to enjoy a decent standard of living. The Belgians asked the European Council to make a statement on the theme of adaptability of the economy. This it did, and the specifics of the Belgian proposals are now being discussed by the social partners as part of the Val Duchesse talks process.

Conclusions

Clearly considerable uncertainty hangs over the future direction of Community social policy. It is difficult to see how the current conflict between those who want to see EC social policy based on social protectionist principles and those who want it to be deregulatory in character can be effectively resolved. Indeed, if anything, the conflict will probably intensify, as a debate about whether or not the 1992 project should have a social dimension has emerged inside Community institutions. It is too hazardous a task to predict what will emerge from this debate. In the short term, however, EC social policy will probably centre around the operation of the Social Fund and the implementation of more policies in the general labour-market area. Considerable worthwhile work can be undertaken in these areas, but in all likelihood it will be overshadowed by the debate about whether or not the Community should have a legislative dimension to its social policy.

Notes and References

1 Commission of the European Community, *The Implementation of the New Community Action Programme on the Promotion of Equal Opportunities for Women*, Com (85) 64 Final Brussels 1985 p 84

2 *ibid*, p 85

3 For more details of this action programme, see the Commission of the European Community, *Employment of Disabled People*, Com (86) No 7 Final, Brussels 1986

4 Commission of the European Community, *Community Policy on Migration*, Com (85) 148 Final, Brussels, 1985

5 Commission of the European Community, *'The Draft Fifth Directive on the structure of public limited companies'*, *Bulletin of the European Community* Supplement 8/75 Brussels 1975, p 2

6 Commission of the European Community; 'The Structure of Public Companies: Amended Proposal for a Fifth Directive', *Bulletin of the European Community* Supplement 6/83, 1983

7 For a detailed discussion of the history of the Vredeling proposal, see BLANPAIN, R *The Vredeling Proposal: information and consultation of employers in multinational enterprises*, Deventer Netherlands 1983

8 Commission of the European Community, 'Employee Information

and consultation Procedures – amended Proposal', *Bulletin of the European community* supplement 2/83 Brussels, 1983

9 See for example 'Community Markets, US Firms oppose Vredeling', *Financial Times*, London, April 1983

10 *Incomes Data Services, International Report*, July 1985

11 See VANDAMME, J (ed) *Pour une nouvelle politique sociale en Europe*, Economica Paris 1984

12 HEPPLE, R 'Community Measures for the Protection of Workers against Dismissals', *Common Market Law Review*, No 14, 1977

13 Commission of the European Community, *Comparative Survey on the Protection of Employees in the event of insolvency of their employer in the member states of the European Community*, Com (76) 305 Final, Brussels 1976

14 Commission of the European Community, *Proposal for a Council Directive on the Protection of Employees in the event of Insolvency* Com (78) 41 Brussels, 1978

15 Commission of the European Community, *Report from the Commission to the Council on the application of the Council Recommendation of 20th December 1982 on the principles of a Community policy with regard to retirement age*, Com (82) 857 Final 10th June 1985

16 Commission of the European Community, *Draft Council Recommendation on the Reduction and Reorganisation of Working Time* Com (83) 543 Final 1983

17 Commission of the European Community *Amended Proposal for a Council Directive concerning the Supply of Workers by Temporary Employment Businesses and Fixed Duration Contracts*, Com 84 (159) Final, Brussels, 1984

18 COLLINS, D 'Social Policy' in LODGE, J *Institutions and Policies of the European Community*, Frances Pinter, London 1983

19 SELLIN, B 'Comparability of Vocational Training Certificates in the Member States of the European Community', *Vocational Training Bulletin* No 18 1985

20 PIEHL, E 'Comparability of Vocational Training Qualifications in EC Member States', *Cedefop Flash* No 2 1987

21 SILLETTI, D 'European System for the International Clearing of Vacancies and Applications for Employment', *Social Europe* No 2 1987 pp 11–14

22 LANDAU, E *The Rights of Working Women in the European Community*, European Perspectives, Brussels 1985

23 HOSKYNS, C 'Women, European Law and Transnational Politics', *International Journal of the Sociology of Law*, Vol 14, nos 3/4 November 1986 pp 299–316

24 PIPKORN, J 'The Draft Directive on Procedures for Informing and Consulting Employers', *Common Market Law Review* No 20 1983 pp 725–55

25 Quoted in the introduction to BLANPAIN, R (ed), *Comparative Labour Law and Industrial Relations*, Deventer Netherlands 1985 p 14

26 CRIPP, L 'The Social Policy of the European Community', *Social Europe*, January 1988 No 1 Brussels pp 51–62

27 Commission of the European Communities, *Report of Social Developments 1986*, Brussels 1987 p 16

Chapter V

The Administrative Dimension

When Britain entered the Community in 1973, the intergovernmental form of decision-making had taken firm root. With the number and range of national administrative inputs into the Community process now extensive, it was more important than ever for the member states to be well organised in relation to EC affairs. For the original member states this was no small task, but for new member states internal organisation on EC matters posed major problems of adjustment, particularly as the Community blurs the distinction traditionally made between domestic and foreign policy. On the eve of Britain's accession one authority wrote a pamphlet arguing that the challenge of Community membership was acute and that there was little time for gradual adjustment.[1] In the short term, Britain had to make the practical commitment of becoming involved in the day-to-day conduct of Community affairs, providing and retraining personnel to work on Community matters, and absorbing Community legislation into national law. The longer-term task was to foster a European policy perspective amongst civil servants.

In 1987, in an article entitled 'Britain needs a European policy dimension', the same author wrote 'there seems to be a secular trend towards an increasing identification in Britain of a necessary and pervasive European dimension. British policy makers feel 'at home' in the European Community. Being part of the European family has begun to feel 'normal'. This is reflected in a series of changes in British government policy, as it increasingly takes as given the need to explore European options more positively'.[2] In this view, British governmental institutions have overcome the problems posed by EC membership and are now constructive on European matters. Yet the evidence produced to substantiate this conclusion is at best anecdotal. The way in which government bodies operate within the European Community is subjected to no detailed examination: surely required before a sweeping conclusion on the above lines can be made.

The purpose of this chapter is to analyse how government and quasi-government bodies in the employment and labour-market policy sphere have adjusted to EC membership and how European matters have impinged on their activity. Only after this survey is complete, will an attempt be made to draw some general conclusions about British national policy-making inside the Community. The national bodies we examine in this chapter are the Department of Employment, the Department of Health and Social Security, the Manpower Services Commission, and the Health and Safety Commission. The chapter starts with a general outline of the administrative links between national government departments and the Community decision-making system.

National Governments in the EC System

Figure Vi outlines the role of national governments and national government departments in the Community decision making system. In this chapter, we are mainly concerned with the linkages between civil servants and Brussels and not with the political role of governments inside the Community. It should be stressed, however, that the distinction between the two is not always clear; as one senior Commission official commented, 'it is always rather difficult to decide how far Ministers are leading their officials or how far officials are leading their Ministers'.[3] The diagram shows that there are two aspects to civil-servant linkages with the Community: the representative role and the policy consultation and implementation role. As pointed out in Chapter II, each member state has a permanent delegation of national civil servants, some with the rank of Ambassador, in Brussels. These civil servants are normally involved with the work of COREPER, putting forward the view of their governments and negotiating with other member states and the Commission to resolve matters of disrepute. Britain is typical in that whilst in most cases the Brussels-based civil servants take the 'lead' in such negotiations, they are normally closely briefed, and on occasions accompanied, by Whitehall-based civil servants. Thus, for example, if COREPER was discussing the Commission's proposals for a future Community programme on health and safety, position papers would be drawn up by the Health and Safety Commission and Department of Employment staff. These national staff would then go to Brussels and brief members of the British delegation and be on hand during the formal discussions in case any further advice and information is required.

In many cases, before proposals arrive at COREPER for formal consideration by the member states, national officials will have already been involved in some capacity with the issue. For instance, proposals may be the outcome of discussions of a Commission committee on which national officials participate. To use the health and safety example again: officials from the Health and Safety Executive are members of the Advisory Committee on Health and Safety which prepares draft Community legislation for this policy area. This involves detailed discussions on technical and administrative matters amongst health and safety experts from the member states and the Commission. Thus

Figure Vi National governments in the Community decision-making system

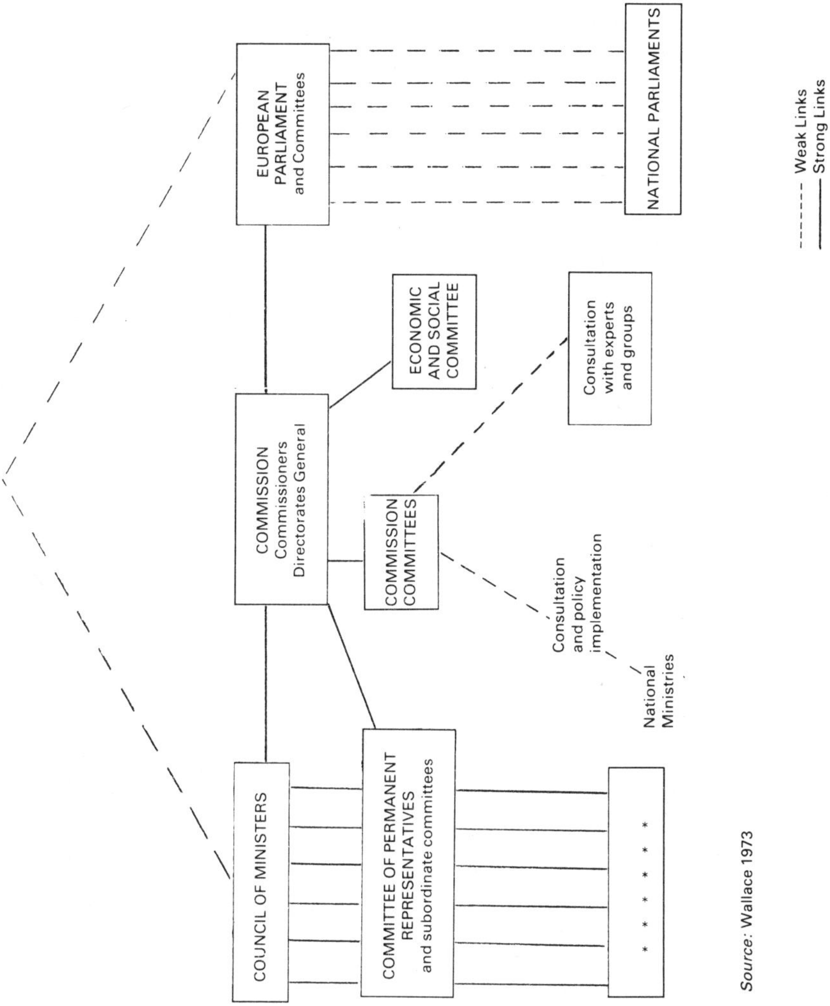

Source: Wallace 1973

national officials are deeply embroiled in the process of formulating proposals for Community action. Even where policy proposals are not the result of the deliberations of a particular committee, national officials are frequently consulted on them by the Commission. The Commission obviously wants to know the legal, administrative and political implications for member states of particular initiatives before formally presenting them. However, on some contentious matters – for instance the 'Vredeling proposal' – the Commission has tended to bypass this consultative role.

Another way national officials are brought into the Community decision-making system is through assisting with the implementation of policies. A clear example of this is the Department of Employment's administration and supervision of the distribution of Social Fund grants in Britain. National officials also play a similar key role in relation to the European Regional Fund. Were it not for the work of national government departments the Community would be unable to operate these funds. National officials are also engaged in implementing Community legislation into national law. This poses considerable problems due to translation difficulties and differences of interpretation between member states. It is also a politically sensitive area, as the British Government has been accused on a number of occasions of not properly or fully implementing Community legislation in Britain (see Chapter VII). Thus, the Community impinges on the work of national government departments and officials in a number of important respects. In the following section, we examine in more detail the linkages between government and quasi-government institutions and the Community decision-making system in the social and employment affairs field.

Governmental Departments

Figure Vii outlines the national administrative network which deals with Community social and employment policies. The Department of Employment is more closely involved with Community social policy than any other part of Whitehall. As mentioned already, the unit that administers the EC Social Fund is housed in the Department of Employment. Another EC unit also exists in the Department, which performs a general policy co-ordinating and initiating role. Specifically, the unit is responsible for briefing ministers about EC developments, getting the relevant functional department to draft policy responses to proposals coming out of Brussels, and maintaining contact with other Departments and relevant British civil servants in Brussels on Community matters.

The second most important department in relation to Community

Figure Vii Administrative Network in the UK dealing with Community Social and Employment Policies

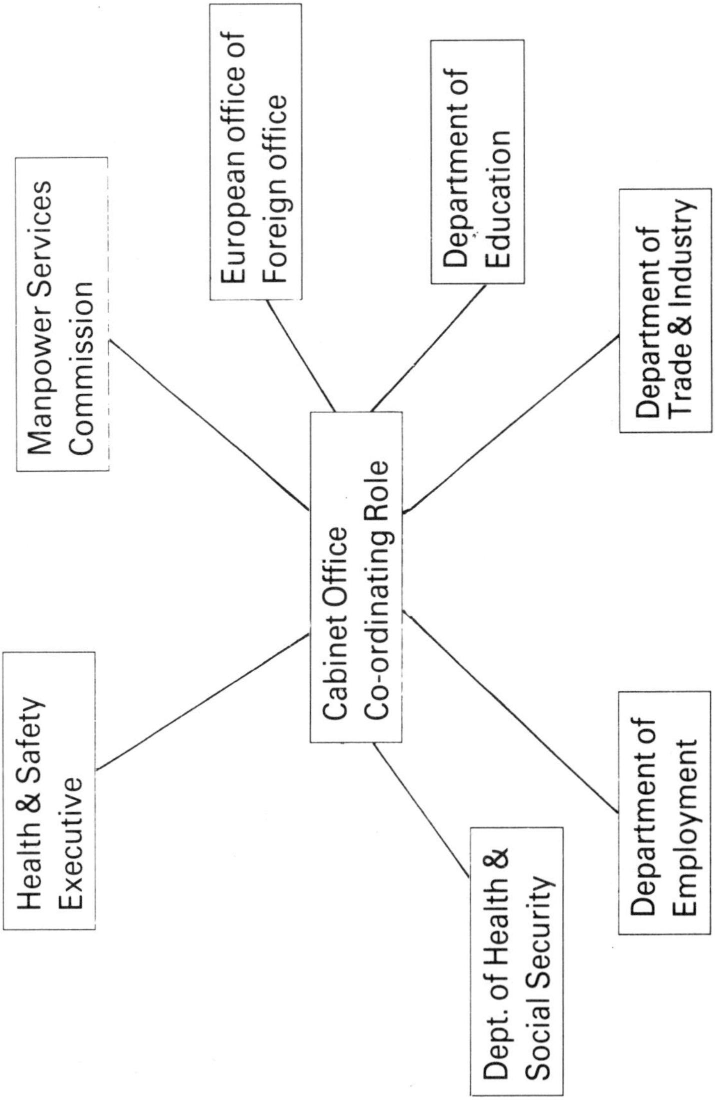

social policy is the Department of Health and Social Security. Officials from this department participate in the regular and continuing discussions on social security matters. The department is organised in a similar way to the Department of Employment with regard to EC matters. A central European unit oversees and co-ordinates the department's policy formation on EC initiatives whilst individual units are responsible for drafting detailed policies.

The other two departments are only marginally involved in EC social policy matters. The Department of Education is involved in a relatively minor way in EC training and educational policy developments, and the Department of Trade and Industry has only an indirect association with EC social affairs in that it is involved with the company law aspects of the proposed Fifth Directive.

For the most part, government departments tend to react to EC proposals rather than to initiate any policies. Thus, if the Commission produces a draft Directive on equal opportunities, the relevant division of the Department of Employment will draft a British Government response. To a large extent, this places civil servants in an unfamiliar role, for it is they who normally initiate policy on employment matters. But this does not unduly worry any of the civil servants themselves. From interviews with officials in all the departments which have a connection with EC social affairs, it is clear that there is general satisfaction with the policy-formation process on Community matters. Probably the only exception to this reactive approach was the British Government-inspired initiative on Employment Growth which was adopted by the Council in December 1986. The background to this initiative was outlined in Chapter IV.

Most of the policy work associated with EC social policy is routine. Officials attend Community committees in Brussels to discuss ways in which policy linkages can be improved between the member states. Officials also write policy papers on EC social proposals, particularly as regards their impact on the UK. In addition to this direct contact on EC affairs, Community social policy also impinges on the work of national governments by imposing legal constraints within which they must develop policy. For instance, a number of policy proposals to increase labour-market flexibility had to be dropped because they infringed EC equality laws. Overall, this constraining influence does not occur very often.

In the following sections, the linkages between these various national organisations are examined in detail. This examination begins with an assessment of how the Community encourages exchanges between the member states to promote co-operation between national employment institutions.

Exchanges of Officials from Member States' Employment Services

Virtually no legal barriers have existed to the free movement of labour inside the Community for twenty years. Yet the actual number of people taking the opportunity to work in another member state remains low. Thus, as things stand, legal provisions alone are clearly not enough to increase the flow of workers between member states. The Commission has responded to this situation by encouraging co-operation between national employment services. One practical way in which this co-operation is being promoted is through regular exchanges between officials of different national departments. The hope is that these exchanges will result in a greater level of convergence between the national administrative bodies, thus enabling them to adopt similar working methods and approaches to certain problems.

Exchanges between officials of national employment services have been going on for about 14 years. In 1986 some 350,000 ecu was expended in such exchanges, involving 275 officials. There are two types of exchanges. One type takes the form of a 1-2 month traineeship, while the other is only a two-day trainee visitation. Visits are normally used as a means of solving specific or immediate problems directly connected with the transfer of vacancies and applications for employment between the member states. The aim of traineeships was until recently primarily to encourage information and co-operation exchanges. In 1986, however, the Commission drew up new guidelines to govern trainee exchanges. From 1987 trainee exchanges have had to involve the study of subjects relating to employment and the labour market policies which are of concern to all member states, so as to reach conclusions useful to the implementation of new national or Community measures in employment. In 1987, traineeships from all member states had to examine one of two topics, namely: 1) recent experiments carried out with a view to improving the operation of the employment market; and 2) unemployment amongst young people – what can be done to ensure transition from training to employment.

The objective of this more coordinated system of exchange is to help bring a convergence, or at least greater co-operation, between member states' employment policies. However, it is too early to assess whether this objective will be fully realised.

In addition to these schemes, the European Centre for the Development of Vocational Training (CEDEFOP) organises study visits for vocational training specialists. The study visits in this area are now in their third year and around 180 grants are shared out in varying proportions amongst member states. In 1987, UK, France and West Germany were each allocated 18 grants. The Manpower Services Commission has a

National Liaison Officer for this programme, whose role is to oversee the distribution of information and application forms to all those in industry, commerce and public service who may have an interest; to select the UK candidates to reflect a balanced range of applicants, taking account of occupation, regional background, sex, employer and trade union interest, to make arrangements for groups of EC nationals to visit the UK; to write a report on the operation of the programme at the end of each year, including an assessment and any recommendations; and to attend meetings at the CEDEFOP offices in Berlin to review the previous year's programme, agree arrangements for the present year and consider plans for the following year.

Each year the National Liaison Officer organises about three UK delegations to other member states, and coordinates the UK programme for approximately five visits from other member states to the UK. UK delegations normally consist of both training policy-makers and practitioners and visits include meeting the relevant national labour market and training body, companies and trade unions, and touring training institutions and schemes. Thus, for example, on a recent visit to Italy, the delegation met officials and staff from: the Ministry of Labour; the SFOL – a government-funded agency with the remit to carry out research projects; Confidustria – the CBI's equivalent in Italy; La Ciliega, a small private organisation concerned with developing creative skills in young people; a government agency appraising and sponsoring proposals for 'young' business projects in South Italy; Coupsind – the large Italian co-operative body engaged in encouraging the growth of small co-operatives; Fonney – an agency established to help alleviate the unemployment problems of Southern Italy; ELIPA, the national organisation for small firms; ECIPA (Bologna) a business enterprise workshop scheme sponsored by the Bologna regional council.

It is difficult to make an accurate assessment of the value of these training visits. Certainly members of the delegations appear to learn a good deal about how national and company-level training initiatives are organised and carried out in other member states. However, it is questionable whether delegation members, particularly those who are training practitioners, learn a sufficient amount to be able to implement some of the approaches and ideas they are shown within the programmes they run in the UK. As one member of a delegation commented, 'Although all visits were worthwhile, they were sometimes too short for us to obtain a deeper insight into the activities.' Perhaps the people who benefit the most from these visits are the training policy-makers. These officials have the time to do the necessary follow-up work to assess whether or not an apparently successful and innovative training measure they come across on a visit could be transferred into the UK. Overall, those who go on these delegations seem to find the experience highly rewarding and worthwhile.

Because the British Government has been unsympathetic to many EC proposals, it is interesting to examine the way the administrators have dealt with some controversial Community social policies. Thus the next section outlines the involvement of Department of Employment officials in discussions on the proposed Fifth Directive.

The Department of Employment and the Fifth Directive

As outlined in chapter IV, the draft Fifth Directive on company organisation and participation is something of an evergreen in EC social policy, being first proposed in 1972. It last went before the Council of Ministers in 1983, when the member states refused to endorse the proposal, primarily because of its sheer complexity. As a result, the proposal was sent back to a Council Working Party to devise a formula on the issue which would be acceptable to all member states. There are both formal and informal aspects to these discussions to reach a compromise agreement. As regards the formal discussions, the 'lead' UK department on the draft Directive is the Department of Trade and Industry, but officials from the Department of Employment are also heavily involved in the working group, as the proposal has important implications for industrial relations.

Officially, the working group should meet in Brussels every six weeks for a two-day session. By and large, each member state which has held the presidency tries to follow this schedule. Thus, during the UK presidency in late 1986, the group met three times; during the following Belgium presidency five times; then in the Danish term four times; and since West Germany has had the presidency, it has met five times. As the British government has major objections to the draft Fifth Directive, officials from the Department of Employment and DTI attend every meeting. To ensure that the British view is properly represented, the same officials attend each time.

Inside the working group, negotiations to try and obtain a draft more or less acceptable to all member states have progressed slowly. The proposal has gone through a first reading. At this stage, the member states voiced their objections to the specific clauses. Thus the Department of Employment officials made clear their general and specific reservations, leaving the other member states and the Commission in no doubt about the UK government's position. The proposal goes on to its second reading, when the discussions and negotiations get extremely detailed, with the member states going through each clause line by line. Because the discussions are so detailed, the working group was only able to work through three articles in the first year. In these detailed negotiations, the Department of Employment officials refrain from continually repeating their opposition to the Directive in general. Instead, they make suggestions on how certain parts of the Directive could be clarified or some practical obstacles overcome. As a result, the British delegation has a reputation for being well briefed and making a valued and important contribution. Occasionally, however, the British officials have to remind the group that the UK remains opposed to the initiatives. Within bounds, every effort is made by the national officials to be constructive.

As can be seen, the formal negotiations to come up with a revised draft Fifth Directive which could be acceptable to all member states leave little manoeuvrability for the construction of compromises. To overcome the overly rigid structure, a range of informal discussions have taken place on the subject. This has involved officials from the Department of Employment holding bilateral discussions with their counterparts in other member states. These informal bilateral contacts have proven to be fruitful, for they have given rise to the proposal that a new section should be inserted into the proposed Fifth Directive. This new section would cover forms of participation negotiated by the social partners at the enterprise level. The practical implications of this new section would be to allow British employers to negotiate their own forms of participation and to avoid having to adopt 'continental models', as proposed in earlier drafts of Directives. This proposal was the subject of informal discussions between the Commission and British officials, which went on alongside the formal deliberations.

Thus, as with policy formation at the national level, informal contacts and discussions are as important in the Community context as are formal sessions for the construction of compromise deals. Another benefit from these informal contacts cited by national officials is that a greater awareness is gained of the industrial relations systems in other member states. This increased knowledge allows the officials to participate more fully and more competently in formal Community committees.

Within the Department of Employment, officials keep senior civil servants, and if necessary Government ministers, briefed on developments both at the formal and informal levels. And every two months or so, a formal internal policy review and update is conducted to assess whether the Department needs to change tack in Community negotiations. For the most part, none of the Ministers associated with the Department are actively involved in this process. It is interesting to note that the officials receive few requests for information on the progress of discussions in the working group from British interest-groups. Of those that are made, most come from employers' organisations. Virtually none come from the trade unions. Equally rare are requests from MPs and MEPs. In giving replies to such requests, the officials only give general information on the discussions, due to the rules of discretion.

Overall, the UK civil servants appear to have a highly professional approach to Community bodies in the labour and employment fields. This assessment coincides with the popular impression of the British amongst Euro-officials in Brussels, namely that they are always briefed and represent their case effectively. Further, although the British Government opposed almost every Commission proposal for social legislation, the national civil servants have endeavoured to be constructive in discussions at the Community level. In addition to participating in formal sessions, national officials place much store on developing informal contracts with officials from other member states.

Manpower Services Commission

The Manpower Services Commission (MSC) is the main labour-market and training institution in Britain. As a result, it is involved in deliberations on Community social policy in a number of ways. In the first place, MSC officials sit on several Community committees relating to training matters. The most important of these committees are the CEDEFOP Management Board which develops every year a work programme of initiatives for vocational and educational training in member countries, and the Advisory Committee on Vocational Training which contributes to the development of Community training policy. While these committees are important, they do not play a dominant role in the Community social policy institutional framework.

Yet Community policies on training have an influence on the form and direction of MSC schemes. The EuroTecNet project is one example. In 1985, the Commission launched a programme on vocational training measures relating to new technologies, called EuroTecNet. For the most part, this programme involved the establishment of a network of demonstration projects across the member states with the goal of 'promoting the development of a united approach to the introduction of new information technologies'.

The demonstration projects were established by national bodies on the basis of a number of criteria defined by the Commission. Originally, the MSC selected a number of Information Technology Centres (ITecs) which had mushroomed during the early eighties, and a number of open learning programmes, as the British contribution to EuroTecNet. The selection of these programmes meant that the MSC had to develop no new initiatives for the Community's programme. But as a result of the exchange of information between the various demonstration-projects and officials visiting some of these initiatives, the MSC made important changes to the form of training undertaken in ITecs, initiated plans to establish new qualifications in the new technologies field, and broadened the scope of technology training. Indeed, so influenced was the MSC by other projects that it established a group of national officials to assess what aspects of new technology training in other Community countries could be imported into Britain. It even co-sponsored and hosted a major conference in London called 'People and Technology', at which the results of the projects from various member states were displayed.

Probably the main EC-related activity of the MSC in the short-medium term will be its contribution to the Community drive to obtain comparability of vocational training qualifications between the member states. In 1983, the Council adopted a Resolution on the compatability of vocational training qualifications. This Resolution provided for a number of things: the adoption of a Community structure of levels of training; the endorsement of the basic methodology for establishing the comparability of vocational training qualifications for given occupations or groups of occupations; common action by the member states to enable workers to use their vocational training qualifications for the purposes of access to related employment in another member state.

The problem of obtaining recognition and comparability of vocational training qualifications was seen as having a number of different but related aspects: the recognition of qualifications for employment purposes; the recognition of diplomas for academic purposes; and the recognition of periods spent at school for general education purposes. To address these different aspects of the problem, the Council's Resolution proposed a five-tier training structure. Level 1 focuses on compulsory education and professional initiation. This form of training must primarily enable the holder to perform relatively simple work and may be fairly quickly acquired. Level 2 covers compulsory education and vocational training (including in particular, apprenticeships). This level leaves the holder fully qualified to engage in a specific activity, with the capacity to use the instruments and techniques relating thereto. Level 3 concerns compulsory education and vocational training and additional technical training or technical educational training or other secondary-level training. This form of training involves a greater fund of theoretical knowledge than level 2, entailing technical work and/or executive and coordination duties. Level 4 relates to secondary training (general or vocational) and post-secondary technical training. This form of training involves high-level technical training acquired at or outside educational establishments. The resultant qualification covers a higher level of knowledge and of capabilities. However, it does not generally require mastery of the scientific bases of the various areas concerned. Level 5 covers secondary training (general or vocational) and complete higher training. This level covers those qualifications which entail a mastery of the scientific bases of the occupation.

The Council Resolution also laid down that each member state was to designate a coordinating body to investigate what changes were required to make training qualifications in similar occupational categories broadly compatible across the Community. For practical reasons, this investigation was limited to a priority group of level 2 occupations, namely hotel and catering, motor-vehicle repair, construction, electro-technology, agriculture/horticulture/forestry. The objective was that from these studies, a European 'vocational training card' would be created, serving as proof that the holder has been awarded a specific qualification which should be recognised throughout the Community.

To fulfil the tasks laid down by the Resolution, MSC officials have become involved in a wide-ranging amount of research and consultation since 1985. In the first place, these officials have had to obtain model job descriptions relating to specific occupations from other member states, so as to assess what changes were required before they could be recognised by UK employers. In addition, they had to hold extensive consultations with employers and training organisations relating to the specific profession, to find out their views on the mutual recognition of diplomas across the Community. As well as these activities at the national level, officials have had to participate in Community-level discussions to coordinate and make coherent the suggestions of each national study. It took nearly three years for all this work to be completed and for a final set of recommendations and conclusions to be forwarded to the Council on the priority group of occupations. As the Community intends to intensify efforts to obtain the mutual recognition of diplomas in the context of 1992, it is highly likely that MSC work in this area will increase significantly.

Health and Safety: Commission (HSC) and Executive (HSE) Involvement

When the European Commission produces a proposal for a Directive concerned with occupational health and safety, the Department of Employment is nominally the lead department. In practice, HSE officials carry out the function of representing the UK at preliminary meetings and negotiations, writing memoranda for Parliament and providing briefing for Ministers.

Where proposals relate to areas in which the UK has adequate domestic legislation, HSE officials always try and ensure in negotiations that the final instrument is, as far as possible, consistent with UK legislation. Take, for instance, the Directive on the protection of workers from lead.

A year before this Directive was adopted by the Council, an HSC regulation on the subject had been passed into law in Britain. In the negotiations leading up to the ratification of the Directive, HSE officials successfully ensured that the European law closely resembled the UK's regulation. As a result, only minimal changes had to be made to the British regulation. On the other hand, where a Commission proposal is in an area in which there is little or no domestic legislation, or which differs radically from existing UK laws, HSC provides advice to Ministers on the line to be followed in negotiations, and generally gives much greater attention to the issue. For instance, when the Commission made proposals on the protection of workers from noise, an area where little UK law exists, the HSC established an ad hoc working group comprising some HSC members and HSE officials to monitor and respond to developments during negotiations at the Community level.

In comparison with UK domestic legislation, the volume of EC health and safety legislation is still comparatively small. But EC negotiations, according to staff, appear to represent a significant and growing claim on the resources of the HSE's policy divisions. It is estimated that in a typical year, the amount of time spent by HSE officials in EC meetings in Brussels and Luxembourg is the equivalent of two full-time posts. This estimation does not include, however, the amount of time spent on preparation for negotiations, including consultation with Government departments, and on the implementation and enforcement of adopted Community legislation.

In addition to the negotiation of EC legislation, HSE officials also attend other EC-related meetings, most notably to advise the Commission on the management of research programmes. For example, the Nuclear Installations Inspectorate has representatives on a number of committees supervising the Community's research effort into reactor safety, and representatives of the Mines and Quarries Inspectorate and Safety Policy Division help to select research projects for support under the aegis of the Community's Safety and Health programme for the Mining and Other Extractive Industries. Overall, officials consider EC work to represent a modest but significant and growing part of the HSC and HSE activity.

In terms of resource burden, the policy divisions are responsible for the negotiations of EC legislation, but it is normally the inspectorate and research and technical services division who provide the representatives for EC advisory bodies. The latter divisions also give specialist advice to policy sections on detailed points of EC law. As well as this involvement, our interviews with HSC officials suggest that as a result of EC membership informal and unilateral contacts with health and safety administrations in other member states has been considerably strengthened and extended.

Conclusions

Britain's membership of the Community has clearly opened up a European dimension to the work of national labour-market and training-related institutions. If Britain had remained outside the EC, contacts and linkages between the Department of Employment, the MSC and so on, and similar institutions in other member states, would not have been nearly as extensive as they are today.

The Community link has meant considerable extra work for many of these institutions. In particular, staff in nearly all labour-market institutions in Britain have had to develop policies so that their organisations can participate fully in European Community discussions. In addition, many of these institutions have to develop initiatives and undertake a variety of tasks so that commitments they have entered into at the Community level are met. At the same time, the impact of the Community membership on Britain's employment and labour institutions should not be overestimated. By and large, work on EC-related matters still represents only a small part of the overall activity of these institutions.

In terms of influencing policy-making in these institutions, the EC connection is also small, but none the less growing. This influence appears to operate in two ways. In the first place, through adopting legislation and policies on certain issues, the Community places constraints on policy development inside national institutions in the social field. Thus the Department of Employment had to shelve an initiative on labour-market flexibility which it was going to implement, as it was considered to contravene EC equality legislation. Secondly, the Community provides a forum in, and the mechanism by, which policy-makers in Britain can more effectively assess innovative and original schemes in other member states. There exists a considerable body of evidence (see Chapter XI) to suggest that national policy-makers are using the opportunity to learn from the experiences of their counterparts in other member states. But again, it needs to be pointed out that while these influences on policy-making are significant, they are not the dominant influences on national policy formation in Britain. And British policy-makers do not allow their increased contact with policy-makers in other member states to prevent them examining schemes in other parts of the world. The recent Department of Employment interest in the Workfare Scheme operating in the USA is a case in point.

Overall, then, can it be concluded that a clear European dimension has been opened up in British policy-making in most areas of government, including employment affairs? The answer is a qualified yes. National labour and training policy-makers are now full and positive contributors to Community bodies, and so on. But a great deal of scope still exists for more concerted action on policy on employment affairs between member states.

Notes and References

1 WALLACE, H. *National Governments and the European Communities,* Chatham House/PEP, London 1973

2 WALLACE, H. 'British Policy-Making Acquires a European Dimension', *Revue Française de Civilisation Britannique* IV 1987 p 148

3 MORLEY, J. *Submission* to the House of Lords Select Committee on European Community in Voluntary Part-Time Work, 19th Report Session 1982 p 302

Chapter VI

The Political Dimension

Most Community decisions are currently made by the Council of Ministers on the basis of unanimity between the member states and, as shown in chapter II, this situation will not change dramatically as a result of the Single European Act. Thus the UK Government has a major say in how and to what extent the Community influences the political, social and economic environment in Britain. For instance, it can undertake diplomatic lobbying at the European level in support of, or in opposition to, particular proposals. If necessary, it can use its right of veto inside the Council of Ministers to block the passage of any initiative. Thus under present arrangements, it is unlikely that the Community could reach a decision which the UK Government firmly opposes. In addition to these powers inside the Community's decision-making system, the UK Government also administers the important legal ports of entry by which EC legislation and European Court of Justice rulings become British statutes. This gives Government the opportunity, if it so wishes, to lessen the impact of EC legislation by interpreting it in a cautious or partial way.

Thus, it is the outlook and behaviour of the political party in Government which determines to a considerable extent the degree of the Community influence within its boundaries. For that reason, it is important to examine how the present Conservative Government, and indeed the opposition parties, view the notion of European integration and how they approach the question of EC social policy. This appraisal constitutes the first part of the chapter.

The focus of the rest of the chapter is on British interest groups – the trade unions, the employers' associations and the related 'single issue' pressure groups like the Equal Opportunities Commission. We examine the way in which these groups have attempted to influence EC Social Policy and whether they have tried to use the Community as a 'third level' forum to further their own interests.

There are two reasons for this assessment. First, to test the thesis prevalent in the academic literature that interest groups will be one of the key dynamics in the integration process by forcing the Community to enter new policy areas as a result of active lobbying at the European level. Secondly, to give practising personnel managers an understanding of the scale of British interest-group lobbying at the European level and some idea of the degree to which these actions are successful.

The Political Parties

The Conservative Government: A minimalist stance

It was a Conservative Government, under the premiership of Edward Heath, which brought Britain into the Common Market in 1973. The political complexion of the Conservative leadership at that time was somewhat different from the one which is at the helm today. In particular, Heath and his ministers represented the 'one nation' tradition inside the Conservative Party, while the current leadership adopts a modern form of laissez-faire politics. A sharp difference exists between these two camps on a wide range of policy issues, including the European Community.[1] Broadly, the 'one nation' Conservatives can be described as European enthusiasts who throughout the late fifties and sixties argued continually for British membership of the Common Market. The extent of their enthusiasm can be gauged by the fact that they were prepared to bring Britain into the Community on what a large body of expert opinion regarded as iniquitous terms.

The radical neo-liberal wing of the Party which gained dominance when Mrs Thatcher was elected leader adopts a more cautious approach to Europe: its stance can best be described as minimalist. This minimalist stance, a product of the Government's highly market-oriented economic strategy, is consistent with the basic EC rules of open markets and free factor movements. But there has been a consistent rejection of the European project to the extent that it goes beyond the integration of markets towards a collective interventionism or towards a close convergence of national economic policies.[2] Thus Mrs Thatcher kept Britain out of the exchange-rate mechanism of the European Monetary System (EMS): the close monetary co-ordination required by the EMS was seen as too restrictive of national policy. The British Government has resisted the political development of the Community and was originally in fact a determined opponent of a revision of the Treaty of Rome. (It was only after the other member states had out-manoeuvred the UK by taking a decision on a majority vote that the process for establishing the Single European Act went ahead.) Expansion of the EC's budgetary resources has also been resisted.

Thus it is hardly surprising to find that the Thatcher administration has been emphatically opposed to EC social legislation. A clear example is provided by the EC Transfer of Undertakings Directive. The past Labour Government agreed this proposal, but it failed to introduce the Directive into national law before the 1979 election. As the new Conservative Government was totally opposed to the initiative, it decided to do nothing on the issue. Eventually, more than a year after the expiry date for the implementation of the Directive, the Commission decided to launch legal proceedings against the United Kingdom. This forced the Conservative Government to introduce legislation on the basis of the Directive. The Minister responsible said he laid this legislation before the House 'with a marked lack of enthusiasm'.[3] There are numerous other examples: just one more will suffice here. Giving evidence to the House of Commons Select Committee on Employment, Kenneth Clarke, then a junior minister, suggested that because of the stance of the British Government Vredeling was dead and buried and as far as he was concerned, it would remain so, and 'if it popped its head above the parapet he would wring its neck'.[4] (Chapter IV detailed the way in which the Conservative administration has been successful in opposing the ambitions of the Commission for further social legislation since 1979.)

The Conservative Government is quite disposed to take the credit for blocking Community social legislation. However, it needs pointing out to both its supporters and opponents that whilst the British Government was at the forefront of the attack on Commission social policy initiatives, other member states were also concerned about the implications of certain proposals, particularly the draft Fifth and Vredeling Directives. They kept silent about their reservations, realising that the UK would use its powers to block the proposals. This allowed them to avoid any possible embarrassments or political difficulties at home. But, at another level, the Conservative Government realised that it was not good politics to be portrayed in the negative light of continually opposing initiatives from the Commission. As an attempt to alter this image, the Conservative Government during its Presidency in the latter part of 1986 formulated the Action Programme for Employment Growth proposals. This initiative, detailed in chapter IV, was a highly subtle piece of political strategy. Not only did it show that the UK Government was trying to break the impasse on EC Social Policy, but it was also a major attempt to redirect the orientation of Community action in this field. As shown earlier, whether the proposal has been successful in that attempt is open to doubt.

The Labour Party

Although there has always been a large number of leading figures in the Labour Party who have favoured Britain's membership of the EC, the majority of party members have been hostile to the Community. This repugnance was expressed in Labour's pamphlets for the 1983 election, which contained a commitment to British withdrawal. Following the outcome of that election, however, and the subsequent course of events, Labour has in effect reversed its position on the EC even if this reversal has yet to obtain the formal endorsement of a party conference. The manifesto for the 1987 election made no mention of withdrawal. Instead, the emphasis was placed on re-orientating the priorities and objectives of the Community towards the fight against European unemployment.

Two main themes can be distinguished in Labour's historical hostility towards the Community; for short we characterise these as the themes of socialism and sovereignty. The Party has seen the EC as intrinsically antagonistic to its socialist values and objectives. The reasons for this vary: Community institutions are sometimes thought to be politically and militarily dominated by the US; sometimes they are regarded as economically instrumental to the expansion of transnational companies; sometimes they are felt to reflect the dark and reactionary aspects of continental history. There is little doubt, however, that the second theme, that of national sovereignty, has been the more important. For Labour, international and – *a fortiori* – supranational decision-making in the Community impeded national politics, and impaired the powers of Parliament, always seen as the most appropriate arena for carrying out Labour's policies. Thus, in the early rejection by Attlee's government of the European Coal and Steel Community, it was considerations of sovereignty that were paramount. A socialist might well object to the bias towards market forces in the later Treaty of Rome, but this was not the case for the Treaty of Paris, which is a highly centralised and interventionist document.[5]

This concern for sovereignty has led the past Labour Governments to work against social and economic objectives at the Community level which would be widely regarded as similar to its own policies. For instance, in 1974 Michael Foot, Employment Minister at the time, made it plain to the Commission that the UK Government would use its veto in the Council of Ministers unless the proposal for a Directive protecting workers' rights in cases of mass redundancies was deferred. Foot did not want the Labour Government to be seen to be introducing such reforms at the behest of the Community. It was only after similar rights were established in the UK by the Employment Protection Act that the Labour Government supported the adoption of the Commission's proposals. Also somewhat surprisingly, the Labour administration proved a willing and able ally for British employers in their lobbying to have the initial proposals for a Directive on the protection of workers' rights in merger and take-over situations narrowed in scope and watered down. In fact, it was largely due to pressure from Labour ministers that the employers were successful in obtaining the changes they wanted. Lastly, while not opposing the intiatives, the Labour Party was distinctly lukewarm about the draft Fifth and Vredeling Directives, although in this case the desire to reject EC authority was combined with a traditional faith in free collective bargaining.[6] The Labour Party has clearly found it hard to come to terms with EC membership.

Although Labour's national leadership have since 1983 clearly dropped the policy of withdrawal, they have not replaced it with a coherent strategy regarding the EC.[7] Occasional statements have been made to the effect that a Labour Government would give its support to the Commission's social proposals which are still on the drafting table. Before the last election the then Shadow Employment Secretary of State, John Prescott, suggested that a Labour Government would implement the provisions of the draft Vredeling Directive within a month of coming to power.

From a purely British perspective it is now to some extent irrelevant whether or not a future Labour Government would support EC social policies. This is primarily because the Labour Party now supports the use of law in industrial relations and its specific proposals are more far-reaching than anything proposed by the Commission. In the TUC-Labour Party Liaison Committee document 'People at Work: New Rights, New Responsibilities' it was stated that the next Labour Government would introduce legislation covering job security and training for new skills, improving protection against unfair dismissal, protecting part-time and temporary workers, developing equal opportunities, attacking low pay and defining fair wages, promoting health and safety in the workplace, strengthening union organisation and collective bargaining, extending workers' influence and responsibility: the conduct of disputes, membership participation in unions.[8] The result of a future Labour Government introducing such legislation would lead to much of the controversy about EC legislation fading into the background as employers tried to cope with the new national law.

The maximalist centre:

The Social Democratic Party and the Liberal Party have undergone much turbulence and change recently, and there is as yet little clarity about the details of the resultant parties' policies and proposals. On Europe at least, the similarities between the SDP and the Liberals by far outweighed their differences. We can refer to them and their manifestations as the centrist bloc. One key facet of this centrist bloc is its interpretation of Britain's relative industrial decline. In particular it regards the obsolescence of Britain's industrial structure as reflecting the archaic nature of the British constitution and government apparatus. From this point of view, the modernisation of British society has been blocked by the failure of a state system, which dates back to the seventeenth century, to put coherent and thorough-going reforms into effect. Thus the centrepiece of its political programme is a comprehensive package for institutional and constitutional reform: the introduction of a system of proportional representation; decentralisation of government; the enactment for the first time of a Bill of Rights.

For the centre, a maximalist, virtually federalist, approach to European integration is of a piece with this general impatience for institutional change: an almost uncritical support for the Community and its policies. The centrist bloc would be quite prepared to see an increase in the authority of EC institutions and a greater presence of the Community in British society. This would unquestionably involve the implementation of many Commission social policy proposals still at the drafting stage. In fact, because the social and economic content of the centre's programme was not well defined, the Alliance parties based many of their proposals before the last election on draft EC directives. For example, the SDP/Liberal Alliance manifesto argued for legislation to oblige directors in all companies to have regard to the interests of employees as well as of their share holders. Moreover, it argued that every organisation with more than 1000 employees should introduce comprehensive arrangements for participation agreements. This new legislation would provide for the establishment of employee councils at each work-place and these would be entitled to full information and the right to be consulted by the company board on strategic decisions. These provisions are clearly drawn from those laid down in the draft Fifth Directive.

In addition, a Government of the centre would introduce a 'new comprehensive framework of positive rights and responsibilities'.[9] This would include better health and safety protection and increased rights to improve the conditions of employment of part-time and other vulnerable workers. The specific proposals in these areas bear a close resemblance to the Commission's proposals on the issues. Presumably, as both the Liberals and the SDP criticised the Conservative Government for not agreeing to the draft Vredeling Directive, which they described as a 'relatively mild proposal', a centrist Government would introduce relevant enabling legislation on this proposal. The centrist parties would prefer British policy-making, including employment and labour relations policy-making, to develop a strong European dimension.

The Pressure Groups

At the level of formal organisation, there has been quite an extraordinary proliferation of pressure groups operating at the European level. Since the formation of the Community in 1958, over 500 pressure groups have been formed with the objective of influencing EC policy.[10] It should be added, however, that about 300 of these groups relate to the operation of the Common Agricultural Policy. In the area of employment and labour affairs, the key interest groups are obviously the

European employers' organisations and the trade unions. The following sections describe the nature of the organisations which represent labour and management at the European level.

The European Employers' Organisations

The principal employers' organisation within the Community is the Union of Industries of the European Community (UNICE). UNICE, which is the European equivalent of the CBI, was formed in 1957 when the Common Market was formed, and its main task is to lobby and attempt to influence the decisions of the main Community institutions. In addition, it provides members at the national level with information on Community developments, carries out studies, adopts positions and promotes them.

Alongside UNICE there are a number of other employers' organisations which cover specific sectors of the economy. A division of labour exists between UNICE and these other employers' organisations: UNICE does not comment or make policy on sectoral questions, and the industrial employers' groups tend to stay clear of issues which are of general concern for employers.

Because UNICE is the main employers' organisation it may be valuable to describe its structure in detail.

The Council of Presidents

The Council of Presidents has full powers, and is the supreme decision-making body. Each member organisation is represented in the Council of Presidents and it meets at least twice a year. In adopting a position or deciding on its own affairs, the Association shall normally seek a consensus amongst its members. Voting takes place, if at all, only after reasonable attempts to reach common agreement have failed. The Association does not adopt a position if this is contrary to the vital interests of one of its members.

The Council appoints the permanent Secretary General.

Executive Committee

The Executive Committee is made up of the Director General of each member organisation, or a designated representative. It meets at least twice a year. The Committee supervises and directs the implementation of policy, approves the work programmes to be pursued by policy committees, and oversees administrative and staffing matters.

Committee of Permanent Delegates

The Committee of Permanent Delegates consists of representatives appointed by the members and acts as a permanent link between the member Federations and the Secretary General. Its main object is to help the Executive Committee carry out its administrative functions and policy activities.

Policy Committees
The policy committees are composed of persons nominated by the members and representing them. The function of the Policy Committees is to monitor developments in their respective fields, help devise the Association's policies in their area, suggest action to be taken and implement the strategies adopted.

In comparison with the ETUC and European trade unionism, relatively little has been written about European employers and how they represent their interests inside the Community. One reason for this lack of attention is that many analysts assume that the interests of business are more or less homogenous and, therefore, it is not worth examining their representative organisations.[11] This view is inaccurate, for disputes regularly occur within UNICE. For instance, differences of opinion emerge between the employers' organisations from southern and northern European member states over the direction of Community economic and social policies, similar to those which surface inside the Council of Ministers. Another reason is that UNICE is quite successful at 'internalising' divisions and controversy. Seldom do employers' representatives air their differences in public, something the trade unions are wont to do. Finally, the fact that UNICE seldom initiates policy but rather responds to Commission or trade union proposals contributes to its low-key image.

In saying that, it should be recognised that UNICE has a coherent set of policies relating to the Community. These are known as 'UNICE's Agenda for Europe' and consist of six priority areas. The first is the creation of the European internal market. UNICE is concerned that companies are ill-informed about the Community's project in this area and, therefore, do not press their governments to make it happen. Thus, it wants to see a major publicity and lobbying drive to ensure that '1992' is a success. The second agenda item is the creation of a more favourable climate for enterprise, involving adaptability of labour markets, reduction of state intervention, lower interest rates, creation of modern economic structures. Thirdly, there is the matter of the promotion of European technology, research and development. The fourth item is the policy of economic and social cohesion. Under this heading, UNICE calls for greater convergence of national economic policies, such as further financial and monetary integration and the reform of the structural funds. Moreover, UNICE wants the Community to play a strong role inside GATT and on the international scene more generally to promote trade liberalisation and to oppose the growing tide of protectionism. The last area relates to the Community's social dimension. Here UNICE is adamant that it opposes the Commission's social proposals of the late seventies and early eighties, but at the same time it states its commitment to the Val Duchesse talks. In relation to the idea of *'le dumping social'* which is at the core of the proposal for a European *l'espace sociale,* UNICE finds it devoid of meaning and, as a result, rejects proposals for the harmonisation or equivalence of social conditions inside the EC. The only area where it regards harmonisation as desirable is the field of occupational health and safety. Thus it concludes 'let the accent be on dialogue and adaptability. Centralisation, harmonisation and European legislation in the social field would create new rigidities and further reduce our ability to compete and to pay for the society we want'.[12]

The ETUC

The trade union equivalent of UNICE is the European Trade Union Congress (ETUC). This organisation was formed in 1973, bringing together a number of different trade union bodies which had been operating at the Community level. Before 1973, trade union organisation within the Community was highly fragmented, being split on religious and ideological grounds. The main European trade union organisation before 1973 was the European Office of the International Confederation of Free Trade Unions, (ICFTU-EO), the regional body of the ICFTU. This body consisted of all social democratic and socialist trade unions in Europe: its main members being the German DGB, the French CFDT and the British TUC. There also existed the European Office of the World Confederation of Labour (EOWCL) which was made up from Europe's Christian Democratic trade unions, most notably the French CGT-FO and the Italian CISL. In addition, there was the EFTA-TUC consisting of the national trade unions from the Nordic countries and the British TUC. This organisation was set up at the instigation of the British TUC, to challenge the EC concentration of ICFTU-EO. Finally, there were the West European communist trade unions, mainly the French CGT, the Italian CGIL and the Spanish Workers' Commissions, who were outside, or who were excluded from, the above organisations.

Three influences encouraged the integration of these different European trade union organisations within the European Trade Union Confederation. One was the growth of regionalism; another was the lessening of ideological perspectives and a general increase in attitudes of detente; and finally there was an increasing awareness that for the trade unions effectively to face the new international commercial environment shaped by the actions of multinational companies they needed to be unified.[13] In the preamble of the ETUC Constitution the founding members laid down the ETUC's major aims as follows:

- 'to represent and promote the social, economic and cultural interests of workers at the European level in general and in particular in respect of all European institutions, including the European Communities and the European Free Trade Association.
- to safeguard and strengthen democracy in Europe.'

The following national trade union confederations are affiliated to the ETUC:

Trade Union Confederations	*Country*
Fédération Générale du Travail de Belgique (FGTB)	Belgium
Confédération des Syndicats Chrétiens (CSC)	Belgium
Cyprus Workers' Confederation (SEK)	Cyprus
Cyprus Turkish Trade Union Federation (TURK-SEN)	Cyprus
Landsorganisationen i Danmark (LO)	Denmark
Fällesrädet for Danske Tjenestemänds-og Funktionärorganisationer (FTF)	Denmark
Deutscher Gewerkschaftsbund (DGB)	Federal Republic of of Germany
Union General de Trabajadores de España (UGT)	Spain
Solidaridad de Trabajadores Vascos (STV-ELA)	Spain
Confédération Générale du Travail-Force Ouvrière (CGT-FO)	France
Confédération Française Démocratique du Travail (CFDT)	France
Trades Union Congress (TUC)	Great Britain
Greek General Confederation of Labour (CSEE)	Greece
Irish Congress of Trade Unions (ICTU)	Ireland
Althydusamband Islands (ASI)	Iceland
Bandalag Starfsmanna Rikis og Baeja (BSRB)	Iceland

Confederazione Italiana Sindacati Laboratori (CISL)	Italy
Confederazione Generale Italiana del Lavoro (CGIL)	Italy
Unione Italiana del Lavoro (UIL)	Italy
Confédération Générale du Travail de Luxembourg (CGT-Lux)	Luxembourg
Letzbuerger Chrësteche Gewerkschafts-bond (LCBG)	Luxembourg
General Workers Union (GWU)	Malta
Confederation of Maltesian Trade Unions (CMTU)	Malta
Federatie Nederlandse Vakbewegining (FNC)	Netherlands
Christelijk National Vakverbond (CNV)	Netherlands
Landsorganisasjonen i Norge (LO)	Norway
Österreichischer Gewerkschaftsbund (ÖGB)	Austria
Schweizerischer Gewerkschaftsbund (SGB)	Switzerland
Christlichnationaler Gewerkschaftsbund (CNG), including Schweizerischer Verband Evangelischer Arbeitnehmer (SVEA)	Switzerland
Toimihenkilö-ja Virkamiesjärinestöjen Keskusliitto (TVK)	Finland
Suomen Ammattiliitto jen Keskusjärejstö (SAK)	Finland
Lansorganisationen i Sverige (LO)	Sweden
Tjästemännens Centralorganisation (TCO)	Sweden
Uniao Geral de Trabalhadores (UFT)	Portugal

The structure of the ETUC is shown in Figure VIi.

Congress

The Congress is the supreme body of the ETUC, making policy and electing the officials of the secretariat. It meets at least once every three years and is composed of representatives of the national trade union centres and European trade union industry committees.

Executive Committee

The Executive Committee has 39 members (and 39 substituting members) representing each affiliated national centre (each centre is entitled

Figure VIi The structure of the ETUC

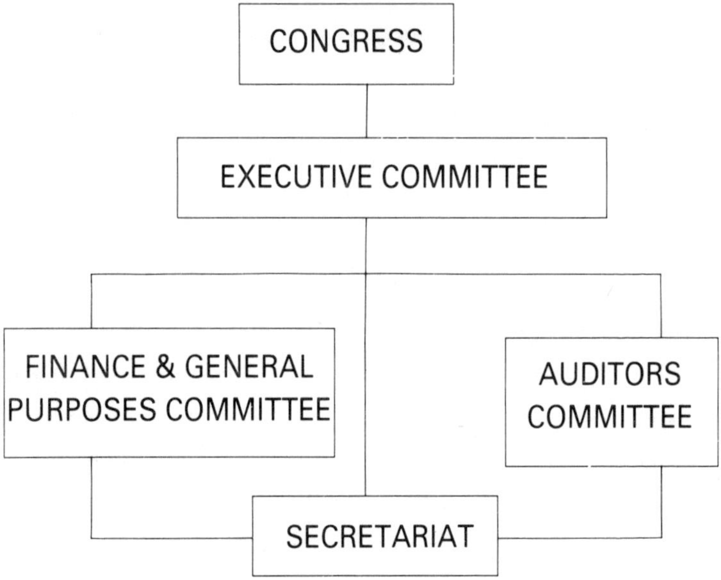

to one representative with the exception of the TUC and DGB who have 3 each). The Committee meets at least six times a year and decides on the measures to be taken to implement Congress resolutions and action programmes and appoints ETUC representatives to Community institutions.

The Secretariat

The secretariat, which has 29 staff, carries out tasks entrusted to it by Congress and the Executive Committee.

Standing Committees and working parties examine and monitor in detail developments within their specific field of competence: they do much of the preliminary work for the formation of ETUC policies.

The following standing committees and working parties are operating at the present time:

- Women's Committee
- Youth Group
- Committee on Migrant Workers
- Committee on the Democratisation of the Economy and of Institutions
- Energy Coordination Committee
- Economic Committee

- Working Party on Working Conditions
- Working Party on Inter-Regional Trade Union Councils
- Working Party on Consumers
- Working Party on Industrial Research and Development
- Working Party on Regional Policy
- Working Party on the Environment and Living Standards
- Working Party on Safety and Health at Work
- Working Party on Agriculture

When ETUC was formed, it was anticipated that it would considerably strengthen trade union action in Europe. Not being affiliated to any of the international trade union federations, it was hoped that it would avoid the political infighting which impedes the work of those organisations. Further, it was seen as being able to give impetus to international collective bargaining within transnational companies.[14] Finally, it was hoped that ETUC would make the trade union voice inside Community institutions more effective. It is questionable, however, whether ETUC has really fulfilled these high expectations.

Several internal organisational factors have impeded ETUC from developing into an efficient and cohesive body. The problem in the mid seventies surrounding the affiliation of European trade union industry committees serves as an example. European trade union industry committees are the regional equivalents of the International Trade Secretariats (ITS): they attempt to organise different national trade unions on an industry basis at the European level. As part of its attempt to reorganise and integrate European trade unionism, ETUC wanted European industry committees to affiliate. In order to qualify for affiliation, industry committees had to become more or less autonomous from their respective ITS and do away with any exclusion clauses which may bar Christian Democratic or Communist trade unions which already belong to ETUC. For some industry committees, these conditions were unacceptable. For instance, the European Textile Workers' Committee refused to accept the affiliation of the Italian CGIL member organisation, as it was Communist in orientation, and the Chemical Workers' International refused to yield any significant degree of autonomy to its European regional organisation. The problem of the affiliation clauses sparked off a major row inside ETUC during 1976/1977. The issue was only resolved when the British TUC persuaded ETUC Secretariat and some national trade union centres that a flexible approach should be taken to the question of affiliation.

Considerable difficulties have also been experienced in the formulation of policy. For example, at the First Tripartite Conference held in 1975 to discuss the economic crisis and possible solutions, major differences of opinion emerged between ETUC representatives. The

Chairman of the German trade unions, who was also President of ETUC, stated that he could not wholeheartedly endorse the concept of investment controls included in the ETUC statement which had previously been rejected by the DGB as unrealistic. And although the ETUC statement refused to endorse protectionism regarding inter-Community trade, the President of the British TUC came out in favour of import controls. These internal divisions, especially aired in front of Commission and employer representatives, did nothing to enhance the image of ETUC.[15]

Since its formation, ETUC has been preoccupied with the behaviour of the multinationals. One of its key objectives in this area has been to support the efforts of its industry committees to persuade multinationals to agree to consultation and collective bargaining at the European level. Developments in this area have been disappointing. Only two agreements have been concluded between European multinationals (Thomson Grand Public and BSN) and European trade union industrial committees. The protocol agreement between Thomson Grand Public and the European Metalworkers Federation is reproduced as appendix 5. As can be seen, a liaison committee was established by the agreement comprised of worker representatives from Thomson subsidiaries in Europe, which is informed of the economic, industrial and trading aspects of the company. In essence, it formalises the exchange of information. Other than these developments, European trade union organisations have met with little success in promoting international forms of collective bargaining.

Overall, ETUC has not fulfilled early expectations. But with the total reversal in the economic climate and the subsequent decline of trade unions within many of the member states,[16] this conclusion should not be surprising. Indeed, it is perhaps a little unfair to assess the organisational development of ETUC against objectives set in the early seventies.

In terms of policy, ETUC broadly supports the Community's drive to complete the internal market by 1992. But it argues that a European social dimension should accompany this programme to abolish remaining non-tariff barriers inside the Community. Without a European social dimension, ETUC argues that the completion of the internal market may lead to accelerated industrial concentration, geographical redeployment of economic and industrial forces and a rationalisation of employment structures, particularly in the poorer member states. For ETUC, a European social programme would include:

(i) the use of the social dialogue at the European level to pave the way for genuine collective bargaining and to undertake the groundwork for Community social legislation that ensures economic and social cohesion;

(ii) the boosting of public and private investments to create employment as well as the establishment of new instruments for the construction of forward employment planning at all levels within the Community;

(iii) the approximation of vocational and educational qualifications amongst Community countries;

(iv) European legislation laying down maximums for daily and weekly working time, and restricting overtime, and the implementation of the proposals relating to the reorganisation and reduction of working time still on the drafting table;

(v) the implementation of comprehensive health and safety measures relating to all aspects of working conditions, and as regards production and plant utilisation and maintenance;

(vi) measures to promote industrial democracy, including the adoption of a European dimension to company law, and Directives on employees rights to ensure that 'every single employee' in the Community is covered by a collective agreement, and to ensure that in the event of bankruptcy the employees are recognised as priority creditors.

This is a comprehensive and indepth range of policies. Even if there was a more favourable economic and political environment, it is doubtful whether ETUC demands would be met in full. But, in the present neo-liberal environment, it is unlikely that the Council will concede many of ETUC's proposals.

Employers and Trade Unions at the European Level: A Case Study of the Vredeling Directive

As can be seen from Figure VIii, the UNICE and ETUC have broadly similar institutional connections within the Community's decision-making system. Within the Community's decision-making structure, the employers by and large have been more successful than the trade unions in defending the interests of their members. An examination of the respective responses to the draft Vredeling Directive bears out this conclusion. The employers were extremely hostile to the proposals. UNICE's objections were based on four main points: 1) the Commission had not proved the need for an EC regulation in this field, and as most multinationals keep to the OECD guidelines no further action was

Figure VIii UNICE and ETUC: institutional links with the Community

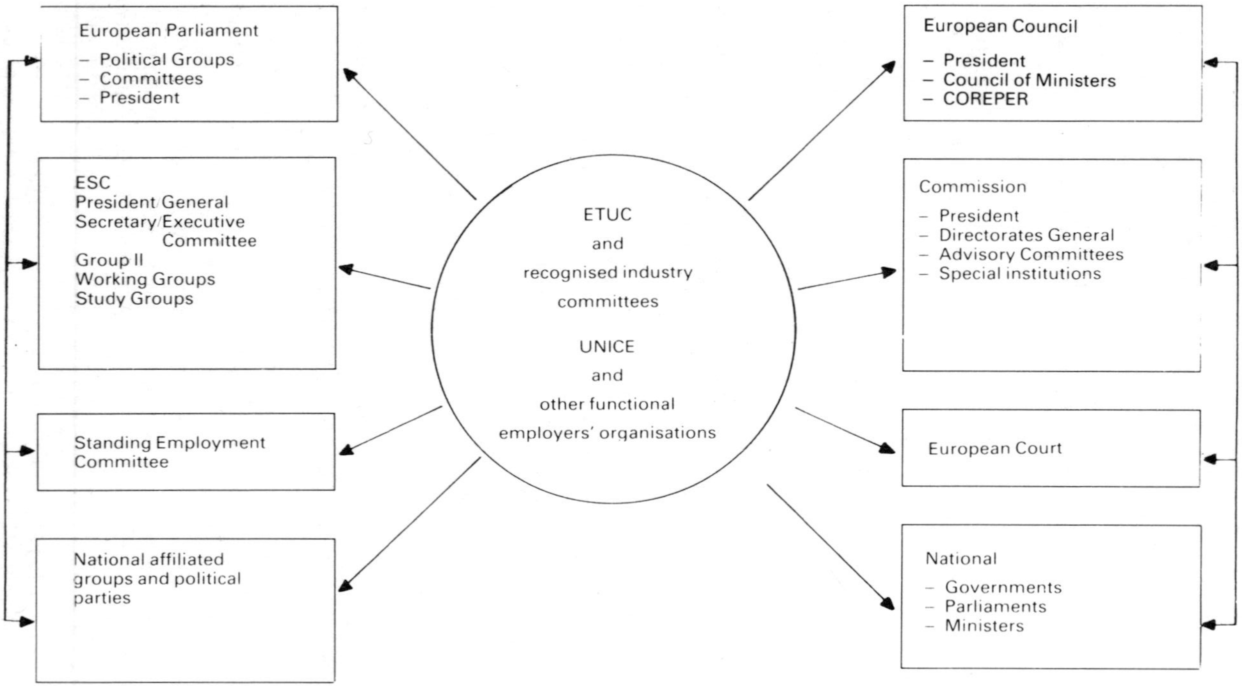

Source: Baranovin 1986

called for; 2) the Treaty of Rome did not provide the legal basis for the Directive; 3) EC enterprises could be jeopardised in competing with firms in non-member states if a stricter law in this field was required in the Community and not in other countries throughout the world. Legal constraints and the absence of an effective guaranteed protection of business secrecy could lead to this problem; 4) as the Directive was an attempt to convert OECD and ILO recommendations into EC law, it would interfere with existing international instruments and could frustrate the policies pursued by the governments of member states.

ETUC was equally emphatic in its support for the proposal. It produced a 50-page document which set down its policy towards multination companies and worker information and consultation. ETUC regarded it as a basic right for employees to be kept informed and consulted about a company's commercial plans which may affect their livelihood. The introduction of Community legislation on the subject was regarded as particularly pressing, given the scale of the rationalisation and restructuring programmes being undertaken by multinational corporations in Europe.

To win support for its views, UNICE launched a major action programme, involving the recruitment of public relations and lobbying experts. Alongside UNICE's campaign, industrial relations executives and lawyers working for multinationals in the US banded together to form a committee of business people from the four largest American trade organisations – the National Association of Manufacturers, US Council for International Business, US Chamber of Commerce, and the National Foreign Trade Council, with the major objective of lobbying against the proposed Directive. This committee organised several delegations to Brussels to express its opposition to Community officials. In another independent move, Congressman Thomas Luken (Ohio) introduced draft blocking legislation in the House of Representatives designed to 'minimise the unfavourable effects of the Vredeling requirement to disclose all manner of confidential information to workers' representatives in Europe'.[17] Furthermore, the Japanese employers' organisation, Keidansen, warned Ivor Richards, the Social Affairs Commissioner in the early 1980s, that Japanese companies might reduce their investment in Europe if the Vredeling proposal was adopted.[18] Plainly, multinational companies, no matter what the country of origin, felt threatened by the Vredeling initiative.

Inside the Community, UNICE urged its members to take effective action against the proposal. The German employers' federation declared that it 'categorically' rejected the concept of the draft. In Britain, like other member countries, especially Italy and Denmark, the CBI encouraged its members to introduce or strengthen existing consultation procedures in order to reduce even further the need for such a Directive. To give weight to this campaign, the CBI conducted a survey amongst its top 836 members. The results, which the CBI conceded were not representative, showed that British companies had increased their consultation efforts with their workforces: about two thirds of the respondents had a company paper or employee report while a small minority had a formal employee involvement structure such as a works council. However, the central conclusion was that 'the survey underlines once again the complexity and variety of business organisations into which patterns of involvement must fit. There can be no one successful model of involvement'.[19] The CBI used this report in their campaign against Vredeling, which involved extensive lobbying of MEPs, Members of Parliament, Government officials and so on. Opposing the Directive was established as a clear priority for the CBI.

For its part, the ETUC also launched a major publicity and lobbying campaign; but in support of the draft Directive. An information pamphlet was produced which it hoped would be distributed on shopfloors across Europe. The basic strategy was to create what the ETUC called a 'general awareness' of the clauses of the Directive and to win solid support at worker level. This ground-level awareness, the ETUC hoped, would bring potentially sympathetic MEPs into line behind the draft. ETUC also relied on sympathetic Commissioners and Commission officials to lend support to the draft. But ETUC could not depend on support from sister organisations outside the Community to the same extent as UNICE: the statement from the Japanese employers' federation warning of an investment strike could not be matched by Japanese trade unions. Nor could ETUC muster the same resources as UNICE and other employers' organisations to support its lobbying activities. A *Sunday Times* correspondent captured this point succinctly when covering the European Parliament debate on Vredeling: he said 'On Tuesday taxis swept up to the Parliament building bearing the most formidable galaxy of professional lobbyists Strasbourg has seen . . . the union lobby consisted of a couple of pleasant individuals from the European TUC handing out leaflets'.

To supplement its activity at the European level, ETUC called on its affiliates to launch separate campaigns on the issue within their respective member states. But within Britain at least, this part of its campaign was not as effective as the one conducted by UNICE. The TUC simply did not undertake as much activity on the issue as the CBI. In fact the TUC action on the Vredeling Directive amounted to an information circular to individual British trade unions, the drafting of a submission to the British Government on the issue, and the release of a few supporting press statements. This stands in sharp contrast to the CBI's highly visible and sustained campaign. It was not that the TUC was disinterested in the subject, but that in the light of major redundancy programmes being implemented at the time and the introduction of national legislation aimed at reducing trade union immunities, it was a low priority.[20]

This assessment, that the employers were more effective at lobbying against the Vredeling Directive than the trade unions were in supporting the initiative, is actually held by some leading trade unionists. In his address to a conference on multinational companies, Mr Herman Rebhan, General Secretary of the International Metalworkers Federation, said, 'We have to be honest and say that the multinational companies beat us to the mark in the battle of the Vredeling Directive . . . Suddenly, their (MEPs') opinions were of great value as the gentleman of the multinationals told them how wise and virtuous they were and how on their slender shoulders rested the responsibility of keeping transfrontier operations of world companies free of any obligation to their workers.'[21] The lesson he concludes from the episode is that the trade unions must learn to become more effective 'manipulators' of the European bureaucracy.

British Interest Groups and the EC

CBI and EC

At the time of Britain's accession to the European Community, it was widely anticipated that membership would have a direct impact on the structure and behaviour of British business groups. The Devlin Commission went so far as to suggest that entry into the EC would lead to the rationalisation and integration of the existing fragmented structure of business organisations in Britain and the creation of a new central organisation: a Confederation of British Business. This view was largely based on the following reasoning: i) decisions in Brussels would greatly affect British commercial and industrial interests, thus forcing the relevant interest groups to become stronger and more efficient; ii) as most European interest groups which represented industrial and commercial interests restricted their membership to one or two organisations per member state, British business would need to streamline; iii) the creation of the EC led to the strengthening of interest groups in the original six member states and as a result this would require British groups to increase their resources and representation to a comparable level if they were going to be equally efficient.[22]

The far-reaching restructuring envisaged by Devlin did not occur: as one commentator noted in 1981 'British employers are remarkable by comparison with other Europeans for their lack of solidarity'.[23] The failure to undertake any restructuring should not be taken as any deficiency on the part of British business, however. The fault, if any exists, lies with the Devlin Commission for exaggerating the impact of EC entry on British interest groups. An examination of the existing literature would have shown that the EC had no fundamental impact on the behaviour or structure of business interest groups in the original six member states. The Devlin Commission's assessment is interesting as a demonstration of the lack of understanding and the naïve views which existed at the time of British entry into the EC.

It would have been more realistic for the Devlin Commission to have assumed that the response of the CBI and other interest groups to EC initiatives would be largely influenced by the way they lobby and campaign at the national level. In other words, any analysis of the CBI response to British membership needs to be prefaced with some remarks about the nature of business interest group representation in Britain. In 1976, some commentators reached the conclusion 'that the CBI had relatively little impact on the major issues which have dominated British politics since its formation . . . it has not been able to extract detailed concessions which are of benefit to its members'.[24] Ten years later the book 'Business and Politics in Britain' put forward the argument that 'Britain has a business sector in which there is an increasing concentration of economic power, but that business remains politically weak.'[25] The main explanation given for this weakness was that business leaders do not in general think strategically in political terms, and thus attach little importance to the activities of the CBI and other employers' groups. But this thesis was qualified by the addition that 'The business community in Britain is capable of acting politically in a cohesive fashion if the perceived level of threat is sufficiently high, as was the case with the Bullock Report on industry democracy in the late 1970s.'[26] Thus, at least in the national context, the overriding conclusion of the academic literature is that for the most part British business does not organise itself effectively to influence public policies. It is interesting to test this thesis in relation to the European Community.

Although it has been a long-standing advocate of British membership of the EC, the CBI's first decisive action in relation to Europe came in 1965 when it established an internal committee on the Common Market. This committee was charged with monitoring all EC affairs and promoting the case for British entry amongst its members, politicians and the wider public. At the turn of the 1970s, British membership of the Community looked imminent. As a result, the CBI decided to set up its own office in Brussels to operate as a listening post, maintain contact with the UK permanent delegation and Community officials and to shadow the work of the various Community institutions. From these activities, the office would feed back information to CBI headquarters in London and thus ensure that CBI representatives were well informed of developments in Brussels.[27]

As well as its Brussels office, the CBI has a European Community Unit within its International Affairs Department. This unit undertakes the administration and organisation related to European affairs, ensures that the relevant specialized department considers all proposals which may emanate from Brussels, maintains a network of specialists and contacts such as MEPs and government officials on European Community affairs, organises and co-ordinates campaigns and initiatives and participates in UNICE meetings.

Unlike the TUC, the CBI has not experienced any significant differences of opinion on European issues. As a result, its overall policy towards the EC has remained more or less unchanged over the years. There are two key themes to the CBI policy on Europe. One is the notion of liberalisation. The CBI is fully in favour of the completion of the internal market, strict limits on the scale of protectionist measures operated by the Community against non-member countries, the simplification of custom formalities, the approximation of technical standards, and the ending of nationalistic public procurement policies and state subsidies. If fully implemented, the CBI feels these policies would 'create an economic and social environment in the Community which encourages profitability and investment and helps the adaptability of trade and industry, creating in turn a solidly based expansion of employment opportunities.'[28]

The other theme is that of harmonisation. The CBI's general view is that harmonisation in any policy area can only be justified if it contributes towards removing obstacles to inter-Community trade and investment: there should be no harmonisation for its own sake. In relation to the Commission proposals so far on harmonisation, the CBI is 'constructively critical'. It regards the legislative output of the Commission in this area as excessive and thinks that some of the specific proposals are inappropriate. As an alternative to the present approach of the Commission, the CBI suggests that there should be greater selectivity in choosing what needs and what does not need harmonising; that the direct economic benefits of future harmonisation measures be demonstrated by conducting a cost benefit analysis of its likely effects; that a guillotine procedure be introduced to decrease the number of Commission proposals that get 'stuck' at the Council of Ministers level at any one time.

In addition to these two key themes, the CBI supports a miscellaneous range of policies. For example, it supports the principle of a European regional policy to reduce the disparity between the regions of the Community. It also favours Community research and development programmes so long as their proposals and objectives are worked out in close collaboration with industry. The EC Environmental Action Programme has also been welcomed by the CBI. Thus there is a range of Community interventions which are endorsed, but these are very much secondary to central policy goals of open markets and liberalisation.

Unquestionably, the *bête noire* of EC affairs for the CBI has been the attempts by the Commission to establish a European social dimension through the use of the Community's legal machinery. While the CBI supported in broad terms the Social Action Programme adopted by the Council of Ministers in 1974, it has opposed, or been lukewarm to, the vast majority of the subsequent specific initiatives. It has been particularly opposed to the draft Fifth and Vredeling Directives and the various initiatives on working time. The only area where the CBI has accepted that it is legitimate for the Community to legislate is in health and safety at work, provided that the legal proposals are based on recognised medical and scientific evidence. For the most part, however, the CBI has consistently accused the Commission of conducting an exercise in 'social engineering' – defined as 'attempts to achieve certain objectives, mainly in the socio-employment field, by imposing on companies conditions governing a wide range of aspects of their relations with employees'.[29] Whether or not the notion of 'social engineering' accurately reflects the nature and scope of Commission proposals, it has certainly been a highly successful campaign slogan, used now by almost everybody who opposes Commission-inspired labour-market proposals.

As seen earlier in this chapter, the CBI has been active at every level in opposing the so-called social engineering proposals. No quarter, of any sort, has been given. As a result of this uncompromising stance, the CBI has earned the reputation of being the fiercest opponent of the 'legislative' approach to EC social policy amongst European employers. This reputation is probably correct, for although the threat of many of the social engineering proposals being adopted as EC law has receded, the CBI continues to monitor developments in the social field at the European level with considerable suspicion. For example, when the Commission produced its Health and Safety Programme, outlining a series of actions and policy objectives to be decided under the new system of qualified majority voting, the CBI was quick to state its reservations. In particular, it questioned whether the Commission had the resources and capacity to meet the targets that it had set itself and, in what was obviously a warning shot across the Commission's bow, it stated that any attempts to formalise participation in the health and safety area would be met with strong resistance by British employers. Thus, if the present trend continues, there will be no let up in the CBI's opposition to any Community regulatory legislation in the social field.

Because the CBI's continual and active lobbying against the Commission's social proposals has been the most visible aspect of its relationship to Europe, it has been accused of being excessively negative in its approach. The CBI has been sensitive to this criticism and as a result in recent years has tried to promote an alternative direction for EC social policy. Two key proposals encapsulate this alternative, which is similar to the British Government's Action Programme for Employment Growth. One is that Community social policy should be tied to the economic objective of restoring competitiveness to European industry. Thus social policies should have no more than a neutral impact on businesses. The other is that social measures should focus on improving the flexibility and adaptability of labour markets.[30] When the UK Government Action Programme was adopted by the Council of Ministers, the CBI issued a statement fully supporting the initiative. It should also be mentioned that in other spheres of EC social policy, the operation of the Social Fund, measures to promote the free movement of labour, encouraging 'concertation' between member states' training programmes and employment policies, the CBI has fully supported Commission proposals. But these policy areas have been overshadowed by the controversy surrounding the Commission's regulatory proposals. Thus, the overall conclusion must be that while supporting some features of EC social policy, the CBI has been, and continues to be, firmly opposed to what most regard as the central aspect of Community social policy, namely the attempts by the Commission to establish a body of EC law on employment and labour-market issues. Moreover, amongst European employers, the CBI has been the most vocal and uncompromising opponent of such proposals, indeed the backbone of UNICE's campaigns against them.

The introduction to this section noted that the CBI only operates cohesively, and effectively influences public policy, when an issue is at stake which is seen as seriously threatening the interests of its members. Clearly the Commission's social proposals were seen in such a light. Given that employers' organisations in other member states did not adopt such an uncompromising stance against the proposals, it is necessary to try and explain why the CBI opposition was so strong and vociferous. One reason appears to be that the CBI is distinctly uncomfortable with the notion that an extra-national institution should be able to legislate about employment and labour issues in Britain. The entire 'social engineering' campaign against the EC proposals was not simply based on objections to specific clauses, or administrative and practical points: rather it rested on the assumption that the nature and pattern of a member state's industrial relations system should be determined by that nation alone. No doubt the historic and cultural detachment of Britain from the rest of Europe fuelled this attitude. But, at the same time, it is a mistake to view British business as xenophobic. As noted in Chapter 1, British managers have long been prepared to incorporate new ideas and approaches which may have originated overseas. But by and large, these influences were of the horizontal kind. The evidence here suggests that British business is hostile to vertical forms of international influences, particularly if they are legal in character.

Another reason for the CBI's opposition is that it regarded Commission proposals as being fundamentally at odds with the voluntarist tradition of Britain's industrial relations. Certainly, despite creeping legislative incursions, British industrial relations continue to be best described as 'voluntary'. For instance, pay and conditions are still primarily determined by collective bargaining outside of the legal framework. But as an explanation for the scale of the opposition to proposals, this reason has its limits. When the voluntarist system was challenged root and branch by the last Labour Government's incomes policy, the CBI response was muted. Instead of directly opposing this statutory regulation of pay, a significant number of British companies tried to devise informal ways to limit its impact. Thus, although the asymmetry between the British voluntarist industrial relations system and the legal orientation of EC proposals is a plausible and legitimate argument for the CBI to use, it cannot be regarded as the main reason why its opposition was so steadfast. Conversely, however, it appears feasible to suggest that the similarities between the Commission's legislative proposals and the highly legalistic basis of Continental industrial relations systems accounts for European employers being not overly concerned by the proposals.

The CBI's trenchant opposition to Commission proposals is more substantially based on the fact that it regarded them as heavily biased towards policies approved by trade unions rather than those advocated by business. The proposals that the Commission produced on working-time broadly approximated to those put forward by ETUC. Having seen the legal immunities of trade unions limited, and other shop-floor powers reduced, the CBI was loath to see British trade unions obtaining a fillip from the EC. It was the desire to entrench and sustain the new-found managerial confidence in Britain that motivated the CBI's approach to Europe. Furthermore, as the trade unions were not the force they were in the seventies, the CBI was given the political space to devote resources and time to sustain its active campaign against the Commission's social proposals.

Another, although more speculative, reason for the CBI's opposition to the Commission's social proposals lies in its distinctiveness amongst European employers' organisations. In particular, while most European employers' organisations have, albeit to varying degrees, some formal role in industrial relations and public policy at the national level, the CBI has virtually no functions in this area. The central conclusion of a recent major cross-national research programme on the work of business organisations was that those organisations which had some type of national responsibilities are those which are most likely to seek accommodation in conflict situations.[31] Thus, it just may be the case that as the CBI has little involvement in national economic and political policy, this fuelled its uncompromising stance towards the EC.

Trade associations and the EC

In its campaign against specific Commission social proposals, the CBI has received important support from trade federations. This has involved these organisations making representations at national and Community level against draft social-policy Directives, and encouraging their members to join CBI campaigns (for instance, urging their members to introduce employee consultative procedures to stave off the need for the Vredeling and Fifth Directives). Senior staff from trade associations have also played a key part in many CBI committees and working parties charged with formulating policy on EC initiatives. Thus although there are some differences amongst the federations about the extent to which they dislike (or like) EC proposals, they are clearly in broad agreement with the stance the CBI has taken against them. Alongside this support for CBI initiatives on EC matters, the trade federations have developed their own independent links with Europe. These links were established out of a desire on the part of the federations to keep abreast of EC initiatives which could have a direct effect on their members. Consequently, their work tends to be less general and less 'political' than much of the CBI activity on EC matters and more specific and technical.

For self-evident reasons, the federations place greater importance on these linkages. Seeking to safeguard their members' interests has meant their becoming actively involved at the European level. Thus for instance when the EC proposed the Banking Harmonisation Directive in the seventies, the British Bankers Association (BBA) opened up direct contacts with Commission officials and lobbied politicians and civil servants at the national level to ensure that nothing detrimental to UK financial institutions was included in the proposals.[32] Indeed as a result of its representations, the BBA was able to secure important changes to the draft Directive. The Retail Consortium is another example of a trade association becoming actively involved in EC affairs and institutions. When the *Comité des Organisations Commerciales de la CEE* (COCCEE), which had represented the interests of the European retailing sector within EC institutions, collapsed in 1978, the Retail Consortium single-handedly took on the role of representing the interests of the British retailing trade inside the Community. Accordingly, the Consortium appointed a full-time officer to work exclusively on EC matters, and retains consultants based in Brussels.

The trade associations which undertake active campaigning and lobbying on EC affairs mostly do so in relation to Commission proposals which have a bearing on the *commercial* interests of their members. Virtually no such action has occurred on Commission social policy initiatives, as these were perceived as having only an indirect effect on their members. From our interviews, we ascertained that only two associations – the BBA and The Engineering Employers Federation (EEF) – have undertaken action which could be construed as being active. In the mid seventies, when the Commission was strongly pushing the Draft Fifth Directive, the BBA toured financial sectors in other European countries which had formal participatory structures to assess how they operated so that it could competently advise its members on what course to follow if the draft directives reached the statute books.

The EEF published a statement on the 'Priorities for the European Community'. In this statement, the EEF argues that before the Commission proposes a social initiative, it should be prepared to demonstrate: (i) its provisions would at worst have a neutral impact on the competitiveness of European industry, measured against the competitive power of extra-EC industry; (ii) its provisions would impose broadly equal obligations on the employer interest and on the union/employee interest so that, for example, any significant benefits or rights given to unions/employees would have to be matched by equally valuable rights given to employers (or by obligations imposed on union/employees).[33] This latter proposal was fairly original and clearly was a thinly veiled attack on what the EEF regarded as an imbalance in favour of trade unions in the Commission's proposals. However, this idea of an 'equalisation' of obligations and responsibility has not been pushed to any significant extent.

These types of anticipatory action in relation to EC social policy were the exception rather than the rule. Thus British trade associations in general have only pursued objectives and goals which were perceived to be directly in their self-interest.

The TUC and the EC

This section examines the trade union response to membership of the EC. The analysis is confined to a consideration of the TUC stance alone, for a comprehensive appraisal would simply not be feasible, as the pattern of individual trade union responses has been very diverse.[34] But this does not limit the interest of the investigation significantly, for many of the differences and debates amongst trade unions on the subject have crystallised within the TUC. In addition, when Britain entered the EC, it was accepted that the TUC would represent the

British trade unions in European forums as it did in national bodies such as NEDC and MSC.

The trade unions within the original six EC member states have been unequivocal in their support for the Community. Indeed on occasions they have been the most vociferous advocates of the European ideal. In the early sixties they openly expressed concern that the pace of integration had slowed down. When the first major crisis erupted inside the EC in 1965 the ICFTU European Office – the European-wide trade union organisation at the time – criticised de Gaulle for causing the conflict and undermining the proposed supranational decision-making process. Even though considerable inertia has crept into the working of the EC, not least in the field of labour affairs, important Continental trade unions such as the French CFDT are still prepared to transfer a limited amount of their functions to supranational European trade union bodies.

A contrasting picture emerges when the focus is shifted to the response of British trade unions to the issue of UK membership. There has been no unity or consistency on the subject. In fact the EC issue has generated deep divisions amongst the trade unions. These divisions first emerged during the sixties when the question of Britain's membership of the Common Market was seldom off the political agenda. Three distinct blocs were formed within the trade union movement at that time which may be characterised as pro-European, anti-European, and pragmatic. Their interactions have shaped a good deal of the subsequent history of the EC debate within the TUC. The pro-EC fraction was the most cohesive and active group, but it was also the smallest, continually failing in its task of getting the TUC to come out in full support of Britain's entry into the Common Market. The anti-marketeers were not as well organised as the pro-EC lobby. This was because the anti-EC camp was made up of divergent political groups. On the one hand there was the traditional left, which opposed entry because it viewed the EC as a capitalist institution. On the one hand there was a section of moderate trade union opinion which rejected EC membership either on the ground that it would lead to a loss of national sovereignty or on the ground that it would loosen Britain's close ties with America. The assortment of views in the anti-EC lobby meant that there was little coherence in its case. Nevertheless, there was widespread support for this general position amongst trade unions. The third group, the pragmatists, neither strongly favoured nor opposed the Common Market. They viewed the argument about loss of sovereignty and the dangers of being enveloped within a federal Europe as secondary. Their central concern was with the terms and conditions on which Britain should enter the EC. This group included most of the TUC General Council.

The interplay of these blocs has largely determined TUC policy towards the EC. Thus during the sixties and until 1972, the pragmatic centre held sway, as the TUC policy was that British membership of the EC should depend on the terms negotiated: it was in essence a 'wait and see' policy. But in 1972, with the announcement of the conditions which the Heath Government had negotiated, and the subsequent defection of some moderates to the anti-EC campaign, the TUC came out in principle against EC membership and as a result refused to participate in any EC-related organisations. This policy remained until 1976, when Britain voted overwhelmingly at the referendum for continued EC membership. The sheer scale of the 'yes' vote forced the TUC to acquiesce and adopt a lukewarm approach to the Community. This reluctant acceptance lasted for about three years. Then in 1979 Congress voted for a motion which urged a future Labour Government to bring Britain out of the Community. Several attempts were made in the early 1980s to soften this position, but they all failed: British withdrawal from the Community remains official Congress policy. However, in practice, the TUC, or at least the TUC Secretariat, has, like the Labour Party, all but abandoned the idea that Britain should withdraw from the Community.

An important distinction has to be made between the actions of the TUC in relation to the EC, and those in relation to the European trade union structure. The TUC played an instrumental role in bringing together the diverse trade union organisations at the European level to form ETUC. Moreover, during the seventies it played a key role in resolving many of the organisational and administrative problems a new organisation like ETUC was bound to face. For instance, it resolved the problem which arose over the affiliation of the industry committees to ETUC. Some Commission officials, who had awaited TUC participation in EC committees after it ended its boycott with some trepidation, remarked that British trade unions had added considerable weight to the ETUC representations at the European level. Within Britain this area of activity caused no controversy. All the factions were agreed that a strong European trade union structure was important.

However, there are some important differences between the TUC and its Continental counterparts on the functioning of ETUC. Inside ETUC, British trade union delegates have continually argued for removing the clause which excludes national trade unions which are communist in orientation from affiliating to ETUC. They have had some success, in that the Italian CGIL has been allowed to affiliate, but most Continental trade unions oppose the admission of the French CGT and the Spanish Workers Commission. Further, there is evidence to suggest that the general anti-European stance of the TUC has on occasions led to tensions with its colleagues. The 1981 TUC Annual Report to Congress stated that relations with other European trade unions were not all they might be. The European trade unions had become somewhat impatient with the TUC wanting to play a key role inside the ETUC, but at the same time wanting to take a back seat on EC affairs.

Although the existing economic and employment situation and the generally difficult climate for trade unions inside the Community has ensured the issue is not a priority, there continues to be a difference of opinion between some Continental trade unions and the TUC on the subject of European collective bargaining: H Vetter, who was President of the ETUC between 1974–1979, expressed the view of the Continental trade unions when he suggested that for ETUC to be effective 'would mean the member confederations gradually transferring their national sovereignty'.[35] This would give ETUC the authority to conclude binding agreements at the European level on employment and labour affairs. In other words, Vetter wanted to see European-level collective bargaining inside the Community. The TUC takes the opposite view. One report of a British TUC delegate to an ETUC Congress: 'he also expressed the view that central international collective bargaining was not necessarily required to counter the power of multinational employers as was suggested in the action programme and he suggested that the ETUC might assist by ensuring that practical information about conditions in industry throughout Europe was available to workers on the shopfloor, that advice was available to national centres regarding possible legislative action to control multinational companies and that the ETUC should ensure that their activities were directed towards meeting the practical needs of the officials and unions'.[36] This speech makes it plain that the TUC believes there are clear limits to the role of ETUC inside the Community. And while ETUC's Social Programme contains a reference to the establishment of Community-level collective bargaining, the TUC would be most reluctant to see practical developments in this direction.

While these differences of view exist, they have not inhibited the TUC from playing an active role inside ETUC. For instance, after it had abandoned the oppositional stance towards the EC and started to participate in Community bodies, the TUC played a major part in getting ETUC to launch a campaign for a Community employment plan. As a result of this pressure from the trade unions the Commission reconvened the Tripartite Conference on Employment to examine whether a policy programme could be developed with the support of the two sides of industry. The TUC delegation was active in these discussions, which continued for several years but did not lead to any concrete policy proposals. This failure to get a European initiative on employment off the group ended the TUC's initial flurry of activity when it entered EC committees. Since the turn of the 1980s, it has been selective in its participation on Community-related bodies. For instance, the TUC only attended one or two meetings of the Val Duchesse working parties on the social dialogue and the new technologies. No doubt resource and administrative reasons played their part in this decision. But it also shows that EC-level deliberations are not a top priority for the TUC.

Gaining first-hand experience of the workings of the EC did make an impact, particularly on individual trade union leaders in the TUC delegations, who became more conscious of the need to monitor directives and proposals coming from Brussels. For instance, at the 1977 Congress, NALGO put forward a motion noting the 'growing influence of the European Community on the day-to-day affairs of the British trade union movement' and urging the General Secretary to 'improve machinery with Congress for monitoring and confirming activities or proposals and developments which could affect British workmen'.[37] Since then, the TUC has organised in relation to the EC along similar lines to those adopted by the CBI. Thus, the TUC international department oversees the organisational and administrative aspects of its contacts with Europe, while the relevant functional department draws up its response to EC policy proposals.

By and large, the TUC has supported all the EC social-policy initiatives. But the legalistic and 'Continental' orientation of some of the Commission's social proposals posed certain problems for the TUC, which has been a stalwart of the British system of free collective bargaining. Thus when the Commission produced the first draft of the Fifth Directive, the TUC argued for a series of revisions so that the role of trade unions in collective bargaining in Britain would not be compromised. Moreover, it was distinctly lukewarm about the idea of transplanting the German works council model into Britain. In 1979, the Commission intimated that it was going to produce a draft Directive on the reduction and reorganisation of working time. As such a Directive, if adopted, would have interfered with free collective bargaining in Britain, the TUC lobbied in Brussels to have the status of the proposal reduced to a Recommendation, which carries no legally binding force. These two episodes demonstrate the entrenched support amongst British trade unions for free collective bargaining.

As regards the Commission proposals the TUC supported, (Vredeling, the Draft Directive on part-time and temporary workers, and parental leave) it has not mounted any sustained action on these issues. As pointed out already, its campaign to promote the draft Vredeling Directive was virtually non-existent. Similarly, no campaigns of any significance were launched on any of the other proposals. In this respect, the CBI can be said to have defended its interests against EC proposals more vigorously than the TUC supported these initiatives. No doubt, the political in-fighting within the trade union movement over British entry affected the ability of the TUC to lobby on EC matters. But probably the most telling reasons for the TUC's low-level action on EC social proposals lie within the British industrial relations environment.

Since Britain joined the Common Market in 1972, the trade unions have experienced two contrasting national political environments which ensured, although for different reasons, that they did not take an active role in Community affairs. For most of the seventies, the trade unions were closely involved in the then Labour Government's economic policies. This brought the unions closer than ever before to government economic and political decision-making, with the result that much of its policy thinking was geared towards national issues. Moreover, enjoying unprecedented leverage in Britain meant that no incentives existed for them to organise fully at the European level. But since 1979, when the Conservative Party took office, the fortunes of the trade unions have been totally reversed. They are now far removed from the centres of economic and industrial decision-making, and their 'shop-floor' power is also decisively on the wane. Not surprisingly, most of their efforts and energies have gone into responding to these changes. As a result, the TUC, along with individual trade unions, has had little time or inclination to participate fully in the Community. In other words, since Britain joined the EC, developments at the national level have operated as a disincentive for the unions to develop an active response to EC social proposals.

Single-Issue Groups

In the French literature on interest-group behaviour inside the European Community much is made of the concept *le troisiéme guichet.* Essentially, this concept refers to the situation where interest groups adopt neither a purely nationalistic nor totally European approach to Community affairs, but a opportunistic European strategy in which the emphasis is on the occasional use of Community institutions as a 'third level' to reinforce their position within the national state. The above analysis shows that neither of the main industrial interest groups adopted such a strategy. The CBI approach and actions were by and large motivated by the desire to check the Community from developing into a meaningful 'third level' institution in the labour and employment field. For its part, the TUC strategy was at best the mechanical projection of its social-democratic Keynesian programme from the national to European level without any regard for the different political and economic circumstances. However, a strategy similar to that encapsulated by the notion of *le troisiéme guichet* emerged in Britain through the actions of a range of single-issue interest groups like the Equal Opportunities Commission and the Child Poverty Action Group.

Faced by what they regard as retrogressive legislation in Britain, these groups are increasingly turning towards Europe to see whether Community law can be exploited to defend, and even further, the interests of their various constituencies. Thus, for example, it was the Equal Opportunities Commission who provided the financial backing and legal expertise for Helen Marshall when she took the case against Southampton Health Authority to the European Court of Justice. The Child Action Poverty Group provided similar support for Jacquie Drake in her case against the DHSS. The use of this strategy should not be overestimated. Exploiting the potential of various aspects of European law is still very much in its infancy, and the strategies pursued by the EOC and the like are still at the experimental stage. Moreover, as Chapter VII will show, major obstacles in terms of legal complexity and in the processing of claims stand in the way of this opportunistic European behaviour becoming standard practice. Nevertheless, the approach adopted by the single-interest groups appears to have influenced the outlook of some trade unions. For instance, BIFU successfully backed an equal-value case against Lloyds Bank in early 1988, *French and others v. Lloyds Bank*, largely as a result of adopting an opportunistic European outlook. If the European Court of Justice is reformed so that the long delays currently experienced by people bringing cases are reduced, and if the interest groups start thinking more astutely about how to use European law, then this type of interest-group action will become more widespread. As a result, there will be an increase in the number of individual companies facing legal proceedings under European law.

Conclusions

The first part of this chapter examined the outlook of the various political parties in Britain towards EC social policy. The main conclusion is that as the current Conservative administration is hostile to Community social legislation, it is highly unlikely that any Directives on employment participation or the reorganisation of working time will be passed by the Council which the British Government opposes. The second part of the chapter examined the response of British interest groups to EC membership. In the formative years of the Community, it was widely held that interest groups would be a key dynamic in the integration process by pressuring the Community to act in an increasing range of policy areas. A by-product of this process, it was assumed, would be that interest groups would become more and more European in orientation until they finally transferred their loyalties to the Community level.[38] The behaviour of British interest groups has not followed this scenario. The CBI was active at the European level, but this was to try and prevent the Community increasing its presence in the social-policy area. The TUC for the most part has been lukewarm on European affairs, giving only minimum attention to Community social and labour initiatives. However, single-issue interest groups have unwittingly pioneered a new model of interest-group behaviour inside the Community which we have entitled opportunistic European action. If this form of action becomes widespread, it could have a far-reaching impact on British companies.

Notes and References

1 For a very readable account of the difference in the Conservative Party see JENKINS, P. *Mrs Thatcher's Revolution: the ending of a socialist era*, Cape, London 1987

2 See GRAHL, J. *'L'évolution de la politique européenne des principales formalités politiques'*, *Revue Française de Civilisation Britannique*, 1987 pp 121–137

3 See IDS, Transfer of Undertakings' Employment Law Handbook, London 1984

4 House of Commons Employment Committee, The European Community's Employment Initiatives – Minutes of Evidence, Wednesday 22 April 1987

5 ROBBINS, L J. *The Reluctant Party: Labour and the EEC, 1961–1975*, ORMSKIRK G W and HESKETH A, London 1979

6 TEAGUE, P. 'The British TUC and the European Community, Millenium.' *Journal of International Studies*, January 1989 forthcoming

7 Interview with Labour Party officials

8 GRAHL, J and TEAGUE, P. 'The British Labour Party and the European Community', *Political Quarterly*, Vol 59 No 1 Jan–March 1988 pp 72–85

9 SDP, 'Industrial Relations: A Fresh Look,' Consultative Paper, London 1986

10 BUTT PHILIPS, A. *Pressure Groups in the European Community*, University Association for Contemporary European Studies, London 1985

11 OFFE C and WIESENTHAL H, 'Two Logics of Collective Action – Theoretical Notes on Social Class and Organisational Form' in ZETLIN, M (ed) *Power, Politics and Social Theory*, Random House, New York 1983

12 TYSZKIEWISCZ, Z. 'The achievement of the internal market by 1992 and European Social Space: Myth or Reality, The employers' view.' Speech given to the Management Centre Europe, 27.11.86

13 ROBERTS B and LIEBHABERG R, 'The European Trade Union Confederation: Influence of regionalism, détente and multinationals,' *British Journal of Industrial Relations* Vol 19 No 3 1976 pp 261–74

14 MARTENS B, 'The European Trade Union Stand' in BRULIKE, J Van Den, *Investment and disinvestment policies of multinational organisations in Europe*, Mantem and Klemmer, Boddeyn, 1982

15 BARANOUIN B, *The European Labour Movement and European Integration*, Frances Pinter, London 1986

16 CROUCH C, 'Future Prospects for the Trade Unions in Western Europe', *The Political Quarterly*, Vol 57 No 1 Jan-March 1986 pp 5–18

17 *Community Markets*, 'US Firms Oppose Vredeling', April Issue No 4 Financial Times Publications, London 1983

18 *Community Markets*, 'Centre Stage for Vredeling', July 1983 p 1

19 Interview with CBI Officials

20 Interview with TUC Officials

21 REBHAN H, General Secretary of the International Metalworkers' Federation, speech to *Financial Times*/International Research of Multinational Conference 1985

22 Devlin Commission 1970, HMSO, London 1971

23 BROWN W (ed), *Changing Contours of British Industrial Relations*, Basil Blackwell, Oxford 1981

24 GRANT W and MARSH D, *The Confederation of British Industry*, Hodder and Stoughton, London 1977

25 GRANT W and SARGANT J, *Business and Politics*, Macmillan, Basingstoke 1987 p 7

26 *ibid* p 8

27 GRANT W, 'British Employers' Associations and the Enlarged Community'. *Journal of Common Market Studies* Vol XI No 4 1983 pp 226–93

28 CBI, *A Europe for Business*, London 1985 p 31

29 CBI, *The European Community and Social Engineering*, 1986 p 1

30 CBI *EC Employment Policy* Internal Paper 1987

31 STREECK, W and SCHMITTER, P L, 'Community, Market, State and Associations? The Prospective Contribution of Private Interests and Government to Social Order', *European Sociological Review* No 1 1985 pp 119–38

32 BUTT PHILIPS, A. *op cit*

33 Engineering Employers' Federation, *Priorities for the European Community*, London 1985

34 TEAGUE, P. 'Labour and Europe, The Response of British Trade Unions to Membership of the Community', unpublished PhD thesis, University of London 1984

35 ETUC Press Release, Interview with H Vetter, 16 April 1979

36 TUC Annual Report 1974 p 117

37 TUC Annual Report 1975 p 222

38 HAAS, E B. *The Uniting of Europe*, Stanford University Press, California

Chapter VII

European Community Legislation And Its Implementation In The UK

European Community law can be regarded as an autonomous legal system, independent of the legal systems of the member states.[1] The sheer scale and complexity of the tasks assigned to the Community meant it could not be administered (and indeed controlled) by a mere extension of national law or through the conventional inter-state arrangements of international organisations. As a result, a decision-making framework with unparalleled authority and powers amongst international institutions was established at the European level. A key feature of the Community decision-making framework was the ability of the institutions to adopt legislation with complete independence from the legal systems of the member states.

This chapter examines the Community's social legislation and its implementation in the UK. It begins by describing the sources of community law and assessing whether or not these can be regarded as superior to the domestic law of member states. Then it examines how various aspects of EC social legislation have been passed into British law and assesses whether employment law in Britain has changed as a result of Community legal intervention.

Sources of Community Law

Probably the most important source of Community law is the so-called *primary legislation* of the European Community, comprising the Treaties establishing the European Community, including the attached annexes, schedules and protocols and subsequent additions and amendments. The Regulations, Directives and Decisions made by the European Council constitute the *secondary legislation* of the Community. As well as these clearly defined aspects of the EC's legal order, there are also *unwritten sources* of Community law. These unwritten sources are based on widely recognised and accepted principles of law throughout Europe and are primarily used to assist and guide the European Court of Justice when performing its tasks.

Finally, there exists what may be regarded as a set of fundamental rights in Community law.[2] Although the Community Treaties contain neither a catalogue of fundamental rights nor a general fundamental rights clause, individual provisions are included in the treaties which come close to such guarantees. This is particularly true of the numerous clauses on discrimination – Article 7 of the EEC Treaty prohibiting any discrimination on grounds of nationality; Articles 48, 52 and 60 of the Rome Treaty, placing EC citizens on an equal footing in the fields of the right to employment, the right of establishment and freedom to provide services. Also worthy of note is the guaranteed right to economic liberty, in the sense of entrepreneurial freedom of action (Articles 9, 52, 67, 85). From the early sixties, a large body of case law, arising from Court of Justice rulings, has been established on issues relating to fundamental rights. But there are strict limits to the capacity of the Court of Justice to create or to define the content and scope of the protection of fundamental rights. Primarily, the guarantees of fundamental rights in the Community legal system are designed to protect EC citizens against possible infringements of such rights by the Community institutions.

Is Community law superior to national law?

No unequivocal answer can be given to the question of whether Community law is superior to national law. In none of the Community Treaties is there a provision to be found which states either that Community law is above national law, or that it is inferior to national law. This uncertainty about the exact status of Community law in relation to national status has been the subject of extensive legal and academic debate.

The idea that Community law has primacy over national laws rests, for the most part, on the notion of *direct applicability*.[3] Although the notion of direct applicability of Community law was referred to on several occasions in the Treaty of Rome, it was not until the *Van Gend and Loos* case in 1963 that it was given an operational definition. As part of its judgement on the case, the Court of Justice declared that 'independently of the legislation of member states, Community law is not only imposing obligations on individuals but it also intends to confer upon them rights which become part of their legal heritage. These rights arise not only where they are expressly granted by the Treaty, but also by reason of obligation which the Treaty imposes in a clearly defined way upon individuals as well as upon the member states and upon the institutions of the Community.'[4] The practical relevance of this ruling is that it improves the position of the individual by turning the freedoms of the Common Market into rights which may be enforced in a court of law in any member state irrespective of whether or not national legislation has provisions on the subject.

This begs the question of the legal position if a direct applicability provision of Community is incompatible with the legislative provision of a member state. The Court of Justice ruling in the *Simmenthal* case to some extent clarified this point. Part of this ruling laid down that 'in accordance with the principle of the precedence of Community law the relationship between provisions of the Treaty and directly applicable measures of the institutions on the one hand and the national law of the member states on the other is such that those provisions and measures not only by their entry into force render automatically inapplicable any conflicting provision of current national law – but in so far as they are an integral part of, and take precedence in, the legal order applicable in the territory of each of the member states, also preclude the valid adoption of new national legislative measures to the extent to which they would be incompatible with Community processes.'[5] What this ruling implies is that the Community is an independent sovereign association with its own sovereign rights and a legal system independent of the member states, to which both the member states and their nationals are subject in the fields of activity assigned to the Community.

But this interpretation of Community law is challenged by other experts. Geoffrey Howe, the UK Foreign Secretary, and also a distinguished lawyer, suggested that Parliament 'could revoke the section of the European Communities Bill which asks the British courts to give precedence to' enforceable Community Rights and, if this happened, the courts would follow that law.[6] And, in two cases decided by the English Court of Appeal, Lord Denning felt able to assert that the EC Treaty is no more than 'equal in force to any statute'.[7] Furthermore, in practice some member states have been reluctant to regard Community law as superior to domestic law. For instance, the legislation introduced in Denmark and Ireland to facilitate their accession to the Communities is ambiguous about whether or not their courts should recognise the supremacy of the Community law. From this alternative viewpoint, Community legislation can only be regarded as superior if member states perceive it as such.

The evidence suggests that by and large member states have been willing to regard Community law as superior. Thus, certain member states have in the past agreed to legislative proposals at the Community level which went further or overrode the prevailing national legislation in the area. In fact one commentator has suggested that the almost unquestioning acceptance by the member states of the supremacy of Community law and of the gradual extension of the Court's influence through judicial interpretation is one of the most remarkable developments of European integration.[8] Thus, in *de facto* terms, Community legislation can be seen to be 'above' and superior to national law. But from a *de jure* perspective, it is best to make the qualification that in the last analysis member states, if they so wish, can reject any piece of Community law.

The Application of Direct Applicability

Because direct applicability is so central to the application of Community legislation this section examines the principle in more detail. As a result of case law established by Court of Justice rulings it is possible to list those legal provisions which typically have direct applicability.

All of the provisions of the Treaty which relate to the elimination of custom duties and tariffs are widely recognised as being directly applicable. But some uncertainty hangs over the extent to which this principle applies to other Treaty provisions, particularly in the area of social policy. For instance one legal commentator suggested that as a result of the judgement in the *Defrenne case*, article 119 'may simultaneously have and not have direct applicability'.[9] This assessment was based on the distinction made in the ruling that Article 119 only covered direct discrimination and not indirect discrimination. However, a subsequent Court of Justice ruling, as will be pointed out later, reversed this ruling by laying down that Article 119 relates to both direct and indirect forms of discrimination. Nevertheless, some confusion still reigns about the scope of the direct applicability principle of Article 119.

In relation to Regulations, Article 189 of the Rome Treaty is much clearer: it states unequivocally that 'regulations are directly applicable'. Subsequent case law has upheld this principle. Thus member states cannot hamper or deflect the application of Regulations by implementing measures of their own. But practice has shown that Regulations are not always directly applicable. This is because many Regulations have clauses reserving the possibility of further measures which conflict with Court of Justice rulings that for any Community legal provision to be directly applicable it must be 'precise' and it must be 'unconditional' in the sense that its implementation must not be subject to any further measures.

As regards Directives, the Court of Justice has never ruled that they are directly applicable. But as a result of several rulings by the Court, considered legal opinion is that if a Directive is unconditional and sufficiently precise and where it has not been properly implemented by a member state, then individuals can bring action to protect their rights as laid down in the Directive against the state. However, Directives cannot be evoked to impose obligations on individuals or be used in cases solely involving individuals. In legal Eurospeak, Directives are said to have 'vertical' but not 'horizontal' direct applicability.

Enforcement Procedures

The legal enforcement of EC labour law takes place both at Community and at national level.[10] As the 'guardian' of the Treaties, the Commission is the main body responsible for ensuring that Community legislation is properly implemented by the member states. It can do this in a number of ways. First, as member states are required to communicate how they have implemented Directives and to forward all the information necessary to draw up reports on their application, the Commission has the opportunity to evaluate whether the national legislation is in full compliance with the equivalent Community law. Most of the infringement procedures initiated by the Commission against member states arise from this evaluation process. The Commission can also commence infringement proceedings following a complaint by a private organisation or an individual. In addition, it can begin an investigation as a result of an intervention by the European Parliament, or by an individual MEP. Finally, it can initiate such action on the basis of a report by an independent specialist who is part of the 'expert network' set up to monitor the implementation of EC equality Directives.

Since the late seventies, the Commission has taken a tough line on the non-compliance with Directives by member states. As a result, the number of infringement procedures initiated by the Commission has grown markedly in the eighties. This growth is portrayed graphically in the Figure VIIi below. Because of this 'non-compliance' problem, the number of cases yet to be resolved by the European Court of Justice has greatly expanded, putting considerable strains on the Community's judicial system. Moreover, as a result of the long queue of cases to be heard, individuals may now have to wait up to two years before their complaint is dealt with. The non-compliance problem is a major disincentive for individuals wanting to take advantage of the Community's legal provisions. However, under the terms of the Single European Act, the Court of Justice is being reorganised so that there is a lower and higher Court. The lower Court would deal with many of the minor legal cases, leaving the higher Court to hear more important complaints. This new system should ease the pressures on the Community's judicial system. Moreover, if effective it could lead to an increase in the number of individuals bringing cases to the Court of Justice. The effect of that, in turn, could be that the Court would assume an even greater role in Community affairs.

At the national level, it is expected that governments should at all times try to apply Community legislation. This may be achieved by constructing national law so as to be consistent with Community obligations, or by national courts themselves applying Community law in favour of individuals. If the national court or tribunal is uncertain about

Figure VIIi Number of infringement proceedings under Community law

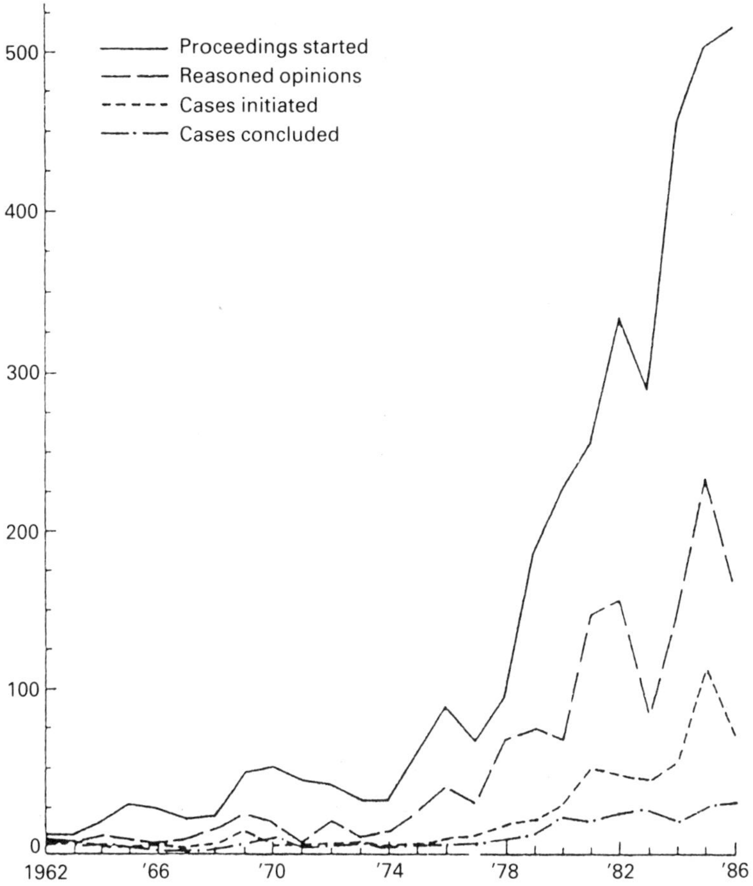

Source: Legal Service of the European Commission

the nature of EC law, particularly whether or not it is directly applicable, then it can refer the issue to the Court of Justice. Of course, this depends on the national judiciary being conversant with EC law. While the situation is improving, the British legal profession has been slow to come to terms with the Community dimension to the UK's legal system. Lord Diplock noted in the Garland case that 'neither the Employment Appeal Tribunal nor the Court of Appeal had attention drawn by counsel, as it should have been, to Article 119 of the EEC Treaty and to . . . (the) . . . Directive dealing with serious discrimination'.[11]

The extent to which this enforcement procedure ensures that member states comply with Community legislation is a matter of some dispute. In particular, it is increasingly being suggested that member states are using a number of devices to escape the full legal implications of certain Community legislation.[12] It will be interesting to see if this is the case as regards Britain and EC social legislation.

The Law in Social Policy

Having outlined the sources of European Community legislation, and the enforcement procedure to ensure their proper implementation, it is possible to assess the implementation of certain Directives in the UK and the effects which they have had on British employee relations. An examination is also made of certain draft Directives which are currently under discussion to assess the effect which they might have on the UK scene in the (unlikely) event that they were to be ratified by the Council of Ministers. It is clear that the legal implications of some of these policies are still being developed; this is indicated, where appropriate, in what follows. Any judgement on the proposals discussed at the end of this section is of course premature, but it was felt that their inclusion here completed an overall picture of the EC legal framework.

Collective Redundancies Directive

Earlier chapters of this book noted that the British Labour Government in the seventies was most reluctant to introduce legislation on collective redundancies at the hands of the Commission. As a result, before it would give approval to the proposed Directive on Collective Redundancies it introduced similar domestic legislation through Part IV of the Employment Protection Act 1975, which was described as 'to all intents and purposes a self-contained Act within an Act.'[13] Because there is such a strong association between the two laws it may be worthwhile to compare the clauses in each piece of legislation. In relation to consultation rights, Part IV imposes more extensive obligations than Articles 1 and 2 of the Directive. There appear to be two main differences. One is that Part IV of the UK legislation imposes no quantitive restrictions on the duty to consult as Article 1 of the European law does. The other difference is that under Part IV, the duty to consult is subjected to a minimum timetable in certain circumstances which probably goes beyond anything implied in Article 2.

But there appear to be areas where Part IV of the EPA is more restrictive than the Directive. For instance, the concept of collective dismissal appears to be broader in the Directive than that in Part IV. In addition,

Part IV restricts the consultative parties to representatives of recognised trade unions: in the Directive the concept of 'worker representative' is used. Part IV also does not include the options given by Article 4 for power to reduce or extend the periods of delay required between notification and dismissal. Nor does Part IV contain the clause in the Directive that consultations must be conducted with a view to seeking solutions to the problems raised by the proposed collective redundancies. These differences should not be interpreted as an attempt on the part of the British Government to water down the contents of the EC Directive. By and large, the differences are the result of the efforts of government lawyers to ensure that the Directive fitted into the British industrial relations system and that it extended employees' rights and strengthened collective bargaining.

One cannot say with certainty whether Part IV of the EPA would have existed if the Commission had not pushed for a Directive on collective dismissals. The only significant legal treatment of redundancy matters before 1975 was the Redundancy Payments Act 1965. This Act allowed for exemption orders to be issued so that redundancies could be discussed by employers and trade unions. Only two orders were ever issued, which indicates that both the employers and the trade unions placed little store by the Act. In the late sixties and early seventies, various bodies recommended that Government should lay down guidelines to promote consultation or bargaining with trade unions about redundancies. Pressure was building up for legislation in the area. However, nothing formally had happened before the Commission made its proposal on the subject. The result of the Commission's drawing up legislation on the subject meant that the national legislation which was introduced (i.e. Part IV of the EPA) was largely framed around EC proposals. Thus the Community had a direct influence in shaping British collective redundancy legislation.

Transfer of Undertakings

The EC Acquired Rights Directive was introduced into British law by the Transfer of Undertakings (Protection of Employment) Regulations 1981/1982, and came fully into force on 1st May 1982 – more than three years after the expiry date of the two-year implementation period laid down by the Directive. It was only after the EC Commission threatened to initiate legal proceedings against the British Government that the latter was moved to take any action on the issue. The UK Government's regulations introduced the principle of automatic transfer of contracts of employment, collective agreements and trade union recognition in the case of certain transfers of commercial ventures; it also rendered automatically unfair a dismissal for a reason, other than an economic, technical or organisational one, connected with such a transfer, and imposed a duty to inform and consult representatives of recognised trade unions.

In assessing the degree to which the UK Government's regulations match the clauses of the EC Acquired Rights Directive, it has been suggested that 'arguably the Regulations are not in full compliance with the spirit or intent of the Directive, itself watered down from the Commission first draft (1974) . . . The 1981 Regulations are significantly less extensive than the draft first laid before Parliament by the Labour government in 1978'.[14] In other words, it is being suggested that the British Government did the minimum necessary to comply with the Directive so as to limit its impact in the UK. There appears to be justification for this conclusion. In the first place, the manner in which the Directive was passed into British law can be questioned. In particular, for the first time in the field of labour law, a Community Directive was implemented into British law by means of a Regulation rather than by an Act of Parliament. With minor exceptions, Regulations do not amend existing legislation, as would have been the case with an Act. As a result, the Regulation simply sits uneasily with a considerable body of existing national law.

Another shortcoming of the British Regulation is that much of the wording is copied directly from the Directive. As much of EC law is written in the manner and style of Continental legal practice, which is frequently incomprehensible in the context of UK law, many clauses of the regulation are unclear and obscure, thus making them difficult for the British courts to use.[15] A further problem arises with the most far-reaching change caused by the Regulation – the concept of automatic transfer of employment contracts when the ownership is changed. As there was little attempt to square this provision with existing national law which laid down that the transfer of a business automatically terminated all existing contracts of employment, a good deal of confusion reigns about the exact legal position.

The rules apply only to transfers involving commercial undertakings, or self-contained parts of undertakings. Transfers of share capital (the main form of takeover in the UK) are excluded from the scope of the Directive. For the purposes of applying the Regulation in Britain, the distinction between a commercial and non-commercial undertaking is the presence or absence of profit. But as there exists a large grey area between these two forms of organisation, it is difficult in some cases to apply such a hard and fast distinction. Another difficulty arising in recent years is that the growth of privatisation in the public sector has raised questions about whether services contracted out by local authorities and other public bodies should be considered as commercial. In the *Rankins v. Initial Service Cleaners* case, a tribunal found that public lavatories contracted out to private contractors could not be considered commercial when under the contract of the public authorities. This ruling has been questioned: 'If there is no possibility of profit or breaking even, then it is difficult to comprehend why private enterprise contractors should show such enthusiasm in presenting and pursuing their tenders to take over such services. Reg. 2 (1) requires that the undertaking or part transferred has to be *in the nature of* a commercial venture, and in any broad construction of these words "in the nature of" could be equated with "something like" a commercial venture'.[16] As things stand, however, the regulations have not been a legal obstacle to the Government or local authorities privatisation programmes.

Probably Regulation 5, which covers the transfer of employment rights, is the most important clause. The EC Directive clearly envisaged that all statutory and contractual rights should be fully transferred in relevant cases. But the general consensus is that Regulation 5 is highly ambiguous on this point. This again presents legal difficulties: the Courts have sometimes interpreted statutory employment rights to be an inherent aspect of employment contracts, and sometimes not. In its 1987 Report, ACAS highlighted and heavily criticized the confusion of the law governing transfer of undertakings. It also argued that the Government should take the necessary action to clarify the precise legal state of play in the area.

The evidence strongly suggests that the British Government, by using a variety of administrative and legal devices, has limited the impact of the Transfer of Undertakings Directive in Britain. But in so doing it has created legal confusion to the extent that industrial tribunals are finding it an almost impossible task to interpret exactly the status of the law in this area. Thus by attempting to marginalise this particular piece of Community labour law, the British Government unintentionally undermined the prevailing legal coherence on the protection of workers' rights in merger and take-over situations. But it's apparent reluctance to restore coherence to this increasingly sensitive area indicates the extent to which the Government wants to keep EC influences on British labour law to a minimum.

The Insolvency Directive

The Directive on the protection of workers' rights in the event of the insolvency of their employer is generally regarded as parallel to existing UK law. None of the clauses in any way changed existing law in the area, established by the Employment Protection (Consolidation) Act of 1978.

Women, Employment and European Equality Law

Equal Pay

The principle of equal pay was introduced into British law by the Equal Pay Act 1970. This piece of legislation established various procedural means for an individual to take a claim of unequal pay to an industrial tribunal. In particular, individuals could pursue a claim of inequality where someone of the opposite sex could be identified as doing 'like work', but getting a higher wage, or where work had been rated as equivalent by a job evaluation scheme, but where this had not been translated into equal pay. Inequality claims could only be made where the 'comparator' worked in the 'same employment'. This has normally been interpreted as including being employed by the same employer in another establishment, if common terms and conditions prevail at the two sites. In other words, the Act only established the legal basis for individuals to make claims within pay structures and not between them, and in relation to 'same work' comparisons but not on 'equal value' comparisons.

The decision to legislate on equal pay was the result of a growing consensus within Britain that a legal framework was required to protect women's rights in this area. European Community legislation had little impact on this decision to legislate, or on the substance of individual clauses of the Act. If any extra-national influence was present it came from the United States, where general anti-discrimination legislation and programmes had been in operation for some time.[17]

In its first years, the Act led to a narrowing of the differentials between men's and women's wages in Britain. But by the early eighties the Act was coming under increasing criticism from women's groups and other bodies like the Equal Opportunities Commission (EOC) for being too restrictive in scope. With a Conservative Government now in power strongly opposed to further extensions in labour protection legislation, it appeared highly unlikely that the demand by the EOC for more far-reaching equal opportunities legislation would be met. Yet as a result of the European Commission taking the UK Government to the European Court of Justice for not properly implementing the Equal Pay Directive, important extensions were made to British equality law.

The essence of the Commission's case was that as the Equal Pay Act did not allow legal claims for equal pay for work of equal value, it contravened the 1975 Community Directive which explicitly held that such claims were permissible. The UK Government opposed the Commission's case, but the European Court of Justice ruled against it. The Equal Pay Act was found to be defective in not providing the necessary changes 'to enable all employees who consider themselves disadvantaged by failure to apply the principle of equal pay for men and women for work to which equal value is attributed and for which no system of job classification exists to obtain recognition of such equivalence'.[18] The Court called upon the British Government to introduce the enabling legislation to reverse this situation.

In response to this judgement, the Department of Employment issued a consultative note in August 1982 and asked for comments by the end of September. About twenty organisations from both sides of industry participated in this exercise. After this consultative process, the Government published the proposed changes to the Equal Pay Act. The changes met with strong opposition from the Equal Opportunities Commission and other women's groups. The Government was accused of not complying with the European Court of Justice ruling because it placed the burden of proof on the employee. In addition, the Government was attacked for trying to stifle debate on the subject by introducing the changes via an order under section 2 (2) of the European Communities Act of 1972, which limited the time for debate by MPs to just ninety minutes.[19]

The extent to which the British Government's Equal Pay Amendment Act complies with the European Court of Justice's ruling is open to question. But what cannot be disputed is that the legal amendments introduced by the Government allowed for the first time claims for equal value. And as chapter VI details, the Equal Opportunities Commission and certain trade unions have started to make use of the legal changes. It is too early to assess the extent of the impact of the amended legislation, as several cases which will define its operational scope are still before the British courts. Only one case with any significance – *Hayward v. Cammell Laird* – has gone through the entire legal process. In this case, Mrs Hayward, a cook employed by Cammell Laird, compared her job with those of skilled craftsmen employed by the company. The EAT (Employment Appeals Tribunal) rejected the claim, basing its interpretation on the argument that equal value is achieved if overall the women's terms and conditions are not less favourable than those of male comparators. This interpretation was upheld by the Court of Appeal. However, the House of Lords unanimously rejected the rulings of the lower courts and held that Mrs Haywards's claim was legitimate and should be met. This judgement is being hailed as a far-reaching success by equal opportunities campaigners, and as a flawed piece of legal thinking by the CBI.[20]

As a result of this judgement, there may be an increase in the number of equal value cases before the courts. Since the British government was obliged to introduce legal provision on equal pay for work of equal value, there has been a steady but not startling increase in the number of such claims.

Of the 3,800 applications made since 1984, about 50 cases have been referred to an independent expert and approximately 12 have gone through the full procedure with claims being upheld in eight cases and rejected in four. Table VIIi outlines the cases referred to an independent expert.

Table VIIi UK Equal Value Cases Referred to Independent Experts

Over 50 cases have been referred to independent experts for consideration. Here we give details of 48 of those, involving approximately 350 employees.

Applicant	Respondent	Jobs compared	Independent expert's conclusion	Tribunal decision	Withdrawn/ settled
Aldridge	British Telecom	Senior drawing office assistant with inspector (engineering)	Work not of equal value		
Allsopp and others (7)	Derbyshire County Council	Audiotypists with photographic technician			
Beattie and others (3)	Kelco Biospecialities Ltd	Production clerk, accounts clerk, administrative assistant typists and telephonist with a warehouseman and a gateman			Settled
Beckett	C R Barron (Meats) Ltd	Packer with labourer	Work of equal value	Claim upheld	
Brown and Royle	Cearns & Brown Ltd	Cash and carry assistants with warehouse hands	Work not of equal value	Claims dismissed	
Brown and others (12)	J H Mudford & Sons Ltd	PVC welders and a machinist with cutters, markers and eyeletters			
Caira	Stott Benham Ltd	Staff worker with manual worker			Withdrawn
Clark	Mersey Docks and Harbour Co	Administration assistant in chief engineers department with administration assistant in estates department			Settled
Coleman	MG Impex	Sales administrator with technical adviser	Work not of equal value		
Copley and others (6)	Lloyds Bank	Typists/secretaries with messengers			
Davies	Francis Shaw Ltd	VDU operator with production clerk	(i) Work not of equal value	Report rejected and new report commissioned from different independent expert	
			(ii) Work of equal value		

Applicant	Respondent	Jobs compared	Independent expert's conclusion	Tribunal decision	Withdrawn/ settled
Eden and others (4)	Almetex Ltd	Packers with loaders			
Ellwood	Northern Ireland Electricity Services	Assistant mains recorder with trainee surveyor, engineer and an industrial worker	Work of equal value to the industrial worker		
Erskine	Hykeham Fareham Supplies	Driver with technical sales representative	Work not of equal value	Claim dismissed	
Everhurst and Boozer	Reed Corrugated Cases Ltd	Despatch clerk (staff) with despatch clerk (non-staff)			
Fleming and others	Short Bros	Clerical grades with kit marshaller, store person, tool store person			
French and others (10)	Lloyds Bank	Print finishers with printers and guillotine operators	Work of equal value	Claim upheld	
Gallagher and others	Adria Ltd	Computer operators clerks with machine operators	Work of equal value		Settled. Gallagher promoted and salary increased from £86 to £115 a week; other clerical workers received increases of up to 20% a week
Green and others (3)	Avon Social Services	Assistant area organiser with registration officer, senior area organiser with team manager grades			
Hall and others (26)	Fraylings Furniture Ltd	Machinists with upholsterers	Work not of equal value		Settled. Bonus earnings parity
Hayward	Cammell Laird Shipbuilders Ltd	Cook with painter, joiner and thermal insulation engineer	Work of equal value	Claim upheld	
Henery	James Howden & Co Ltd	Licensee co-ordinator with a senior progressor, progress engineer and a shop loader	Work not of equal value		Withdrawn
Hogan and Newton	Micropore Insulation Ltd	Senior operative and skilled machinist with basic process operator, skilled process operator and mixer operator	Work of equal value		
Holden and others (60)	Buoyant Upholstery	Sewing machinists with upholsters	Work not of equal value		Withdrawn

Applicant	Respondent	Jobs compared	Independent expert's conclusion	Tribunal decision	Withdrawn/ settled
Holmes and others (55)	Britfish Ltd	Packers with labourers			
Jackson and others (11)	F&M Ducker Ltd	Office workers with shopfloor worker, clerks with general labourer		Withdrawn	
Jervis and others (5)	J&C Moores	Unskilled manual workers with skilled and semi-skilled workers; clerical workers with machine operators and craft and semi-skilled workers			
Langley and others (14)	Beecham Proprietaries	Assistant laboratory technicians with craftsmen			Some settled (upgrading); some withdrawn
Lim	The Post Office	Senior nursing officer with welfare officers and information officers			
McAtamney and Barr	Goven Shipbuilders Ltd	Ship cleaners with messenger steward, runners and steel work labourer			
McAuley and others (4)	Eastern Health and Social Services Board	Part-time domestics with full-time porter and groundsman			
McInnes and Kane	Walter Alexander & Co (Coachbuilders) Ltd	Coach trimmer machinists with painter, trimmer and cross-cut saw operator	Work of equal value	Claim upheld	
McMaster	John C Walker Ltd	Forewoman with foreman and HGV drivers	Work not of equal value	Claim dismissed	
Miller and Fernandes	Forex Neptune (Overseas) Ltd	Accounting clerk and management cash clerk with assistant accountant			Settled
Murry and Kerr	AG Barr plc	Branch clerks with checker clerks			
Quinton and Case	Hemsec Manufacturing Ltd	Ledger clerk and wages supervisor with assistant accountant	Work not of equal value	Claim dismissed	
Read	University College, London	Computer assistant with senior store keeper	Work of equal value		Settled
Scallay and others (2)	Jaeger Tailoring	Supervisors with supervisors	Equal value to some comparators but not to others		
Schofield	Church Army	Matron and a principal care assistant	Work not of equal value		Withdrawn

Applicant	Respondent	Jobs compared	Independent expert's conclusion	Tribunal decision	Withdrawn/ settled
Scott	Beam College	House mother with house father	Work of equal value	Claim upheld	
Silberry and Smith	Sheffield Metropolitan District Council	Group school meals organisers with site service officer, inspector street cleansing, multi-trade supervisor and senior cleansing assistant			
Stuart and another	Galen Research Laboratories Ltd	Process operatives with process operator			
Thomas and others (9)	GE Shouler & Co Ltd	Packers with labourers	Work of equal value		Settled. £15.20 rise in basic pay: increase in overtime rate of 57p per hour; and an ex gratia payment of £1000
Todd	Tennants Textile Colours Ltd	Laboratory assistant with laboratory technician	Work of equal value	Claim upheld	
Wells and others (13)	F Smales & Son (Fish Merchants) Ltd	Fish packers with labourers	Nine applicants do work of equal value; five do not	All claims upheld	
White and others (22)	Alstons (Colchester) Ltd	Machinists with upholsterers	Work of equal value	Claims upheld	
Williamson and others (6)	GEC Reinforced Plastic Ltd	Clerks and receptionist telephonist with progress chaser, semi-skilled workers, skilled production workers, buyer, production control clerk and labourers			
Wressell and others (16)	Christian Salvesen (Food Services) Ltd	Factory operatives with checkers			

Table VIIii details the equal pay for work of equal value claims made between 1984 and 1987.

Table VIIii Industrial Tribunal Equal Value Claims, 1984–7

Year	Applications	Employers
1984	229	30
1985	381	68
1986	1481*	62
1987	1738†	179**

* Including 1115 applications for British Coal employees
† Including 1395 applications from speech therapists
** Including 126 district health authorities/boards

The table shows the strong tendency for equal claims to involve large number of employees in the public sector.

The evidence suggests that British women have yet to make full use of the equal value legislation introduced by the British Government at the behest of the Community. But as many of the legal uncertainties about the operational scope of the law will be resolved in the next year or so and as equal opportunities interest groups and trade unions are stepping up their action in this area, it is highly likely that the number of equal value cases before the courts will increase appreciably in coming years.

From the viewpoint of equal opportunity campaigners, other important advances have been made as a result of Community law. For instance in *Garland v. British Railways Engineering*, the applicant claimed that British Railways operated in a discriminatory way by excluding retired women employees from benefits enjoyed by retired male employees – in this instance the availability of cheap travel. The EAT ruled that Article 119 of the Treaty of Rome covers all emoluments in cash or kind or payable, or conditions provided, even indirectly, by the employer, as a result of employment. Therefore, British Rail was found to have been operating in a discriminatory way. The wider significance of the ruling, however, was that it defined pay in sufficiently broad terms to open up fringe benefits to equal value claims.[21]

For some time confusion prevailed about the position of discrimination in EC law, particularly as to whether the concept was covered by Article 119. To a large extent, this confusion was sparked off by the judgement in the second Defrenne case when the European Court of Justice drew the distinction between 'direct and overt discrimination' on the one hand and 'indirect and disguised discrimination' on the other. As regards 'direct and overt discrimination' the European Court ruled that 'Article 119 is directly applicable and may thus give rise to individual rights which the courts must protect' (paragraph 14 of the second Defrenne judgement). In relation to 'indirect and disguised' discrimination the Court deemed that further legislative provisions were necessary.

This ruling appeared to lay down that Article 119 did not give directly applicable rights before the national courts in relation to 'indirect or disguised discrimination'. But this interpretation of the ruling created considerable unease within the Community's judicial circles. Thus in the *Worringham v. Lloyds Bank* case, the Advocate General suggested that no case before the Court of Justice which distinguished between direct and indirect discrimination had any bearing on whether the relevant provision of Community law had direct applicability or not. He invited the Court to clarify this point in its judgement. Accordingly, the Court ruled that Article 119 is directly applicable as regards indirect or disguised discrimination as well as in cases of direct discrimination.[22]

The Equal Treatment Directive

The Equal Treatment Directive is the EC legislation which parallels the UK's Sex Discrimination Act (SDA). This Directive expands the forms of discrimination capable of legal challenge within the UK, particularly in the area of pensions (pensions are examined in a later section). In addition to pensions, several other clauses of the Sex Discrimination Act have had to be revised in the light of European Court of Justice rulings. As a result of infringement proceedings brought by the Commission, the Court of Justice ruled that section 5 (3) of the SDA which exempted private households or undertakings with five or fewer persons, was in violation of the Equal Treatment Directive. In the same ruling, the Court also found Britain to be in breach of section 4 (6) of the Directive which holds that any provisions contrary to the principle of equal treatment in collective bargaining agreements which are legally binding or otherwise 'shall be, or may be declared null and void or may be amended'. To comply with this ruling, the British Government introduced the Sex Discrimination Act of 1986. And in a separate hearing, *Johnson v. the Chief Constable of the Royal Ulster Constabulary*, the Court enlarged the scope of sex discrimination prohibitions by putting strict limits on the derogations from EC regulations. Thus the Equal Treatment Directive has had a direct impact on British anti-discrimination legislation by forcing changes which otherwise would not have occurred.

The Equal Treatment Directive was at the heart of the widely known *Marshall v. Southampton and South West Hampshire Area Health Authority* case brought before the Court of Justice in 1986. The normal practice in the Health Authority was for women to retire at 60 and men at 65. But occasionally this practice could be postponed by mutual agreement. Such an agreement was reached in the case of Miss Marshall, who thus continued to work after age 60. However, when 62 she was dismissed on the basis that she had passed the normal retirement age applied by the employers to women. Marshall immediately complained to the Industrial Tribunal that her dismissal amounted to unlawful discrimination, contrary to the Sex Discrimination Act and the Equal Treatment Directive. Although the Tribunal ruled that her complaint did not fall within the scope of the SDA, it held that her dismissal was contrary to EC laws. However, an EAT held that while Marshall's dismissal violated the Equal Treatment Directive, such a violation could not be relied upon before a UK court or tribunal. In other words, the Directive was not directly applicable. Marshall appealed to the Court of Appeal who in turn applied to the European Court of Justice for a ruling. The Court of

Justice held that 'dismissal of a women solely because she has attained or passed the qualifying age for a state pension, which age is different under national legislation for men and women, constitutes discrimination on grounds of sex, according to that Directive'.

But the second part of the ruling is probably the most important in terms of its far-reaching implications. It laid down that 'Article 5 (1) of Directive 76/207, which prohibits any discrimination on grounds of sex with regard to working conditions, including the conditions governing dismissals, may be relied upon as against a state authority acting in its capacity as employer, in order to avoid the application of any national provision which does not conform to Article 5 (1)'.[23]

The implication of this ruling is that the Equal Treatment Directive is only directly applicable as regards public sector bodies. Employees in the private sector cannot evoke the EC Directive in claims alleging discrimination, as its contents are not binding and enforceable upon private persons or bodies. However, in response to the ruling, the British Government announced that it would introduce legislation making it unlawful both in the public and private sector to dismiss a woman on grounds of age when a man of the same age and comparable circumstances would not be dismissed. These changes were put into effect by the Sex Discrimination Act 1986.

It has been suggested that a major issue presently outside the scope of the UK discrimination law, but arguably within the scope of the Equal Treatment Directive, is sex-based wage discrimination. On this argument, sex-based wage-discrimination may have taken place 'if the pay differentials are not commensurate with the differences in job values and this discrepancy is due either directly or indirectly to the sex of the workers performing the work . . . (or) . . . if the women are doing work of greater value than the men, but the difference in value is not reflected commensurately in their relative pay'.[24] At present there is a clear loophole in national law on this point. The Sex Discrimination Act excludes complaints relating to pay, while sex-based wage discrimination is not actionable under equal pay law. The Equal Treatment Directive may be used to close this loophole and in particular, Article 5 (1), which provides that 'Application of the principle of equal treatment with regard to working conditions, including the conditions governing dismissals, means that men and women shall be guaranteed the same conditions without discrimination on grounds of sex.' This could be used as the relevant legal clause for sex-based wage discrimination as it can be argued that wages form part of working conditions mentioned in the Article.

Pensions, Social Security and the EC Equality Legislation

As mentioned earlier, pensions were excluded from the Sex Discrimination Act (1975). The only concession to the notion of non-discrimination in this area was the requirement of 'equal access' to occupational pension schemes. The EC Social Security Directives of 1978 and 1986 lay down that all discrimination based on sex either directly or indirectly by reference in particular to marital or family status should be eliminated both in state and private sector occupational schemes. But Article 9 of the 1986 Directive allows member states to defer the compulsory application of the equal treatment principle in the following areas:

(i) determination of pensionable age for the purposes of granting old-age or retirement pensions, and the possible implications for other benefits:
 – either until the date at which such equality is achieved in statutory schemes
 – or, at the least, until such equality is required by a Directive;
(ii) survivor's pensions until a Directive requires the principle of equal treatment in statutory social schemes in that regard;
(iii) the application of the first subparagraph of Article 61(i) to take account of the different actuarial calculation factors, at the latest until the expiry of a thirteen year period as from the ratification of this Directive.[25]

However, these exceptions may be nullified as a result of some far-reaching rulings in this area by the European Court of Justice. The first legal intervention of the Court of Justice into pension matters was in *Worringham v. Lloyds Bank*. In this case, the claimant argued that her employer operated a discriminatory pension scheme and that this contravened Article 119 of the Rome Treaty. The Court of Justice avoided giving a ruling on whether Article 119 covered pension provisions, but it did declare on the specifics of the case that the bank was operating a discriminatory scheme. The importance of this ruling was that it further broadened the concept of pay under Article 119 to cover sums included in the gross salary of employees which had repercussions for the calculation of other benefits linked to salaries (e.g., redundancy payments and credit facilities). Equally significant, however, was that it did not take the opportunity to *exclude* pension provisions from Article 119.

From the standpoint of the equal opportunities lobby, a major advance was made by the Court of Justice ruling in the *Bilka-Kaufhaus v. Weber von Hartz* case. Karin Weber von Hartz worked for Bilka, a group of department stores in West Germany, as a sales assistant between

1961-1972 full time, and then between 1972-1976 part time. Under the pension scheme operated by Bilka, a part-time worker was excluded if he/she had not worked full time for 15 years in the previous 20-year period. On her retirement, Weber von Hartz applied for a pension from the Bilka scheme, but was turned down on the grounds that she had not worked the requisite 15 years. Weber von Hartz challenged at the German Labour Court the legality of Bilka's refusal to pay the pension, on the grounds that it contravened Article 119 of the Rome Treaty. The German Court referred the case to the European Court of Justice for a ruling. The decision of the Court of Justice fell into two distinct parts. The first part related to the applicability of Article 119. Here the Court held that the pension scheme was an integral part of the contract between Bilka and its employees, and thus fell within the scope of the second paragraph of Article 119. The second part concerned the exclusion of part-timers as indirect discrimination. The Court held that an employer which excludes part-time workers from its occupational pension scheme prima facie is in breach of Article 119 if this exclusion affects significantly more women than men.

Some general principles emerge from the judgement: (i) Article 119 applies only to questions of equal pay between men and women, and not conditions of work and employment: but pensions are regarded as 'pay' rather than 'conditions' and thus subject to Article 119; (ii) an employer who adopts a 'pay' practice having an adverse impact on more women than men, must show a legitimate business or economic objective for doing so and that the practice must be appropriate and necessary to achieve that objective. If the employer cannot demonstrate these 'objectively justifiable' grounds, then the practice will be regarded as indirectly discriminatory and hence in breach of Article 119. The Court of Justice left it to national courts to determine what constitutes 'objectively justifiable' grounds; (iii) the Court decision seems to have the effect of leap-frogging the occupational pension provisions contained in the Social Security Directive 1986 which were not expected to come into effect until 1990.[26]

One authority argues that the 'objectivity justifiable' criteria are very different from the 'loose and largely subjective test of *sound and tolerable* reasons previously used by British courts to determine whether or not an employer had discriminated indirectly'.[27] Since the Bilka ruling by the Court of Justice, British courts appear to have changed their approach in such cases. For instance in *Rainey v. Greater Glasgow Health Authority*, the Law Lords ruled that as Bilka was an authoritative ruling they had to apply it in British cases. In particular, the Court of Justice ruling held 'the principle of prepertanality must be observed'. That principle requires that the derogations remain within the limits of what is appropriate and necessary for achieving the aim in view and that the principle of equal treatment be reconciled as far as possible with the requirement which underlies the exception.

If any one overriding conclusion can be made about European equality legislation it is that it forms a highly complex and uncertain legal subject. Many of the operational and definitional parameters to these laws appear to be fixed by European Court of Justice rulings in particular cases. In this respect, this situation places the Court in a key position, for through its interpretation the particular equality laws can have a limited or far-reaching impact. So far, the Court has tended to give a broad rather than a narrow interpretation to equality legislation. These rulings have resulted in important changes being made to British law in equal opportunities and discrimination. But it would be wrong to overestimate the impact of Community legislation and Court of Justice rulings on Britain. Because of the cumbersome procedure associated with launching a legal case under EC law many are deterred from doing so. Thus since the Equal Value Amendment was introduced into British law, there has been no major increase in such claims.

Health and Safety Dimension

In 1980, the then chairman of the Health and Safety Commission, Mr Bill Simpson, stated 'my own assessment of the situation is that the best posture for us to adopt is to be slightly in front of the EEC but not out of sight. This would give us the advantage of being able to set the mood for the legislation which is going to come from the EEC.'[28] By and large, Simpson's statement accurately reflected the state of play of UK health and safety legislation in relation to the EC Directives during the seventies. In this period, only small-scale changes were required to UK law in the area as a result of Community legislation. Moreover, the likelihood is that such changes would have been implemented domestically in the course of time. In the following section, we detail the extent to which some of the Directives passed by the Council of Ministers since 1980 have affected Britain's health and safety regulations. An exhaustive examination of each individual piece of Community health and safety legislation that has impacted on Britain is not feasible here, as this would entail a separate study. For instance, there are seventeen individual Directives relating to the classification, packaging and labelling of dangerous substances. Thus the focus is on the more substantive and representative pieces of Community legislation.

First, however, it may be worthwhile briefly to outline the process by which EC Directives on health and safety are transferred into UK law. The normal procedure is for a Community health and safety Directive to be implemented by making Regulations under the Health and Safety at

Work Act. In practice, the Health and Safety Commission consults appropriate interested parties (mainly trade unions and employers) about the implementation of the Directives. From these discussions, it draws up exact proposals for the enactment of the Directive into UK law which are passed to the Secretary of State for Employment. The following sections examine how several pieces of EC health and safety legislation have been implemented in Britain.

The Lead Directive

In 1979, the Commission produced a draft Directive which sought to introduce strict controls over the circumstances in which workers were exposed to lead. This proposal met with immediate opposition from some member states. Anticipating a protracted round of negotiations on the issue, the HSC decided to push ahead with the unrelated discussions on lead controls in the UK with a view to the enactment of national legislation on the subject. As a result, the UK regulations over the control of lead at work were introduced in 1980. These regulations were less stringent than the controls proposed by the Commission. However, after several rounds of negotiations these original proposals were watered down so much so that the final provisions of the lead Directive adopted by the Council of Ministers in 1982 were more or less equivalent to the UK regulations. As a result, only small changes to the HSC Approved Code on the control of lead at work were required.

The Seveso Directive

In 1982, the Council of Ministers adopted a Directive on major hazards of certain industrial activities – the 'Seveso Directive'. To some extent, this paralleled existing UK legislation, particularly the Hazardous Installations (Notification and Survey) Regulations enacted in 1978. However, there were also signficant differences between the two pieces of legislation. In the first place, the Directive makes the distinction between the requirements for stored dangerous substances as opposed to those involved in processes. It also includes a long annex of particularly hazardous substances selected for special attention, absent from the UK Regulations. Furthermore, the Directive, unlike the existing UK legislation, includes provisions covering the reporting of accidents, the issue of warnings to the population neighbouring major hazard installations, the setting up of an EC register of accidents and provisions for the transfer of accident experience from one member state to others. However, the Directive did not lay down any specific requirement for the carrying out of hazard assessments/risk analyses, as did the UK legislation.

Asbestos

The Asbestos Directive, which seeks to give workers protection in all situations where they may be exposed to asbestos, was passed into UK law by supplements to the 1974 Health and Safety at Work Act: the Control of Asbestos at Work Regulations 1984 under section 65 and a new approved Code of Practice under Section 16. Broadly, the Community's Directive is in line with UK policy based on the Health and Safety Commission's advice following the recommendations of their Advisory Committee on asbestos. In some instances, the existing legal standards in Britain are higher than those laid down in the Directive. The only provisions contrary to UK practices are a requirement that all asbestos work must be notified to the competent national authority and that there be a single hygiene standard for all major forms of asbestos.

Noise Directive

In 1981, the Health and Safety Exective published a consultative document recommending that national legislation should be introduced to regulate noise levels at work. At the same time, the Commission produced a draft Noise Directive. To avoid overlap and duplication, the HSC (Health and Safety Commission) decided to shelve its proposals and engage in Community-level discussions on the subject. Initially there were wide differences of outlook and approach between the two organisations. Whilst negotiations reduced the differences between the European Commission's and the HSC proposals, the Noise Directives ratified by the Council in 1986 did not completely close the gap between the two sides.

Firstly, the Directive imposes specific requirements at noise levels of 85db(A), and makes statutory the provision of information to workers and the availability of personal ear protection. Apart from a general requirement to reduce, as far as reasonably practical, any risk of hearing damage, the HSC proposal would not have imposed any requirements below 90db(A). Secondly, initially the Commission wanted compulsory audiometric examinations for all workers exposed to over 85db(A). But a compromise was reached that workers exposed to such noise levels should be able to have their hearing medically checked, a provision already available under the National Health. As a result of this compromise, the Directive falls short of the HSC proposal for routine industrial audiometric examinations for workers exposed to over 105db(A). Thirdly, the Community's Noise Directive requires no action below a daily exposure of 85db(A), yet the HSC proposals included an open-ended requirement for all exposures likely to be injurious to hearing to be reduced as far as reasonably practical.

The Noise Directive was implemented by the introduction of new regulations under Section 15 of the Health and Safety at Work Act. But as the above analysis shows, it cannot be concluded that the Directive introduced far-reaching new provisions. Indeed, in many important respects, the initial HSC proposals were more regulatory than those contained in the Directive. Thus this piece of Community legislation should not be seen as supranational in character; rather it is merely introducing a series of legal measures which otherwise would have been adopted at the national level.

The above analysis shows that most of the main Directives passed by the Council of Ministers since 1980 have more or less paralleled British legislation or practice in the same field. This does not necessarily imply that Community legislation in the area has had a far-reaching impact on health and safety matters in Britain. What *is* beyond dispute, however, is that certain Directives amending pre-existing Community statutes, particularly in relation to the handling of dangerous substances, have had important implications for companies in certain sectors. Furthermore, with health and safety matters coming under the new qualified majority voting regime introduced by the Single European Act, the possibility exists that Community influence will grow in this area. It will be interesting to monitor the progress of forthcoming proposals in this area as their fate will give a strong indication of how the qualified majority voting will work in practice.

Draft EC Social Legislation – Possible Impact on Britain

So far the examination has focused on formal Community social legislation and in its impact on Britain. In this section, we assess the likely impact of some of the Commission proposals for social legislation which, although widely known, have not yet reached the Community's statute book. Many of the proposals in this category have received so much publicity that it was deemed necessary to gauge the exact legal implications for Britain if they were adopted as formal Community policy. The assessment focuses on four particular proposals – Part-time Work Directive, Temporary Work Directive, Parental Leave for Family Reasons Directive and the Vredeling Directive.

Part-time Workers Directive

If the draft Directive was adopted, it would introduce several important changes to the existing parallel UK law. In the first place, the draft

Directive requires that any provisions which contravene it and are included in collective agreements shall be declared null and void. But as collective agreements are not legally enforceable in the UK, wholesale changes would have to take place. Several revisions would also have to be made to the Employment Protection (Consolidation) Act 1978. In particular, the present law laying down a minimum hours qualification for rights against unfair dismissal would have to be repealed. An amendment would also be required to comply with provisions on vocational training, promotion, social facilities and medical care as well as obliging occupational pension schemes to admit part-time workers.[29]

Temporary Work Directive

The draft Directive on temporary work aims to give such workers a measure of protection by regulating employment businesses supplying workers to 'user' undertakings on direct fixed-term contracts of employment between employers and workers. The Employment Agencies Act 1973 provides for registration and inspection of these businesses. But the draft Directive would extend the scope of this Act. For example, Article 5 of the draft Directive would prohibit a 'user undertaking' paying the employment business a fee if they decided to take one of the latter's temporaries on to the staff, a practice which is widespread in Britain. Furthermore, large-scale changes would have to occur to comply with Articles 4, 6 and 9 of the draft Directive which require the employment conditions of these temporary workers to be comparable with those in the user undertaking. In terms of the regulation of fixed contracts of employment, there is some confusion, arising largely from interpretation problems over the exact legal implications for the UK. It has been argued that UK law would have to change in order 'to identify certain types of activity in which limited duration work is permissible'.[30] At the moment there is no such limitation and the effect of such a provision, if introduced, would be to increase the number of workers who would be protected by the law. For example, a worker employed for the duration of a building contract or for a harvest would be afforded new rights.

Parental leave and leave for family reasons Directive

This draft Directive would establish a new set of legal rights for workers, although there would be some overlap between some provisions of the Directive and the maternity leave rights given by the Employment Protection Act 1975. In comparison with other EC countries, the UK offers a relatively generous period of maternity leave, but by the same standards the conditions and benefits attached to it are not generous. It is difficult to assess the likely impact of the draft Directive on existing practice because in some cases collective agreements supplement and add to the UK legal requirements. For example, while the CBI claim that legal parental leave provisions would increase the operational costs of businesses, the House of Lords concludes that 'there is no convincing evidence one way or the other that parental leave would raise industry's costs.'[31] Similarly, in relation to the clauses relating to leave for family reasons, it is difficult to assess their impact accurately. It can reasonably be argued that such provisions would create few difficulties, as many employers already grant such leave. However, the Directive would bring legal prescription into an area which is traditionally settled by collective bargaining or by contractual arrangements between the individual employee and the employer.

Vredeling Directive

If implemented, the draft Vredeling Directive would have a far-reaching impact: it goes way beyond the existing provisions in the United Kingdom for disclosure of information for collective bargaining purposes and the requirements for notification and consultation on impending redundancies contained in the Employment Protection Act 1975. The precise contents of this proposed Directive, both in its original and revised forms, is discussed in Chapter II, while Chapter XI assesses its likely impact on UK practice.

Clearly, if implemented, these proposed Directives would have major ramifications for British employment law and practice. But in the current political environment inside the Community, it is highly unlikely that any of these proposals will be adopted by the Council. Indeed, in Commission circles it is widely accepted that the Vredeling proposal is for all intents and purposes no longer on the negotiating table. Similarly, as mentioned earlier in the book, Commission officials in interviews with the authors, indicated that the Part-time and Temporary Work Directives are not now being pursued with any vigour.

Conclusions

Four main points arise from the discussion in this chapter. First, most of the proposed Directives which would have required far-reaching changes to British law have yet to be ratified by the Council of Ministers. Secondly, and following on from the above point, most of the social legislation that has been passed by the Community has either only paralleled existing UK legislation or, given time, would have been introduced domestically anyway. The only exception to these two general conclusions is the Community's equal opportunities legislation. Both as a result of Article 119 of the Treaty of Rome and subsequent secondary legislation on the subject, the Community has been able to have a direct impact on British equality laws. However, and this is the third conclusion, the full impact of the Community equality legislation as well as its Transfer of Undertakings Directive on the British employment environment has been cushioned as a result of actions by the UK Government. The current Conservative administration has successfully used its control over the legal ports of entry by which Community law is passed into national law to limit the influence of these aspects of European law. The final conclusion is that where the Community legislative machinery has been successfully used by individuals – for instance the Marshall and Hayward cases – the results owe more to the persistence and patience of those involved than to the easy accessibility and operation of the EC judicial system. In other words, the complex and drawn-out procedures which have to be gone through fully to exploit the advantages of European law act as a major disincentive to people using that system.

Overall, then, it can be concluded that although the EC has obliged British Governments to introduce labour and equality legislation which otherwise probably would not have been implemented, the Community's legal influence on the UK employment environment has failed to reach its maximum feasible level. Despite minor changes introduced by the Single European Act, it is highly unlikely that the Council will ratify any legislation in the near future which will have any substantial impact on Britain. The only possible way the Community's legal influence could increase is if the Court of Justice, particularly after the reforms contained in the Single European Act are implemented, makes rulings which could have wide-ranging repercussions. This is only a speculative prediction, and the most likely scenario is that the Community legal influence on Britain's employment environment will not change dramatically.

Notes and References

1 Relatively few comprehensive introductory texts exist on EC law. Probably the best is USHER, J. A. *European Community law and national law: the irreversible transfer*. London University Association for Contemporary European Studies, London 1981

2 See DAUSES, M. 'The Protection of Fundamental Rights in the

Community Legal Order', *European Law Review* Vol 10 No 6 1985 pp 398–421

3 For a discussion of the notion of direct applicability *see* PESCATORE, P. 'The Doctrine of "Direct Effect": An Infant Disease', *European Law Review*, Vol 8 No 3 1983, p 155–179

4 Case 26/62 Van Gend & Loos (1963) ECR, (Nature of Community Law, Rights and Obligations of Individuals)

5 Case 106/77 Simmenthal (1978) ECR 629 (Community Law, direct applicability: primacy)

6 HOWE, G. 'The Future of the European Community', *International Affairs*, Spring 1984, p 37

7 See KOVAR, R. 'The relationship between Community law and national law', in *European Commission, Thirty Years of Community Law*, European Perspectives, Brussels 1981

8 WALLACE, W. 'The EC: More than a regime, less than a Federation', in WALLACE, W. *et al 'Policy-Making in the European Community'*, Wiley, London 1982 p 318

9 'Arnull, Article 119 and Equal Pay for Work of Equal Value', *European Law Review*, Vol 11 No 3 1986 p 203

10 See DOCKSEY, C. 'The Enforcement of Community Law at National Level', *Social Europe* No 1 1988 pp 21–27

11 cited in DOCKSEY, C. 'The Promotion of Equality', in McCRUDDEN, C. (ed) *Women, Employment and European Equality Law*, 1987 p 7

12 HEPPLE, B. 'The Crisis in EEC labour Law', *The Industrial Law Journal* Vol 16 No 2 1987 pp 77–78

13 See *Industrial Relations Review and Report*, October 1978

14 HEPPLE, B. The Transfer of Undertakings (Protection of Employment Relations) *The Industrial Law Journal* Vol 11 No 1 1982 pp 29–42, p 29

15 See IDS Labour Law Report 'The Transfer of Undertakings Regulations', London 1985

16 See DAVIES, P. 'European Equality Legislation, UK Legislative Policy and Industrial Relations, in McCrudden, *op cit*

17 ibid p 33

18 Case 61/81, Commission of the European Communities v United Kingdom (1982) I.C.R. 578 (E.C.J.)

19 See McCRUDDEN, C. 'Equal Pay for Work of Equal Value: the Equal Pay (Amendment) Regulations 1983, '*The Industrial Law Journal* Vol 12 No 4 1983 p 197-220

20 *Financial Times* June 8, 1988

21 LEENAN, A. 'Equal Treatment of Male and Female Employees under European Community Law', *Legal Issues of European Integration No 1* 1986 pp 91-115

22 For a full account of this legal episode *see* ARNULL, A. *op cit*

23 RUBENSTEIN, R. 'The Equal Treatment Directive and UK Law', in McCrudden, *op cit*, p 99

24 ATKINS, S. *et al.* 'Pensions and the European Community Equality Legislation' in McCrudden *op cit*

25 These points were made during the course of interviews with Senior Officials from the DHSS

26 See *Equal Opportunities Review* No 18 March/April 1988 p 8-12

27 cited in *Industrial Relations Review and Report* February 1980 p 3

28 House of Lords Select Committee on European Communities Temporary Work, 6th Report Sesson 1982-83

29 HEPPLE, B. memorandum to the House of Lords Select Committee on European Communities Voluntary Part-Time Work, 19th Report Session 1981-82 p 24

30 See House of Lords Select Committee on European Communities, Temporary Work, 6th Report Session 1982–83 p 37

31 See House of Lords Select Committee on European Communities, Parental Leave and Leave for Family Reasons, 3rd Report Session 1984-85 paragraph 115

Chapter VIII

The EC and the Local Authorities

So far, consideration of the effects on Britain of the European Community's social policy has been focused on the national level. The general pattern set by other studies on the impact of the EC on Britain and different policy areas is for the analysis to finish here. But it is important to look beyond the national level and identify and assess the impact of the Community on employment policies and practices within organisations. This and the subsequent chapter detail the principle research findings in the public sector; Chapter X outlines the results from the private sector.

The public sector is of particular significance in relation to the European Community in at least three respects. First, as indicated in Chapter VII, the public sector has a unique constitutional position. There is certain legislation, and in particular there are certain legal judgements, which in effect apply directly to all aspects of governmental employment. Secondly, aspects of EC administration have been more relevant for the public sector than for the private sector. This and the next chapter will show the range of EC institutions which deal with specific aspects of public sector operation and the way in which elements of EC funding are in practice targetted upon public sector bodies. Thirdly, the public sector in the UK not only has distinctive industrial relations machinery not found in the private sector, but has been used quite consciously for 'experiments' in employee relations. These experiments have in many cases had a noticeably 'European' flavour, in that they have been built upon developments in the other European states or proposals made by the European Community. The obvious example is provided by the 'Working Director' approaches in the public enterprise sector, and there are less visible but equally real links in the development offices and equal opportunities offices of the public authorities.

Two broad categories were examined within the public sector: local authorities and public enterprises (as at 1987). These two categories are quite distinct in their organisation, function and control, so this chapter deals with the local authorities. Chapter IX examines the public enterprises.

Local Authorities

This chapter examines the linkages between the local authorities and the EC. The analysis focuses mainly on: the direct institutional linkages between local councils and their representative organisations; the degree of convergence or similarity between EC legislation and policies on employee relations matters and those which actually exist in the local government sector; and the success of local government in attracting monies from the various EC structural funds to assist their economic development projects. To obtain the necessary information for this examination, we conducted a series of interviews with officials from the national representative bodies for local government, and with staff in six local authorities throughout Britain, and extracted data from the Community's computers on the dispersion of EC Social Fund grants in Britain.

In order to examine the contacts between the local authorities and the EC it is necessary first to remind ourselves of the local government institutional structure in Britain. For the purposes of this chapter it is probably best to mention the International Union of Local Authorities (IULA): British section. This is the organisation which brings together local authorities and municipalities at the world level. It organises both international and regional congresses which decide general policies and broad principles of interest to local government. The organisation also makes an impact on the work of international organisations, for example the EC, the OECD and the ILO. The IULA: British section is the body which formally organises British local government contacts and linkages with international institutions. Policies and initiatives of the British section are determined by a governing council made up of the various national representative organisations for local governments. The Council also organises international and bilateral delegations and meetings. In addition, the British section, by producing regular information bulletins and briefings and occasional detailed pamphlets, also operates as an information service for local authorities so that they remain abreast of international developments and issues which may affect them.

At the national level, local authorities all belong to one or more local government associations. These associations are:

Association of County Councils (ACC)
Association of Metropolitan Authorities (AMA)
Association of District Councils (ADC)

These organisations are political in character. There are internal elections determining whether the Labour Party or Conservative Party has the majority on the national boards, though the custom and practice is that the Party which is in the majority tends to avoid pushing a totally partisan line. Each association has its own secretariat whose tasks are to develop policy, and undertake research for the various national committees, and to give technical advice to individual local authorities. The main purpose of these associations is to represent the view of their members at the national level, particularly within Government.

Alongside these national associations is the Local Authorities Conditions of Service Advisory Board (LACSAB), the employers' organisation for local government. Its main task is to co-ordinate the employers' position in national negotiations, and advise individual local councils on industrial relations and labour law matters. The supreme decision-making body of LACSAB is the Council of the Board; made up of locally elected councillors representing local government associations. The Council formulates the employee relations policies to be pursued by employers in forthcoming negotiations. The actual negotiations with trade unions are conducted in over 40 joint councils which are more or less sub-committees of the Council. These joint councils are serviced by a Secretariat which monitors industrial relations developments, and carries out research on specific topics designated by the Council. Fairly close relationships exist between the secretariat of LACSAB and the national associations.[1] However, considerable efforts are made to ensure that the activities of LACSAB and the national associations remain distinct: LACSAB confines itself to industrial relations issues, while the national associations concentrate on policy issues such as local government finance or economic development.

The Local Authorities and Europe

The formal connection between British local government and Europe is shown in Figure VIIIi:

Figure VIIIi

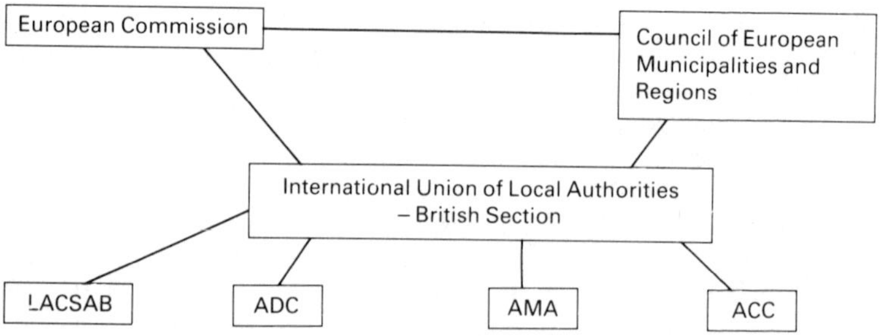

The Council of European Municipalities and Regions consists of local authority organisations from the member states of the EC. At present it is outside the official EC framework, but moves are being made to designate the Council as a social partner. In practice, this will make little difference, for Commission officials already attend its meetings. In addition, the Commission relies heavily on the Council for obtaining information. The British delegation is made up of representatives from LACSAB and the national associations who sit on the IULA: British section's governing body. When attending meetings in Europe these representatives put the view of IULA: British section and not those of their own organisation. Policies within IULA: British section are reached on the basis of consensus and unanimity. Meetings of the Council of European Municipalities and Regions occur about two/three times a year. The general view of this Council, and British participation within it, is that it is important to have a formal organisation representing the interests of local authorities at the European level. But in terms of practical benefits, the informal contacts between different national local government associations, and between national associations and Commission officials arising from these meetings, is considered to be more important.

Each national association also undertakes work in relation to EC activity independently of this formal structure. For the most part, this work mainly relates to the Community's structural funds, especially as regards their impact on local authority economic development policies. For example, the associations lobby government departments, particularly the Department of Employment, in an effort to obtain changes in the administration and implementation of the structural funds which would favour local authorities. As well as mounting pressure at the national level to obtain changes to the operation of EC funds, the national associations also advise individual local authorities, by producing information guides and answering individual enquiries on Community matters. National associations do not have extensive contacts with Commission officials, but there is occasional communication between the two on an ad hoc basis. Some national associations have started to organise delegations to Brussels with the aim of increasing knowledge of the Community.

National associations on occasion lobby MEPs to canvas their support on issues relating to local government inside the European Parliament. Individual councillors who sit on national associations use their political contacts towards this end. Thus national associations appear to have an active stance on EC matters in so far as these affect British local government.

LACSAB officials keep abreast of general Community developments which effect British local government, through formal and informal links with IULA: British section. In relation to EC industrial relations initiatives they mainly keep informed by reading secondary sources such as specialist magazines, and information bulletins from the Commission. But on an issue which they regard as particularly important, they seek further information from the Commission and the British

Government and then study in detail what should be LACSAB's response. Thus for example when the draft Vredeling Directive was proposed by the Commission, LACSAB wrote requesting clarification of whether the proposal applied to the local government sector. After the Commission considered the issue, Ivor Richards, the Social Affairs Commissioner, replied by saying that the draft Vredeling Directive does not apply to local and national government departments.[2] At the same time, LACSAB tries to avoid commenting on the merits or otherwise of particular proposals. For example, on the EC proposals on parental leave, part-time and temporary workers, LACSAB did not commit itself to any particular position, and did not join with other employers' organisations in campaigning against these positions. Probably the main reason for this neutral response to EC initiatives has been to avoid unnecessary friction amongst elected councillors from different political parties who sit on LACSAB committees.

An interesting development in recent years has been for individual local authorities, or groups, within Britain to combine with the IULA: British section to make contacts with other local authorities in different members states to co-ordinate activity on specific economic development issues. For example, local authorities in the West Midlands joined together to organise a conference for local authorities in each member state where the car industry was the main manufacturing employer, to assess whether they could develop a joint European economic programme for the industry.[3] It would appear that the membership of the EC, and the various institutional contacts this involves, is gradually having an impact on the local authorities, as policy-makers begin to think increasingly in a European context.

Thus various formal and informal links exist between national local government associations and the EC, but these links are not extensive, nor do they amount to a major aspect of the work of national government institutions. In most of these organisations, the EC portfolio constitutes only one aspect of the workload of an official in the policy division. The organisations do keep abreast of EC developments and when it is considered necessary they make representations to Government on EC-related matters. Overall, the attitude of these national organisations towards the EC is positive. Most of the local government associations fully support the EC activities in the sphere of employment initiatives. When interviewed, LACSAB officials expressed a view neither for nor against the nature of EC policies and proposals on employee relations. This agnostic view was primarily due to the political character of the organisation.

Local Authority Industrial Relations and EC employee relations initiatives

This section examines how the industrial relations practices in the local authorities compare with EC initiatives in the areas of equal opportunities, working time arrangements, employment involvement and individual rights (mainly health and safety). This analysis will give some insight into the extent to which EC initiatives in a particular area mirror actual practice, and will allow an assessment to be made about whether the Community is a catalyst for change in the industrial relations field. In addition, it allows an assessment to be made of the extent to which local government industrial relations policies were influenced by the Community.

In relation to their industrial relations practices, the local authorities can be divided into four categories, namely, those with active policies, those with semi-active policies, those who have passive policies and the 'non-policy' situations. Active policy refers to the situation where a particular area has become a priority for action, or where a far-reaching policy programme is being implemented; semi-active policy describes the situation where a policy is drawn up, but the envisaged action is of a limited scale, or does not have priority status. The passive policy scenario is when the local authority has a policy in name only; 'no policy' is self-explanatory.

Equal Opportunities

Before examining the equal opportunities policies of the six interviewed local authorities, it is useful to outline where the local authorities stand in equal value cases. There have been a number of settlements at preliminary tribunal stage: for instance *O'Dougherty v. Clwyd County Council* was settled in favour of the applicant, who received £12,000. However, only one equal value case of any signficance has come before the Courts in the local authority sector, namely *Leverton v. Clwyd County Council*. In that case a nursery nurse claimed that she was doing work of equal value to that done by male clerical workers employed by the Council in different establishments. But the applicant and her comparators were covered by the same local authority conditions of service, and there were many common terms and conditions of employment; for example, holiday provisions, notice and special leave. However, the Employment Appeals Tribunal decided that because there were differences in hours of work and holidays between Mrs Leverton and her comparators, common terms and conditions were not observed and therefore her claim was not allowed to go ahead. As a result of this ruling, cross-establishment claims for equal value have been severely limited.

Two out of the six local authorities interviewed had active policy action programmes in relation to equal opportunities. Those programmes have involved the establishment of new council committees on equal opportunities, the creation of new posts such as Women Officers and Ethnic Minority Officers and the rigorous implementation of equal opportunity and anti-discrimination policies more generally. These policies are enacted at two different levels. One relates to the internal practices of the local authorities. The policies implemented at this level are wide-ranging, including equal value studies, examination of the 'sex and race structure' of higher-paid managerial posts, the introduction of positive-action programmes in certain areas which amount to preference being given to either women or ethnic minority candidates, and training awareness schemes, particularly for personnel managers in charge of recruitment and promotion. The other level concerns the implementation by local authorities of contract compliance policies – their use of public procurement to ensure that suppliers are also equal opportunities employers. Contract compliance policies are essentially codes of conduct, a checklist against which the local authority examines such issues as how many women and ethnic minority people are employed in supplying companies and the nature and scope of their equal opportunities policies. If a company is found not to be an equal opportunities employer, it may not be awarded local authority contracts. These policies have generated a good deal of controversy: they have been criticised as unwarranted interference in the affairs of independent companies; the effectiveness of the policies has also been questioned.

Two of the other local authorities pursued semi-active policies. This entailed adopting a formal equal opportunities policy and introducing some affirmative action policies on the issue. The adoption of the policy in these local authorities did not however lead to any significant organisational changes – the policy was administered by the existing personnel staff. Awareness training sessions were held for managers and other senior staff on the issue. A number of job-evaluation exercises relating to equal pay have been conducted on an ad hoc basis. But it was by no means a fully-fledged policy.

In neither local authority was there a formal evaluation mechanism to review the effectiveness of the policy. Senior personnel managers and the relevant administrating staff undertook such a review on an ad hoc basis. The degree of the centralisation of the personnel function appeared to affect the execution of the policy in the two authorities. In the less centralised authority, the execution of the policy was, for the most part, in the hands of department officials. As a result, the central personnel unit had not extensive knowledge of the operation of the policy. Moreover, because of the devolved personnel structure, the policy according to the senior personnel manager was being implemented in an uneven way. The centralised local authority did not experience these problems, or at least not to the same extent. Having responsibility for recruitment interviews, being able to introduce policies on a uniform basis, and so on, unquestionably gave his local authority a better opportunity to monitor the policy.

Of the remaining two local authorities, one had an equal opportunities policy, but adopted a passive approach to the subject, while the other had no policy on the issue. In both cases, it was felt that a formal active approach to the question was not required, as the personnel department were deemed to be sufficiently professional not to act in a discriminatory way.

Thus the equal opportunities pursued by local authorities are extremely diverse – ranging from active policies to no policy whatsoever. The main influences on whether or not a local authority pursues an equal opportunities policy appears to be the political composition of the majority group in the council. It goes without saying that the EC had no influence on the two local authorities which had done next to nothing on the issue. Amongst the local authorities which were semi-active on the issues, the view was expressed that their equal opportunities policy was not inspired by the EC. Instead, it was argued that the adoption of the policies was the outcome of a political belief that firm action was needed to ensure that women and minority groups were not discriminated against. However, personnel managers in both authorities in this category did say that specific legal binding EC Directives did force them to undertake a limited amount of additional action. For example, the European Court of Justice ruling on equal pay for equal value in cases against the British Government induced the local authorities to carry out job evaluation studies.

One might expect those local authorities implementing active equal opportunity policies to be influenced the most by the Community initiatives. But this is not a straightforward correlation. Certainly those officers charged with enacting the policies fully supported the Community's action in the area. The various legally binding Directives on equal opportunities were seen as establishing a very important floor of minimum rights for women across the Community, and the various action programmes drawn up by the Commission were regarded as providing an additional support to those working in the area. But in terms of helping the officers implement equal opportunities programmes it was suggested that the experience of local municipal administrations in the USA in encouraging greater racial equality was of more value than the provisions of EC law. (Policies such as contract compliance, and internal equality audits now being pursued by a number of local authorities in Britain were pioneered in the United States during the late sixties and seventies).

It is worth noting that these local authorities adopt a much broader notion of equal opportunities than the one which underpins many of the Community's actions. In particular, while Community initiatives focus almost exclusively on women, the 'active' local government authorities in the survey adopt a wider definition, covering ethnic minorities, the disabled and gay and lesbian people. This is a further indication that the approach adopted by these local authorities was only superficially influenced by the Community.

Working Time Arrangements

Five out of six local authorities simply adhered to the working time arrangements negotiated at the national level. Only one authority tried to supplement the national agreement with local action. This authority embarked on several initiatives. One was to bring the manual workers' working week into line with white-collar staff – i.e. 35 hours. This policy was based on a decision made by the ruling Labour group and not one developed by the officials. The same council, also as a result of a political decision, had introduced a policy on parental leave which owed a great deal to the Community's proposed Directive on the subject. In an interview with the councillor responsible for the policy, it was stated that the Community proposal on parental leave motivated her to propose a similar initiative for the Council.

In the other five local authorities, no formal policy existed on matters such as a parental or compassionate leave. The common view was that these policies were best administered in a flexible and informal way. In fact, amongst this group of five councils, only one initiative was undertaken on working time. This was the outcome of a policy development by one of the senior personnel managers. The scheme was to provide early retirement for certain occupational categories, and then fill the vacant posts with 'young blood' candidates. Although the policy had only been in operation for two years, 30 people had taken the opportunity to retire early (and 30 new appointments had been made). But this scheme was the exception. The reason most often given for so closely following nationally determined agreements was that in the present political environment, it was important to show that national negotiations are essential to the smooth functioning of local government.

None of the local authorities were unduly concerned with the contents of the draft Commission legislation on the protection of part-time and temporary workers, as they thought it would make no significant difference to their existing practice. However, all the personnel managers interviewed did say that they were against the principle of such legislation. This was a constant theme in all interviews with personnel staff – Community legislation, or proposed legislation, was regarded as an unwarranted intrusion into the British voluntarist system of free collective bargaining.

Employee Involvement

As mentioned earlier, because of the particular status of local authorities – the fact that councillors are elected to run and control their operations – they have been declared exempt from the Vredeling and Fifth Directives, if these were ever to be implemented. Thus in the formal sense, the Community initiatives on employee involvement have no bearing on local authorities. However, the local authorities do have formal structures at the local level. Although these take a variety of forms, they all amount to negotiating forums for the discussion of local issues. Four out of the six local authorities made determined efforts to limit the scope of local negotiations; partly because they were reluctant to see the trade unions gaining extra local leverage. Personnel managers in the other two authorities, although keeping a firm limit on what was negotiated, stated that they encouraged wide-ranging discussions in their consultative committees. They felt this gave them the opportunity to know what were the main grievances of members, and also facilitated the establishment of a close informal working relationship with the trade unions. These different approaches were mainly the result of the differing managerial styles adopted by individual personnel officers, and were totally unrelated to EC deliberations.

Health and Safety

The local authorities had very similar formal structures covering health and safety. Each had a central health and safety unit, usually composed of four or five people responsible for developing the council's health and safety policy and ensuring that it was effectively implemented. Beneath this level, elected or nominated safety representatives in all departments were charged with ensuring the policy was put into practice. Without observing the operation of the health and safety policies over a period of time it is difficult to make an accurate assessment of their effectiveness. However, what is clear is that all the officials interviewed stated that as far as they were aware, there was no direct influence from the Community.

Personnel Policies

It appears that the nature and type of the personnel policies pursued in local government are largely determined by the political composition of the majority group in individual councils. In Labour-controlled councils, far-reaching policies on such things as equal opportunities are encouraged, whilst in Conservative-controlled authorities the tendency is to follow national agreements on such issues. Characteristics such as the size of the authorities and the willingness of the personnel officers to initiate policies have an impact, but perhaps this is not as large as in the private sector.

On the day-to-day running of the personnel function, most officials interviewed thought that the influence of the Community was virtually non-existent. But in terms of forming the context within which personnel policies are developed for local government, most thought that the EC did have an influence. In particular, the EC influenced two areas. It exerted a legal influence, especially in the equal opportunities area, by laying down certain statutes. It also influenced the outlook of local councillors on certain issues.

Although the evidence suggests that the EC policies and labour law have only a marginal influence on employee relations policies in local government, this may not always be the case. For example, two recent publications suggest that many local authorities may be vulnerable to claims for equal pay for work of equal value. One of the studies indicates that despite the incorporation of equal value principles into the revised grading structure for local authority manual workers, many women will still earn less than men on the same grade.[4] The second study shows that job evaluation schemes in the Greater London Whitley Council, which covers white collar employees in most London boroughs, is discriminating, because it consistently under-rewards those jobs typically performed by women and over-rewards those characteristically done by male professionals.[5] Thus it is by no means beyond the bounds of probability that local government trade unions will seize this opportunity and use EC law to increase the pay and conditions of their women members.

Direct contact with the EC

Since the turn of the eighties, economic development has become a key local authority objective. Before then, initiatives in this field were limited to the provision of factory units. Now a wide range of activities, from the provision of financial support for small business to the establishment of original employment and training projects, are a common feature of the work of local authorities. To help finance some of their economic development initiatives, many local authorities have tried to obtain grants from the various European structural funds. EC liaison officers have been appointed by a number of local councils to co-ordinate activities in relation to Europe. As the links between local authority and the EC structural funds are now so significant it is worth examining in more detail the three key sources of finance: the Social Fund, the Regional Development Fund and the European Investment Bank.

The EC Social Fund

For most of the early and mid eighties the UK was one of the countries which received most from the EC Social Fund. It has been suggested that this situation arose as the result of the Commission's attempts to placate British protestations about the size of its contribution to the Community budget. While this cannot totally be ruled out, an equally plausible reason was put forward by Commission officials in interviews with the authors, namely, that the UK applications for Social Fund grants are superior to those from other member states. Approximately two-thirds of the Social Fund allocation to Britain goes to the MSC to help fund some of their programmes, particularly those relating to youth training. But as already mentioned, since 1981 local authorities have been increasingly active and successful in trying to obtain Social Fund grants.

The tables in Appendix 4 detail the amount of monies local authorities have obtained from the Fund between 1981–1985. The figures were extracted from the Community's computerised data base. It should be pointed out that some local authorities have a better chance of obtaining social funds that others, for the rules of the Fund stipulate that areas of high and long-term unemployment and/or of industrial restructuring should be given priority. There are 36 'priority' local authorities in Britain. These are designated by the Commission from an analysis of the most recent labour-force statistics: a list of these local authorities is also included as Appendix 5. As would be expected, the figures show that all the priority areas have benefited from the Social Fund. But it also shows that 24 non-priority areas have also received grants: indicating that non-priority local authorites which are well organised in relation to Europe can be successful in attracting money from the various structural funds.

In accordance with the established guidelines (see p 84) the bulk of the Social Fund grants go to training projects. Britain's regional unemployment blackspots receive the lion's share of the money. But there are indications that grants are guided towards those regions which are considered to be important in the national context. Thus, for example, when the plight of Merseyside hit the headlines after the 1981 riots, Social Fund grants increased from £864,590 to £2,226,944 in one year.

Similarly, when the deindustrialisation problems of the West Midlands were highlighted, allocations increased sharply from £1,662,385 in 1983 to £4,999,526 in 1985. Beyond this peculiarity the depressed regions appear broadly to have benefited equally from the Social Fund. The only possible exception is Wales, where local authorities received lower levels of cash aid than the other regions. The level of grants given under the employment grants section of the Social Fund are smaller than the amounts allocated to training projects, and for the most part they are targeted to the 'priority' local authorities. Strathclyde, which placed more emphasis on this instrument as a means of employment creation, received the most from this section.

It has been argued that a 'learning curve' effect has operated in relation to the attempts by local authorities to get money from the Social Fund; in other words, the local authorities will become more efficient at getting money once they have made several applications.[6] At one level this is right: the tables show that numerous authorities have gradually increased the amount of money they have received from Brussels. But there are also examples where local authorities have received money one year and nothing the following year (as with Nottinghamshire, in 1982–3), or where the actual amount of cash aid received declines from one year to the next (West Glamorgan 1983–4), and finally where the local authority has benefited only once from the Fund. Thus gaining experience of the Social Fund application process does not in itself guarantee future success, nor does it seem to indicate that local authorities become more ambitious when making future applications.

It would be misleading to overstress the role played by the Social Fund in Britain. Compared with the Manpower Services Commission budget, the amounts channelled to training initiatives from the Fund are miniscule. But within the local context the Fund does have a positive impact: the £3,853,834 training grant given to Greater Manchester in 1985 is bound to have added value to such initiatives in the area. Overall, the grants appear to go to the areas that need them most. But local authorities who are enterprising and organised in relation to the European Community tend to benefit disproportionately from the Fund. The fact that Britain receives more grants than any other member state other than Italy indicates that the applications from UK local authorities are of a high professional standard. However, other member states are trying hard to catch up and if Britain wants to stay near the top then local authorities must continue making improvements in their approach to the EC.

The European Regional Development Fund

The type of schemes eligible for ERDF assistance are capital-intensive-projects involving the provision of new or improved facilities which make a contribution to the economic development of the area. (Projects such as housing, schools and hospitals are excluded.) Essentially, the schemes relate to all forms of transportation and communications, energy supplies, water, sewage, land drainage and flood protection, and tourist infrastructures.

One of the most contentious aspects of the operation of the ERDF is the problem of additionality. At its simplest, additionality is the principle that Community resources should complement those given by member states through their own financial instruments for regional development projects. Problems arose, however, when the Conservative administration under Mrs Thatcher challenged that principle, at least implicitly. On the industrial side, the Government seeks ERDF grants on projects which have already received national aid, thereby taking ERDF money as partial reimbursement for its own aid. Similar difficulties arise with infrastructure projects, although in a somewhat different form. If a local authority receives ERDF grants for a capital project, it is allowed to use that grant to reduce the interest charges and debt service costs it would otherwise have to pay. However, it is stated policy not to allow ERDF monies to fund any new projects.

European Investment Bank

Table VIIIi shows the major UK borrowers from the EIB and reveals that, relative to other organisations, local authorities have actively sought money from the EIB – with a good deal of success.

Table VIIIi Major UK borrowers from the EIB, 1973-85

Group	Amount borrowed £m)	% of total
Electricity boards	1124.1	28.9
Water boards	606.0	15.6
Local authorities	519.54	13.4
British Nuclear Fuels	328.1	8.4
GPO/BT	256.9	6.6
BSC	205.85	5.3
BR	132.5	3.4
British Gas	93.7	2.4
Other state industries	34.95	0.9
Oil & chemical industry	174.5	4.5
Other private industry	221.1	5.7
Global loans	191.5	4.9
TOTAL	3888.74	100.0

Source: Barnes and Campbell 'UK Local Authorities and the European Investment Bank' '*Local Government Studies* Jan/Feb 1987'

Table VIIIii breaks down the local authority borrowers on a regional basis, although the results need to be interpreted with caution. The dominant position of Scotland is mainly due to Scottish local authorities

Table VIIIii Local authority borrowing from the EIB, 1973-85

Region	Amount (£m)	% of total	No of LAs who borrowed Upper tier	Lower tier
Scotland	280.275	54.0	12	2
N West	58.2	11.2	2	5
Wales	57.8	11.1	6	1
Yorkshire & Humberside	38.69	7.4	2	4
W Midlands	54.8	10.5	2	0
S West	11.8	2.3	1	0
S East	10.0	1.9	2	1
North	7.97	1.5	2	7
TOTAL	519.535	100.0	29	20

Source: Barnes and Campbell 'UK Local Authorities and the European Investment Bank' '*Local Government Studies* Jan/Feb 1987'

having responsibility for water (the English water boards are the second biggest UK borrower from EIB). Nearly half of the amount borrowed by Scottish authorities was for water projects. But even allowing for this factor the Scottish local authorities are still the biggest borrowers from the EIB for 'conventional' projects amongst British local authorities. Most of the capital finance in English and Welsh local authorities went towards road schemes and industrial estate developments in assisted areas (only four authorities were not designated assisted areas at the time when they borrowed EIB money). Of the 49 local authorities obtaining finance from the Bank, some 25 used it for the first time between 1982–1984, indicating that the use of the EIB by authorities is a relatively recent development.

While the EIB still represents only a very minor source of local authority borrowing, there are clear benefits for local authorities from using this resource. In particular, because of the relatively cheap interest rates, local authorities could be expected to save about £400,000 in every £1m if the money is borrowed from the EIB rather than from the more conventional sources. However, there are also drawbacks. First, the EIB, like most other EC funds, has been criticised for having a cumbersome and complex application and administrative procedure. Second, the main beneficiaries of EIB cheap money appear to be the county councils and the larger city councils. The smaller authorities, which may appreciate this type of finance more, have not so far received a lot of EIB finance. Part of the reason for this is that a lot of local authorities still remain ignorant of its existence. The appointment of CIPFFA Services Ltd as the Bank's agents for local authorities in Britain may go some way to alleviating this deficiency. Despite these criticisms, the evidence suggests that local authorities welcome the opportunity to use the EIB facility – approximately two-thirds of the local authorities which had borrowed from the EIB by 1982 have successfully negotiated more than one loan. At the same time, the EIB can hardly be described as an alternative to the traditional sources of local authority borrowing. Rather it is a useful addition, giving more options.

Getting Cash from Europe

All but one of the local authorities interviewed has applied for and been successful in obtaining money from Europe. The only exception was the Conservative-controlled shire county. However, at the time of the interview, that authority was in the process of appointing an EC Liaison Officer, and the anticipation was that before long it would be benefiting from European money. The other councils either had EC Liaison Officers, or assigned the EC portfolio to some existing members of staff. These officers relied heavily on the Department of Employment's Social Fund Office and the various local authority-related national bodies to be kept informed of the seemingly ever-changing rules and regulations governing the funds. All were of the view that these bodies provided an indispensable service, and that without them their authorities would not have been nearly so successful in obtaining funds from Europe.

There are a number of ways projects come to form the basis of the local authority's applications for EC grants. One is via the EC Liaison Officers, working closely with the economic development offices (which most authorities now have) to assess whether any of their projects could possibly qualify for EC money. This approach has given rise to some interesting EC funded projects. For example, one firm was given half the costs of sending three workers to Switzerland to learn how to operate new computerised machinery. Another firm which had invented a method of producing animal feed from chicken feathers received a grant to do further research in the area. Another way of developing projects for EC money is to build on ideas and schemes proposed by voluntary organisations. Most of these relate to training projects – for example 'women only' training workshops. Two of the authorities were quite ingenious in this area. They had set up quasi-independent voluntary training organisations through which they make applications for EC money: (voluntary organisations in Britain tend to avoid the weighted reduction scheme which is now in operation, see p 86). The Liaison Officers also do considerable animating work – encouraging their colleagues and voluntary organisations to develop projects which could attract EC money. This type of activity has been much less successful.

Work specifically geared to attracting EC funding does not appear to interest local authority staff other than those who have direct responsibility for EC affairs.

Most of the officers interviewed did air the general complaints about the Social Fund – that it is excessively complex, and that the local authority has to wait unduly long before actual grant payments are made. Some did say, however, that the situation was improving. The contentious question was raised: would EC-funded projects have proceeded anyway, even if no money from Europe was forthcoming? Officers in three of the local authorities suggested that the vast majority of projects put forward for EC money had already been earmarked for funding by the council, and those that had not probably would have ended up obtaining council money. In two local authorities the point was made that the nature of the application procedures made it very difficult for the local authority not to fund a project if it failed to get EC money. This was because projects have to be well-developed, which means spending considerable time planning the scheme, and in the process raising the hopes of many people, before an EC grant application can be made. For the local authority to abandon a project if it failed to secure EC money would cast it in a very bad light. So local authorities tend to fund the project totally if it is turned down by the EC fund administrators. Thus, EC funds do not appear to add directly to the number of schemes developed at the local level. Of course, where projects are successful in obtaining EC grants, local authority money is released to fund other schemes, which gives the authority the opportunity, at least, of increasing the number of projects it funds.

Other less tangible benefits also arise from local authorities applying for EC Funds. For instance, officers begin to think in an innovatory way about projects so that they will stand a better chance of receiving money. This original and innovatory thinking has resulted in new instruments being established to counter unemployment at the local level. In this sense, the mere existence of the funds may be acting as a catalyst for change.

For the most part, local authorities do not tend to lobby on the matter of rules and regulations of the various EC funds – they simply accept the framework as devised by the EC officials. The only exception to this was a local authority which is an active member of the Coal Communities Campaign which, amongst many other things, is trying to persuade the EC to direct money the entire year round to those areas which have recently experienced pit closures.

Local Authorities: Conclusions

The most direct and tangible link between British local government and the EC centres on the operation of the Community's structural funds. Since the early 1980s, British local authorities have considerably increased their efforts to obtain grants and loans from EC sources. These efforts have not been motivated by an upsurge of Europeanisation on the part of the local councils, but by the need to obtain new sources of revenue as the financial situation for local government in Britain has become gradually more constrained.[7] Although most of the local authorities complained about the cumbersome and complex rules and regulations governing the various funds, most had a positive attitude towards these Community initiatives. The general view was that Social Fund grants had only an indirect impact: most of the projects financed by Social Fund grants would have proceeded even if no such monies had been secured. There is evidence that as a result of greater contact with the Community, some councillors have changed their views about Europe. For example, some Labour Party councillors who were previously lukewarm towards the Community have as a result of their involvement in EC affairs at the local level revised their stance and are now in the forefront of changing Labour Party policy on the matter.[8]

Direct institutional as well as informal links exist between local government national associations and Community and other European organisations. These links have been established so that local government organisations can lobby and influence the direction of Community policies on matters like local economic development. Community officials also find these links fruitful for keeping in touch with practical developments in Britain. Both sides regard these linkages as useful and worthwhile, but officials from the local government national associations do not view the connection with Europe as a key aspect of their role. In relation to other national matters, the connection is regarded as very much secondary. However, the attempt to obtain a concerted European local government policy towards the car industry can be seen as evidence of the fact that a more strategic and calculating strategy is beginning to be adopted by some local government bodies and officials.

In terms of direct impact on employment policies and practices in the local authorities, EC influence is negligible, though indirectly the legal framework may have some impact. Much less direct, but perhaps more long-term, influences may be suggested, in that policies and proposals produced by the Commission have influenced the 'policy outlook' of certain councillors interested in employee relations in local government. For example, one councillor interviewed stated that the Council's policy on parental leave and leave for family reasons stemmed directly from reading the Commission's proposals on the subject. Thus, in sum the

EC has a minor influence on employment policies and practices in UK local authorities, but one that is growing and developing.

Notes and References

1 Interviews with officials from LACSAB and national associations

2 See Association of District Councils, *EEC Policies: Views on issues of Concern to District Councils,* London 1985

3 See the chapter on International Activities of Local Authorities in COATES, K *Joint Action for Jobs,* Spokesman Books, Nottingham 1986

4 London Equal Value Steering Group, *A Question of Earnings,* London 1987

5 London Equal Value Steering Group, *Job Evaluation and Equal Value,* London 1987

6 GLASSON, J and McGEE, T. *EEC Aid and Local Authorities: Some Research Findings – an Interim Report,* Oxford Polytechnic 1984

7 This finding coincides with the findings of several of the papers in MELLORS, C *Promoting local authorities in the European Community,* IULA Discussion Paper No 1 1987, London

8 See GRAHL, J and TEAGUE, P. 'The British Labour Party and the European Community', *Political Quarterly* Vol 59 No 1, Jan-March 1988

Chapter IX

Public Enterprises and the European Community

This chapter focuses exclusively on public enterprises and the European Community. A public enterprise – or 'public undertaking' in the EC's vocabulary – is defined by the Community as one 'over which the public authorities may exercise directly or indirectly a dominant influence by virtue of their ownership of it, their financial participation therein, and on the rules which govern it'.[1] There is, of course, a wide spectrum of different types of public enterprise, diverse in function, organisation and size, but they share, inter alia, two features of relevance here. Unlike private sector businesses, public enterprises are established for the most part to achieve a wider social, or politically defined, or economic, goal. Thus, public enterprises have been set up to establish state influence or control over strategic areas of the economy, to assist regional development, to promote wealth, to reduce perceived inefficiency and the misallocation of resources, and to stave off industrial decline. Moreover, in the UK at any rate, public enterprises have been used as the testing ground for experiments in industrial and employee relations. For instance, in the seventies when workers' democracy was much in vogue, the idea was first experimented with in British Steel and the Post Office. These distinctive features are sufficient grounds to justify a specific examination of how UK public enterprises relate to the European Community.

This chapter addresses the connection between four British public enterprises – British Coal, British Steel, British Rail, and British Shipbuilders – and the European Community. It focuses on how the latter may have influenced the employment practices in these companies. First, the institutional links are outlined: both those common to all public enterprises and those between the various companies and the EC. Then an appraisal is made of how key personnel in the various public enterprises view these links, and how much signficance is placed upon them. After this, there is an examination of how the companies have adapted to formal EC legislation in the sphere of employment practices. Finally, an appraisal is made of how informal EC pressures or possible EC policy have impinged upon the behaviour of personnel managers. The conclusion tries to place the discussion in context by gauging the signficance of EC influences on recent employment policy developments within the various organisation.

Public Enterprise at the Community level

The significance of public enterprises has always been recognised by the Commission and other Community officials. These officials were instrumental in the establishment of the European Centre for Public Enterprises (CEEP) in 1965, and in the conferring upon it of the status of a social partner. In strict constitutional terms, the representatives of public enterprises have an equal voice with the trade unions (ETUC) and the employers' organisation (UNICE) inside the EC machinery, although in practice they will on occasion combine with UNICE and organisations representing agricultural employers and the liberal professions in a European Employers' Liaison Group. The Statute of CEEP states its principal objectives to be:

(a) to keep public enterprises informed of the activities of the institutions of the European Communities, especially those aspects of particular interest to public enterprises;
(b) to keep under review the position and problems of public enterprises in the light of the progressive development of European organisations and to propose common solutions which, as a prior requirement, serve the general interest;
(c) to maintain close contact with the Community institutions; to convey to these institutions in the form of opinions, the view of public enterprises on the development of the European Community, to advise the Community institutions of the experiences and problems of public enterprises; to secure adequate representation of public enterprises in any consultative or specialist committees set up, or which may be set up in the European Communities;
(d) to develop contacts and cooperation with other 'social partners'.

CEEP's formal contacts with EC institutions take the following forms:

i advisory Committees;
ii representation on the governing boards of the European Centre for Vocational Training and the European Foundation for the Improvement of Living and Working Conditions;
iii the Economic and Social Committee;
iv the Standing Committee on Employment.

Obviously, the Centre also has a wide-ranging set of informal contacts with the Commission and the other social partners, though whether or not CEEP has any influence on EC policy-making is open to question.

Community industrial and employment policies and the public sector

Several inducements exist for national public enterprises to participate fully in EC affairs. One is that the Commission has attempted to establish fully-fledged industrial policies in sectors dominated by public enterprises. This is particularly the case in the steel and coal industries. Between 1974 and 1984, the workforce of the steel industry was, for example, slashed by two-fifths.

The Community's Steel Policy

Not long after Britain entered the Community the European steel industry fell into a deep slump with an immediate and dramatic impact on output, employment and investment. So severe was the reversal of fortunes, that by mid 1975 the European steel-makers (with the exception of the German producers) were pressing the Commission to use its powers and declare that the industry was in a state of 'manifest crisis'. Initially, the Commission rejected these calls, but due to mounting pressure it was forced to make a more positive response. Henri Simonet, the Commissioner responsible for industrial policy at the time, drew up a set of measures which became known as the Simonet Plan, obliging the Commission to provide a better and quicker statistical service on production, prices and investment. The hope was that with more complete information the steel producers would be able to put their own house in order. To assist this process of voluntary re-adaption, a European steel cartel called 'Eurofer' was established. And in a significant shift from its old style neo-liberal outlook, the Commission welcomed the creation of this body, and said it hoped that both bodies could work together.[2]

Originally, the Simonet Plan was only to last for the first four months of 1977, but due to the continuing deterioration of the steel market it was extended initially to June and then to December. Probably the most significant development of 1977, however, was the replacement of Simonet by Viscount Etienne Davignon as the Commissioner responsible for industrial policy. Almost immediately after taking up the post Davignon came to the conclusion that the crisis in the European steel industry was structural and not cyclical and that a major restructuring and modernising programme was required to solve the problem of chronic overcapacity. However, he was also of the view that the costs of redressing the market situation by purely neo-liberal policies were too high both in economic and social terms. Instead, he wanted a positive adjustment strategy for the European steel industry: that is, a series of market interventions to give the industry manoeuvrability to restructure in an orderly and politically acceptable way. Of course, the logic of this argument meant that the Community should abandon the passive stance it had taken until then and get actively involved in the adjustment process.

At the end of 1977, Davignon introduced a series of measures to replace the Simonet Plan. These measures – labelled the Davignon Plan Mark 1 – went some way to implementing the strategy of positive adjustment. For the first time, the Commission was to regulate steel imports into the Community by relating them to the production costs of the most cost-effective producers from non-member states. Any imports found below this price would be automatically subject to an anti-dumping suit. In return for this greater policing of steel imports the Commission expected the Community producers to cut back on existing capacity. To facilitate this internal restructuring the Commission was to publish production target guidelines for each member state. No doubt helped by the mild recovery in the world economy, the Davignon Plan Mark 1 was relatively successful in 1978 and 1979. Community producers appeared to be following Commission output guidelines and exporters from third countries were deterred from dumping. But when the world demand for steel plummeted in 1980, some member states (particularly Germany and Italy) began openly flaunting voluntary production targets. The danger existed that a highly damaging price war could be triggered amongst European producers.

In this climate, Davignon thought that he had no alternative but to recommend to the Council of Ministers that they declare the steel industry to be in a state of manifest crisis, thus allowing the Commission to use the full powers invested in it by the Treaty of Paris. The Council of Ministers ratified the recommendation, thereby giving rise to the Davignon Plan Mark II. Under this new phase, greater attention was paid to speeding up the rate of structural adaption instead of enforcing market regulations. Thus compulsory production quotas were introduced for each member state. In addition, at the end of 1981, a 'subsidies code' for the industry was adopted by the Council of Ministers. The aim of the code was the abolition of state subsidies to the steel industry by December 1985. In the interim, only state subsidies facilitating rationalisation and modernisation were to be allowed. The Davignon strategy of positive adaption was now fully operational, with the Commission having extensive powers of intervention.

Although the overall picture for European steel remained bleak throughout 1982 and 1983, the Commission was satisfied with the attempts made by firms to reduce their output. In fact, it commented that some member states (most notably Britain) had committed themselves to capacity reductions which went far beyond the designated targets. But because the market situation deteriorated markedly during the middle of 1983, the Commission was forced to announce another round of rationalisation measures. A new system of mandatory common prices and certificates to monitor intra-Community trade was introduced. These measures further strengthened the hand of the Commission, by allowing it to intervene directly in cases where firms broke production targets. Thus the pressure on producers to implement rationalisation plans was maintained. By mid-1984, signs were emerging that the steel industry was recovering: for the first time in almost a decade, supply and demand in the industry looked like moving back to equilibrium. Although the Commission continues to think that the industry is in a state of 'manifest crisis', the producers are confident that the new favourable market conditions will continue.

The key objective of the European steel policy has been to prevent a highly damaging private war in the steel industry between member states. To a large extent the Community succeeded in this objective, as no serious infighting has occurred amongst the member states. In adopting a strategy for the steel industry, the Community moved away from its traditional free market approach to a strategy of positive adjustment. The main emphasis has been to cushion the steel industry from the full vagaries of the market to allow producers to restructure in an orderly fashion. Initially, the hope was that the producers would voluntarily restructure. When this did not happen, the Commission was forced to take a more interventionist role, by implementing a range of supranational policies.

As a result of the restructuring programmes adopted by the Community and individual member states, the numbers employed in the steel industry were reduced by two fifths between 1974 and 1984. It should be stated, however, that there were wide variations between the member states. In the United Kingdom, the total workforce fell from 194,500 in 1974 to 67,700 by the summer of 1983, while the corresponding figures in Italy were 95,200 and 91,200. Despite the variations amongst the member states, the overall effect was that at the beginning of 1984, the community was producing less steel than it was twenty years previously.

EC Coal Industry

When Britain started negotiations to enter the Community, the general consensus was that it was only a matter of time before oil totally replaced coal as the source of energy in Europe. During the previous decade, the share of coal in the Common Market's energy consumption had fallen from 70% to 16%. However, in the first year of Britain's membership, dramatic events occurred in world energy markets. The Yom Kippur

War between Israel and Egypt in 1973 resulted in a spectacular increase in the price of oil. This caused major problems for the member states, in particular leading to soaring energy bills. As a response, the Community proposed that member states reduce their energy imports from outside the Community. In practise, this meant increased reliance on coal-producing nations within the EC. Coal-consuming countries were opposed to these measures as they thought cheaper coal could be obtained from outside the Community.

This stalemate continued until the early eighties, resulting in not a single policy proposal being agreed to by the member states in seven years. In an attempt to break the deadlock, the Commission in 1982 drafted a new energy programme for the Community. This document departed completely from previous Commission thinking on the European coal industry. Instead of calling for an expansion of coal output inside the Community, the new programme proposed that the industry should undergo modernisation and rationalisation, with some 15–20% of existing capacity being removed. In addition, the document recommended that a 'safe' supply of coal imports should be secured from either Canada, Australia or one of the Lomé Convention countries. The Commission's rethink on coal appears to have been heavily influenced by the emerging divisions inside OPEC. All the signs were that OPEC could no longer exercise effective control over world oil markets. In this situation, the Commission seems to have been reluctant to commit the Community to a policy of satisfying its energy requirements from internal EC coal supplies.

This policy, like the previous one, failed to get the backing of the Council of Ministers. However, by the mid-eighties important political and economic developments were to significantly reduce the appeal of a Community energy strategy centred around coal. The oil price was becoming more and more influenced by the workings of the market rather than the dictates of OPEC. Moreover in the coal-producing countries, most notably in Britain, a strong neo-liberal approach was being adopted towards the coal industry. These developments influenced Commission thinking, for in 1986 it put forward a plan which proposed a major reduction in the Community's coal output. Somewhat surprisingly, given past experience, the Council of Ministers agreed to this programme. For the first time since 1974, the Community had ratified a policy for the coal industry. Currently the Commission is busy drawing up specific measures which some experts suggest will reduce coal output in the Community by about 45%. For more than a decade the Community operated without an effective energy policy. It was only at the end of the period under study that the Council of Ministers were able to agree firm proposals for the European coal industry.

Readaption Programmes

Articles 49, 54 and 56 of the Treaty of Paris empower the Commission to raise funds from the capital markets to assist the redeployment of workers made redundant as a result of rationalisations in the ECSC. Table IXi shows the amount of ECSC Funds for the readaptation of workers both in the coal and steel industries affected by rationalisation since 1973. By and large the money was used as a fiscal transfer to fund national programmes for early retirement, redundancy programmes, and the retraining and mobility of workers. Neither British Steel nor British Coal received any direct funding from these programmes. However in recent years, British Steel Enterprises and British Coal Enterprises, the two enterprise agencies set up to encourage and assist redundant workers to establish their businesses, have received some ECSC money which they have used to organise training programmes.

Table IXi ECSC appropriation for the readaption of workers in Britain

	Coal Industry		Steel Industry		TOTAL	
	workers	Aid ECU	Workers	Aid ECU	Amount Made Available	Workers
1973	11,921	19,445,686	7,704	3,143,467	22,589,153	19,625
1974	2,357	8,367,323	3,307	2,141,950	10,509,273	5,664
1975	4,998	8,424,000	2,633	1,844,379	10,268,379	7,631
1976	n/a	n/a	2,792	1,722,750	1,722,750	2,792
1977	9,121	17,735,000	13,025	11,378,000	27,113,000	22,146
1978	n/a	n/a	14,366	21,609,250	21,609,250	19,366
1979	2,346	8,039,350	20,102	48,244,750	56,284,000	22,448
1980	2,426	8,986,000	29,258	88,199,750	97,185,750	31,684
1981	6,880	34,328,500	12,102	60,337,000	94,665,500	18,982
1982	5,495	28,644,750	7,392	62,355,500	90,999,250	12,887
1983	481	4,096,500	4,477	19,226,500	23,323,000	4,959
1984	12,673	76,098,500	1,770	22,205,000	98,303,500	14,443
1985	34,371	80,907,000	2,891	9,706,750	90,614,500	38,212
1986	n/a	38,784,750	2,161	8,492,000	47,276,750	2,161

Shipbuilding Industry

The clauses of the Treaty of Paris undoubtedly made it easier for the Community to pursue active industrial policies for the coal and steel sectors. There were no similar clauses which the Commission could evoke when trying to establish a policy role in other industrial sectors, and as a result, the Commission has met with limited success there. The shipbuilding industry is a case in point.[3] Since about 1976 the shipbuilding industry has faced chronic international over-capacity, despite successive waves of capacity reductions, reduction in price levels and redundancies. The shipbuilding industries of the member states were adversely affected by the crisis. In 1976–77, the Community still held about 18 per cent of the new-build market but in the ensuing decade this sphere dropped to about 10 per cent.

Despite the dire situation facing most Community shipbuilders, the member states have been unable to agree to a European policy for the industry. Although a good deal of superficial evidence exists to suggest that Far Eastern nations are engaging in unfair trading practices by heavily subsidising their shipbuilding producers, the Community remains steadfastly opposed to introducing anti-dumping or protectionist measures. During the last decade, the Commission has made several proposals to reduce surplus capacity amongst Community producers: aids for scrapping, a scrap and build policy, a guarantee fund to promote scrapping and to set up scrap yards. However, none of these proposals have been adopted by the Council. Thus, beyond allowing member states to give their producers export credits and various other forms of subsidy, the Community has been unable to devise concrete industrial or labour market policies for the sector.

In 1987, however, the Commission forwarded to the Council another proposed labour-market programme for the industry. This programme was designed to give assistance to all shipbuilding workers made redundant or threatened with redundancy inside the Community. In particular, the programme proposed:

(i) that any workers made redundant or threatened with redundancy should be eligible for financial assistance of 2,500 ECU (subject to an equivalent amount being provided by the member state). Assistance may be granted for expenditure in respect of the following: recruitment aid; income maintenance allowance (to compensate for the differences in wages between the old and new jobs); subsidies to promote the setting up of new businesses; assistance towards consultancy services; recruitment aid for schemes to provide work in community service projects; tide-over allowances;

(ii) the establishment of a mobility premium, up to a maximum of 1500 ECU (subject to member states contributing an equivalent amount) to cover eligible expenditure on moving house;

(iii) to ease the transition to permanent retirement from working life of older workers, whether retiring early on a pension or receiving a 'tide-over' allowance designed to supplement unemployment benefit.

This proposal was adopted by the Council of Ministers. However, it is too early to assess its effect.

Transport Policy

In accordance with its Treaty obligations, the Commission sent in 1961 a memorandum to the Council relating to the development of a common transport policy. The Commission declared in this document, which became known as the 'Schaus Memorandum', that 'a transport policy applying to the Community as a whole must therefore gradually replace national transport policies. In the very progress of economic integration, the difference between national and international transport within the Community will disappear'.[4]

It is clear from this statement that the Commission wanted nothing less than a fully-fledged supranational Community transport policy. Yet, over 25 years later, the European Parliament initiated proceedings against the member states for failing to comply with clauses of the Treaty of Rome obliging them to establish a common Community transport policy. The contrast between intent and achievement could not be more stark; the Community had only progressed marginally towards a European transport policy since 1961.

Some measures have been introduced, however. For instance, a uniform system of maximum lorry weight, set at 44 tonnes, has been established. After a long legal and political wrangle, the EC forced British hauliers to introduce tachographs in their lorries in the face of opposition from the British Government. A quota and licensing system has been introduced for intra-Community lorries. Certain measures have been adopted to make railways across the Community less dependent on subsidies, but to no great effect. Monies have been set aside to finance transport infrastructure projects. And after years of infighting, the member states have agreed to initial steps towards the deregulation of air fares. While these measures have made some difference, they hardly add up to a comprehensive Community transport policy.

Institutional Links

By virtue of being a part of the European Coal and Steel Community, which has its own internal decision-making framework, British Coal and British Steel have more extensive links with Europe than any of the other public enterprises studied. The central ECSC framework is shown in Figure IXi.

A host of other smaller committees (some 20 in all) also exists. These committees, for the most part, deal with separate specific technical matters.

The main committees outlined above meet quarterly. Both British Steel and British Coal make efforts to ensure continuous representation in the Consultative Committee, as this is perceived to be an important

Figure IXi

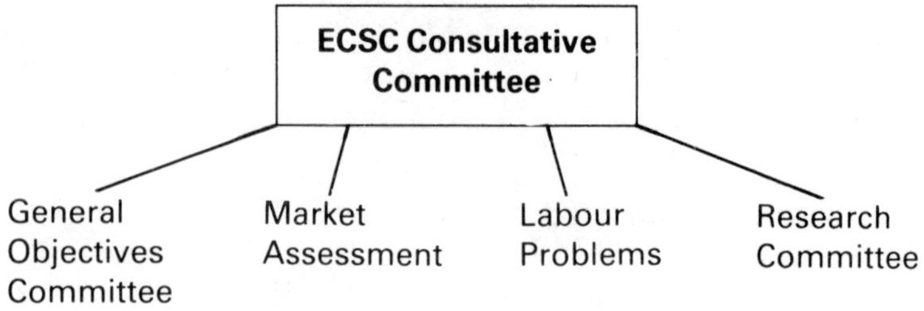

and active body.[5] Normally, in both cases, the Chairman, a Vice Chairman and a senior policy-maker represent the organisation on the committee. The other sub-committees are seen to be less important, and as a result, representation varies a great deal. British Coal appears to be the more structured and formally organised of the two in relation to Europe. Inside the organisation, there is a European Community Unit, of five people, with the sole responsibility for monitoring EC developments in relation to the coal industry, and formulating responses and policies towards any relevant initiatives emanating from Brussels. The Director of this Unit is permanently based in Brussels, which no doubt means he enjoys considerably more formal and informal contacts with the Commission officials and others in the EC machinery than would be the case if he were situated in London.

British Steel, on the other hand, has no similar unit. In fact, there is nobody within the company who deals specifically with international matters. This is somewhat surprising, given that the industry is increasingly being influenced by extra-national pressures, and given that most of the other public enterprises (and, indeed, private sector companies of similar size) have such people. Of course, this does not mean British Steel pays scant attention to EC developments. Such matters are dealt with on a functional basis within the company: those EC proposals concerning industrial relations would be dealt with by the industrial relations directorate, while matters relating to statistics would be handled by the statistics branch, and so on. This system no doubt ensures that all relevant EC initiatives are carefully and promptly considered by the company, though with the danger that consideration may be fragmentary and lacking a common thread. A central unit, like the one which exists in British Coal, may facilitate a more consistent and coordinated approach to EC issues. British Steel has no permanent representative in Brussels to remain in frequent contact with EC officials and to be aware of possible changes to EC steel policy (it has only a Sales Office there). The company clearly believes that a lot of this monitoring role can be done from London.

As well as being involved within the ECSC decision-making structure, the two companies are also members of their respective European-wide producer organisations – Eurofer (the European steel cartel) and CEPCED (the Association of Coal Producers in the EC). It is probably fair to say that Eurofer is the stronger of the two organisations because, for over a decade, it has actively assisted the Commission with its rationalisation plans by setting production quotas for the European steel industry and by cajoling members to abide by decisions reached at the EC level. The coal producers' organisation has never had to undertake this type of activity, although this may change now that the Community has developed a restructuring programme for coal. This difference is reflected in perceptions of the respective organisations. British Coal views CEPCED as a weak organisation with members having divergent interests and policy outlooks, and as a result, attaches little importance to its deliberations. British Steel's attitude to Eurofer is the opposite. Because this organisation operates in essence like a cartel, British Steel actively participates within it, and tries, as far as possible, to comply with its decisions.

The development of EC policies for coal and steel has meant the creation of additional committees and organisations at the European level. Although considerable time is spent preparing for, and attending, meetings of these bodies, British Coal and British Steel staff normally take a reactive approach to European deliberations. Very seldom do they initiate policy proposals inside the EC machinery. Because the trips to Europe are frequent, involving a large number of staff and covering a wide range of subjects, both organisations have found it difficult to maintain an integrated and coordinated approach to Europe. To comprehensively brief and get a full report-back from staff travelling to and from Europe would create an administrative nightmare for both organisations. Thus, coordination and briefing are confined to the most important meetings, and the more routine committees are not covered. This means in many instances that staff who participate in meetings in Luxembourg are unaware of, or at least not familiar with, the European activities of other departments. Only a select few members of staff in British Coal and British Steel have full knowledge of the extent and nature of their links with Europe.

The EC policy-making framework is not so integrated for other economic sectors in which public enterprises dominate. Thus for instance, British Shipbuilders has to keep abreast of the developments in the Commission's Internal Market, Competition and Social Policy Directorates, as proposals from any one of these sources could impact on shipbuilding. The company deals with EC-related issues in a number of ways. A senior staff member has particular responsibility for international matters. This person spends considerable time in Brussels and, hence, has many contacts with Commission officials, which ensures he is well informed of developments. He also plays an active role in the general discussions about the future of the industry, which take place inside the Commission. But much of the detailed work on specific EC proposals is done by functional departments. Thus the health and safety unit was responsible for deciding the organisation's response to the proposed Noise Directive, while a Social Affairs Unit administers the tasks relating to European Social Fund grants. Senior managers are also involved in various CEEP committees, although these are generally regarded in a poor light. Indeed, the general opinion of these committees was so low that senior managers have seriously discussed withdrawing British Shipbuilders from CEEP.

The company's general attitude towards the Community is ambivalent. On the one hand, it recognises fully that decisions with far-reaching effects can be taken at the European level, and as such it is important to be attuned to developments and to respond accordingly. On the other hand, however, the Community's consultative framework is considered to be cumbersome, with the proceedings at times showing no apparent relevance to the company.

As well as using the channels of communication at the European level, British Shipbuilders also use the various mechanisms available at the national level to influence EC policy. For instance, senior managers of the company liaise with DTI officials in relation to Community initiatives for the shipbuilding industry. These meetings give the company's management the opportunity to brief civil servants on their views. These civil servants will normally push to defend the company's interests inside the sub-committees of the Council of Ministers. Thus the overriding stance of British Shipbuilders appears to be that while it is important to monitor EC development diligently, it is not altogether enthusiastic about the European connection.

A more positive attitude towards the Community is adopted by British Rail. This attitude stretches back to when Britain first joined the Common Market, and is partly due to the fact that BR always enjoyed extensive links with other European railway administrators. The Chairman at the time was eager for the organisation to play an active role inside the Community machinery, and over the years, this outlook has evolved into standard practice. As a result of this commitment towards Europe, British Rail have played a key role in some Community committees. For example, officials have, in the past, been Chairmen of a number of CEEP and sector bodies.

As shown above, progress towards establishing an EC transport policy (of any description) has been painfully slow. In the absence of any substantive policy discussions within CEEP, committees as well as sector committees have focused on employment-related issues. The discussions on employment matters fall into two categories. The first essentially has involved an exchange of views on personnel management and employment policy developments within the different member states. While these exchanges undoubtedly kept British Rail abreast of the developments in other countries, it is questionable whether they influenced the company's approach to these issues. The company specialists tend to believe that because their Continental counterparts operate within a different industrial relations system, their approach to particular issues is of limited applicability in Britain. Nevertheless, the discussions are considered to be valuable because they alert British Rail management to the type of demands Continental trade unions are making; demands which their British counterparts may pick up in due course. They also give personnel managers insight into European policies and practices in employment.

The second type of discussion aims to establish a common policy amongst EC railway employers on social policy proposals from the Commission. This has proven to be no easy task. More often than not, a common position is obtained only after protracted bargaining. To some extent it can be argued that this is based upon the different frameworks and conditions in each country. Such an argument would point to the fact that French railways (SNCF), accustomed to law in industrial relations practices, is less hostile to the Commission's legislative approach than the British Rail, which operates in the voluntarist environment in the UK. For the most part, British Rail has been happy with the compromise policy stances adopted by the European Railway Employers.

Thus British Rail plays an active role in the EC machinery, particularly that part relating to transport. This active role is adopted, partly out of a desire to be good Europeans, and partly out of a realisation that only through full participation will the company be able to fully protect (and promote) its interests. But the company feels under no obligation to transfer into its own practice the decisions and recommendations of European-level committees. Changes in existing industrial relations practices are normally the result of developments inside the company, or within the transport industry or in the national political and economic environment. In other words, there are limits to British Rail's apparent pro-European stance.

Approach to EC Employment Policy

Although there is no formal system in any of the companies to monitor EC Social Policy developments, most of the personnel specialists interviewed remain generally informed through their internal structures, via their involvement in the various EC committees or by reading reports in the industrial relations journals and literature. However, once a decision on an employment-related matter is made at the European level, even before it is incorporated into UK legislation, each company takes immediate action to assess the likely impact on its organisation. Thus, to take a recent example, when the European Court of Justice decided that it was discriminatory to oblige women to retire at an earlier age than men, all companies took action to see what changes were needed to existing policies on such matters as retirement, and the impact of the ruling on their pension schemes. From these deliberations, an action plan was developed on how the company structure should adjust to incorporate the ruling. None of the companies ever considered for one moment not complying with the Court's decision. All legally-binding Directives and decisions made by the EC are regarded in the same light as national legislation, something with which the company has no alternative but to comply. Beyond making adjustments to accommodate Community policies, some of the companies have on occasions attempted to assess how particular Commission proposals, if adopted by the Council of Ministers, would affect their operations. Thus, while the companies do not keep in touch with EC developments on an on-going basis, they do remain aware of the proposals which are most likely to affect them. Most companies are satisfied with this ad hoc issue-orientated approach. As one interviewee put it, 'We have never been taken unawares by any piece of EC legislation, which means that our system in broad terms must work OK.'

All the personnel managers (and other managers) interviewed, opposed the EC policies and proposed policies relating to employment and industrial relations matters. In fact, not one had a single positive comment to make about any of the EC initiatives in this field. The arguments used against them were those put forward by managers in other sectors. The Commission was accused of being insensitive to the fact that many of their proposals, if implemented in full, would add significantly to a company's costs, and also inhibit flexibility which, in a highly competitive commercial environment, might have disastrous results. Furthermore, the Commission also came in for criticism for not giving proper consideration to the voluntaristic nature of British industrial relations which made the UK unsuitable for the EC's legislative approach. These criticisms are widely held amongst industrialists and managers. But there were other specific reasons why the personnel managers in the public enterprises are lukewarm to the EC record in the employment field.

In particular, most felt there was a major contradiction between the industrial policies promoted by the Commission for the coal, steel and shipbuilding sectors, and the initiatives it has put forward in the field of social affairs. The industrial policies implemented have been highly neo-liberal in character, and have reinforced the large-scale redundancies programme initiated by successive British Governments, whilst the employment policies adopted or proposed have focused on social protectionist measures and conferring greater rights to consultation in establishments. Having on the one hand to enact large-scale redundancies, while on the other hand, having to increase the rights of those who remain in work, was regarded by the interviewed personnel managers as not an entirely consistent approach. Indeed, because of this perceived inconsistency, many were critical, and in some cases even disdainful, of the Commission and the entire EC machinery.

Another factor contributing to the general opposition of the interviewed personnel managers towards EC social policy is the present Government's drive to 'commercialise' managerial practice in the public sector. Since the early eighties the Thatcher administration has encouraged senior managers in the public sector to adopt policies which would make their organisation more efficient and less dependent on state finance. Most of the personnel managers were of the view that they and their colleagues had eagerly embraced these principles and that as a result they were lukewarm to the idea of external intervention. This new-found feeling of independence, the argument went, made them hostile to the idea that the Community should legislate in a particular area, with the effect of constraining the possible choice of policies open to them.

Influence of EC Social Policy

The EC has directly influenced the personnel and employment systems in all the interviewed companies in a number of ways. One way was through employees, usually with the backing of their trade unions, taking advantage of European law to pursue equal opportunities cases against three of the public enterprises – British Shipbuilders, British Coal and British Railways. In relation to British Rail two cases were brought before the courts where EC legislation was evoked, namely *Arthur Burton v. British Rail* and *Garland v. British Rail Engineering*. In the late seventies, as part of a reorganisation plan, British Rail (the British Railways Board) offered voluntary redundancy to some of its employees on certain terms (men aged over 60 and women over 55). In August 1979, Mr Burton, aged 58, applied for voluntary redundancy. But his application was rejected on the ground that he was under the minimum age of 60. Mr Burton refused to accept this decision, maintaining that he had been treated less favourably than a female employee, inasmuch as the benefit would have been granted to a woman aged 58. Accordingly, he complained to an Industrial Tribunal, but this rejected his claim. Not deterred, he appealed to the Employment Appeal Tribunal, invoking Article 199 of the EEC Treaty, Article 1 of Directive 75/117/EEC and

Articles 1, 2, 5 of Directive 76/207/EEC. The Employment Appeal Tribunal, realising that the case would have set a precedent, asked the European Court of Justice for a number of rulings. Without entering into the precise legal arguments which followed, the net result was that Mr Burton lost his case.

The other case involved British Rail Engineering (a wholly-owned subsidiary of the British Railways Board) and a Mrs Garland, a married woman employed by the company. As part of their employment, all employees of British Rail Engineering enjoy certain valuable travel facilities which are also extended to their spouses and dependent children. On retirement, former employees, men and women, continue to enjoy travel facilities but they are reduced in comparison with those which they enjoyed during the period of their employment. However, the previous practice was that although male employees continued to be granted facilities for themselves and for their wives and dependent children as well, female employees did not have such facilities granted in respect of their families.

Mrs Garland brought a case against British Rail Engineering to an Industrial Tribunal claiming that this practice was discriminatory. Three different tribunals in turn, using the provisions of the Sex Discrimination Act as the legal framework for the issue, decided against Mrs Garland. But the case reached the House of Lords where issues of Community law were raised. The House of Lords requested the European Court of Justice for several legal rulings. Again leaving aside the ensuing legal technicalities, the Court ruled that where an employer provides special travel facilities for former male employees to enjoy after their retirement this constitutes discrimination against former female employees who do not receive the same facilities. Of course, BR (Engineering) immediately changed its practice to comply with these decisions.

As well as these rulings against it, British Rail was also found to be presiding over both direct and indirect discriminatory employment practices and procedures by an Equal Opportunities Commission Research Report. British Rail responded to these two episodes by establishing an 'equal opportunities' project. As a result of this project, a positive action programme is being implemented inside the company on the issue, involving a review of existing employment practices and collective agreements, a new system of monitoring the application of the policy throughout BR by regular statistical analysis of employees and applicants, and new training schemes on the issue. The Hayward case, which is described in more detail on p 165, did not prompt British Shipbuilders to take any action on its existing equal opportunities policy. The attitude of the personnel department was simply to play down the incident, and hope that another similar case would not arise.

British Coal has also faced a legal equal pay for work of equal value case. This occurred in 1987 when a consolidated equal pay case was lodged, with the backing of the NUM, by over 1500 women canteen assistants employed at collieries throughout the country, comparing their work to that of a named comparator, a Mr Tilstone, employed until his retirement in 1985 as a canteen assistant.

In 1966, because of recruitment difficulties, it was decided to treat nightwork in canteens in North Staffordshire as surface work and pay a higher rate. Mr Tilstone was recruited on this rate in 1975. In 1977, two women employed as canteen assistants at the colliery brought a successful equal pay claim using Mr Tilstone as a comparator. The consolidated equal value claim attempted to use this case as the springboard for a much larger legal case. Thus first an industrial tribunal and then an Employment Appeals Tribunal held that the risk and additional responsibility of unsupervised nightwork as a canteen assistant justified unequal pay with day work. This case is still at the higher appeals court stage. But like the British shipbuilders in regard to the Hayward case, British Coal was not moved to rethink its equal opportunities policies as a result of the case.

Various other pieces of EC legislation, mostly in the health and safety field, directly influence the public enterprises. To illustrate the point we examine how the EC's Noise Directive affected British Shipbuilders. Long before the Noise Directive reached the statute book, British Shipbuilders were studying how the initiative would affect them. An ad hoc committee made up of the senior safety officials was established to devise a company response to the initiatives. They undertook several actions: the noise levels in all subsidiaries were checked to see whether or not they would infringe the noise ceilings imposed by the Directive. It was found that several important pieces of machinery produced noise levels far above those laid down in the Directive. As a result, it was decided to remove the machines (at considerable expense) so that the company could effectively implement noise-control standards. In addition, the Purchasing Departments were given the responsibility to give preference when purchasing new equipment to those which produced low levels of noise. Finally, a major drive was made to increase awareness amongst the workforce of the potential hazards arising from high noise levels. Thus when the Directive was finally implemented, the company had already made many of the adjustments to comply with the Directive. Several other examples could be outlined where diligent attention was paid to the prospect of EC legislation, and anticipatory action taken. But the general point to note is that the public enterprises appear to be well organised to deal with initiatives coming out of Brussels which have a specific and direct bearing on their operations.

Apart from the above influences, the personnel managers interviewed were of the view that the EC had no impact on the formulation or the implementation of personnel and employment policy within their specific enterprise. None could think of an instance when their thinking was influenced by any EC proposal or document. However, it was recognised that EC influences would probably be greater on national institutions and interest groups – Manpower Services Commission, the TUC and CBI – than individual companies. For them, the biggest influences on the personnel function were the drive to establish more commercially orientated policies, which in most cases involved a degree of decentralised pay bargaining, and the effort to become more responsive to market conditions.

Conclusions

Three main conclusions arise from the discussion in this chapter. First, most public enterprises have extensive formal institutional links with the Community. This is partly because the Community has adopted wide-ranging industrial restructuring policies, which the public enterprises have to monitor closely, particularly in the coal and steel sectors, and partly because numerous committees and bodies exist at the European level which require the attendance of representatives from public enterprises in Britain. Thus, as a result of membership, a clear European dimension has opened up to the work of these enterprises. The way the public enterprises organise in relation to Community affairs constitutes the second conclusion. There appears to be no consistent pattern to how the enterprises organise in relation to Europe. Some enterprises, most notably British Coal, appear to be better organised than others, e.g. British Rail. But all the enterprises appear to deal effectively with those aspects of Community affairs, particularly legal issues, which have a direct impact on their operations. It is in the more general areas of policy coordination, briefing representatives on Community committees, reporting-back procedures, and monitoring developments, where some enterprises are more effective than others. None of the enterprises paid much attention to launching initiatives inside Community institutions. Thus the approach to Community affairs is primarily reactive in nature: the enterprises will undertake the changes required by Community law, but few will do more than that.

The third conclusion is that several of the enterprises have experienced a direct EC influence as they have had equal pay for work of equal value legal cases brought against them. Such cases would not have been possible if the Community had not intervened in British labour law on the issue. For the most part, however, the personnel managers interviewed were of the view that the Community only marginally, if at all, influences the personnel and manpower policies pursued inside their respective organisations. From a professional point of view, none of the personnel managers could be regarded as enthusiastic Europeans, as they opposed many of the Community social policies. Indeed, the overall approach appeared to be practical and hard-headed: Community membership had placed certain obligations upon them which had to be met, but these could be done without embracing the Europeanisation fervour frequently associated with Community affairs. Thus the personnel managers in the public enterprises can be best described as diligent Europeans.

Notes and References

1 Cited in KIRCHNER, E *Interest Groups in the European Community*, Gower, Farnborough p 14

2 For a good account of the development and effectiveness of EC steel policy *see* STRAUSS, R and TSOUKALIS, L 'Crisis and adjustment in European steel: Beyond laissez-faire' *Journal of Common Market Studies* Vol 33, No 3 pp 207–28 1985

3 For a detailed account of the problems of establishing a Community policy for the shipbuilding industry *see* TEAGUE, P *Labour and Europe: The Response of British Trade Unions to Membership of the European Community* Chap 6, Unpublished thesis, London University 1984

4 Cited in DESPITCH, N *The Transport Policy of the European Communities*, PEP, London p 33

5 For an account of how the relevant British trade unions – the National Union of Mineworkers and the Iron and Steel Trades Federation – have responded, *see* TEAGUE, P 'Trade Unions and Extra-national Industrial Policies, EC coal and steel policies: A case study of the NUM and ISTC inside the European coal and steel Community', *Economic and Industrial Democracy*, February 1989

Chapter X

The EC and the Private Sector

British managers are often ridiculed for being inward looking and even on occasions for being xenophobic. In relation to the EC, this 'Little Englander' outlook is seen to be reinforced by the general anti-European sentiment which purportly pervades British society. Of course, this depiction of British managers is specious. But, while little evidence may exist to substantiate this view, there is equally a dearth of evidence to show that it is wrong. Since one of the central findings from our interviews with personnel managers in the private sector is that they are virtually unanimous in their opposition to the nature of the EC social policies, it is necessary to ask whether the opposition is the product of a 'Little Englander' outlook or is based on a genuine concern about the likely impact of such policies? Thus, in the first part of this chapter, we address this issue by assessing the degree of compatibility between some EC social initiatives and the actual employment and personnel practices in the private sector in Britain. If a large measure of difference is found to exist between the two, then it can be reasonably assumed that opposition towards EC policies was not simply, or even largely, based on xenophobic reasons. The second part of the chapter details the results of the interviews held with personnel managers in the private sector.

The compatibility of EC social initiatives with British employment practices

In this section we cover both adopted and proposed EC social policies, for both have played an important role in shaping British personnel managers' perceptions of the Community's social dimension. The comparison made covers four controversial areas: equal opportunities; consultation and communication; parental leave; and part-time and temporary work.

Equal Opportunities Policies

There is widespread acceptance within industry that women (as well as black and disabled people) experience discrimination in the labour market.[1] Partly out of a general desire to combat these practices, and partly out of a recognition that discrimination does not make good business sense, both the CBI and the IPM encourage their members to adopt and operate equal opportunities policies. As pointed out in earlier chapters, despite legislation existing on the matter, women continue to be disadvantaged in the labour market relative to men. Although employment growth trends favour women, this is largely due to the expansion of part-time work. The Manpower Services Commission has calculated that between 1986–1987, out of the net increase in paid jobs of 198,000, 22,000 went to full-time men, 20,000 to part-time men, 46,000 to full-time women and 110,000 to part-time women.

The initial impact of the Equal Pay Act was substantial: women's pay as a proportion of men's improved from 63.1 per cent in 1970 to a peak of 75.5 per cent in 1981. However, during the past decade this ratio has stayed more or less constant: hourly earnings for women remain at 73.6 per cent of male earnings.

Table Xi outlines average earnings of full-time employees by sex and occupation in 1987 where valid occupational comparisons can be made. The figures show that in every occupational category, male average earnings are higher than female average earnings. Moreover, the table indicates, bar a few exceptions (e.g. nurses and police constables), women's gross earnings are less than men's basic earnings. As regards occupational location, women are over-represented in low-paid manual jobs and under-represented in high-paid white collar or professional employment. Thus three quarters of all those employed in catering, cleaning, hairdressing and other personal services are women, while in professional and related occupations in science, engineering and technology only nine per cent of employees are women. Clearly despite equal pay and equal value legislation and despite the fact that employers' organisations have encouraged their members to introduce equal opportunity policies, women continue to be disadvantaged in the labour market.

Employers responded in a low-key manner to the European Court of Justice ruling in 1984 which forced the British Government to introduce the Equal Value Amendment to the Equal Pay Act. At the same time, they were distinctly nervous about the implications of this legal change. As the figures in Table Xi show, significant wage differentials exist between men and women in similar occupational groups. Thus, on paper, the equal value legislation could have a far-reaching impact, with major cost implications for employers. So far, the impact of the amendment has not been large-scale. But this situation could soon change: if the equal opportunities bodies and trade unions do begin to make full use of the legislation (see p 149) and if many of the test cases that are still going through the Courts are resolved in the employee's favour, then the equal value amendment could have a telling impact. In these circumstances, employers' anxieties about the cost implications of the amendment could be justified.

Table Xi Average Earnings of Full-Time Employees by Sex and Occupation (1987)

	Men		Women	
	Excluding Overtime PBR & Shift	Overtime PBR & Shift	Excluding Overtime PBR & Shift	Overtime PBR & Shift
Non-manual	£pw	£pw	£pw	£pw
Further education teachers	284.2	2.2	239.7	0.4
Secondary teachers	249.4	0.6	218.1	0.2
Primary teachers	242.2	0.2	209.3	0.1
Other teachers	241.6	2.4	202.1	0.3
Welfare workers	204.0	8.0	164.5	7.0
Nurse administrators and executives	228.7	24.1	199.0	13.9
Registered and enrolled nurses, midwives	151.3	24.3	137.2	13.8
Literary, artistic & sport	254.0	29.7	198.1	14.9
Laboratory technicians (scientific, medical)	179.6	15.9	148.8	5.5
Office managers	311.3	19.8	209.9	8.8
Supervisors of clerks	208.0	15.0	174.9	7.8
Costing and accounting clerks	156.7	9.9	128.3	5.1
Cash handling clerks	150.4	21.2	127.1	8.8
Finance & insurance etc clerks	181.0	21.6	139.9	8.6
Shipping & travel clerks	157.3	28.5	123.3	12.2
Records & library clerks	140.6	12.3	124.4	3.3
General clerks & clerks not identified elsewhere	147.7	12.4	125.1	5.0
Sales supervisors	178.3	20.6	130.3	8.3
Sales staff, shop assistants, shelf fillers	113.7	26.2	94.5	4.5
Police constables	240.5	24.4	225.7	14.8
Manual				
Chefs/cooks	127.0	17.7	101.9	11.4
Barmaids/barmen	110.4	23.3	83.3	10.4
Materials processing (excluding metals)	136.4	53.8	97.4	21.8
Footwear workers	77.8	89.2	49.4	59.1
Processing, making, repairing & related (metals & electrical)	153.5	50.9	106.2	24.1
Repetitive assemblers (metals & electrical)	130.7	41.6	102.8	20.2
Inspectors & testers (metals & electrical)	161.1	42.8	118.4	22.9
Packers, bottlers, canners, fillers	123.7	42.3	98.8	19.8
Storekeepers etc	124.8	32.1	108.8	7.9

Source: *New Earnings Survey*, Part D, 1987

Consultation and Communication in British Industry

In many Community countries, legislation obliges companies to establish works councils or other similar institutions. Such legislative provision in many of the member states ensures that there is a large measure of uniformity in employee rights to information and consultation, as well as in some cases to formal participation in company decision-making, across the economy. Until recently, there existed little labour law in the UK regarding the information and consultation rights of employees. As a result, the workplace consultative machinery in the UK is 'all over the place'.[2] The British Workplace Industrial Relations Survey 1986 gives the most authoritative account of consultative and communication provisions in the British economy. It found that the overall proportion of workplaces with joint consultative committees stands at about one third. For the private sector the figure was rather less.[3]

Three main topics – production, employment and pay issues – are most frequently discussed by establishment-level joint consultative committees. By and large, all sides of industry, where joint consultative committees exist, regard them as valuable. Only two per cent of managers, three per cent of non-manual representatives and five per cent of manual representatives said that they felt the meetings to be unimportant. Other forms of communication with the workforce were found to exist in addition to these formal institutional mechanisms for employee consultation. The most common communication method reported by respondents was either the systematic use of the management chain or regular newsletters distributed to all levels of employee, or a combination of the two. The topics which are the subject of most communication are terms and conditions of employment and major changes in working methods or work organisation. Staffing or manpower is next, whilst investment plans were reported to be the subject of least communication. The survey also found that private sector organisations tended to give less extensive information to their employees than the public sector did.

The survey also attempted to solicit from management whether or not they had developed any initiative during the past four years or so aimed at increasing employee involvement or improving the communication and consultation machinery within the enterprise. Relatively few of the managers reported the establishment of formal participation structures during the eighties. However, most managers did report an increase in *two-way communication*; a finding corroborated by the responses from worker representatives. Initiatives in this area were primarily qualitative in character, some involving the implementation of quality circles, some face to face meetings between managers and employees.[4]

British law obliges companies to furnish information to worker representatives for the purpose of collective bargaining, if requested by them. Numerous annual reports of the Central Arbitration Committees suggest that the number of occasions in which this legislation is evoked declined in the early eighties.[5] This view is substantiated by the Workforce Survey which shows that there occurred an initial decline and then a levelling off in the number of occasions workers' representatives used the provisions of this legislation. The most likely explanation for this fall-off in the use of the information disclosure legislation is that management has increased the quality of information and communication to employees in recent years.

Thus there are a number of distinct features to the form and scope of consultative procedures in British industry. First, while employers use a wide range of procedures to keep employees informed of company developments, the overall tendency is to use informal arrangements rather than formal mechanisms such as joint consultative committees. Secondly, the evidence suggests that terms and conditions of employment are the most common topics covered by the consultation or communication process. Thirdly, there appears to have been an increase both in the number and quality of consultation arrangements in recent years, resulting in a fall-off in the demand by employees and their representatives for information for collective bargaining purposes.

If the earlier versions of the draft Fifth and Vredeling Directives were to be implemented, the above consultative practices of British industry would be disrupted in a far-reaching way. In the first place, the Fifth Directive, as originally drafted, would oblige a uniform system to be introduced by all British companies with 500 or more employees, bringing to an end the highly diverse pattern of consultative arrangements. The two-tier board system first proposed by the Directive would change, root and branch, the consultative procedures in the affected companies. This model of employee involvement, largely based on the West German and Netherlands experiences, is virtually non-existent in British companies. Thus considerable time and resources would have to be employed to ensure that the model was implemented in such a manner as not to undermine the smooth running of companies. Even in its amended form where there could be a choice of systems of employee participation at board level, the Fifth Directive would require significant change to existing systems of information and communication within companies. Another change that the Directives would bring about is the formalisation, and an increase in the power, of employee representatives. For example, under proposals made by the Fifth Directive, employee representatives would for the first time have a say on such things as the appointment and dismissal of the members of the management board. As regards the Vredeling Directive, at least in its early form, the range of information to be given to UK employees would greatly broaden in scope.

Clearly, during the seventies there was a considerable gap between the Commission's proposals on employee involvement and information and consultation procedures and related practices within British industry. As a result, the opposition of British employers to these initiatives cannot be put down to simple myopia. Whether or not one agrees with the CBI's and other organisations' campaigns against these initiatives, it cannot be disputed that employers opposed these proposals as a result of being deeply concerned about their likely impact on existing personnel practice and business performance more generally. A measure of their concern is that the prospect of these initiatives motivated the employers' organisations to encourage, even exhort, their members to improve their consultation and communications systems in the hope that this action would stave off the need for this Directive.

Parental Leave

In its policy response to the Commission's proposal for a Directive on Parental Leave and Leave for Family Reasons, the CBI argued that such legislation would place added cost burdens on employers. The argument rests on the belief that significant numbers of employees would take advantage of the Directive if it became law. However, there are too many imponderables, and a lack of appropriate statistics, for precise figures to be calculated. As a result, it is unclear how the CBI could reach its unequivocal view on the issue. By comparison, in its review of the Directive, the House of Lords Select Committee on European Communities estimated that the initial impact would be small.

This view was based on the following arithmetic. In 1982 there were 14 million men and 9.5 million women in employment in Britain. In the same year, there were 692,000 births, equivalent to 4.9 per cent of the population and 7.3 per cent of employed women. In other words, only a small proportion of the labour force have a baby in any year. Moreover, in all probability partly because many parents would be ineligible (e.g. self-employed workers are not covered by the proposed Directive) and partly because some parents may not choose to take up their right to parental leave, only a small proportion of the initial small proportion would be likely to take advantage of parental leave. The House of Lords Committee estimated that on 1982 figures, 69,200 men or 0.6 per cent of the male employees, and 128,578 women or 1.4 per cent of women employees might have taken up these legal rights to leave. Thus the view of this committee was that the initial impact of parental leave would be limited. This interpretation is completely at variance with the CBI assessment that employers' costs would rise appreciably if the proposed Directive became legislation. It can therefore be concluded that a question mark hangs over this view. Sufficient evidence exists to suggest that employers in the UK could have adjusted with relative ease to the clauses of the Directive.

Part-time and Temporary Work

The Part-time and Temporary Workers Draft Directives have been strongly opposed by the employers' organisations on the basis that they would increase costs and reduce the amount of such forms of employment without any compensatory increase in permanent jobs. As detailed in chapter VII, these Directives would increase and make more comprehensive the legal rights afforded to part-time and temporary workers in Britain. As a result, employers' labour costs would almost inevitably increase. But short of conducting an elaborate econometric exercise, it is impossible to estimate the extent of this increase in labour costs. The employers' claim that the Directives would increase British industry's costs may be valid, but would they, as claimed by the employers' organisations, deter employers from recruiting part-time and temporary workers?

A number of factors have been identified to account for the steady rise in part-time work since the Second World War, and the more recent increase in temporary work. In the first place, some authors put this growth of 'atypical forms' of employment down to structural shifts in the British economy away from manufacturing activity to services. Thus, whilst five per cent of the manufacturing workforce are part-timers, the equivalent figure for the service sector is 22 per cent.[6] In other accounts, part-time and temporary work is seen as reflecting the demand by employers for greater flexibility and a desire to improve the utilisation of capital equipment.[7] Another supply-side explanation put forward for the growth of non-permanent jobs is the efforts of employers to escape the influence of employment legislation as well as the complexities of the tax, benefits and National Insurance systems.[8] A final view places more emphasis on the demand side, such as the increased number of married women or men approaching retirement age preferring not to work full time.[9]

These factors were brought together in an econometric model to evaluate the employment impact of the Part-time Work Directive.[10] The results of the simulations suggest that the implementation of this Directive would have little detrimental impact on part-time employment, nor would it have any significant impact on other forms of employment. Thus the most detailed examination of the employment consequences of the Directive fails to substantiate the claims made by the CBI. The predominant impression is that employers would accept the added cost burden of the Directive and continue to employ and deploy part-time and temporary workers.

Overall, a mixed picture emerges about the extent to which employer's responses to EC social policies and proposed policies are based on a genuine concern about the potential disruptive impact these policies would have on British employment practices. It can hardly be disputed that the employers' view of the likely disruptive impact of the early versions of the Fifth and Vredeling Directives was an accurate assessment of the situation. In this instance, employers' anxieties about the nature and direction of the Commission's social proposals can be regarded as well founded. Moreover, the anxieties employers have about the potential cost implications of some of the Community's equal opportunities legislation and Court of Justice rulings in the area could be well founded if the British courts give broad operational definitions to these laws in the various legal test cases that are awaiting their consideration. But the examination also found that the employers' responses to the Parental Leave and Leave for Family Reasons, and to the Part-time and Temporary Directives exaggerated the cost implications of these proposals, particularly in the case of the Parental Leave initiative. To some extent, political exigencies forced the CBI to inflate the cost burdens of these initiatives – you cannot vociferously oppose EC initiatives and at the same time say that they could only have small cost implications. But the evidence suggests that as regards these proposals, the employers used the cost implications argument too blandly and too opportunistically. As a result, one must go beyond the costs thesis in an attempt to explain why the employers opposed these initiatives. In chapter VI, it is suggested that the pro-trade union orientation of the policies and reluctance to see the Community developing a significant presence in the field of industrial relations are more convincing explanations for the opposition of employers to these initiatives.

The compatibility of EC social initiatives with developments in British industrial relations

So far, the analysis has focused on the relationship between Community labour policies, as well as proposed policies, and industrial relations practices in the UK to assess the degree of change the Community has brought about or could bring about within Britain. This investigation was largely motivated by the wish to find out whether or not the uncompromising opposition of British employers was based on genuine concern over the likely disruptive impact of Community social initiatives. A related but at the same time distinct issue is addressed in the next section, namely the degree of symmetry or overlap between EC social policies and proposals and the current trends and key themes in

British industrial relations. This is an important issue to examine since, as later sections will show, the almost unanimous views of personnel managers interviewed is that EC social policies are outdated and do not reflect current trends in company-level employment practices.

Material detailing UK industrial relations developments is drawn substantially from a survey conducted by 'Industrial Relations Review and Report'.[11] This survey suggests that since the beginning of the eighties, and particularly since the mid eighties, several important changes have taken place in British industrial relations. To begin with, there appears to have been a major shift away from nationally determined wage agreements towards decentralised forms of pay bargaining. Increasingly, the trend is towards performance-related pay schemes where an employee's remuneration and career path is largely determined by individual merit and the arrangements made to assess such merit. Another significant development is what the survey team call new industrial relations packages. These new packages mainly cover the establishment of single-union deals, pendulum arbitration and single status for manual and white collar workers. A third source of change is the introduction of flexibility arrangements within firms. On this point, the survey was at pains to stress that while flexibility was a prominent feature of change, no blueprint for flexibility emerged from the survey. Rather the trend is for organisations to devise their own particular brands of flexibility, largely dictated by pragmatic concerns.

The survey found that profit-related pay and employee share-ownership schemes were on the increase in British industry, though not to the extent hoped for by the Government in its White Paper on the issue. The aim of these schemes is to increase employee involvement and attachment to the enterprise in the hope these will yield positive productivity increases. The evidence of the survey, reinforcing the conclusion of other reviews,[12] suggests that the envisaged benefits do not materialise in every instance.

Overall, the evidence is that important changes are occurring in British industrial relations. These developments can be associated with the emergence of human resource management policies in British companies. The key aspect of HR policies is that they relate personnel and manpower policies more closely to the commercial objectives of the business. To a large extent, the development of HR strategies has been brought about by the increasingly competitive commercial environment. This is forcing employers to reduce costs, while at the same time striving to improve productivity and quality by increasing the attachment of employees to the company.[13]

Comparing these developments with the content of EC initiatives shows that in several important respects, there is little complementarity between the two. In the first place, there is considerable mismatch between what the Community has adopted and what the Commission is proposing, and actual ground-level developments in the UK. Thus the trend towards flexibility and performance-related pay has, so far, no reflection in Community initiatives. Furthermore, there is a clash between the policy direction and objectives of the Community – which is largely concerned with economic, social and political issues – and enterprise strategies primarily motivated by commercial considerations. Whilst companies want to obtain better labour deployment within the enterprise through the encouragement of part-time and temporary workers, the Community is much more preoccupied with the distributional aspects of such flexibility policies. As a result, a sharp contrast in approach exists between the policies espoused by the Commission and the practices implemented by companies.

This gap between the Community and British companies on employment and labour affairs is reinforced by the focus in Community policies on the national and European industrial relations framework within which companies operate, whilst the companies themselves are concerned with operational policies directly concerned with production and service. The Commission is, therefore, focusing on an issue which from the company viewpoint in the present climate is only a constraint to its main objectives.

Thus the overriding conclusion from this section is that a large gap exists between the nature and direction of Community policies, and trends and developments in British employee relations. The stalemate on Commission social proposals since the early eighties to some degree contributed to this situation. It is self-evident that with no substantive new policies and legislation being adopted, Community social legislation would be overtaken by ground-level development in employee relations. Equally obvious is that if Community social legislation is out of tune with developments on the ground, then its ability to influence them declines sharply. The rest of the chapter is given over to assessing the degree of Community influences on company-level personnel and manpower policies in Britain.

Community influence on private-sector personnel policies

When preparing the research strategy for the private sector, it was considered essential to interview a range of companies of different sizes and nationalities in separate economic sectors. The sectoral classification was regarded as important since it was assumed that the commercial location of companies may affect their responses to ratified and proposed EC social legislation. For example, as there is a disproportionately large number of part-time workers in the distributive trades, it might be thought that companies in this sphere of economic activity would be more concerned about the proposed Directive on part-time work than companies in manufacturing. In other words, as well as uncovering a number of general or common responses to EC social policy initiatives, it was anticipated that the research would uncover several sector-specific strategies in relation to the EC. As well as this sectoral breakdown of the interviews, nationality of ownership was also seen as a potentially important factor influencing the responses of firms. For instance, personnel managers in a subsidiary of a Belgian or Dutch firm located in Britain might be assumed to be less hostile to EC initiatives than their counterparts in British firms, since many of the proposals made by the Commission are already in place in their headquarters' labour markets. Finally, it was regarded as necessary to study a range of companies based on size classification, incorporating both multinationals and small firms. Large, particularly multinational, companies would almost certainly have more developed and more active views relating to EC social initiatives than small firms, but it was seen as important to include the latter as they are a growing sector in the British economy and essential to an assessment of the extent to which EC influences have penetrated the commercial environment in Britain.

The research findings did not fully support these assumptions. In particular, whilst it was initially assumed that the research would produce certain sector-specific findings, this turned out not to be the case. The sectoral location of the companies interviewed appears to have had little relevance to the manner in which they responded to EC social initiatives. The interviews did show that the size and nationality of firms have a bearing on how personnel managers responded to the proposals emanating from Brussels, although perhaps not strictly on the lines first anticipated. The rest of this chapter outlines the findings from the conducted interviews in some detail. The discussion is organised as follows: the first section examines company *responses* to the EC social proposals; then company *perceptions* of the impact or likely impact of EC social policy are analysed. The following section outlines the *actions* undertaken by companies in relation to these initiatives. Finally, the discussion assesses the extent to which company personnel policies and strategies have been influenced by the Community's deliberations on social policy.

Company responses to EC Social Policy Initiatives

The most striking finding of the study is that with the exception of equal opportunities and certain health and safety policies, where an agnostic rather than supportive view was held by some respondents, the personnel managers interviewed did not support the direction of EC social legislation during the seventies and early eighties. A variety of reasons was put forward to explain this unease with Community proposals on worker participation, information disclosure and labour-market regulation. The most frequent comment made by the respondents was that as the Commission's thinking on employment and labour affairs was heavily imbued with the legislative-orientated practice of the member states on mainland Europe, it was insensitive to the voluntarist tradition of British industrial relations. For example, the proposals contained in the draft Fifth Directive for formal participation structures at the enterprise level were widely regarded as being fundamentally at odds with collective bargaining practices and other informal consultative and communication arrangements in Britain. In a similar way, attempts to encourage the reorganisation and reduction of working time through the legislative route were deemed to be inappropriate for the British context of free collective bargaining.

Another reason cited for opposing many of the Commission's proposals for social legislation was that they were insufficiently business orientated. The Commission's proposals were seen to be motivated by social objectives which would only, the argument went, add burdens on businesses and thus reduce their ability to remain or become competitive in world markets. By contrast the personnel managers saw themselves motivated by commercial objectives, which meant they had a completely different set of priorities. Instead of promoting regulatory policies, they were devising ways in which jobs and tasks could be made more flexible: rather than creating new formal structures, they wanted to make existing ones more adaptable. As shown in an earlier section, aggregate trends give substance to this view. Thus, a genuine asymmetry does appear to exist between the personnel policies of British companies and the Commission's proposals, which by their own admission are regulatory in character. Some of the more forthright personnel managers said that they were unable to support the Commission's proposals, as they were in all but name trade union policies. Although not always explicitly stated, the general impression gained from the interviews was that the Commission was widely regarded as too supportive of the trade union point of view on employment and labour matters.

An argument put forward by many respondents was that as some of the Directives were introduced in response to certain industrial relations problems which have now passed, they are in effect no longer salient. The most common example cited was the Mass Dismissals Directive. This piece of legislation was seen as an initiative on the part of the Community to give workers certain protective rights when large-scale redundancy and rationalisation programmes were being enacted across European industry during the late seventies and early eighties. But this 'shake-out' period, it was argued, is now over, and as a result the importance of this piece of legislation has declined. In other words, the personnel managers appeared to be suggesting that if Community social legislation was to have any influence it had to be much more in step with or responsive to actual ground-level developments in personnel and employment policies.

Few of the personnel managers interviewed believed that the EC institutions were in touch with developments. The prevalent view was that much of the EC legislation is based on an industrial relations approach increasingly regarded by personnel managers in Britain as redundant. In particular, it was argued that the EC's involvement in employment and labour affairs rests on the assumption that an *external* body of legislation and initiatives is required to complement or reinforce personnel policies and practices within the enterprise. In this view, legislation is required to enforce positive action on such issues as equal opportunities at the workplace, worker participation and communication. Again, as we saw in an earlier section, there is evidence to challenge the relevance of this view, in the UK.

While the nature of the personnel policies implemented varied considerably, a key goal of the majority of the companies interviewed was the creation of a decentralised enterprise-specific employment system. Under these *internalised* employment systems, pay, conditions and so on are fixed locally. There has been, for instance, an increase in the use of individual performance and merit criteria. Comprehensive company policies frequently exist on such things as equal opportunities which go beyond those recommended nationally. Thus personnel managers designing and implementing human resource strategies are increasingly taking a cool view of national external influences on their enterprise-level employment and labour affairs: for example, industry-wide agreements are now regarded as inappropriate and as a result less and less importance is being attached to them. In this context, the Commission's attempts to establish above the national level a body of legislation laying down certain Community-wide employment rights were regarded by the personnel managers as an unwarranted and unnecessary intrusion. As a result of the trend towards decentralisation, EC deliberations on employment were seen as remote and distant, with practically no bearing on the day to day personnel matters in companies.

Most of the respondents emphasised that whilst they were opposed to the direction of EC social policy, they supported Britain's membership of the Community. For them, Britain's economic and commercial integration with Europe was a positive and worthwhile goal. They did not, however, believe that this entailed any significant social dimension.

The argument often evoked by the Commission to justify its activity on social and employment affairs – that social harmonisation on such things as employment rights and practices was necessary to make the internal market work more effectively – was seen by most personnel managers to be highly dubious. A common response was that different employment conditions and arrangements existed in companies in the same industries within Britain without widely disrupting the workings of the market: why could not these principles apply within a wider European market? More specifically, some suggested that the standardisation of employment rights and practices across the Community was an outmoded, even regressive, policy goal. Any proposals towards that goal should be seen as time-consuming and as a waste of scarce staff resources. In other words, the personnel managers questioned the very legitimacy of the Community's involvement in manpower and personnel related issues.

An instructive example is provided by the Community initiatives on equal opportunities and health and safety. Most of the personnel managers did not seriously question the contents of the initiatives. They did, however, query whether this type of initiative was something with which the Community should involve itself. In general terms, whilst the personnel managers said that they had no serious objections to Community equal opportunities and health and safety policies, they did have a firm belief that their company's policies in these areas were comprehensive and adequate. As will be shown in the next section, this reply fits somewhat uncomfortably with the anxiety some respondents expressed about the implications for their companies of Court of Justice rulings on equal opportunities matters. But the main point should not be lost: personnel managers were reluctant to support Community initiatives even in areas where they perceived there to be no conflict between these policies and the practices they were implementing in their companies. For the most part, the personnel managers regarded employment rights and practices at the workplace as something outside the scope of Community competence.

By contrast, there were no dissenting voices raised against the Commission's general labour-market initiatives – obtaining concerted policies between member states on matters such as training, social security, and the free movement of workers. Similarly, general support was expressed for the Commission's efforts to encourage and sponsor employment-creation initiatives throughout the Community. The respondents were of the view that these were the social policy issues on which the Community should focus.

The Impact of EC Social Policy

Having established that few personnel managers support EC social initiatives, this next section outlines how the same personnel managers perceived the impact of adopted and potential EC social initiatives on their manpower and employment policies. Since adopted EC social policies are transferred into national law before becoming operational, the possibility exists that a personnel manager may be unable to differentiate a national influence from an EC influence. In other words, a personnel manager may not know that a piece of national legislation obliging certain changes to the company's employment system had its origins in Brussels. As a result, the way that personnel managers perceived the impact of EC policies on their organisation's employment system may not accord with the actual impact. To overcome this problem, the personnel managers were questioned about individual EC social policies as well as some proposed policies and also the subject matter of these policies. The objective was to identify what influenced the shape of their company policies in each area so as to find out what motivated them to make major changes to their policies. This approach, by a process of elimination, made it possible to identify whether any EC influence was present in the employment policies of the companies.

In detailing the results of the interviews on these questions, there is a distinction between operational influences and structural influences. Operational influences refer to the manner in which EC social legislation and policies have affected or may potentially affect company-level employment policies or the day to day management of the personnel function. Structural influences refer to the way in which the EC social policies have impacted on the general industrial relations framework within which companies formulate their employment and management policies. Although this distinction is to some degree arbitrary, it is useful in making clear both the way in which the EC affects employment policies and practices, and the views of personnel managers on the subject.

The consensus view is that since the early eighties, EC influences and potential EC influences on British work practices have receded considerably. This is widely attributed to the UK Government taking a firm stance against Commission social policy proposals. As other parts of the book show, this view reflects reality – few significant social policy measures have been adopted by the Council since the Conservative Government has filled the British seat. This decline in EC social policy initiatives has led the personnel managers to adopt the view that it is no longer necessary to undertake detailed analysis of what is being proposed by Community institutions in the employment and labour fields. It is confidently assumed that any proposal made which is not in the interests of business would be successfully blocked by the UK Government.

During the late seventies, the approach was very different. At that time, every likelihood existed of the Commission's draft Fifth Directive being adopted, and the proposed Vredeling Directive was taking shape. The Community was regarded then by many companies, particularly multinationals, as an institution which could have a far-reaching impact on their employment systems. Nearly all of the personnel managers in MNCs said that during this period their companies closely monitored EC social proposals and had active strategies on the issues. Among foreign-owned MNCs in Britain, most of the 'strategic' work in relation to EC social policies was co-ordinated by special teams at the headquarters location. The tasks of such teams were to assess the likely impact on the company of the Commission proposals if adopted, and to devise implementation plans to enable the company to adjust with the minimum degree of disruption. Personnel managers in the UK subsidiaries played a role in these activities, particularly in the multinationals with decentralised employment systems, by evaluating what changes would be required in Britain. Within UK multinationals, the reverse situation was the case, with the UK personnel department being responsible for corporate-wide policy on EC matters. In some companies, this involved a personnel team working full time for over a year on devising strategies, advising managers in subsidiaries, and giving support and assistance to 'umbrella' employers' groups and lobbying organisations campaigning against EC proposals.

The proposal which the transnationals regarded as the most threatening was the draft Vredeling Directive. The common view was that the initiative would give a big boost to trade union attempts to open up international forms of collective bargaining and to pave the way for further Commission initiatives designed to regulate international business within the Community. The Vredeling proposal was seen as very much the thin edge of the wedge and accordingly had to be stoutly opposed. None of the other Directives were regarded in the same menacing light. Indeed, personnel managers in these companies were of the view that they could adapt to many of the EC Directives, if implemented, with relative ease. For example, the UK personnel director of a large USA multinational said that although he regarded the Commission's draft Fifth Directive to be inappropriate to Britain's industrial relations context, its proposals could be introduced without the distinct employee relations culture of the organisation being disrupted too much. The company, he stated, was able to operate effective employee relations strategies in West Germany, where it had had to establish an internal employment regime similar to that proposed by the Fifth Directive. Another personnel manager said that the Commission proposal for a Directive on Parental Leave and Leave for Family Reasons would, if adopted, be an 'administrative inconvenience' rather than a cost burden, since existing company policies on these issues were in some respects more extensive than those contained in the Directive.

Personnel managers in foreign-owned multinationals were more inclined to take this attitude to the potential impact of EC social policies than were personnel managers in UK multinationals. The latter tended to suggest that EC social proposals, particularly on worker participation and information provisions, would have a far-reaching and disruptive impact on their organisation. The reason for this difference in assessment may be that the UK personnel managers were more closely involved in the CBI's and other campaigns against the Commission's proposals. This may have tempered their assessment so that they were more sceptical about the possibility of translating participation practices, which may have been successful in the very different German and Dutch contexts, into the UK employee relations environment.

How have the companies reacted to existing Community social policy? This can only be assessed issue by issue. Most of the companies regarded the health and safety Directives as fairly benign. Only companies in the textiles and chemical industries said that they had to adapt their practices as a result of EC Directives, but these adjustments were not substantial. On the other hand, the personnel managers interviewed in one company in this sector said that if the newly-adopted health and safety programme was implemented in full, then they would most likely have to introduce far-reaching changes to existing arrangements. An examination of the new Community health and safety programme shows that this is probably an accurate view. The more general conclusion to be drawn here is that in the future it is likely that the EC influences on health and safety, and on other issues for that matter, will be uneven across sectors.

Equal opportunities was generally considered to be the area where the Community has the most direct influence on British employment practices. Most personnel managers regarded this influence as structural rather than procedural. In other words, the widely held view was that the EC had been to a certain extent successful in reshaping British equality law. It had not, however, influenced company equal opportunities policies. Most personnel managers said the changes that the British Government were obliged to make to existing equality laws as a result of the Court of Justice rulings did not lead to a significant revision in their company's policies in this area. For instance, few made any major revisions to their job evaluation programmes, the principal method used to implement equal pay policies inside many of these companies as a result of any Court of Justice rulings. It should also be added, however, that most of the personnel managers regarded operating an effective and comprehensive equal opportunities programme as a high priority. The majority of these companies had started monitoring the effectiveness of their policies in this area, and were putting on training courses for selection interviewers. Some had also begun organising 'women only' training courses for their female employees so that they could obtain a range of skills to enhance their career prospects within the company.

The increasing number of equality cases going before the Court of Justice was regarded as a new development: potentially the most significant change. While this was regarded by the personnel managers as important, few had undertaken any specific action to ensure that their company would not fall foul of this type of action, nor had many of them worked out any company strategy in the event of such action. Most personnel managers were of the view that, for a number of reasons, it was unlikely such action would be taken against their company. Most regarded their equal opportunities policies as sufficiently effective to ensure that no basis exists for such actions. Furthermore, as the trade unions in their companies were seen as not giving priority to equal opportunities policies, it was thought unlikely that the necessary 'ground work' to devise such claims would be undertaken. Finally, some took heart in the Court of Justice ruling on the Marshall case, which laid down that Directives were only directly applicable in the public sector. In other words, equality claims based on Community Directives could not be initiated against their private sector companies. The common view amongst the personnel managers was that their companies were secure from being taken to the European Court of Justice.

Whether this view is justified is open to question. To begin with, the personnel managers interviewed appeared not to give due weight to the fact that equal opportunities cases, particularly relating to equal pay (which the Court of Justice has defined fairly broadly), can still be initiated against private sector companies under Article 19 of the Treaty of Rome. Thus the ruling in the Marshall case in no way makes the private sector immune from European legal proceedings on equal rights issues. Secondly, there is growing evidence to suggest that trade unions and other single-issue groups will in the forthcoming period increasingly exploit the opportunities available in certain aspects of European law.

The main difference between the responses of personnel managers in multinational companies and those within other private sector companies was that the former were more aware of the way in which the Community worked. They had a better understanding of the exact nature of EC social policies and proposals and their likely impact. Most of the personnel managers in the purely British companies were only broadly familiar with these issues. Thus, the majority were unaware, for instance, of the exact contents of the proposed Directives on part-time work and parental leave. Most took the view that EC social legislation required no special attention: nearly all kept abreast of developments, casually rather than rigorously, by reading the various personnel and industrial relations publications. As a result of this informal monitoring, most personnel managers had some understanding of which aspects of employment practices and legislation had direct EC influence, most notably with regard to equal opportunities.

The predominant view amongst personnel managers in national companies was that existing employment legislation did not inhibit to any great extent company personnel practice, particularly as regards the drive to obtain more flexible employment systems. It was suggested that in all likelihood this situation would change if some of the Commission's labour-market proposals were to be adopted. This conclusion was based more on a reading of CBI and other employers' organisations' responses to these initiatives rather than a close study of the Directives themselves. In fact, most of the views expressed by these personnel managers corresponded closely with the CBI views on EC social legislation. A general expectation existed amongst these personnel managers that employers' organisations would both lobby against EC social policy proposals which would adversely affect businesses, and keep them fully informed of the possible implications of any initiative emanating from the Community. As long as the employers' organisations fulfilled these functions, and the consensus was that they did so fairly well, then it was widely felt that there was little value in individual organisations independently monitoring EC developments.

None of the personnel managers interviewed regarded the EC as having any significant influence on the operational employment and personnel policies of their companies. However, it was recognised that the EC had an influence on the national industrial relations framework, particularly through influencing national legislation. Moreover, some regarded the Community as having what can best be described as a 'promotional' influence. In other words, while not directly influencing employment policies in companies, the fact that particular issues were raised by the Community was seen to influence, indirectly and over a period of time, how personnel managers perceived these issues. This line of argument should not be pursued too far, since clearly there are limits to the degree to which the Community can influence the outlook of personnel managers. For example, in their pursuit of greater employment flexibility, the personnel managers remain undeterred by the Commission's regulatory proposals. By and large, the Community will have a promotional influence only when there is a high level of consensus that active policies are necessary on such issues as, for instance, equal opportunities and health and safety.

Strategies towards the European Community

All of the multinational corporations interviewed either had international industrial relations advisors or somebody in the personnel policy research department with a brief to monitor international developments. Some of these officials were actively involved in EC social policy deliberations either as an employers' representative on an EC committee or by being a member of one or more of the many employers' organisations at the Community level. The first-hand involvement obviously gave these officers a considerable insight into the state of play as regards EC social policy, which benefited their companies considerably. International officers who were not so closely involved kept in touch with developments in Brussels by contact with such bodies as national and European employers' organisations. By and large, the MNCs are fairly well organised in relation to Europe. As regards national firms, they attach much less importance to EC social policy developments, and rely heavily on the employers' organisations to represent their views in the EC and to keep them informed of developments.

Conclusions

Detailed research amongst personnel specialists in the private sector found them to be sanguine about the impact of EC social policy: particularly at the operational level within their organisations. Only personnel managers in the textile and chemicals industries regarded EC social policies, in particular certain health and safety Directives, as having a direct influence on operational personnel policies. With the exception of this case, the almost unanimous view was that the impact of the EC on personnel practices was extremely limited. It was widely recognised that Community social policy had influenced British labour legislation and other parts of the British industrial relations framework. In this area, however, as in so many others, legislative probity is not the major concern of the personnel specialists operating in the UK. For organisations in the UK private sector, it is the need to maintain market competitiveness which is the main driving force behind personnel policies, and not aspects of national labour law. Hence it is unsurprising to find, for example, that whilst operationally there is some evidence that employee involvement is becoming more widespread,[14] the (structural) requirement to identify participative practices laid down by section 1 of the 1982 Employment Act is obeyed by less than half the relevant companies.[15]

The inescapable conclusion is that the EC has only a marginal influence on company-level employment policies and practices in Britain. Indeed, formidable obstacles exist against an increase in its presence at this level. As outlined in chapter VII, the current Government has endeavoured to limit the influence the Community could have on British labour law by using its control of the legal ports of entry to water-down or undermine the objectives of Directives and so on. In addition to this obstacle, as this chapter shows, personnel managers on the ground do not feel constrained by national legal provisions. It is unlikely in the short-medium term that this situation will go away. Thus, if the Community wants to increase its influence on business at the ground level, it has radically to rethink its approach to social policy.

Notes and References

1 Income Data Services, *Women's Pay and Employment*, Study 402, January 1988

2 *European Industrial Relations Review*, November 1987 p 23

3 MILLWARD, N and STEVENS, M *British Workplace Industrial Relations 1980–1984*, Gower, London 1986 pp 138–141

4 *Ibid* p 147

5 See successive ACAS Annual Reports 1980–84

6 HAKIM, C 'Trends in the Flexible Workplace', *Employment Gazette*, November 1987

7 BREWSTER, C and CONNOCK, S *Industrial Relations: Cost Effective Strategies*, Hutchinson, London 1985

8 See LINDAY, B *New Terms and Areas of Employment Growth: A Comparative Study*, European Commission, Brussels 1987

9 ROBINSON, O and WALLACE, J 'Relative Pay and Part-Time Employment in Great Britain', *Oxford Bulletin of Economics and Statistics* Vol 43 May 1981

10 DISNEY, R and SYKEZCZAK, E 'Protective Legislation and Part-time Employment in Britain,' *British Journal of Industral Relations* Vol XXII No. 1 March 1984

11 *Industrial Relations Review and Report*, June 1987

12 BLANCHFLOWER, D G and OSWALD, J A, *Profit Sharing – Can it work?* New Bridge Street Consultants

13 BREWSTER, C and CONNOCK, S 1985

14 MILLWARD, N and STEVENS, M 1986

15 IPM, *Annual Reports – Employee Involvement Statements*, IPM, London 1985; see also the different interpretation in 'Involving the Staff', *Employment Gazette*, March 1987, pp 147–9, and 'Employee Involvement Statements – Current Practice', *Industrial Relations Review and Report* 396, July 1987, pp 2–7

Chapter XI

Harmonisation: Problems and Prospects

As outlined in earlier chapters, a 'narrow' interpretation of European integration reflected in the Rome Treaty guided the policy actions of the Commission and other Community institutions during the sixties, and possibly even the early seventies. After the Paris Summit of 1972, however, when the Council of Ministers declared that the development of a fully-fledged Community social policy was to be a top priority, a 'wider' view of integration came to the fore. As a result, new policy objectives, such as the upwards harmonisation of social provisions and employment practices, were adopted by the Commission.

The concept of social harmonisation, as shown earlier, aroused a good deal of opposition, mostly from employers' organisations. They did not see this concept as a benign policy instrument to reduce economic and social disparities amongst the member states. Rather, they considered it to be a potential licence for the Commission to press-gang employers into uprooting long-established and widely-accepted industrial relations practices and replace them by more costly, less efficient 'foreign' methods. Because social harmonisation has proven to be so controversial and because actual achievements in this area have fallen far short of Commission ambitions it is important to examine the notion in detail. For the most part, the literature published so far on social harmonisation is unsatisfactory, as it provides partisan and highly judgemental assessments of the concept. In addressing the issue here, a different, hopefully more rigorous, approach is adopted. The question analysed in this chapter is whether social harmonisation is a realistic policy goal that can be made fully operational.

To answer this question the chapter compares different aspects of employment conditions, practices, policies and legislation in the member states to assess the extent to which these converge and diverge. It is our thesis that social harmonisation in large measure depends on whether convergence exists in specific aspects of the employment sphere amongst the member states: if there is considerable divergence then it will be practically impossible to obtain social harmonisation without highly disruptive and far-reaching policies which may not necessarily yield beneficial results.

The chapter is organised as follows: it begins by outlining certain general developments in the European labour market to see whether there are any discernible Community trends. It then goes on to examine the degree of convergence or divergence in a number of different areas:

(i) labour market flexibility; (ii) social protection; (iii) collective bargaining institutions; (iv) public policy and the labour market. In the conclusion, we bring together the trends found in each area and assess the feasibility of harmonising labour and employment matters across the member states.

The European Labour Market: An Overview

In the preamble to the Treaty of Rome it states that a principal objective of the Community is 'to strengthen the unity of economies and to ensure their harmonious development by reducing the differences existing between the various regions and the backwardness of the less-favoured regions'. Nobody could seriously claim that this objective has been realised. Even the most ardent supporters of the Community concede that wide differences in terms of economic and social conditions and economic performance exist between the member states. If anything, the divergences have widened since the signing of the Treaty of Rome. To a large extent this is accounted for by the recruitment of countries from the Mediterranean basin into the Community, but even among the more industrialised member countries trends towards convergence as a result of economic integration have not been spectacular.[1]

A number of economic indicators can be used to show the extent of economic divergence or convergence amongst the member states – differences in macro-economic policy, industrial structure, trade specialisation ratios, and research and development potential. Here we are primarily concerned with examining the scale of divergences of some aspects of the Community labour market. The most appropriate starting point is trends in employment. Figure XIi shows the employment/population ratios in 1986, amongst selected member states, and the percentage change between 1979 and 1986. The employment/population ratios indicate that proportion of the working-age population which actually has a job. (They are distinct from activity rates, which indicate the proportion of the working-age population which has a job or is seeking employment).

Two points are worthy of note. Firstly, in most member states, the ratio declined. In fact, the drop was significant in Ireland, Spain, France, Germany and the United Kingdom, although in the latter two countries most of the fall occurred between 1978 and 1982. Second, as a result of these patterns, the variance of the ratio across countries has increased, indicating that the employment creation potential of the member states now differs considerably. As an aside, when the ratios for Community states are placed against ratios for other countries, the picture is depressing, for the Nordic countries, the United States and Canada have

Figure XIi Employment/Population Ration in 1986[a] and percentage point changes 1979–1986

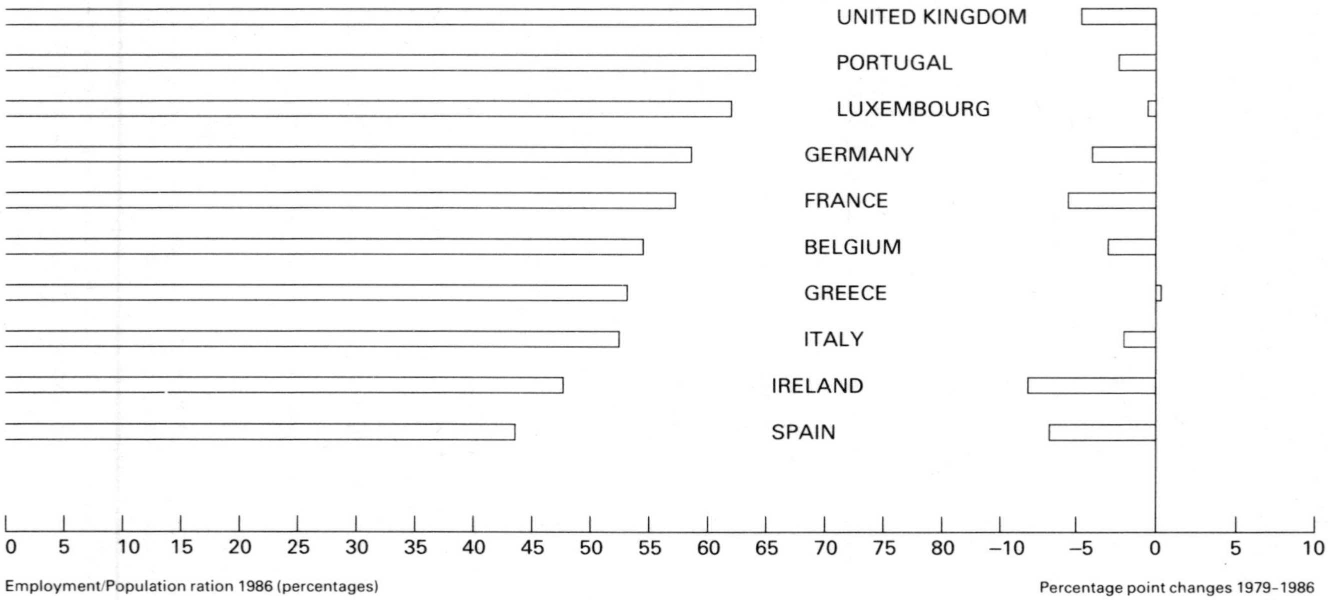

a. Defined as total employment divided by the population of working age (15 to 64).

Sources: *OECD Labour Force Statistics ; Quarterly Labour Force Statistics.*

experienced increases in this measure. Thus in terms of employment growth, the statistics indicate that there will be no one Community pattern in the future.

Full and Part-time Employment

The broad trends in part-time work in the Community labour market are shown in Table XIi. This details size and composition of part-time employment, 1979-86, amongst a number of Community countries. Several interesting points can be discerned. First, since 1979 part-time employment has increased relative to full-time employment in every country except Italy, though Germany and Ireland have experienced a decline since 1983. Secondly there are large differences between the member states: the part-time ratio is highest in the United Kingdom and the Netherlands, accounting for over one in five people in employment in comparison with around one in twenty in Italy, Ireland and Greece. Third, most part-time workers are women, although there has been a marginal decline in part-time employment as a proportion of female employment in Germany, Ireland and Luxembourg since 1983. The proportion of men employed part time is low, but since 1979 has increased virtually everywhere.

Table XIi Size and composition of part-time employment, 1979-1986

	Part-time employment as a percentage of:											
	Total employment			Male employment			Female employment			Women's share in part-time employment		
	1979	1983	1986	1979	1983	1986	1979	1983	1986	1979	1983	1986
France	8.2	9.7	11.7	2.5	2.6	3.5	17.0	20.1	23.1	82.0	84.6	83.0
Germany	11.2	12.6	12.3	1.5	1.7	2.1	27.6	30.0	28.4	91.6	91.9	89.8
Greece	--	6.5	--	--	3.7	--	--	12.1	--	--	61.2	--
Ireland	5.1	6.7	6.5	2.1	2.7	2.4	13.1	15.7	15.5	71.2	72.0	74.3
Italy	5.3	4.6	5.3	3.0	2.4	3.0	10.6	9.4	10.1	61.4	64.8	61.6
Luxembourg	5.8	6.7	7.3	1.0	1.0	2.6	17.1	18.8	16.3	87.5	90.0	76.6
Netherlands	11.1	22.0	24.0	2.8	7.8	8.7	31.7	50.5	54.2	82.5	76.2	76.1
United Kingdom	16.4	19.1	21.2	1.9	3.3	4.2	39.0	42.4	44.9	92.8	89.6	88.5

Source: *OECD Employment Outlook* 1987

Table XIii shows where part-time workers are located. With the exception of Ireland, the proportion of industry specific employment that is part-time increased in some two-thirds of the industry groups. The table does show up some country-specific trends. For example, the UK has a much larger number of part-time workers in the distributive trades than anywhere else; the Netherlands and the UK have a large

Table XIii Part-time employment as a proportion of total employment by industry, 1983 and 1985

	All Industries	Agriculture forestry fishing, hunting	Energy & water	Mineral extraction & chemicals	Metals engineering manufacture	Other manufacture	Construction	Distributive trades	Transport-ation & communi-cation	Finance insurance real est & business services	Other services	Public admins
Belgium												
1983	8.1	6.2	1.0	1.9	1.9	3.8	2.1	11.0	2.4	10.1	17.6	4.7
1985	8.6	7.2	1.2	1.7	1.6	4.3	2.7	11.2	2.8	10.0	17.4	7.4
France												
1983	9.7	16.5	3.5	2.1	2.2	5.6	3.9	10.6	5.4	9.2	17.5	10.2
1985	10.8	15.6	3.8	2.6	1.2	5.8	4.4	12.1	6.7	10.8	19.4	13.4
Ireland												
1983	6.7	9.4	1.8	1.8	2.5	3.6	2.6	10.2	4.0	4.0	10.8	2.7
1985	6.5	7.9	1.2	1.3	1.6	2.9	1.8	9.7	4.3	4.7	12.5	2.5
Italy												
1983	4.6	13.3	1.2	1.1	1.2	3.6	2.7	4.2	1.4	2.9	6.7	0.9
1985	5.3	14.3	2.2	1.6	1.6	4.3	3.5	5.1	1.6	3.3	7.7	1.7
Luxembourg												
1983	6.7	15.9	0.0	1.2	2.0	4.7	1.5	7.3	3.2	5.1	13.2	7.4
1985	7.3	13.4	0.0	1.8	5.1	5.0	4.5	8.6	4.3	5.7	12.5	7.0
Netherlands												
1983	22.0	17.7		6.5			5.8	23.3	12.8	16.8	40.9	33.8
1985	24.0	17.6		10.3			6.6	24.9	12.1	19.8	45.5	33.7
United Kingdom												
1983	19.1	14.9	3.3	5.6	5.0	12.2	4.5	33.5	5.8	14.4	36.3	8.9
1985	21.2	17.8	2.9	5.7	5.1	13.8	6.3	35.5	6.5	15.3	38.8	10.3

Source: *OECD Employment Outlook* 1987

proportion of part-timers in 'other services' relative to the other countries.

Trends in Temporary Employment

In recent years, there has been an increasing trend towards temporary employment. Much interest is focused on whether this form of work gives rise to job instability and insecurity. Figures for the member st·tes suggest that while temporary employment has increased in all countries except Italy, it remains relatively small. Yet its contribution to employment changes has been important in several countries. For example, in Belgium, France and Ireland, the number of people in permanent employment fell, whereas temporary employment increased. In Luxembourg and the Netherlands, over half of the total change in the number of wage and salary earners was accounted for by those who considered their jobs to be temporary. Moreover, temporary workers tend to be disproportionately located in the distributive trades and other services, and under-represented in manufacturing. Table XIiii shows the demographic composition of wage and salary workers with temporary jobs. Young people account for a large proportion of temporary employees, although the dispersion is quite large, from under a third in Italy to almost two thirds in Denmark, France and Luxembourg. Two factors account for the over-representation of young workers: (i) the expansion of fixed-term government programmes for young people; (ii) the tendency for this age group to prefer temporary forms of work. The table also shows that in almost every member state there is about a 50/50 split in the male-female share of temporary jobs. However, with the exception of France and Denmark, women are over-represented in temporary employment relative to their proportion of all wage and salary employees.

Table XIiv attempts to clarify where these workers come from. It outlines the composition of labour inflows into permanent or temporary work (i.e. the status one year earlier of employees in a permanent or temporary job at the time of the survey). The table shows a sharp contrast between the two inflows. In every country, over 90 per cent of those currently in what they considered to have been a permanent wage and salary position had been employed a year earlier. Among those in temporary jobs, only about half had been employed a year earlier in France, Ireland and the United Kingdom (while this proportion was as high as 70 per cent in Italy and Luxembourg).

A superficial examination of the figures may lead one to the conclusion that similar trends are emerging amongst the member states – growth of part-time work, or the slowing down of employment generation potc· tial. But such a conclusion should not be taken too far: a closer

Table XIiii Demographic composition of wage and salary workers with temporary jobs (1985)

Percentages
(Percentages of permanent jobs are given in brackets)

	Age 15 to 24	Age 25 to 54	Age 55 & over	Men	Women
Belgium	47.4 (15.5)	50.5 (77.5)	2.1 (7.0)	44.8 (65.2)	55.2 (34.8)
Denmark	62.8 (23.1)	33.3 (66.6)	3.9 (10.3)	50.2 (53.2)	49.8 (46.8)
France	62.9 (15.6)	35.5 (77.5)	1.6 (6.9)	58.7 (57.5)	41.3 (42.5)
Ireland	58.3 (30.0)	37.8 (61.6)	3.9 (8.4)	48.9 (64.6)	51.1 (35.4)
Italy	30.8 (15.3)	57.6 (75.4)	11.6 (9.3)	50.9 (66.5)	49.1 (33.5)
Luxembourg	65.6 (23.0)	34.4 (61.5)	0.0 (5.5)	49.2 (66.0)	50.8 (34.0)
United Kingdom	51.1 (22.1)	41.3 (64.8)	8.6 (13.1)	45.3 (56.2)	54.7 (43.8)

Source: *OECD Employment Outlook* 1987

examination reveals that important differences exist between member states. For instance, the employment creation potential of the member states varies considerably. Similarly, the growth of part-time employment is highly uneven amongst the member states – the trend being most significant in the UK and least significant in Germany. The divergent trends raise a number of implications for Community policy. In particular, it will be difficult for the Commission or some other Community institution to gain a consensus for a Community labour-market strategy among member states which have their own individual priorities.

Policy issues within the Community labour market

Obtaining greater flexibility and adaptability in labour markets is currently a major concern of governments and employers almost everywhere in Europe. On the face of it, therefore, the management of human resources in the member states would appear to be converging

Table XIiv Labour force status one year earlier among current employees with a permanent or temporary job

Current Status and Country	Wage and Salary Employee	Other Employ	Unem-ployed	Not in labour force
Belgium, 1985				
Permanent job	95.6	0.3	1.8	2.3
Temporary job	58.5	0.4	18.0	23.1
Denmark, 1985				
Permanent job	94.1	0.2	2.6	3.1
Temporary job	68.1	0.3	13.4	18.2
France, 1985				
Permanent job	94.0	0.5	2.4	3.1
Temporary job	48.2	1.0	19.4	31.4
Ireland, 1985				
Permanent job	94.0	0.6	2.5	2.9
Temporary job	50.4	0.5	19.4	29.7
Italy, 1983				
Permanent job	94.4	1.2	2.1	2.3
Temporary job	71.8	0.9	15.5	17.8
Luxembourg, 1984				
Permanent job	95.4	0.2	1.2	3.2
Temporary job	70.0	0.0	3.3	26.7
Netherlands, 1985				
Permanent job	95.3	0.1	1.4	3.2
Temporary job	61.6	0.9	12.7	24.8
United Kingdom, 1985				
Permanent job	91.0	1.7	2.5	4.8
Temporary job	48.5	6.2	14.2	31.1

Source: *OECD Employment Outlook* 1987

around a fixed group of issues and problems. Again, however, this is not necessarily the case, since a more detailed examination shows that the drive towards flexibility can take many forms and can focus on different issues.

In this section we examine developments in a number of areas which are at the centre of the drive towards greater labour-market flexibility:

labour cost flexibility;
regulations governing the recruitment and dismissal of employees;
temporary and fixed-term employment;

self-employment and off-site working;
developments in working time.

Labour Cost Flexibility

Neo-classical economic theory treats the market for labour as similar to that for any other commodity, where equilibrium is achieved through the interplay of demand and supply. In this view, wages should adapt to changing conditions in industries, occupations and regions to maintain labour-market equilibrium (conventionally now defined as the non-accelerating inflation rate of unemployment (NAIRU)). Thus, if an industry falls into recession leading to a fall in product prices, wages should fall by an equal amount to avoid unemployment in the industry and/or to give the incentive to workers to switch to more buoyant industries. Similarly, if a region is experiencing an economic downturn, then wage levels should fall, and hence wage differentials should be established between depressed and prosperous regions to encourage labour mobility. This view has gained currency amongst some member states' Governments, particularly that of the UK in recent years. A UK Government White Paper suggests:

'To think of workers as part of a market is not to devalue them; it is to recognise that the realities of economic life are not waived just because the factors are people, not things. Skill and effort are traded between workers as sellers and employers as customers; and here as in all other markets, the customer cannot be expected to pay unless he is getting what he needs at a price he can afford. In the labour market the employer as customer is looking for the right people at the right price in order to carry on his business.'[2]

From this neo-liberal view, the labour market should gravitate towards equilibrium: if it does not, then it is a result of imperfections and rigidities. One of the imperfections which inhibits wage adjustments in the face of changing patterns and trends in employment is seen to be wage-fixing arrangements. These include such measures as statutory minimum wages, and indexation agreements which keep wages in line with inflation. The wage-fixing systems of the member states, together within recent trends, are outlined in Table XIv.

Probably the most striking point in Table XIv is the difference in the wage-fixing systems of the member states. Some member states, like Italy and Belgium, have legally binding minimum wage and indexation arrangements, while in others, such as Germany and the UK, these matters are left to collective bargaining. In terms of wage-fixing, the UK is the least regulated. It has no indexation mechanism, and by denouncing the ILO conventions – No. 94 on labour clauses (public contracts), No. 95 on the protection of wages, and No. 26 on minimum wage-fixing machinery – it has gone further than any other member state in liberalising this area. At the same time, in most member states where minimum wages are fixed by law, the rules governing minimum wages have been amended downwards. Furthermore, in all the countries where wage indexation rules exist, either on the basis of legislation or contained in collective agreements, these arrangements have been restrained. Thus the general trend appears to be towards a loosening up of wage-fixing arrangements. It should be noted, though, that the scale of the move in this direction varies considerably amongst member states, with Belgium being the most regulated system and the UK the least.

The above analysis suggests that any attempt to construct a Community approach to the issue of labour cost flexibility would run into major problems. For a start, although there is a general trend towards deregulation inside the Community, important differences exist in the degree to which member states have introduced liberalisation policies. Clearly, Belgium and the Netherlands or the South European member states would be unhappy with a Community deregulation strategy similar to the one being implemented by the UK Government. In turn, the UK Government would have reservations if the Community adopted a pragmatic stance on the issue as some member states appear to have done. In other words the Community would face major problems in determining the level at which labour cost flexibility policies should be aimed.

Regulations on the recruitment and dismissal of employees inside the Community

One of the key assumptions of the case for greater labour-market flexibility is that regulations governing the recruitment and dismissal of employees – 'hiring and firing rules' – undermine the ability of firms to adapt to market conditions. Thus, for proponents of the flexibility thesis, there should be a European drive towards deregulation in this area. Alternatively, from a social protectionist point of view, it is argued that regulation of recruitment and dismissal procedures should be supported in order to afford employees a degree of job security. Indeed the argument is continually being made by trade unions and others that 'hiring and firing rules' should be harmonised on a European basis. Both arguments assume that it is possible to obtain a single Community regime in this field. The extent to which this can be achieved depends on the scale of divergence in existing regulations amongst the member states. This section focuses on that issue.

In 1985, the Commission financed a detailed survey of 50,000 companies in EC countries to obtain detailed information on whether or not

Table XIv Wage-fixing Systems in the Member States of the EC

Country	Pay increases of Employed persons – 1986 Trend National	 Real	Negotiating level	Minimum Wage	Indexation
Belgium	3.0	1.8	Interprofessional agreements (2 years) taking account of wage-moderation and competitiveness	Statutory minimum Wage since 1975	Indexation reduced since Royal decree 178 of 30/3/86 – 2%
Denmark	3.1	0.6	National agreements taking account of government recommendations	Agreed minimum wage in very few agreements	Indexation suspended since March 1983
Spain	8.6	0.6	Local & Sectoral collective agreements (1–2 years), major state involvement	Statutory minimum wage	No official indexation mechanism but safeguard clauses
France	4.3	1.9	Sectoral agreements and agreements at company level (1 year), major state involvement	Statutory minimum wage (SMIC) (Law of 2 January 1970)	No official indexation but safeguard clauses which are tending to disappear
Greece	15.2	–5.9	Central agreement for private sector and sectoral agreements in a number of branches	Statutory wage since 1982	'A priori' indexation since May 1983

Country	Pay increases of Employed persons – 1986 Trend National	Real	Negotiating level	Minimum Wage	Indexation
Ireland	6.6	3.6	Sectoral agreements and agreements at company level (12–18 months)	Minimum wage rates fixed by joint labour committees (*)	No wage-indexation mechanism
Italy	7.6	1.8	Three year sectoral agreements taking account of 1983 protocol	Agreed minimum wage in each industry	Automatic indexation since 1957, in low year since 1983
Luxembourg	4.2	3.3	Sectoral negotiations, major state involvement	Statutory minimum social wage since 1944. Statutory minimum income since July 1986	Return to automatic wage indexation in in Jan 1986
Netherlands	2.2	2.2	Sectoral agreements and agreements at company level (1 or 2 years) Considerable state intervention limited, however, by law of April '86	Statutory minimum wage since 1986	Automatic indexation tending to disappear from agreements and be replaced by a single payment
Portugal	17.2	4.6	Sectoral agreements (1 year)	Statutory minimum wage	No indexation mechanism
F R Germany	4.0	4.0	Sectoral agreements (1 year)	No statutory minimum wage	Prohibition of sliding scale
UK	7.7	3.6	Negotiations at sector and company level	Minimum rates fixed by Wages Councils (*)	No indexation mechanism

(*) Wage committees statutorily authorised to fix minimum rates for workers not covered by collective agreements.

Source: *EC Internal and External Adaption of Firms* 1987

employers regarded regulations on the recruitment and dismissal of employees as a disincentive to employing more staff.[3] Table XIvi below ranks the responses in order of countries according to the importance enterprises attached to 'insufficient flexibility in hiring and shedding labour as a reason for not employing more staff.' It shows that employers' perceptions of the problem varied significantly across the member states. Only 26 per cent of UK employers interviewed regarded 'hiring and firing' regulations as causing a rigidity, indicating that they faced few problems in the area. On the other hand, Italian employers must regard recruitment and dismissal regulations as a major constraint: 83 per cent of those interviewed thought such rules were an important obstacle to employing more staff. As such a wide variance exists in employers' perceptions on the subject, it is worthwhile examining the matter in more detail.

Table XIvi Percentage of firms considering 'insufficient flexibility in hiring and shedding rules to be an important obstacle to employing more staff'

	Country	%
1.	Italy	83
2.	France	81
3.	Belgium	75
4.	Greece	67
5.	Ireland	68
6.	Luxembourg	56
7.	Germany	56
8.	Netherlands	51
9.	United Kingdom	26

Source: *European Economy* 1986

Rules of Recruitment

Although affirmative action legislation has been passed in a number of states in the USA, this form of regulation is not widespread in Europe. Only one European country, Italy, has attempted to regulate precisely whom is to be recruited. The so-called 'numerical' system in principle lists candidates by order of merit, according to certain social criteria. The system is regarded by employers and labour economists both inside and outside the country as burdensome and impractical. Some public authorities in member states, like local authorities in the UK, have attempted to develop employment policies which favour certain groups, but no evidence exists about how extensive and how successful are such initiatives.

Systems for Individual Dismissals

The procedures for dismissing individuals on economic and professional grounds (i.e. most of those cases not involving criminal acts and gross misconduct) differ considerably inside the Community. One key factor is the degree to which trade unions, works councils, government or the courts can undermine the employer's prerogative to make such decisions. In Germany, the trade unions have to be consulted, and a social plan agreed with the works council in cases of dismissal for economic reasons. In individual dismissals, if the works council does not agree, the dismissed employee may take the case to the labour court, where procedures are sometimes very long drawn out (up to five years) during which time the employee must be retained on full pay. In Italy, appeals to the courts are likely to be treated favourably, particularly if the applicant's family conditions are not good. Until 1986, works councils and trade unions had to be consulted before individual dismissals, but this requirement was removed by legislation in that year.

In the United Kingdom, dismissed individuals have the right to appeal against unfair dismissal, but employers win a large majority of the cases. This evidence suggests that compared to other EC countries, the UK has a fairly liberalised system, in that the external appeals procedure does not appear to constrain employers' termination decisions. In other member states, the system for individual dismissals appears to be heavily regulated, although how this operates in practice may differ significantly.[4]

Temporary Work and Fixed-term Contracts

Table XIvii outlines the regulations which apply to private sector temporary work agencies inside the Community. There is some divergence amongst the member states, but largely in the extent of the regulatory structures. The most restrictive regime exists in Italy where the law on private temporary work agencies severely restricts direct employment on the basis of non-permanent contracts. Most of the other member states – Germany, France, Belgium, Netherlands and Denmark – regulate and restrict temporary work companies quite strictly.

During the 1970s, comprehensive legislation restricting fixed-term contracts was introduced throughout Europe. But since 1982, the general trend has been to loosen these regulations. For instance, in Germany legislation in 1985 extended the maximum duration of fixed-term contracts from six to eighteen months, also removing the need for any particular justification of such contracts. Spain had adopted similar measures in 1984. Italy in 1984 increased opportunities to offer fixed-

Table XIvii Regulation of private sector temporary work agencies

France	Restricted under licensing system
Germany	Restricted under licensing system
Italy	Prohibited; law strongly prefers permanent employment contracts
United Kingdom	Regulated under licensing system
Belgium	Restricted under licensing system
Netherlands	Restricted under licensing system
Denmark	Restricted under licensing system (only permitted in business and office branches)
Norway	Restricted under licensing system (only permitted in business and office branches)
Sweden	Prohibited; direct temporary employment severely restricted since 1974
Switzerland	Unregulated
Ireland	Regulated under licensing system
Greece	Restricted to specific activities

Note: Temporary work companies hire personnel to a third company for limited periods of time. Direct temporary employment involves only employer and employee in a contract of fixed duration.

Source: *Emerson* 1987

term contracts to young people, and in 1986 liberalised their previous restrictive regime. However, the Commission's survey in 1985 showed that there is considerable divergence of opinion amongst the Community employees on the likely positive employment impact from measures facilitating temporary contracts (Table XIviii)

Moves have been made to liberalise regulations relating to the recruitment and dismissal of employees across the Community, but the pace and scale of liberalisation differs significantly amongst the member states. In addition, while some deregulation measures have been introduced in most member countries, these have not amounted to the dismantling of the pre-existing policy regime: most member states, with the possible exception of Britain, continue to have regulated hire and fire systems. What is more, there appears to be a wide difference of opinion amongst Community employers about the possible benefits arising from deregulating these systems. This evidence tends to suggest that rules applying to recruitment and dismissals in individual member states are the outcome of national industrial relations practice and

Table XIviii Percentage of firms expecting a positive employment impact from measures facilitating temporary contracts

	Country	%
1.	Germany	74
2.	Luxembourg	69
3.	Italy	63
4.	Belgium	63
5.	France	53
6.	Greece	50
7.	Ireland	47
8.	Netherlands	32
9.	United Kingdom	27

Source: *European Economy* 1986

preference and as such are not readily amenable to European-wide harmonisation.

Self-employment and off-site working

As part of its programme of research into the development of the labour market, the Commission financed five separate studies concerning the development of new forms of employment and new areas of employment growth in France, Germany, Italy, the Netherlands and the United Kingdom. Each study addressed the issue of whether new forms of contractual arrangements were emerging. The key issues arising out of the country studies relate to: (i) the nature of 'self-employment' and prospects for its future growth; (ii) the forms of 'off-site working' which straddle the boundary between self-employment and employee status; and (iii) the flexible use of employees through contracts which vary working time. The overall conclusion 'is that while these forms of work may be *marginal* relative to the mainstream patterns of full-time and part-time employment, they are certainly not small taken together, and changes in their rates of growth will make substantial differences to the quantity and quality of paid work in the economies concerned'.[5]

i) Self-employment

The country studies show that non-agricultural self-employment in France, Germany and the Netherlands has remained roughly constant, while in the UK and Italy it has grown at almost 1.5 per cent and 2 per cent per annum respectively. By 1984 Italy had by far the highest share of self-employment in total non-agricultural employment at 25 per cent, whilst the Netherlands had nearly 5 per cent: the other three countries fell in the 8-12 per cent bracket. The case of Italy is clearly distinctive simply because of the scale of self-employment.

The country studies reflect these figures in the relative signficance they attach to self-employment. Thus, little reference is made to this area of employment in the Dutch study. In France, the stabilisation of self-employment in the first half of the 1980s and employer strategies for contracting out were seen to have reached their limit. The small rise in self-employment between 1980-1985 for Germany is expected to continue alongside a moderate decline in manufacturing. But this process is regarded as the result of conventional growth in small enterprises' self-employment activity, structural shifts towards the service sector, and some recession-induced movement into self-employment. For the UK there has been a significant increase in the number of self-employed; this is seen in an increased penetration of self-employment within certain industries, reinforced by industrial change in favour of employment in the service sector. The country study suggests that these structural shifts arise partly through changes in contractual arrangements involving producers contracting-out some service activities and production related work. The growth of franchising in the service sector also has a limited impact on the increase in self-employment at the expense of employee jobs. In addition, legislative (and particularly tax) changes by the Conservative government have acted to encourage self-employment.

An important distinction emerged in the country studies between the growth of the self-employed working on their own account, and the growth of self-employment where the person becomes an employer of others. The first form is expected mainly to be a response to high unemployment, while the second is more likely to be a response to improvements in the entrepreneurial climate. Thus it is worth noting that whilst UK self-employment grew at four times the German rate during the decade up to 1983/84, by the final year only 36 per cent of the self-employed in the UK had paid employees, compared with 62 per cent in Germany. This distinction is seen as important, for if the form of self-employment growth experienced by the UK is associated with large firms contracting out in response to market difficulties, it could be undermined by a cyclical market upturn. Alternatively, the form of self-employed experienced in Germany is more likely to be a better long-term guide to the intensity of job-creating entrepreneurial activity. Despite this observation, the conclusion is that self-employment in Italy and the UK will continue to rise faster than total employment.

ii) Off-site Working

Off-site workers straddle the boundary between self-employment and employee status. Certain industries, for example textiles and clothing, are traditionally associated with off-site workers. But this form of employment has now spread to a wide range of industries and occupations. Large numbers in services and in professional, clerical and sales occupations are involved. The country reports suggest that there have been substantial increases, particularly in the UK, with growth being concentrated in white collar occupations. On the distinctive forms of growth, and future trends, the research is equivocal. On balance, the trend for off-site workers is positive and mainly associated with the service sector. In addition, developments in communications and information technology do open up new possibilities for extending off-site working. Thus, like other sections, the evidence suggests that the degree and form of new employment arrangements vary across the member states. And once again, in this area, diversity poses problems in establishing a harmonised Community policy.

iii) Working Time

In a major survey of working time developments in 17 countries, conducted by the European Industrial Relations Review, the main conclusion was that it is becoming less and less easy to generalise about the length of the working week in many West European countries. Gradual reductions in contractual hours have been accompanied by a variety of arrangements allowing greater flexibility in actual working practice. Taken together with special provisions for shift workers, this means that time actually worked varies from week to week for more and more groups of employees. In this section, we use (with permission) the survey results on West Germany, France, Greece and Ireland to compare working time developments in two of the richer member states with those in two of the poorer member states. The part of the Table XIix relating to statutory working time shows that in Germany and Ireland the legislation dates from a considerable time ago: the relevant laws being passed in the case of Germany in 1938 and in the case of Ireland 1936 and 1944. French legislation relating to working time, however, was enacted more recently: a law establishing a statutory working week was passed in 1982 by the then socialist government. For its part, Greece follows the general trend in the overall survey of laying down in law a 40-hour week.

The part of the table relating to collective agreements shows that unions in France and Germany tend to enjoy lower working hours than workers in Ireland and Greece. But this needs to be qualified: when it

Table XIix Statutory Working Time in Europe

France	West Germany	Greece	Ireland
	STATUTORY WORKING TIME		
39 hours a week 10 hours a day Decree dated 16 January 1982 (Article L212-1 of the French Labour Code) Article L212-2 adds two further limits, extended again in 1987.	48 hours a week 8 hours a day Working Time Order (Arbeitszeitordnung) 30 April 1983, amended on numerous occasions since.	40 hours a week 8 hours a day (exceptionally 9 and in the case of weekend fourth shift systems only, 12 hours. Royal Decree 10 of 10 September 1937 and covering weekend fourth shifts – ruling 25/1983 of Athens Arbitration Court.	48 hours a week industrial 9 hours a day Conditions of Employment Acts of 1936 and 1944 covering 'industrial work'; shops (Conditions of Employment Acts of 1938 and 1942, covering shop assistants, other acts cover other sectors, such as mining, transport and so on. The Hours of Work Bill (1984) not yet enacted, would limit the statutory working week for most workers of 40 hours.
	COLLECTIVE AGREEMENTS		
Average blue and white collar 38-39 hours Engineering: 38½ hrs Chemicals: 38 hours Banking/insurance 39 hours (may be less at company level).	Average blue and white collar 38½-40 hours (By the end of 1987, 39% of all workers will have a working week of under 40 hours. Engineering: 38½ hours average Chemicals: 40 hours (employees over 58 have an extra 2 days off per month) Banking/Insurance: 40 hours.	Average blue and white collar 40 hours (a very few collective agreements grant 39 hours. Engineering: 40 hours Chemicals: 40 hours Banking/Insurance: 38 hours 20 minutes.	Average blue collar 40 hours Average white collar: 38 hours Engineering: 40 hours Chemicals 40 hours (manual) 37 hours 54 minutes (clerical) Banking: 36¼ hours.
	FLEXIBLE WORKING TIME		
Most Collective Bargaining agreements allow flexible working of two or three hours above or below the statutory working week, provided that over a specified time limit – usually 8 to 12 weeks – the average does not exceed the statutory 39 hour week. In addition, there are some notable agreements on	There are very few agreements on flexible working time at company level. At sector level – notably engineering and printing. though some others as well – weekly hours must average a certain number over a negotiated period. For example, in engineering, weekly hours must average 38½ over a period of	There are no agreements on annualised or flexible working hours.	There are no agreements on annualised or flexible working hours.

Table XIix Statutory Working Time in Europe (cont.)

France	West Germany	Greece	Ireland
annualised hours. In the public works sector, there is an annual limit of 1770 working hours, while at company level there is one of 1739 hours at Lhotellier-Montrichard (industrial packaging) and one of 1585 hours for shift workers at Cegedur-Pechiney (aluminium). The length of the actual working week is limited by the statutory limits in the two companies.	two months. However, in 1984 agreement also allowed two other formulae to reduce working time – the continuation of a 40 hour week with additional days off, or an average 38½ hour working week across the company, with different groups of employees working below and above the average. In engineering, overtime rates are applied after 38½ hours up to a maximum of 10 hours a week 20 hours a month.		
	TRENDS IN WORKING TIME		
There has been a trend towards flexible working notably in the metalworking agreement of 17 July '86 which covered reorganisation of working time, extension of shift systems, and time off in lieu (EIRR 151 p 9). This agreement is the mode for the new law on working time currently under scrutiny by the Constitutional Court. The Unions continue to stress working time reductions in their bargaining claims.	In recent years there has been increasing variety in the ways in which working time has been reduced: for instance, reductions in the working day, the introduction of free shifts or early retirement have all been used. A survey by the Engineering Employer's Association in July 1985 revealed that about 70% of companies reducing or reorganising working time had also maintained or increased their use of plant – evidence of greater flexibility in working time. Unions still aim for an eventual 35 hour week, and in the current round most are going for hours cut or early retirement though they are concentrating more on pay.	The unions emphasise reductions in working time as a means of reducing unemployment. The National Council for Development Policy (ESAP) considered a new approach towards flexible working, but no action has yet been taken.	Unions continue to look not only for reduced working hours but also – in some cases – for greater flexibility. Companies are beginning to take an interest in annualised working hours.

Source: *European Industrial Relations Review*, March 1987

comes to specific sectors, contractual working hours vary from country to country. In chemicals, French workers have a contractual 38½-hour week while in the other countries they work 40 hours. In banking, the average of negotiated working week agreements in Ireland is 36¼ hours, while in other countries, it is nearer the 40-hour mark.

In relation to flexible working time, the table shows there are virtually no developments in this area in Ireland and Greece. While there have been moves towards flexible working time both in Germany and France, they differ both in scale and character. In France, a number of agreements have been signed both at national and company level which have introduced annualised hours systems. But perhaps more significant was the law of 1982 which introduced flexible working over a negotiated period. Legislation extended this in 1987 so that up to 48 hours a week may be worked in certain cases, provided that working hours over a year average 39 per week.

Probably the most wide-ranging innovations amongst these four have taken place in West Germany, where major sector agreements allow not only for different working patterns but also for alternatives based on a variety of flexible systems. The 1984 collective agreement reached in metal working in Germany allowed working time to be reduced in three different ways: an average 38½-hour week spread over two months; an average 38½-hour week for the company's workforce as a whole but with some categories of employees working above the average matched by others working below; or the retention of the 40-hour week, but with more days off.

Pressure will increase in all the countries for the reduction and reorganisation of working time. The trade unions will obviously be pressing for shorter working hours, while the employers will be emphasising greater flexibility in working time. The exact path and developments taken will depend on the nature of the sector, the strength of the trade unions, and the structure of collective bargaining.

This brief examination shows that there is considerable variation in the nature and extent of developments in working time arrangements, not only between rich and poor member states, but also within rich countries and poor countries. This implies that a Community model for the reduction and reorganisation of working time may not be feasible. Any action undertaken by the Community in this sphere would need to be highly flexible so as to allow for the differences in approach and objectives which exist amongst the member states.

Retirement Age

In most West European countries, the retirement age ranges from 60–65. Although some economists suggest that a reduction in the retirement age would reduce labour supply, thereby having a beneficial impact on employment, this is not currently an important collective bargaining issue in any member state. However, early retirement is now widespread across Community countries. Belgium, France, West Germany and Spain have general provisions through which employees may retire early on a proportionally reduced pension. In addition many countries have special pension schemes for unemployed and disabled workers which may sometimes be limited to job creation (as in France and West Germany). Partial pension schemes also exist in some member states – UK, France, Spain and Denmark. In these schemes, workers can go part-time in the lead-up to full retirement. At the sector and company level, there exists a wide range of early retirement programmes, but these usually relate to sectors which are in difficulty, or are characterised by tough physical requirements. The general move is towards more flexible, and hence overall earlier, retirement arrangements. Overall, therefore, although there has been a general move towards earlier retirement, and a general trend towards more flexible retirement arrangements, there have been substantial differences in the approaches adopted in the various member states. In particular, there are noticeable differences in the extent of early provision of a state pension and in the relative roles of state and employer. The nearest that the Community is likely to get to harmonisation is the general Recommendation of 1984 which simply encouraged member states to facilitate flexible retirement.

Annual Paid Leave

Article 120 of the Treaty of Rome lays down that 'member states shall endeavour to maintain the existing equivalence between paid holiday schemes'. To what extent does this equivalence still exist? With the exception of the United Kingdom, where holiday entitlement is determined by collective agreement, all member countries have legislation which guarantees workers minimum annual paid holidays. Legislation on holiday entitlement falls into two categories. One category sets a basic minimum which then is improved through collective bargaining arrangements. West Germany, Ireland and the Netherlands are the countries in this category. The other category establishes a relatively high holiday entitlement which is usually only slightly supplemented by collective bargaining. Legislation of this type can be found in Denmark, France, Greece and Luxembourg. The countries within 'the golden triangle' inside the Community have five or more weeks annual holidays, while the other member states have four weeks annual holiday arrangements. It is apparent that there are significant differences in holiday entitlements between member states. Increasingly, holidays are being considered in relation to the package of annual working time and remuneration. In this more complex scene it is unlikely that the Commission could even take an equivalent step to the modest Recommendation for a minimum four weeks annual entitlement made in 1976.

Social Protection

Social protection is a term used in a number of contexts. Here we use the term in the narrow sense of situations where certain guarantees or rights and protections are afforded to the worker. In this section we examine the possibilities for Community harmonisation in three areas: introduction of new technology; health and safety; social security.

i) Introduction of new technology

The joint opinion adopted by the Val Duchesse working party on new technologies stressed the importance of informing and consulting workers in relation to technological change. Table XIx below details the forms of regulation used for introducing new technology.

This table shows that in most member countries there exists some form of information and consultation legislation relating to technical change. In addition, legislation in France, Germany and the Netherlands relating to co-determination is also of relevance. However, only Belgium and Denmark have a national agreement shaping the role of the parties in negotiating over new technology.[6] For most EC countries it is the sector, company or plant level which is most important for the establishment of agreements relating to technological change. Two studies financed by the European Foundation for Living and Working Conditions throw further light on the methods of regulations used to introduce new technology. These studies show that the key strategy of European trade unions in this area is the negotiation of new technology agreements. But the research also highlights that there were wide variations in the form, content and objectives of such agreements between and within member states. One important finding was that over two thirds of the companies researched had consultation procedures relating to the introduction of new technology. But again the specific consultation mechanism varied considerably; from the formal works council model in West Germany to the informal consultation processes based on work groups typical in the UK. Furthermore, the studies found that procedures for disclosure of information were much less common, and where they did exist, the process tended to be ad hoc with no clearly established pattern of involvement of workers or their representatives. No national, let alone European, pattern could be discerned. This suggests that the process of consulting and informing workers in rela-

Table XIx Procedures on Informing and Consulting Workers in Relation to Technological Changes

COUNTRY	LAW	MULTISECTOR AGREEMENTS	SECTORAL AGREEMENTS	COMPANY AGREEMENTS
BELGIUM	Works Council informed A.S. 27.11.1973	Works Council informed c.c. No 9, 9.3.1972 Information, consultation, and deliberation with representative bodies c.c. No 39, 13.12.1983	Printing Textiles Banking and insurance Distribution	Agreements national agreements
DENMARK	Information and consultation of technological committee 1981 Agreement for private sector 1981 Agreement for public sector and administrative bodies	Banks and Savings Banks Consumer Cooperatives Breweries	Agreements to implement national agreements	
GERMANY	Information and consultation of Works Council Law of 15.1.1972		Metalworking Footwear Leather Paper	More than a hundred collective agreements
FRANCE	Information and consultation of Works Committee Auroux Laws of 1982		Banking and insurance	Undertakings in the following sectors: chemicals, oil, cement, banking and insurance
SPAIN	Information and consultation of staff representatives or Works Committee – Workers' Statute – Law 8 1980 of 10.3.1980			
GREECE	Information for trade union representatives Law No 1264 of 1.1.1982 Information and consultation of health and safety committee Law 1568 1985		Agreement of July 1980 for the press and printing industry	
IRELAND			Press, printing, graphic arts, banking	Joint Committees
ITALY		Public sector IRI-Agreement 18 December 1984 EFIM-Agreement, July 1986	Employees' rights to information	Numerous agreements
LUXEMBOURG	Information and consultation of Works Committee Laws of 6.5.1974		Iron and steel industry	
NETHERLANDS	Information and consultation of Works Council Laws of 1971, 1979 and 1982		Metal working Building Printing	
UNITED KINGDOM			Public services	Several hundred agreements
PORTUGAL	Information and consultation of workers' committees Law 46/79 of 1979			

Source: *EC Internal and External Adaption of Firms* 1987

tion to technological change is highly flexible, and is determined primarily by factors such as enterprise size, industrial classification, the form of collective bargaining, the strength of trade unions, and managerial style.

ii) Health and Safety

Approaches to occupational health and safety in the member states reveal a surprising degree of diversity. Apart from Britain, only Denmark has opted for a unified government organisation which is wholly and exclusively responsible for policy and administration in the area of health and safety. Other countries' systems reflect differing federal structures, a mix of responsibilities between government agencies and insurance systems, a broader definition of the role of labour inspection, or a distinction between health inspection and safety inspection.

These differences in organisation make direct comparisons between countries extremely difficult. The problems of comparison may be best illustrated by considering the occupational and health and safety systems in two of the largest EC member states, France and Germany.

The French system is complex, comprising a number of government agencies with different but partially overlapping responsibilities. The largest element is formed by *Services Exterieures du Travail et de l'Emploi* – SETE, part of the Ministry of Social Affairs. SETE is responsible for inspection of employed people (as opposed to the self-employed) in most of industry and commerce. However, the responsibilities of the SETE inspectors go much wider than those of the British Health and Safety Executive, and in addition to health and safety, cover conditions of work and many industrial relations activities including, amongst other things, conciliation and arbitration in disputes and the sanctioning of collective dismissals on economic grounds.

Thus, the role of French inspectors is fundamentally different from that of HSE's field staff. The French inspectors spend the major part of their time on labour relations matters. It was estimated that health and safety may take up only 15-20 per cent of their time. An additional difference between France and Britain seems to be that most inspectoral effort is devoted to investigating accidents and complaints, leaving little scope for preventative inspection. French inspectors see their health and safety role as primarily concerned with enforcing the law.

In Germany there is a dual system of inspection. Each of the eleven Lander has an inspectorate responsible for enforcement of industrial safety legislation in a wide range of industries. These inspectorates, or *Gewerbeaufsicht* (GAs), are principally concerned with the prevention of accidents and ill health, including the enforcement of federal and state legislation, social conditions such as hours of work and, in most states, environmental protection.

The second part of the system is the network of mutual insurance bodies (*Berufsgenossenschaften* – BGs). There are 95 of these altogether, mostly covering specific sectors, although some are also regionally based. They are financed by employers' contributions and managed jointly by employers and employees, but their existence is based on law, and overall supervision is exercised by the Federal Ministry of Labour. The BGs can draw up accident prevention regulations which, after they are approved by the Federal Ministry, may be formally adopted and published, whereupon they become legally binding on firms covered by the relevant BG.

No other member state gives such a prominent role to insurance in the setting and enforcement of occupational health and safety standards. One direct consequence of the regulatory powers of the BGs is that the total volume of health and safety legislation is much greater than in Britain and much more detailed. Both the GA and BG inspectors spend much of their time on visits in response to complaints, or requests for advice, especially, in the case of the BGs, reported accidents. Both have similar powers to issue administrative fines for minor offences, to issue notices and ultimately to ask the public prosecutor's office to pursue offenders through the courts.

Health and safety is the only area which indisputably comes under the qualified majority voting system introduced by the Single European Act. Thus, there is every chance that health and safety will become an increasingly important aspect of Community policies on employment conditions. This brief review suggests that the Community will have considerable difficulty in establishing a uniform system or machinery for the implementation of health and safety legislation across the member states. It is likely that the parameters of the Community's health and safety programme will be fixed around establishing common policies across the member states. A general consensus exists that the approximation of health and safety standards is possible at the Community level.

iii) Social Security

As outlined in an earlier chapter, the member states are now facing similar problems in the area of social security. One is the increased numbers of the elderly as a proportion of the population, which puts strain on the operation and financing of social security systems. Secondly, the need to fund persistent and historically high unemployment is faced by all the member states. Thirdly, as many European social security systems were established before single parenthood existed on anything like its present scale, most member states are facing increasing demands from this quarter and other sections of what is termed the 'New Poor'. In combination, these problems mean that the operation and financing of the social security system will be a major problem in all member states. Given that the issues of concern appear to be broadly similar across the Community, does the possibility exist of a co-ordinated Community response?

The evidence suggests that formidable barriers exist to complete harmonisation of social security provision inside the Community. To begin with, social security provisions are based on different assumptions in the different member states. Take, for instance, the system of family benefits in France and Great Britain. A major difference exists in the structure of family benefits, varying with family size and age of children. In France no benefit is paid for the first child, and in the case of a two-child family, there is no premium for the elder child. This means that one- and to a lesser extent, two-child families in Britain are definitely better off. On the other hand, in France there is a higher additional amount for the third and subsequent children so that the level of assistance rises from 32 per cent of the base amount for the two-child family to 73 per cent of the base amount for the three-child family and then by a further 41 per cent for each additional child. Thus there is a strong 'tilt' in favour of larger families in France. Significant differences also occur in other aspects of the social security provisions in France and Britain. This is only a two-country comparison on one issue. Multiplied, it indicates the scale of problems that would arise if setting common social protection standards becomes a Community objective.

A second difficulty lies in the administrative and organisational differences between the EC countries in the field of social security. Occupational pension schemes are but one example. In the United Kingdom and Eire, for instance, the basic state provision may be regarded as a pension which covers the fundamental requirements of life with no luxuries. But Spain, Italy and Portugal provide a state pension which is earnings related and which would provide an adequate pension related to earnings for all. Other countries would fit in between these two systems. Another difference is that the British system of means tested aid is the only centralised comprehensive system in the EC. Other systems are to a greater or lesser degree localised and segmented, in the sense that there are different systems for different categories of pensions. This situation led the National Association of Pension Funds to comment 'the state pension arrangements in the EEC are so different that it will be almost impossible to achieve harmonisation of benefit levels or indeed benefit at least within a feasible time span'.[7]

A further problem is that if social security harmonisation meant the equalisation upwards of the level of benefits, then enormous burdens would be placed on the poorer member states. They would face a major increase in their financial bill in this area. Some analysts suggest that if such a policy was to be considered seriously, then the richer member states would have to transfer resources to the poorer member countries.

The conclusion must be that as each European social security system has been established in a different set of historical circumstances and different inherited sets of traditions and priorities, the possibility of complete harmonisation hardly exists in the short run. As pointed out in chapter IV, this appears to be accepted by the Commission, although attempts are being made to obtain a degree of partial harmonisation on specific subjects, such as the portability of pensions. Overall, the evidence suggests that formidable obstacles exist to the harmonisation of social security across the Community, to the establishment of a set of Community guidelines or even to a Community model for the introduction of new technology. In health and safety, the diversity in administrative systems appears to limit Community action in this area to the harmonisation of policies. These conclusions cannot give heart to those who argue that a social dimension linked to the internal market should be based largely on the harmonisation of social protection areas such as social security.

Collective bargaining and the labour market

During the sixties, and indeed the seventies, a considerable body of academic opinion was of the view that as a result of industrialisation and the dynamics of market forces, national industrial relations systems would tend towards uniformity or convergence.[8] Although this view is increasingly criticised, it still has adherents. At the same time, many of the earlier writers on European integration suggested that with the creation of a Common Market, information exchange would increase amongst trade unions, industrialists and governments leading to industrial relations matters being dealt with in a similar manner across countries.[9] Thus both from the perspectives of industrial relations and European integration there were expectations that industrial relation systems would converge. How is this thesis standing up to the test of time?

The evidence suggests that there remains a sharp divergence in the manner in which collective bargaining is organised in the member states. For a start, there are differences in the type of agent the employer has to deal with. In Britain, for example, employers normally bargain with shop-floor trade unionists; in Germany and France, the bargaining agents are essentially non-union, as the activities of local works councils are carefully laid down within a legal framework; in Denmark most major negotiations are conducted at the national level. There are also differences in the relationship between work-place bargaining and multi-employer bargaining. In Britain, there has been a decisive shift toward decentralised forms of bargaining.[10] Yet in most other countries, centralised multi-employer bargaining continues to be the norm. Any local bargaining that does occur in these systems is mainly of an administrative or supplementary type.

The role of law in managing collective bargaining is another important source of difference. In Britain the legal system plays a minimal role in collective bargaining: the employer makes rules unilaterally in many areas, and collective agreements have no legally binding status on the parties to them. By contrast, in other EC countries there are quite detailed substantive rules about the conduct and procedure of collective bargaining, especially multi-employer collective bargaining; and normally all agreements concluded carry some degree of legal force. Not that there are no differences between the systems in the Continental member states: for example, the law in West Germany allows employers to engage in sympathetic lock-outs, while such actions are in broad terms illegal in France and Italy. Similarly, what is known as the 'peace obligation' is more or less absolute in collective agreements in Germany, while French and Italian legal systems uphold the individual's right to strike. These differences in collective bargaining arrangements reflect significant differences in the more fundamental aspects of industrial relations: the trade unions are stronger in some countries than others, central arbitration is more common is some than in others and the Labour Ministries adopt quite different roles.

Public policy and the labour market

During the 1960s and 1970s public policies towards the labour market focused mainly on the training of manpower to produce a more efficient match between the supply and demand for labour, and the provision of training for disadvantaged groups. Although these policies have not been abandoned, they have been broadened considerably across the Community, mainly in order to cope with rising unemployment. In this section, therefore, we examine the degree of similarity of member states' policies in two key areas: measures in favour of the long term unemployed; and vocational training.

i) Measures in favour of the long-term unemployed

Measures to bring the long-term unemployed back into the labour market have been identified by the Commission as a priority area for employment policy within member states. Although exact definitions of the notion differ, it is broadly accepted that once people have been out of work for a year or more they can be considered long-term unemployed. The long-term unemployed are believed to be distinctive for a number of reasons. First they are seen to have fallen out of the labour market: they do not actively search for jobs nor attempt to get retrained or reskilled to enhance their employment prospects. Secondly, they represent a large segment of the new 'under class' for whom coping with poverty has become a way of life. Thirdly, they are more vulnerable to ill health, both physical and mental: there is a strong association between unemployment and ill health. For such reasons, long-term unemployment is regarded by the Commission as an unacceptable social (and economic) problem.

Given that the number of specially targeted programmes for the long-term unemployed has mushroomed amongst the member states, it would appear that most if not all of them share the Commission's anxieties on the issue. Table XIxi lists the range of programmes introduced by the member states for the long-term unemployed during the 1980s. It shows that every member state has introduced some type of scheme for this group. In addition, it can be seen that although there is a wide variety in the type of programmes that have been established, there is a significant similarity between the member states. One form of intervention that is widespread is the special work programme: with the exception of Denmark and Greece, every Community country has introduced a scheme in this category. For the most part, special work programmes focus on creating temporary jobs, lasting six months to a year, in 'non-market' organisations. The intention is to refamiliarise the long-term unemployed person with work routines.

An equally popular method of helping the long-term unemployed appears to be subsidising normal work. Most schemes in this area offer subsidies for a limited period to employers who recruit long-term unemployed people. To a large extent, this and the other schemes outlined above are fairly conventional instruments used to address the problems of disadvantaged groups in the labour market. A more novel approach to the specific problem of the long-term unemployed, which is gaining increasing support across the Community, is fostering self-employment. These schemes normally take the form of offering financial assistance to those who want to start up in business. The philosophy which underpins these schemes is that instead of looking for traditional forms of employment in large factories, people should consider creating their own work. Amongst the other programmes devised to tackle the long-term unemployed question, there are counselling sessions to restore people's confidence, self-help schemes to provide practical assistance, and training schemes to improve employment prospects and opportunities.

Thus, in this sphere of employment policy, dealing with long-term unemployment, the conclusion must be that there is considerable convergence amongst the member states.

ii) Vocational Training

In the eighties an ever-increasing amount of the Commission's social policy work has related to vocational training. Amongst the factors that made this subject a priority were the need to help young people obtain more adequate and suitable qualifications, the need to retrain and reskill traditional workers made redundant as a result of the structural changes in European industry, and the need for special training programmes for women and minority groups to facilitate their access to occupations where they have been traditionally under-represented. For similar reasons, individual member states also began placing greater emphasis on activity in this area: the budgets of public bodies responsible for training have increased substantially, and policy papers on training schemes and the establishment of new initiatives are now voluminous. A principal objective of the Commission is for these developments in training to occur in a concerted fashion across the Community. To what extent has this happened?

Youth training was the first area where the Community attempted to establish some degree of coherence. Part of a 1983 Council Resolution stipulated that member states 'will do their utmost that all young people who so wish . . . can benefit over a period of at least six months and if possible one year following full time compulsory education from a full time programme involving basic training and/or an initial work experience to prepare them for an occupation . . . moreover, will pursue their efforts, in the context of their national policies and practices, to see that for young people without sufficient qualifications, including particularly those who are looking for work, adequate opportunities of vocational training to improve their skills and qualifications are available'.[11] The Commission was asked to monitor progress towards what was called the social guarantee for young people, by undertaking a specific comparative analysis of youth training in the member states. The Commission published this review in 1986 and it concluded that most member states have met – or will shortly meet – the minimum commitment to offer some basic vocational training to all young people at the end of the period of compulsory schooling. But, more cautiously, the review also suggested that existing provisions may not be meeting the challenges thrown up by technological and economic change.

The Commission analysis made clear that beyond the establishing of

Table XIxi Measures in member states to help the long-term unemployed

	Belgium	Denmark	Germany	Spain	France	Greece
Personalised counselling			*Personalised counselling* after every three months of unemployment		Personal interviews assessment and programme after 13 months unemployment	
Fostering self-help			*FdA financial aids* for travel etc to enable LTUs to find and take up jobs			
Fostering self-employment		*Enterprise allowance scheme* to help start up own firm instead of receiving a second Job Offer	*Bridging allowance* for three months	*Reduction of interest* on loan and technical assistance grant	Helping the unemployed set up own business *Departmental youth initiative fund* for LTUs aged over 25	
Financing specialised training			*Training* to improve placement prospects. Grant for training period within an employment contract	*Basic and vocational retraining* for LTUs over 25 years (75 per cent of statutory minimum wage)	*Modular traineeships* 300 to 1200 hours for over 25-year-olds *Training and reinsertion and programme:* 550 hours training plus two months in enterprise for young people; and 300 to 700 hours for adults	
Insertion into existing training		*Training allowance* for up to two years for under 25-year-olds *Training allowance* instead of second Job Offer	LTUs are encouraged to participate in existing courses only once they have come to grips with their personal and vocational situation so as to reduce the number of drop-outs	*Vocational training in rural areas:* LTUs over 25 years receive 75 per cent of minimum wage. Free VT for LTUs aged over 45 after being given indefinite employment contracts	18-25 traineeships Employment-training contracts *ANPE* upgrading *FNE* traineeships	Priority on courses to LTUs

	Belgium	Denmark	Germany	Spain	France	Greece
Work contracts			Fixed-term trial employment	*Indefinite contracts* for LTUs aged over 45 Indefinite contracts for employing women aged over 45 in under-represented occupations		
Special work programmes	*TCT-Third work circuit:* new permanent, non-market community jobs. State pays 95 per cent of wage, plus social security (1982-86) Promoting employment in the non-market sector		Public interest job creation	Priority in *collaboration* contracts of public sector bodies with INEM: maximum grant of 100 per cent	*Part-time collective utility jobs* for 16 to 21-year-olds (1984) extended to 21 to 25-year-olds *Part-time work* for LTUs aged over 25 years for six months	
Subsidising normal work		*Job offers* for jobs lasting at least seven months in public (nine in private) sector after two years	*Wage subsidies* for over 50-year-old LTUs hired for additional jobs Loans or subsidies for organising, extending and equipping firms and departments aimed at providing work for older workers Settling in allowance Occupational trial periods	In co-operatives: loan interest reductions for LTUs Encouraging local employment initiatives for LTUs *Work experience contracts* for 25-year-olds with dependants	*Aids to employer* and topping up unemployment benefit for part-time employment *Financial compensation* for LTUs accepting part-time jobs at wages below unemployment benefit levels	12,000 12-month grants to firms for hiring LTUs
Fostering early retirements	*Early retirement* by collective agreement for workers aged 57 or over replaced by unemployed people	*Voluntary early retirement scheme:* replacements by LTUs are encouraged	*Early retirement scheme* enables LTUs to be hired in replacement			
Extending unemployment allowance			Extension of maximum duration of receipt of unemployment benefit over 42 years old	Over 55-year-olds on unemployment assistance qualifying for retirement pension	LTUs of over 57 years get unemployment benefit without signing on until age 60, when	

	Ireland	Italy	Luxembourg	Netherlands	Portugal	United Kingdom
Personalised counselling	*Direct action (pilot) programme:* integrated package of counselling, plus job for place on training programme					*Restart* offering all LTUs practical advice and help to secure jobs
Fostering self-help	*Job search scheme:* coaching in job-search techniques					*Jobclubs* providing LTUs with meeting place, coaching and material facilities
Fostering self-employment	Enterprise allowance *LTUs constitute 40 per* cent of participants			*Start-up assistance scheme:* income supplement plus loan	*Self-employment aids* programme *Capitalised unemployment insurance scheme* for enterprise creation	*scheme:* £40 (ECU 55) a week allowance for one year to set up own business – not just LTUs
Financing specialised training	*Building on experience* for LTUs aged 25 to 44: six months alternating formal training and on-the-job training *Management development programme* for LTU managers		Vocational training or re-education, general education courses For under 25-year-olds: introductory courses in companies; temporary manpower programme contracts; initiation traineeship contracts			*Restart* training course for updating basic skills and job search techniques of one week plus one day for 13 weeks
Insertion into existing training	*Special employable skills* programme *Enterprise training* programmes *Educational opportunities scheme* for over 25-year-olds				Priority access to reconversion and upgrading courses of state training centres	*Wider opportunities training programme* *Job training scheme:* six months training and work experience *Training for enterprise*
Work contracts	*Part-time job allowance scheme* for LTUs having found regular part-time work of less than 24 hours a week	*Training-work contracts* for 18 to 29-year-olds with 15 to 30 per cent wage subsidies (1983-86)		*Temporary work contracts* of 20-32 hours a week for young LTUs through national agency (*START*) enable employers to receive subsidy of 33 per cent of youth minimum wage	Grants (12 times the minimum wage) to firms giving LTUs aged over 25 open-ended employment contracts	

	Ireland	Italy	Luxembourg	Netherlands	Portugal	
Special work programmes	*Social employment:* part-time work in non-profit-making organisations, paid ECU 92-112 on half-weekly basis	*Enhancing cultural assets:* finance for projects hiring additional LTUs aged under 29 on fixed-term contracts for maximum of 36 months	Aids for creating jobs of socio-economic usefulness	*Temporary jobs* for LTUs in non-profit bodies (1979-83)	programme of temporary employment (six months) in community activities for over 25-year-olds Local employment initiatives finance	*Community programme* offers jobs for up to one year of value to the community to help raise LTUs job prospects
Subsidising normal work	*Employment incentives scheme:* subsidy to employers hiring additional workers, premium) in favour of LTUs	Jobs in state administrations, autonomous bodies, local authorities: priority to LTUs unemployed for over six months	*Incentive premium* to hire LTUs – 200 per cent of reference minimum social wage	Employers hiring a LTU for at least six months receive up to ECU 400 a month for six months for training, etc., costs *Plough back scheme:* Job creation in building, financed by unemployment benefit and public funds, 70 per cent must be LTUs *Social security exemption* for hiring LTUs unemployed over three years on indefinite contract, or a work contract for over two years, plus grant for retraining costs		*Jobstart allowance:* £20 (ECU 28) a week to LTUs who find a full-time job paying less than £80 (111 ECU) a week
Fostering early retirements					*Early retirements* for over 62-year-olds (no replacement required)	*Job release scheme:* early retirers replaced by unemployed (not just LTUs) *Part-time JRS* (1983-86)
Extending unemployment allowance			Possibility of extending unemployment compensation for 182 days for particularly difficult to place unemployed people		Extended unemployment assistance payments for over 50-year-olds	

Source: *Employment Gazette* No. [illegible] 1987

a minimum floor of training provision, important distinctions in training and vocational educational structures continue to exist amongst the member states. At one end of the spectrum, some members combined vocational training and work experience (for instance the German and Danish training systems). At the other end, some member states, most notably France, have full-time vocational education within the formal education system. In between, there are the countries like the UK which have a mixture of the two systems. These divergent systems give rise to different forms of training and qualifications. It is almost impossible to compare qualifications across the Community. Some assessments have been made of the quality of such training; usually comparing just two countries. The conclusion of some of these studies is that the quality of Britain's training provision for young people, for example, is behind its Community partners, particularly West Germany.[12]

The quality and distribution of education and training across the Community have been identified by the Commission as issues which should dominate the Community's activities on youth training over the next two to three years. But details of means to achieve these objectives are conspicuously absent from the Commission's appraisal.

Table XIxii shows the vocational training programmes having an impact on the labour market which have been introduced by the member states since 1983. It can be seen from this table that there is a good deal of similarity amongst the programmes established by the member states. Every member state has developed initiatives for the youth labour market. For the most part, these fall into two categories: (i) the extension of existing apprenticeships schemes; and (ii) the development of general educational and vocational schemes. The other areas for which policies have been developed include initiatives for the long-term unemployed; training in the new technology; and reskilling programmes for traditional workers.

Conclusions

In 1986 Jacques Delors, the President of the Commission, established a group of independent experts to investigate the economic consequences of the decisions taken in 1985 to enlarge the Community to include Spain and Portugal, and to create a market without internal frontiers by the year 1992. The group was invited to identify the problems that could arise in implementing these decisions and to suggest solutions. The outcome of the deliberations of the group is the Padoa-Schioppa Report. Although the report is largely concerned with narrow economic questions such as those concerning the European Monetary System and market integration, it does address, albeit briefly, the question of the

Table XIxii Recent vocational training measures having an inpact on the labour market

	B	DK	D	ESP	F	GR	IRL	IT	L	NL	P	UK
1983	Law-Compulsory education raised to 18 Apprenticeship system extended to industrial sectors	*General:* – Higher co-ordination council – Short combined work training scheme – Combined work training scheme for unskilled young people – Further vocational training for adults – Interim courses for unemployed	*General:* – Compulsory education until 18 – 'Dual' system – Possibility part-time education at 15 16 – Additional continuous vocational training for part-time workers – Special courses for unemployed skilled manual workers and graduates and persons made redundant through restructuring		*General:* – Leave for retraining (jobs threatened) – State-company agreements (on SME, investment and training, aid for training in EDP technology Agreement: employment contracts – training (young unemployed)	Law: increased number of apprenticeships Law: network of apprenticeship schemes	*General:* Anco courses: 33400 trainees 200 course for		*General:* – School reform – secondary level – Vocational guidance and induction courses for 15–17-year-olds – Regulation-apprenticeship in order to obtain certificate of manual skills (CCM)	*General:* – Short vocational courses in secondary education – Measures for young unemployed Open consultations between teachers and world of work (e.g. on funds and EDP technology) Agreements: creation sectoral training funds	Decree-Laws: New system of apprenticeships	*General:* – Youth Training Scheme: 2 years – Adults: improvement of information system (computer network) – ITEC network (EDP) – Permanent training programme for adults – Consolidation vocational training programme – EDP
1984		Law: apprenticeship contracts – basic vocational training			Youth integration (900 reception centres and 100 offices at local level)	31 new technical and vocational establishments		Law: employment-training contracts				
1985	System of paid day release replaced by paid educational leave			Order: PLANFIP (vocational training and integration) —— Decrees on harmonisation ESF assistance and initiatives in progress	Five-year plan extension of vocational and technical instruction —— Decrees on harmonisation, ESF and initiatives in progress	Law: technical and vocational training	Social guarantee youth integration integration Creation COMTEC (Community training & employment schemes) ——	– Planned reforms: – school-leaving-age: 16 – educational and vocational guidance (with social partners & use EDP technologies)		Recommendation: decentralized tripartite management structure (OBA) labour market and vocational training	Decree Laws: increase in and for IEFP (Employment and Vocational Training Institute) IEFP Governing Board begins operation	
1986		Law: training for long-term unemployed	Programme 1986-88 equipment of intervocational training centres with EDP technology	Law: establishment General Council on Vocational Training (tripartite)	Law: establishment General Council on Vocational Training (tripartite)	Introduction of EDP into technical training —— Vocational guidance programme for 15–18-year-olds ——	White paper: White paper: Labour policy —— Youth training initiative				Compulsory education until 16	Experimental technical and vocational training programme to become national programme
1987		Law (not yet passed): advanced technical training with management and adaptation structure vocational training extended from 2 to 2½ years				Combined work training schemes Schools-use of electronic systems		Law: labour market 'monitoring stations'				

Source: *EC, Internal and External Adaption of Firms* 1987

labour market. On the subject of labour-market policies, the report argues that 'countries should be free to experiment with policy adjustment in the search for more efficient means of achieving the double objectives of a high level of employment and high standards of social security. Harmonisation of policies would not seem to be recommendable, especially where the situation is one of massive labour market disequilibrium'.[13]

Our assessment here supports the overall conclusion of the report that there should be a move away from the monolithic harmonisation approach to Community policy-making prevalent in the 1970s towards a decentralised pluralistic and pragmatic model in which national policies and legislation are framed within wider Community rules.

In many areas a wide measure of diversity persists. Even in areas where superficially there appears to be some convergence, e.g. in labour-market flexibility, important distinctions exist between the number and type of strategies pursued by the member states. Only in the public policy area is a degree of convergence found. On the basis of this evidence, the conclusion must be that it would be a major strategic error for the Community to embark on a large-scale harmonisation programme in social policy. Past experience and the scale of labour-market divergences inside the Community indicate that such a programme would get bogged down in administrative and technical complexities.

In relation to public policies for the labour market there appears to be a high level of convergence between the member states, although the institutions and mechanisms by which they are implemented continue to be different. This suggests that the way forward for the Community may be to identify a range of public policy objectives which could be implemented simultaneously across the Community, but not to attempt to specify appropriate mechanisms.

Notes and References

1 WALLACE, W and HODGES, M *Economic Divergence in the European Community*, Macmillan, London 1983

2 Department of Employment, *Employment: The Challenge of the Nation*, HMSO CM49474, London 1985, p10

3 Commission of the European Community, 'Employment Problems: View of business men and the workforce', *European Economy*, No 27, March 1986

4 EMERSON, M 'Regulation and deregulation of the labour market:

policy regimes for the recruitment and dismissals of employees in industrial countries', Harvard University Mimeo, June 1986, and GENNARD, J 'Job Security, Redundancy Arrangements, and Practices in selected OECO Countries', Paper prepared for OECD September 1985

5 LINDLEY, B *New Forms and New Areas of Employment Growth: a comparative study,* Commission of the European Communities, Brussels 1987, p 40

6 LEVI, H *Trade Unions and Technological Change: A Comparative Survey,* European Centre for the Improvement of Living and Working Conditions, Dublin 1985

7 National Association of Pension Funds, Submission to the House of Lords Select Committee on the European Communities on Social Security in the European Community, Session 1987–88 3rd Report 1986 p 162

8 See the first chapter in BAMBER, G and LANSBURY, R *International and Comparative Industrial Relations,* Allen and Unwin, London 1986

9 DEUTSCH, K *Political Community at the International level, Problems of definition and measurement,* Random House, New York, 1970

10 MILLWARD, M and STEVENS, M *British Workplace Industrial Relations 1980–1984,* Gower, London 1986

11 Commission of the European Community: 'Youth Training in the European Community', *Social Europe* Supplement No3 1987

12 LAYARD, R *How to Beat Unemployment,* Oxford University Press, Oxford 1986 and PRAIS, S J *Vocational qualifications of the labour force in Britain and Germany,* National Institute of Economic and Social Research, London 1981

13 PADOA-SCHIOPPA, T *et al., Efficiency, Stability and Equality* Oxford University Press, Oxford 1987.

Chapter XII

EC Social Policy: Current Impact, Future Prospects

Introduction

Assessing the impact of EC social policy on Britain's employment environment is clearly a difficult task. The previous chapters have emphasised the point that this a complex and varying field, open to many interpretations. Looking forward, at future prospects, is fraught with even more risks. Nevertheless, this chapter attempts both to emphasise some of the more important and general conclusions that can be drawn from the discussion so far and to assess future developments.

The conclusions, in the first part of this chapter, serve two functions. In the first place, they can act as an 'executive summary' of the arguments in each of the preceding chapters. Secondly, they consolidate those arguments in a succinct form, thus providing a springboard for the leap into the assessment of what the next few years will hold for EC social issues.

This assessment of the future is made with some trepidation, but also with some confidence. It is based upon the range of interviews with many key players that formed part of the research as well as on a detailed appraisal of policy statements. The future will always include surprises, but the cautious well-founded assessment here is likely to contain most major developments.

Conclusions

The European Community was borne out of the spontaneous emergence of the Europeanisation fervour after the Second World War. But the political development of the Community has not lived up to early expectations. In particular, the initial hope that the Community would develop into a supranational institution has not materialised. As a result the EC is at present, as outlined in Chapter II, a fully-fledged intergovernmental body. Although the Single European Act will speed up the decision-making process in certain areas, it will not alter this basic political character of the Community. Within an intergovernmental organisation, the scope and nature of policies will depend on the outlook and approach of participating countries: if a group of countries, and on occasions even a single country, is opposed to a particular proposed policy direction, then it is highly unlikely it will be adopted by the organisation. Thus in relation to the EC, the Governments of member states are in the practical position of deciding what is and what is not adopted as Community policy.

The development of the EC's Social Policy was shown in Chapters III and IV. Two distinct phases were indicated. The first phase, which lasted until the early 1970s, focused on removing obvious restrictions to the free movement of labour and on establishing the Social Fund, but otherwise involved few major initiatives. The high economic growth rates enjoyed by all the member-states relegated social policy matters to secondary importance. The second phase was more interventionist, concerned mainly with extending the individual and collective rights of employees and with addressing the widespread problem of unemployment. The legalistic orientation of social policy in this phase began to run into opposition in the early 1980s and no very coherent development has taken place since. The last few years have seen a consolidation and deepening of existing links and arrangements on non-legalistic aspects of Community social policy, but as yet no alternative has been worked out to the principle of obtaining harmonisation of employment matters through the use of the legal machinery.

Despite this, the impact of the EC has been felt in a number of areas. In the bureaucratic arena, for example, the EC membership imposed a range of obligations and duties on policy-makers and administrators in government departments, and other organisations, dealing with national employment. In Chapter V it was explained that these involved drafting British policy responses to Community-related proposals, participating in EC deliberations, undertaking the necessary tasks to ensure that Community policies are implemented in Britain and helping to administer certain EC programmes. While these activities are a significant part of the workload for these departments, they remained minor, relative to other tasks. Moreover, in the years just after joining the EC, these functions were for the most part carried out in a self-contained niche, having only a modicom of influence on tasks relating to national affairs. This has changed, for it now appears that national officials to some degree adopt a European perspective when considering policies for the national context. But this is more often than not a 'negative' perspective, in that they assess whether or not European law allows them to develop a particular scheme. Thus, for example, during the past few years several proposals relating to labour-market flexibility had to be shelved as it was considered that they might be in breach of EC equality legislation. In this respect the EC can be seen as being a constraining influence. When developing new policies, officials on occasions do adopt a 'positive' perspective and scan other member states to see if similar initiatives have been implemented. It should, however, be pointed out that British civil servants also look beyond

Europe to get ideas about employment schemes – for instance, the investigation into whether or not the 'workfare' initiative operated in the USA could be transplanted into Britain is a good case in point. Thus, although policy-makers have adopted a European dimension to their work, it has not been to the exclusion of examining experiments in other countries further afield.

The Community policies that the civil servants administer are those which are deemed acceptable by the Governments of the member states. It was for this reason that the views of the major political parties in Britain towards the European Community were examined in Chapter VI. It was found that the present Conservative Government has a 'minimalist' stance towards EC affairs: reluctant to see the Community's institutions obtaining increased powers or to countenance any significant European social harmonisation programmes. The preference of the Thatcher Administration is for the Community to concentrate almost exclusively on removing remaining barriers to trade and promoting 'open markets' more generally. The implications of this outlook for Community social policy cannot be underestimated, for as long as the present Conservative Government is in power in Britain, it is extremely doubtful that the Council will make any further extensions to existing EC labour law. Certainly the possibilities are remote for the adoption of legislation of a 'social protectionist' kind.

The Labour Party, after years of being at best lukewarm towards Community membership, now appears to accept that withdrawing Britain from the EC is no longer a viable policy option. Moreover, recent statements from the Party's front bench suggest that Labour is now actively considering the type of policies it would like to see implemented by the Community. Some place much store on this policy shift. One commentator suggests that to regain electoral popularity in Britain, Labour should become the Party of Europe.[1] As part of this emerging new European outlook, there can hardly be much doubt that a future Labour Government would give its assent to Commission proposals on such things as the re-organisation and reduction of working time and the Vredeling Directive being adopted as formal Community policy. But we suggest that while this may be a significant development in terms of extending and strengthening Community policies on employment and labour affairs, it will do little to increase EC influences on Britain's employment environment. This is essentially because a Labour Government, if it follows its current Party policies, would be enacting similar or even more far-reaching industrial relations and labour-market policies at the national level. Thus a Labour Government could have the paradoxical effect of helping to increase the range of EC employment policies, while at the same time defusing the controversy in Britain over the EC's involvement in this area, by making national institutions the initiators of new and possibly even more controversial labour-market proposals.

Although on present trends it is doubtful whether the centrist parties will form a Government in the foreseeable future, for completeness it is noted that they adopt a maximalist approach to European affairs. The industrial relations proposals of the Alliance Parties at the 1987 election bore a close resemblance to some Commission social policy proposals, particularly as regards workers' participation. The centrist parties would encourage the EC to play a more prominent role in British society, not in the sense of increasing the presence of Community institutions, but by bringing Britain closer to the broad industrial-relations model which exists in other member states.

In the early years, after the establishment of the Common Market in 1958, one major school of academic thought suggested that interest groups would be a key dynamic in the European integration process. None of the principal industrial interest groups – the CBI, TUC or the trade federations – correspond to this model on interest-group behaviour inside the EC. Although working from different standpoints, both British employers and trade union organisations have been reluctant to transfer any of their powers or functions to their relevant European umbrella bodies. Nor have they been willing to see the EC's competencies grow in the field of employment and labour affairs *at the expense* of national institutions and practices.

The most interesting insight of the study, as regards British interest groups and the EC, has been the way 'single issue' pressure groups like the Equal Opportunities Commission have increasingly tried to use European law to defend and further the interests of their various consituents in the face of what they see as regressive policies at the national level. This strategy has not involved these bodies transferring some of their powers and functions to European-level organisations, nor for that matter their embracing the European ideal. The emergence of this strategy was more straightforward. Key staff in the Equal Opportunities Commission and other similar organisations started to recognise that whilst European law would never replace national law, it did represent another legal tier which could be used to much greater purpose and effect than hitherto had been the case. These organisations began encouraging and sponsoring legal cases evoking European law.

We suggested that by adopting this approach these organisations were acting in an *opportunistic European* manner – involving the intermittent use of Community law and institutions to further the interests of a particular group or interest within a nation state. As this approach has yielded some notable successes, it is highly likely that an increasing number of interest groups will begin acting in a similar way. For instance, given the unfavourable climate that currently exists for trade unions in Britain, it appears, on paper at least, that they have nothing to lose by trying to utilise certain aspects of the EC machinery more than they do at present. If this opportunistic European behaviour becomes more widespread, it will open up a new dimension to EC social policy. In particular, rather than Community institutions attempting to implement social policies from above, national interest groups may be more successful in developing the scope and effectiveness of EC law by action from below.

Chapter VII examines by far the most direct way the EC can influence Britain's employment environment, which is by passing legislation which changes or substantially reverses existing UK law. To date, this has occurred only to a limited extent. This is partly because some of the initiatives which would have required far-reaching changes to British labour law and practices have yet to be adopted by the Council of Ministers, and partly for other reasons outlined below.

The legislation that has been adopted in the field of labour and employment affairs falls into several categories. In the first place, there is the Community legislation that simply parallels existing British law, and as such has not required any adjustments. The 1976 Mass Dismissal Directive and 1978 Insolvency Directive are two examples of this form of legislation.

A further category is the body of EC law which has brought about small-scale changes to British statutes. For the most part, these changes have not been controversial. This is primarily because the topics covered are of an administrative and technical nature. Examples of legislation in this category are some of the health and safety Directives which broadened the scope of existing national legislation for certain scientific reasons.

A final group of Community laws should, on paper at least, have necessitated substantial changes and additions to British labour law, for they are quasi-supranational in character. Some of these laws are limited to particular spheres of economic activity while others are intended to have a more pervasive impact. The former particularly relate to some health and safety legislation, which covers a narrow range of issues, although it has a major impact on certain companies and organisations, particularly in the chemical industry. As long as established scientific evidence exists to indicate that such legislation is required, the British Government has tended to comply closely with the details of the law when implementing it within British law. The same cannot be said of the British Government's approach to Community legislation designed to have a more general impact on member states' employment environments. Community legislation in this area mostly relates to equal opportunity matters, but in relation to Britain at least, also included is the Transfer of Undertakings Directive.

Because the British Government controls the legal ports of entry by which the Community law is passed into national law, it has tended to do the minimum necessary to comply with the more general Directives and Court of Justice rulings so as to limit their impact in Britain. On several occasions, the Court of Justice found that the UK had failed to comply fully with the texts of Community equality Directives, and there is a large body of legal opinion which argues that the changes made to British law in response to these rulings still do not bring Britain into line with European law. Furthermore, the British Government introduced the Transfer of Undertakings Directive by a specific legal device which resulted in this law co-existing with existing national law in a way that was contradictory in several important respects. The result has been to create confusion in the UK courts and tribunals over what actually is the legal position in such cases. The 1987 ACAS Report heavily criticises the Government for allowing confusion to reign in part of this employment law. Another constraint on this body of EC law obtaining its maximum feasible impact in Britain is the tendency of British courts and tribunals to lay down restrictions on the situations where EC law can be evoked. Thus, as a result of the approach of the British Government and of British judicial practice, EC equality and transfer of undertakings rulings are having less impact than theoretically they might. The argument should not be taken too far: this body of extra-national law does have an impact on Britain's employment environment. The recent Court of Justice rulings in the Marshall and Drake cases are good examples.

Whilst the arenas summarised so far are complex enough in themselves, they beg the even more complicated question of the effect that the EC social policies have within employing organisations. The results of the research on this topic were outlined in chapters VIII, IX and X.

The analysis of the public sector and the EC in Chapters VIII and IX was limited to local authorities and certain nationalised industries. We found that a number of concrete connections exist between these various public organisations and the Community. In the first place, both the local authorities and the nationalised enterprises examined received grants from one or more of the EC's structural funds, most notably the Social Fund. Although there was general dissatisfaction about the way in which the various funds were administered, the consensus view was that the monies received from European sources had a positive and beneficial impact. British Rail and British Shipbuilders, and all but two of the local authorities interviewed, employ people to organise and develop schemes specifically earmarked for EC funding. Whilst in the nationalised industries these staff mainly play an administrative role, in the local authorities their role is more dynamic, encouraging departments to develop new schemes and programmes which may be eligible for some EC grants. Thus, as well as having a quantitive impact, the link between the local authorities and Europe has the qualitative benefit of encouraging officials, particularly in economic development units, to think in a novel and creative way.

It is the various national representative organisations in the local government sector, and not individual authorities, which deal with EC affairs at governmental level, and have direct contact with EC institutions and officials. The EC dimension to their work is regarded by officials of these national organisations as useful and worthwhile, but not overridingly important. The nationalised companies, with the exception of British Steel, have international officers or units who remain in regular contact with Commission officials in various Directorates. As a result, these enterprises are normally fully aware of Community initiatives and policies for their industries. In addition to these day to day informal contacts, staff from these enterprises, particularly from British Coal and British Steel, participate in a wide number of EC committees and bodies, dealing mostly with technical and scientific matters. Participation was regarded simply as an obligation which went with EC membership. As in the local government sector, the deliberations of these committees are regarded as useful and productive, but not really central to the operation of their respective enterprise. The public enterprises also participate in CEEP, a designated 'social partner' inside the EC structure. Views vary considerably about the efficiency of this body. This difference does suggest that little communication and co-ordination occurs between British public enterprises in relation to EC matters.

Claims for equal pay for work of equal value have been launched against British Rail, British Shipbuilders and British Coal. As these claims were only legally permissible due to Court of Justice rulings against Britain, they can be regarded as instances where the EC directly influenced employment practices within each organisation. Some of the decisions in these claims have in themselves affected the scope of EC equality law. In relation to local authorities, there have been few legal cases which have evoked EC law. If one adopted a fairly broad definition of EC social policy to include the labour-market impact of EC industrial restructuring policies, then, with the exception of British Rail, all the public enterprises have faced direct EC influences. This is because the highly neo-liberal character of EC industrial policies has given added weight and impetus to the rationalisation and redundancy programmes first initiated by British Governments.

This is very much the model for EC influence on the public enterprises and the local authorities. None of the organisations' manpower or personnel policies and practices were influenced directly by the EC policies in any major aspect. The main non-market external influence on these organisations continued to be Government policies. Thus, in relation to local authorities, new personnel and manpower strategies have had to be developed fairly rapidly in response to the Government's contracting-out programmes. For the public enterprises, the Government-imposed tight fiscal policy requirements have led managements to devise strategies to increase efficiency and productivity. In comparison with this influence, the EC played only a marginal role in the shaping of employee relations strategies inside public sector organisations.

Chapter X examined the impact of EC social policy on the private sector. The first part of that chapter assessed to what extent the opposition of British employers to EC policies and initiatives was due to a 'Little Englander' attitude or to a legitimate concern over the likely impact of such measures. It was argued that on a number of issues, particularly the draft Fifth and Vredeling Directives, the employers' case that these would be highly disruptive to existing British industrial relation practices was an accurate assessment of the situation. But on other proposals, most notably the Parental Leave Directive, the employers tended to overestimate the cost burdens they would place on British business. The reason for opposing these initiatives was that the employers, by the early eighties, did not want any type of regulatory social legislation adopted by the Community. As a result of this point of view, the employers tended to exaggerate the potential impact of such proposals. Overall, however, the employers cannot be regarded as adopting a 'Little Englander' attitude to EC initiatives.

The following sections of the chapter reported the findings of interviews conducted with personnel managers in industry. The main conclusion from this research was that none of the personnel managers interviewed were supportive of Community social legislation. The arguments used by the managers were virtually identical – insensitive to the voluntarist tradition of British industrial relations, too regulatory in character, insufficiently business orientated, and so on. At the same time, most thought that the influence of the EC on company-level employment policies and practices was marginal. None of the managers could think of an instance where the formulation of policy was influenced by the European Community. However, it was recognised that the Community had an influence on the broader industrial relations framework in Britain. As most of the Commission's more interventionist proposals have been sidelined, largely as a result of the stance taken by the British Government on the issue, most of the companies did not continuously monitor developments in social policy inside the Community. For the majority, the threat of Vredeling and the Fifth Directive had all but disappeared and thus there was no need to regard Community deliberations on social policy as a priority issue. Overall, the Community is currently seen as a distant and remote institution, far removed from the day to day concerns of practising personnel managers, and the consensus view is that this situation should be continued.

Future Prospects

The above summary of the extent and nature of EC influences on the employment environment in Britain is valid as this is written in 1988. But what of the future: will the EC influences on member states' employment and labour affairs grow or diminish in forthcoming years? To a large extent, the answer to this question hinges on the form EC social policy takes in the context of completing the internal market project, and on the present deliberations on the future direction of social policy in Community institutions. However, at this stage it can be fairly confidently predicted that the strategy of 'monolithic harmonisation' which underpinned many Commission social-policy initiatives in the late seventies and early eighties will have no further role in EC social policy. The presence of the British Conservative Government and other right-wing Governments inside the Council of Ministers constitutes an insurmountable institutional barrier to the enactment of social policies in this mould. The aim of the member states with Conservative Governments (which include two of the 'big three' member states – Britain and West Germany) is to decrease, or at least to hold in check, the powers of EC Community institutions and officials. Their vision, particularly in the context of 1992, is for a neo-liberal Europe. As one advocate of this outlook put it 'let there be no mistake. The Europe of 1992 must be the Europe of Competition. Let us be vigilant and beware of Euro-bureaucrats. We are currently kicking out bureaucracy and inefficiency from both our countries: we do not want to see them back through the Brussels door. We are reducing our tasks, our expenses, slimming down our administrations; we do not want to have a Europe with heavier institutions, heavier budgets, more European civil servants and rising taxes. Europe is a liberal area . . . it must not be a super state following the pattern of the dirigiste nation states of the 1960s'.[2]

Even if a dramatic shift did occur amongst the member states, it is highly doubtful that the 'monolithic harmonisation' approach would be relaunched to any significant degree. The Commission, or at least key officials in the Commission, have come to realise that attempting to harmonise industrial relations policies and structures across the member states is an administrative and technical nightmare. The experience is that most of the monolithic harmonisation social policy proposals have ended up as embarrassing failures. Thus there is little danger that companies will have to uproot existing employment practices as a result of bureaucratically imposed Directives.

This is not to say that the idea of a fully-fledged Community social policy has been abandoned by the Commission and others with a similar outlook on the matter. Rather, they have reformulated, in a far-reaching way, what should provide the basis and direction of EC social policy. Although there are differing views on the subject, a consensus appears to be emerging around the notion of a Community Charter of Fundamental Social Rights or a Community Social Constitution. Michel Hansenne, the Belgian Minister of Employment and Labour, proposed that the Charter should include existing pertinent international labour standards, and lay down requirements that in cases of large-scale enterprise and industrial restructuring, prior information to, and consultation with, both the competent authorities and the workers should be promoted within the framework of national regulations and current practices. Moreover, he argued that workers should, whatever their working arrangements, be given the opportunity of being covered by collective agreements in each occupational sector and in small and medium-sized enterprises.[3] What Hansenne appears to be proposing is a revised and updated version of the European Social Charter, detailed in Chapter 1.

Chapter VII explained that certain fundamental rights are already legally enforceable under Community law, for example in respect of discrimination on grounds of nationality. Although the scope of existing EC law on this issue would almost certainly have to be expanded, it has been argued that it is feasible for EC institutions to be given the legal powers to review national law and practice against the yardstick of fundamental social rights. 'Since under Article 5 of the Treaty, member states must take all 'appropriate measures' to fulfill their Treaty obligations and these are said by the Court of Justice to include those fundamental rights which are enshrined in the (European Social) Charter and the European Convention (on the Protection of Human Rights), there seems to be no reason why member states should not be compelled to observe such rights that are not simply pragmatic. Those capable of enforcement in this way include some aspects of the right to just conditions of work, to safe and healthy working conditions, to reasonable notice before termination of employment, to organise, to bargain collectively and the right of children and young persons to protection.'[4]

Changes along the above lines would make EC social policy more federalist in character. In practice this would mean that instead of attempting to standardise aspects of employment practices and policies across the member states, the Community would establish an EC-wide legal framework within which companies and governments would have to operate. If fully implemented, this type of EC policy could have far-reaching implications for British business. In the first place, it would lead to a substantial increase in the opportunistic European behaviour of interest groups who want to challenge particular aspects of labour law in a member state, or to call into question a specific company practice. Furthermore, it would give a more central role to the European Court of Justice, which would presumably have the task of deciding whether or not a fundamental right has been breached. If past experience is anything to go by, then the Court of Justice will do its utmost to ensure the effective implementation of such rights. In other words, a federalist form of EC social policy would by-pass the political decision-making process which has been used until now with great effect to block a good many interventionist policies.

However, unless this approach can be ushered in via Court of Justice rulings, it is highly unlikely that it will come into force. Some member states, not least the UK, are fundamentally opposed to the idea of a European Social Constitution. They would almost certainly use their veto within the Council of Ministers to block such a scheme. Faced with this practical reality, the Economic and Social Committee has produced a report (the Beretta Report) which proposes a compromise. In particular, Beretta suggests that in the context of 1992, the Community should establish a Charter of Social Rights but with no legally binding status. Instead, the Charter would be 'exemplary' in character. The Beretta proposals in essence reduce the concept of a European Social Constitution to a set of voluntary guidelines, which would have a minimum impact on company policies.

An important influence on the future shape of EC social policy will be the project of completing the internal market by 1992. Since 1985, the almost exclusive concern of Community institutions and officials has been to develop programmes and initiatives aimed at creating a totally liberalised trading regime inside the Community. These programmes not only involve an assault on a wide range of tariff barriers, but also the promotion of the free movement of factors of production – capital and labour. Obtaining a high level of labour mobility must be one of the most daunting objectives of completing the internal market programme.

Although Community citizens have legally been able to work in any member state since 1968, only a small minority have availed themselves of this opportunity. Clearly, linguistic, cultural and social barriers are important here. It is also argued that differences in, and non-recognition of, training and professional qualfications, and disparities in social security systems, are reasons why little progress has been made on the free movement of labour. Therefore, in the context of 1992, the Commission has launched a major drive to obtain greater *mutual recognition* of training, professional and educational qualifications inside the Community. This will involve the labour market institutions, professional bodies and government bodies from each member state identifying the obstacles to mutual recognition in a wide range of occupations and professions, and drawing up plans for their removal. In many instances, obtaining mutual recognition will be a long and complex process, such is the degree of divergence in the nature and context of some professional and occupational training programmes. It is probably accurate to say that progress in this issue will be incremental, lasting for more than a decade. In addition to these initiatives as regards training and education, greater efforts are being made to draw together the different social security regimes that exist inside the Community. Again, it is unlikely that significant developments will be very rapid, even though the Commission has placed a high priority on removing these obstacles to labour mobility. But as a result of the Council giving priority to these areas, policy co-ordination and contact between national employment and labour-market bodies will become a central feature of European social policy. As a result, EC influences are likely to increase at the administrative level in Britain.

To provide the legal basis for the internal market project and to increase the efficiency of the Community's decision-making process, the member states adopted the Single European Act. Amongst other things, the Act introduces qualified majority voting in several policy areas. As regards social policy, it has already been pointed out that health and safety matters will be subject to qualified majority voting. One immediate effect of this new voting procedure will be to speed up decision-making in this area, previously tortuously slow. Furthermore, if the Commission's present health and safety programme is anything to go by, then the quantity of Community health and safety initiatives and Directives will increase substantially. Some employers' organisations have expressed the fear that the Commission will use the label of health and safety as a flag of convenience to introduce policies on other aspects of the working environment. It is much too early to say whether or not this strategy will be used to broaden the scope of employment issues covered by qualified majority voting. In any event, there are clear limits to such a strategy, since the number of wider aspects of working conditions which can be linked to health and safety are relatively few.

The general legal consensus is that apart from health and safety no other aspect of the 'working environment' will be subject to majority voting. But as the relevant clause (Article 118A) is loosely and confusingly worded, the possibility exists that a legal test case will be mounted in the near future in an effort to extend the majority voting principle to other employment issues. If such a test-case was successful, the political environment in which EC social policy is developed would be significantly changed. On the basis of present interpretations, such a legal challenge would almost certainly fail: but inside the Community legal interpretation and perspectives have been known to change with the passage of time. The indications are that the Commission will attempt to use the Single European Act to increase the range of EC social policies. In a reply to a question put to it by an MEP in the European Parliament, the Commission argued that initiatives on the 'rights and interests of workers' were covered by provisions of the Single European Act – although it did not specify which ones – and said that it 'will not fail to adopt the appropriate initiatives with a view to protecting them (workers' rights) when the time is ripe'.[5]

So far, the shape and extent of EC social policy has been determined by the deliberations and proceedings of Community institutions. In other words, EC social policy has largely been an exercise in 'European integration from above'.[6] However, if the objective of completing the internal market by 1992 is realised, then a new set of factors, namely non-institutional, commercial and market forces, may have a bearing on the direction of social policy – 'European integration from below'. Spontaneous developments within the economy will create pressures for new policies or regulatory structures at the institutional level. Consider the example of financial markets. If financial and capital markets are fully liberalised within the EC without any new Community-wide institutional changes, then the opportunity is opened up for widespread tax-evasion practices. Furthermore, increased capital mobility could have serious 'decoupling' effects on member states' monetary policies, which will increase pressure for a European central bank and perhaps a single European currency. In the same way, market dynamics and commercial decisions by companies may have far-reaching implications for the European labour market which may only be addressed by Community-level action.

Most economic forecasts suggest that trade expansion produced by the completion of the internal market is unlikely to be as painless as the trade expansion produced by the formation of the Community and its subsequent enlargements. The general prediction is of growing income distribution problems created by the changes, as well as real costs in terms of employment. These effects could arise in a number of ways. For instance, if a completely open trading regime was established inside the Community, then multinational enterprises may decide to relocate from the richer member states in Northern Europe to the poorer countries in the south of the Community in the pursuit of labour-cost savings. This may trigger demands from the trade unions, politicians and even industrialists from the richer countries for Community action to bring about greater equivalence in pay and working conditions amongst the member states. To a large extent, such effects depend on the full ramifications of liberalisation working themselves through the system fairly quickly. Some doubt that this will be the case. For instance, UNICE argues that such economic ramifications will emerge only over a considerable period of years. Whichever of these forecasters are proved right, pressures will emerge for the Community to adopt a more consistent and coherent approach to social policy.

This broad overview suggests that although uncertainty remains about the future of EC social policy, in the short to medium term its influence inside Britain will most probably grow mainly at the national administrative level. The ground-level personnel and employment policies of companies in Britain will remain largely unaffected by Community social policies. It is unlikely that the Commission will return to its 'monolithic harmonisation' strategy, which caused the vast majority of British personnel managers to hold the Community in such a negative light in the social policy field; and with this approach now a thing of the past, the opportunity exists for the emergence of a more constructive attitude towards the European Community. In particular the British personnel profession could start examining in greater detail those employment practices in other EC countries which may be beneficial in the UK. This approach could pay considerable dividends, especially in the context of 1992, which will bring Britain commercially much closer to the rest of Europe than ever before.

Notes and References

1 See SASSON, D 'Labour and Europe', *New Statesman*, 13th November, 1987

2 MADELIN, A 'Creating a Single European Market: A French View', *World Today*, London Royal Institute of International Affairs, March 1988, p 42

3 HANSENNE, M 'Is the EEC afraid to guarantee fundamental Social Rights as flexibility takes over?', *Social and Labour Bulletin*, International Labour Organisation, Geneva, No 3, 1987 pp 369–73

4 HEPPLE, B 'The Crisis in European Labour Law', *Industrial Law Journal*, 1987, p 87

5 See *European Industrial Relations Review*, May 1988, p 2

6 PELKMANS, J 'Economic theories of integration revisited', *Journal of Common Market Studies*, Vol XVIII, No 4, June 1980 pp 333–54

Appendix 1: Social Provisions of the Treaty of Rome

Health and Safety

Article 30

Basic standards shall be laid down within the Community for the protection of the health of workers and the general public against the dangers arising from ionizing radiations.

The expression 'basic standards' means:

(a) maximum permissible doses compatible with adequate safety;
(b) maximum permissible levels of exposure and contamination;
(c) the fundamental principles governing the health surveillance of workers.

Article 31

The basic standards shall be worked out by the Commission after it has obtained the opinion of a group of persons appointed by the Scientific and Technical Committee from among scientific experts, and in particular public health experts, in the Member States. The Commission shall obtain the opinion of the Economic and Social Committee on these basic standards.

After consulting the Assembly the Council shall, on a proposal from the Commission, which shall forward to it the opinions obtained from these Committees, establish the basic standards; the Council shall act by a qualified majority.

Article 32

At the request of the Commission or of a Member State, the basic standards may be revised or supplemented in accordance with the procedure laid down in Article 31.

The Commission shall examine any request made by a Member State.

Article 33

Each Member State shall lay down the appropriate provisions, whether by legislation, regulation or administrative action, to ensure compliance with the basic standards which have been established and shall take the necessary measures with regard to teaching, education and vocational training.

The Commission shall make appropriate recommendations for harmonising the provisions applicable in this field in the Member State.

To this end, the Member States shall communicate to the Commission the provisions applicable at the date of entry into force of this Treaty and any subsequent draft provisions of the same kind.

Any recommendations the Commission may wish to issue with regard to such draft provisions shall be made within three months of the date on which such draft provisions are communicated.

Article 34

Any Member State in whose territories particularly dangerous experiments are to take place shall take additional health and safety measures, on which it shall first obtain the opinion of the Commission.

The assent of the Commission shall be required where the effects of such experiments are liable to affect the territories of other Member States.

Article 35

Each Member State shall establish the facilities necessary to carry out continuous monitoring of the level of radioactivity in the air, water and soil and to ensure compliance with the basic standards.

The Commission shall have the right of access to such facilities; it may verify their operation and efficiency.

Article 36

The appropriate authorities shall periodically communicate information on the checks referred to in Article 35 to the Commission so that it is kept informed of the level of radioactivity to which the public is exposed.

Article 37

Each Member State shall provide the Commission with such general data relating to any plan for the disposal of radioactive waste in whatever form as will make it possible to determine whether the implementation of such plan is liable to result in the radioactive contamination of the water, soil or airspace of another Member State.

The Commission shall deliver its opinion with six months, after consulting the group of experts referred to in Article 31.

Article 38

The Commission shall make recommendations to the Member States with regard to the level of radioactivity in the air, water and soil.

In cases of urgency, the Commission shall issue a Directive requiring the Member State concerned to take, within a period laid down by the Commission, all necessary measures to prevent infringement of the basic standards and to ensure compliance with regulations.

Should the State in question fail to comply with the Commission directive within the period laid down, the Commission or any Member State concerned may forthwith, by way of derogation from Articles 141 and 142, bring the matter before the Court of Justice.

Article 39

The Commission shall set up within the framework of the Joint Nuclear Research Centre, as soon as the latter has been established, a health and safety documentation and study section.

This section shall in particular have the task of collecting the documentation and information referred to in Articles 33, 36 and 37 and of assisting the Commission in carrying out the tasks assigned to it by this Chapter.

Wages and Movement of Workers

Article 68

1. The methods used for fixing wages and welfare benefits in the several Member States shall not, in the case of the coal and steel industries, be affected by this Treaty, subject to the following provisions.
2. If the High Authority finds that one or more undertakings are charging abnormally low prices because they are paying abnormally low wages compared with the wage level in the same area, it shall, after consulting the Consultative Committee, make appropriate recommendations to them. If the abnormally low wages are the result of governmental decisions, the High Authority shall confer with the Government concerned, and failing agreement it may, after consulting the Consultative Committee, make a recommendation to that Government.
3. If the High Authority finds that wage reduction entails a lowering of the standard of living of workers and at the same time is being used as a means for the permanent economic adjustment of undertakings or as a means of compensation between them, it shall, after consulting the Consultative Committee, make a recommendation to the undertaking or Government concerned with a view to securing, at the expense of the undertakings, benefits for the workers in order to compensate for the reductions.

This provision shall not apply to:

(a) Overall measures taken by a Member State to restore its external equilibrium, without prejudice in such case to any action under Article 67;

(b) wage reductions resulting from the application of a sliding scale established by law or by contract;

(c) wage reductions resulting from a fall in the cost of living;

(d) wage reductions to correct abnormal increases that occurred previously in exceptional circumstances which no longer obtain.

4. Save in the cases referred to in paragraph 3 (a) and (b), any wage

reduction affecting all or a substantial number of the workers in an undertaking shall be notified to the High Authority.

5. The recommendations provided for in the preceding paragraphs may be made by the High Authority only after consulting the Council, unless they are addressed to undertakings smaller than a minimum size to be defined by the High Authority in agreement with the Council.

If in one of the Member States a change in the arrangements for the financing of social security or for dealing with unemployment and its effects, or a change in wages, produces the effects referred to in Article 67 (2) or (3), the High Authority is empowered to take the steps provided for in that Article.

6. The High Authority may impose upon undertakings which do not comply with recommendations made to them under this Article fines and periodic penalty payments not exceeding twice the amount of the saving in labour costs improperly effected.

Article 69

1. Member States undertake to remove any restriction based on nationality upon the employment in the coal and steel industries of workers who are nationals of Member States and have recognised qualifications in a coalmining or steelmaking occupation, subject to the limitations imposed by the basic requirement of health and public policy.

2. For the purpose of applying this provision, Member States shall draw up common definitions or skilled trades and qualifications therefore, shall determine by common accord the limitations provided in paragraph 1, and shall endeavour to work out arrangements on a Community-wide basis for bringing offers of employment into touch with applications for employment.

3. In addition, with regard to workers not covered by paragraph 2, they shall, should growth of coal or steel production be hampered by a shortage of suitable labour, adjust their immigration rules to the extent needed to remedy this state of affairs; in particular, they shall facilitate the re-employment of workers from the coal and steel industries of other Member States.

4. They shall prohibit any discrimination in remuneration and working conditions between nationals and migrant workers, without prejudice to special measures concerning frontier workers; in particular, they shall endeavour to settle among themselves any matters remaining to be dealt with in order to ensure that social security arrangements do not inhibit labour mobility.

5. The High Authority shall guide and facilitate action by Member States in applying this Article.

6. This Article shall not affect the international obligations of Member States.

Social Provisions

Article 117

Member States agree upon the need to promote improved working conditions and an improved standard of living for workers, so as to make possible their harmonisation while the improvement is being maintained.

They believe that such a development will ensue not only from the functioning of the common market, which will favour the harmonisation of social systems, but also from the procedures provided for in this Treaty and from the approximation of provisions laid down by law, regulation or administrative action.

Article 118

Without prejudice to the other provisions of this Treaty and in conformity with its general objectives, the Commission shall have the task of promoting close cooperation between Member States in the social field, particularly in matters relating to:

- employment;
- labour law and working conditions;
- basic and advanced vocational training;
- social security;
- prevention of occupational accidents and diseases;
- occupational hygiene;
- the right of association, and collective bargaining between employers and workers.

To this end, the Commission shall act in close contact with Member States by making studies, delivering opinions and arranging consultations both on problems arising at national level and on those of concern to international organisations.

Before delivering the opinions provided for in this Article, the Commission shall consult the Economic and Social Committee.

Article 119

Each Member State shall during the first stage ensure and subsequently maintain the application of the principle that men and women should receive equal pay for equal work.

For the purpose of this Article 'pay' means the ordinary basic or minimum wage or salary and any other consideration, whether in cash or in kind, which the worker receives, directly or indirectly, in respect of his employment from his employer.

Equal pay without discrimination based on sex means:

(a) that pay for the same work at piece rate shall be calculated on the basis of the same unit of measurement;

(b) that pay for work at time rates shall be the same for the same job.

Article 120

Member States shall endeavour to maintain the existing equivalence between paid holiday schemes.

Article 121

The Council may, acting unanimously and after consulting the Economic and Social Committee, assign to the Commission tasks in connection with the implementation of common measures, particularly as regards social security for the migrant workers referred to in Articles 48 to 51.

Article 122

The Commission shall include a separate chapter on social developments within the Community in its annual report to the Assembly.

The Assembly (Parliament) may invite the Commission to draw up reports on any particular problems concerning social conditions.

The European Social Fund

Article 123

In order to improve employment opportunities for workers in the common market and to contribute thereby to raising the standard of living, a European Social Fund is hereby established in accordance with the provisions set out below; it shall have the task of rendering the employment of workers easier and of increasing their geographical and occupational mobility within the Community.

Article 124

The Fund shall be administered by the Commission.

The Commission shall be assisted in this task by a Committee presided over by a member of the Commission and composed of representatives of Governments, trade unions and employers' organisations.

Article 125

1. On application by a Member State the Fund shall, within the framework of the rules provided for in Article 127, meet 50% of the expenditure incurred after the entry into force of this Treaty by that State or by a body governed by public law for the purposes of:

(a) ensuring productive re-employment of workers by means of:

- vocational retraining;
- resettlement allowances;

(b) granting aid for the benefit of workers whose employment is reduced or temporarily suspended, in whole or in part, as a result of the conversion of an undertaking to other production, in order that they may retain the same wage level pending their full re-employment.

2. Assistance granted by the Fund towards the cost of vocational retraining shall be granted only if the unemployed workers could not be found employment except in a new occupation and only if they have been in productive employment for at least six months in the occupation for which they have been retrained.

Assistance towards resettlement allowances shall be granted only if the unemployed workers have been caused to change their home within the Community and have been in productive employment for at least six months in their new place of residence.

Assistance for workers in the case of the conversion of an undertaking shall be granted only if:

(a) the workers concerned have again been fully employed in that undertaking for at least six months;

(b) the Government concerned has submitted a plan beforehand, drawn up by the undertaking in question, for that particular conversion and for financing it;

(c) the Commission has given its prior approval to the conversion plan.

Article 126

When the transnational period has ended, the Council, after receiving the opinion of the Commission and after consulting the Economic and Social Committee and the Assembly, may:

(a) rule, by a qualified majority, that all or part of the assistance referred to in Article 125 shall no longer be granted; or

(b) unanimously determine what new tasks may be entrusted to the Fund within the framework of its terms of reference as laid down in Article 123.

Article 127

The Council shall, acting by a qualified majority on a proposal from the Commission and after consulting the Economic and Social Committee and the Assembly, lay down the provisions required to implement Articles 124 to 126; in particular it shall determine in detail the conditions under which assistance shall be granted by the Fund in accordance with Article 125 and the classes of undertakings whose workers shall benefit from the assistance provided in Article 125 (1) (b).

Article 128

The Council shall, acting on a proposal from the Commission and after consulting the Economic and Social Committee, lay down general principles for implementing a common vocational training policy capable of contributing to the harmonious development both of the national economies and of the common market.

Appendix 2: The Single European Act

Subsection III – Social Policy

Article 21

The EEC Treaty shall be supplemented by the following provisions:

Article 118A

1. *Member States shall pay particular attention to encouraging improvements, especially in the working environment, as regards the health and safety of workers, and shall set as their objective the harmonisation of conditions in this area, while maintaining the improvements made.*

2. *In order to help achieve the objective laid down in the first paragraph, the Council, acting by a qualified majority on a proposal from the Commission, in cooperation with the European Parliament and after consulting the Economic and Social Committee, shall adopt, by means of directives, minimum requirements for gradual implementation, having regard to the conditions and technical rules obtaining in each of the Member States.*

Such directives shall avoid imposing administrative, financial and legal constraints in a way which would hold back the creation and development of small and medium sized undertakings.

3. *The provisions adopted pursuant to this Article shall not prevent any Member State from maintaining or introducing more stringent measures for the protection of working conditions compatible with this Treaty.*

Article 22

The EEC Treaty shall be supplemented by the following provisions:

Article 118B

The Commission shall endeavour to develop the dialogue between management and labour at European level which could, if the two sides consider it desirable, lead to relations based on agreement.

Subsection IV – Economic and Social Cohesion

Article 23

A Title V shall be added to Part Three of the EEC Treaty, reading as follows:

Title V

Economic and social cohesion

Article 130A

In order to promote its overall harmonious development, the Community shall develop and pursue its actions leading to the strengthening of its economic and social cohesion.

In particular the Community shall aim at reducing disparities between the various regions and the backwardness of the least favoured regions.

Article 130B

Member States shall conduct their economic policies, and shall coordinate them, in such a way as, in addition, to attain the objectives set out in Article 130A. The implementation of the common policies and of the internal market shall take into account the objectives set out in Article 130A and in Article 130C and shall contribute to their achievement. The Community shall support the achievement of these objectives by the action it takes through the structural Funds (European Agricultural Guidance and Guarantee Fund, Guidance Section, European Regional Development Fund), the European Investment Bank and the other existing financial instruments.

Article 130C

The European Regional Development fund is intended to help redress the principal regional imbalances in the Community through participating in the development and structural adjustment of regions whose development is lagging behind and in the conversion of declining industrial regions.

Article 130D

Once the Single European Act enters into force the Commission shall submit a comprehensive proposal to the Council, the purpose of which will be to make such amendments to the structure and operational rules of the existing structural Funds (European Agricultural Guidance and Guarantee Fund, Guidance Section, European Social Fund, European Regional Development Fund) as are necessary to clarify and rationalise their tasks in order to contribute to the achievement of the objectives set out in Article 130A and Article 130C, to increase their efficiency and to coordinate their activities between themselves and with the operations of the existing financial instruments. The Council shall act unanimously on this proposal within a period of one year, after consulting the European Parliament and the Economic and Social Committee.

Article 130E

After adoption of the decision referred to in Article 130D, implementing decisions relating to the European Regional Development Fund shall be taken by the Council, acting by a qualified majority on a proposal from the Commission and in cooperation with the European Parliament.

Appendix 3: Methodology

Some aspects of the methodological approach are outlined in various parts of the book. But to give the reader a more comprehensive and fuller insight into how the study was conducted, this appendix describes the methodological approach in some detail. When the IPM International Committee first conceived of the project, it gave it the working title of the EC influences on the Employment Environment in Britain. While this title was broad and open-ended, it also had the considerable merit of incorporating the reality that EC influences take various forms and that EC employment and labour market policies do not solely relate to employment practices or to the situation of people at work. If the IPM International Committee had adopted a narrower working title, it might have excluded some important issues from the study.

Obviously when the research work started on the project, the first task was to establish some satisfactory and operational definitions to the terms 'EC influences' and the 'employment environment'. It became apparent almost immediately that a formal legalistic definition of the notion of EC influences would be too restrictive. At that early stage, it was already realised that several of the Commission's social policy proposals had affected the behaviour of British business even though they had not been officially ratified by the Council. The obvious case in point is the draft Vredeling Directive. Limiting the notion of EC influences to formal Community legislation and policies would exclude an assessment of this type of influence. To overcome this problem, it was decided to develop different categories of EC influences which together would cover all the circumstances in which the Community could potentially influence aspects of the employment environment in Britain.

Four different forms of influences were developed. First, *formal legal influences*. Under this heading, the major issue that required examination was the extent to which Community legislation on social and labour affairs had led to changes to employment law in Britain. At the outset, it was expected that this form of influence would be the most straightforward to detect and report. But as the study shows, this initial expectation could not have been further from the reality.

Secondly, *political influences*. As many people are not fully aware of the political and economic nature of the Community, a static conception sometimes pervades discussions on the issue. From this point of view, Community institutions are perceived to be a monolith existing at the international level, occasionally imposing its will on political and economic affairs in Britain. But this concept of the nature of the Community is highly misleading. Community institutions should not be regarded as existing 'above' the nation state in some unconnected way.

Rather, they should be seen as entrenched in a two-way political and economic integration process in which not only Community institutions and bodies try to influence developments within the respective member states, but also national political parties and interest groups try to have an influence on Community-level deliberations.

To take the interest group dimension as an example, the European integration process gives rise to a wide range of political linkages between national and community organisations and involves groups in new types of action which they would not undertake if outside the Community. Thus, in the industrial and labour spheres, Britain's membership of the Community has strengthened employers' organisations and trade unions' ties with equivalent bodies at the European level and has led them to campaign at the European level for and against policies. These connections and linkages between national and European interest groups and the action they take on Community-related matters may be regarded as political influences. Thus under this heading of political influences, the research agenda was to assess in what ways Community membership has brought a new perspective to the thinking of the main employers' and trade union bodies and to explore what type of action they have undertaken on European matters. In addition, it was also regarded as necessary to examine how the political parties in Britain viewed Community-level developments in the social and labour fields. This is because, as Chapter II explains, the Community is an inter-governmental type of organisation which means that it is unlikely to adopt any policies which are strongly opposed by any member state. Thus as things stand, one member state can effectively block any policy direction which it dislikes at the Community level.

As well as the elaborate web of linkages between national and European interest groups, the Community has also given rise to a dense network of connections between different government and quasi-government bodies in particular policy areas. Thus in the social policy area, the different labour-market and training bodies from the various member states come together at the Community level to examine ways their policies and programmes could be better coordinated and to discuss Community-wide training initiatives. These institutional linkages place two types of obligations on national bodies in the employment field: (i) they commit them to develop policies on how to obtain greater co-ordination between the member states on employment and on what they regard as the most appropriate direction for Community training policies; (ii) they commit them to take action on policy decisions resulting from Community meetings. Thus, in theory at least, Community membership opens up a new European dimension to the work of national government and quasi-government institutions in the employment field which may lead them to approach policy issues in a different way or may constrain them in the actions they take on certain issues. The connections which national labour-market bodies have with Community affairs can be regarded as *institutional influences.* This is the third category of influences which was developed for the study.

The almost universal trend in studies which assess the extent of the impact of Community membership on Britain is to focus on aggregate issues – the impact on national political parties, interest groups, the national legal system and so on. While these studies have produced worthwhile and interesting findings, it was decided that this approach was too limited for a comprehensive assessment of how the EC has influenced the employment environment in Britain. This was essentially because focusing purely on the national level would leave unexplained how the EC, if at all, influences companies on employment and labour affairs. To examine this dimension, the notion of *company-level influences* was developed. Under this heading, it was regarded as necessary to interview personnel managers in industry to find out their views about Community employment legislation and policies, and their assessment of the extent to which company personnel and manpower policies were influenced by Community policies.

These four categories of influences – legal, political, institutional and company – were thought to cover all the ways the EC may influence the employment environment in Britain, thereby allowing a thorough examination of the issue. Having identified the type of influences requiring study, it was relatively straightforward to tackle the problem of the open-ended nature of the term 'employment environment'. Simply, the term employment environment was broken down in a similar way. Thus, the employment environment was separated into legal, institutional, political and company dimensions which together make up that environment. This categorisation of the terms influence and employment environment into discrete but related areas was seen as a comprehensive and operational research framework.

With the task of establishing a research framework complete, the next problem was how to collect the necessary information for the four separate categories. As regards the legal, institutional and political, no major problems were foreseen. It was anticipated that the required data could be obtained through the standard practice of interviewing officials in political parties, government departments and trade unions; and other experts, and by carrying out a detailed literature search. However, the company dimension was seen as the area posing the most problems. For instance, one potential problem identified was that as European social legislation is transferred into national labour law before it impacts on companies, personnel managers may feel that any changes they are required to make are as a result of national rather than European law. In other words, some personnel managers might perceive there to be no EC influence, when actually one exists. Because of this factor, and others such as the complicated subject matter, we decided against using a questionnaire to find out the view of companies. Instead, we chose to conduct structured interviews with a range of companies. Obviously, this limited the range of our sample, but it was strongly felt that the nature of the subject area did not lend itself to the questionnaire approach.

The structured interviews scheduled were divided into three parts. The first part asked questions about the company's view of EC social policies in the various areas: health and safety, equal opportunity policies, workers' rights, and participation. The second part asked questions about whether the company had any direct linkages with the EC, for example, whether any company personnel sat on any EC body or other related Community organisation (for instance a European employers' body). The third and main part of the interview schedule attempted to assess the degree of EC influences on personnel and management policies in companies. The first sub-section assessed whether the personnel manager was conscious of any EC influences at work. The interview form focused on the subject area of EC initiatives, and the personnel manager was asked to outline any changes that had taken place in recent times and if so for what reasons. Through this approach it was hoped that we would be able to identify those changes which might have come about at the behest of the Community, but which were not recognised as such by the personnel manager. The second sub-section asked the personnel manager what he regarded as the most important influences operating on the formulation and implementation of personnel policies. This was to give us some insight into whether the EC is influencing working practices, and if not, what are the factors in operation. This interview schedule form was considered to be sufficiently rigorous to allow us to investigate the extent of EC influences on companies. Some prior adjustments had to be made to the questions to take account of the different size of companies, their sector location and their nationality of ownership.

In drawing up the list of the companies we wished to interview, we regarded it as important to select a sample which included companies in different sectors, of different size and of different nationality of ownership. The sectoral classification was regarded as important, since it was assumed that the commercial location of companies may affect their responses to ratified and proposed EC social legislation. For example, as there is a disproportionately large number of part-time workers in the distributive trades, it was thought that companies in this sphere of economic activity would be more concerned about the proposed Directive on part-time work than companies in manufacturing. In other words, as well as uncovering a number of general or common reponses to EC social-policy initiatives, it was anticipated that the research would uncover several sector-specific strategies in relation to the EC. As well as this sectoral breakdown of the interviews, nationality of ownership was also seen as a potentially important factor influencing the responses of firms. For instance, personnel managers in a subsidiary of a Belgian or Dutch firm located in Britain might be assumed to be less hostile to EC initiatives than British firms, since many other proposals made by the Commission are already in place in their headquarters' labour markets. Finally, it was regarded as necessary to study a range of companies based on size classification, incorporating both multinationals and small firms. Large, particularly multinational, companies, would almost certainly have better developed and more active views relating to EC social initiatives than small firms, but it was seen as important to include the latter as they are a growing sector in the British economy, and also as they provide a yardstick by which to assess the extent to which EC influences have penetrated the commercial environment in Britain.

As regards the sector classification, an initial breakdown was made on manufacturing sector, private services sector and the public sector. Then a further breakdown was made into categories. The manufacturing sector was subdivided into extractive, low technology, medium technology and high technology subsectors. In each subsector we interviewed three small firms (except in the extractive subsector) six UK-owned large companies or multinationals and six foreign-owned multinationals. In total, 57 organisations were interviewed in the manufacturing sector. The private service sector was disaggregated into financial and banking services, distributive trades and private producer services (leisure activity etc). Again three small companies, six UK-owned large or multinational companies and six foreign-owned companies were interviewed. Thus 45 companies in total were interviewed in the service sector.

In the public sector we decided to adopt a different approach. Instead of interviewing a sample of companies representing the full range of public sector activity, we decided to concentrate on two sectors where the links with the EC appeared to be strong, namely the local authority sector and the public enterprise sector. It was decided to interview six local authorities and four public enterprises. In total, therefore, 112 organisations were interviewed.

This is a brief outline of the methodological approach adopted for the study. If people want further information on any aspect of the methodological approach, please contact either author. Unfortunately, we cannot list the companies interviewed, as many wished to remain anonymous.

Appendix 4: Geographical Breakdown of Social Fund Allocations

Table i: Training Grants to Local Authorities (£)

	1981	1982	1983	1984	1985
Avon		19,946	98,239	977,371	1,125,989
Berkshire			108,137		
Borders				210,261	
Cambridgeshire				149,267	53,335
Cheshire		6,006	181,240	446,914	498,866
Cleveland	15,258	100,000	768,063	1,212,508	1,099,173
Clwyd		29,600	232,929	22,323	546,836
Cornwall			56,531	662,562	1,190,585
Cumbria	51,217	59,406		59,791	64,593
Derbyshire			44,879	34,020	129,340
Devon	225,813		7,000	450,074	695,048
Dorset					8,498
Durham	47,044	65,550	142,235	102,368	202,522
Dyfed			173,093	121,324	467,458
Essex	80,849		105,230	243,599	339,072
Fife				4,738	395,837
Gloucestershire				80,284	57,617
Grampian				31,054	70,986
Greater London	153,517	815,420	1,516,636	2,906,598	5,662,229
Greater Manchester	70,617	3,822,603	362,832	8,647,404	3,853,834
Gwent			127,250	168,803	320,307
Gwynedd					51,911
Hampshire		15,000			12,767
Hereford & Worcester		467,500		50,776	260,735
Hertfordshire	51,000	81,225	63,380	469,904	154,129
Highlands & Islands			202,450		590,288
Humberside				479,582	
Kent			32,320	50,760	29,773
Lancashire	9,256	13,935	617,411	553,318	2,822,893
Leicestershire	3,879	61,098	378,056		96,729
Lincolnshire				16,763	97,730
Lothian		112,927	262,239	2,762,851	2,905,367
Merseyside	214,590	1,276,170	1,637,865	3,964,378	6,736,215
Mid Glamorgan			147,908	12,500	666,016
Norfolk		51,348	106,067	17,396	31,256
North Yorkshire	36,225		38,005	3,640	80,143
Northamptonshire			142,200	262,658	35,950
Northumberland				71,479	409,086
Nottinghamshire		1,366,550		375,619	23,160
Powys				20,000	91,012
Salop			235,389	196,232	86,022
Somerset					110,721
South Glamorgan		22,082	56,250	34,345	206,758

	1981	1982	1983	1984	1985
South Yorkshire	32,238	50,284	1,035,335	938,263	2,746,532
Staffordshire	6,850	245,290	264,582	146,470	234,514
Strathclyde	138,085	297,727	3,172,799	3,532,164	7,938,498
Surrey				164,000	281,158
Tayside	12,000		736,565	384,645	419,486
Tyne & Wear	178,450	945,913	991,400	960,100	3,304,755
Warwickshire				125,249	353,745
West Glamorgan	45,875	232,696	28,550	140,705	
West Midlands	111,510	402,107	1,662,385	2,872,624	4,999,526
West Sussex				73,785	
West Yorkshire	636,041	806,459	2,188,693	2,326,686	6,875,585
Wiltshire				149,529	367,179

Table ii: Employment Grants to Local Authorities (£)

	1981	1982	1983	1984	1985
Cambridgeshire					185,964
Central			273,000	169,975	
Cheshire					
Cleveland	31,575	282,247	144,242	142,766	327,267
Clwyd			50,000	4,968	117,167
Cornwall				344,760	79,479
Cumbria	809	34,990	70,543	78,000	75,503
Dumfries & Galloway		3,696		47,151	52,103
Durham	100,000	231,618	231,847	176,505	220,252
Dyfed			48,121	9,652	61,780
Fife					210,218
Grampian			100,974	13,500	
Greater Manchester	21,050	3,729,132	322,722	469,683	710,328
Gwent		78,000	152,507	205,060	
Gwynedd		10,882			
Highlands & Islands			189,150	53,000	203,388
Humberside			117,000	126,360	
Lancashire			4,624	12,675	41,061
Lincolnshire					11,823
Lothian			120,000	26,486	136,768
Merseyside	650,000	950,774	640,999	360,234	225,713
Mid Glamorgan	9,051	9,359	248,666	61,285	78,760
North Yorkshire				20,000	29,773
Northamptonshire				167,310	
Northumberland				30,420	
Nottinghamshire		48,750			
Salop			24,085	37,933	
South Glamorgan			5,359		
South Yorkshire	17,000	32,900	158,201	335,325	373,252
Staffordshire				32,651	7,215
Strathclyde		1,041,000	1,870,050	745,875	986,745
Tayside		507,000	250,000	55,575	107,672
Tyne & Wear	69,634	108,706	216,877	407,940	617,874
Warwickshire					24,811
West Glamorgan			56,880		402,323
West Midlands				58,283	610,756
West Yorkshire		202,762	66,193	207,006	225,963

Table iii: Grants for other Social Action to Local Authorities (£)

	1981	1982	1983	1984	1985
Cheshire				103,275	
Cleveland	66,325	133,425			
Devon	28,700				
East Sussex		96,000			
Essex				13,020	114,945
Gloucestershire				21,000	
Grampian		86,700			
Greater London	31,379	267,810	144,444		
Hampshire		18,500	26,900		
Highlands & Islands	49,500	48,750			
Lancashire				5,755	
Lothian	21,750	30,500	48,900		
Merseyside					4,978
Oxfordshire				23,500	
South Glamorgan		89,500			
Staffordshire		14,535			
Tayside			25,750		
Warwickshire		9,575			
West Midlands				45,067	126,585
West Sussex			232,750		
West Yorkshire	27,600	3,900		144,270	
Yorks & Humberside				26,865	51,765

Table iv: Employment Grants to the Different Regions (£)

	1981	1982	1983	1984	1985
South East					
(Greater London)					
East Anglia					185,964
South West				344,760	79,479
West Midlands			24,085	10,408,981	10,052,260
East Midlands		48,750		167,310	11,823
Yorks & Humberside	17,000	235,662	341,394	9,438,084	8,375,745
North West	671,050	4,679,906	968,345	842,592	4,830,886
North	202,018	657,061	663,509	835,631	1,240,896
Wales	9,051	98,241	561,583	280,965	660,030
Scotland	1,524,696	2,803,174	1,098,062	1,696,894	

Table v: Grants for Other Social Action to the Different Regions (£)

	1981	1982	1983	1984	1985
South East	31,379	382,310	404,094	36,520	114,945
(Greater London)					
East Anglia					
South West	28,700			21,000	
West Midlands		24,110		45,067	126,585
Yorks & Humberside	27,600	31,900		53,230	51,760
North West	–	–	51,755	108,253	
North	66,325	133,425			
Wales		89,500			
Scotland	71,250	165,950	74,650		

Table vi: Training Grants to the Different Regions (£)

	1981	1982	1983	1984	1985
South East	285,366	911,645	1,825,704	3,744,646	6,479,128
(Greater London)					
East Anglia		51,348	125,784	17,396	31,250
South West	225,813	19,946	161,770	2,170,291	3,188,458
West Midlands	118,310	1,114,897	2,162,356	38,660,656	21,777,326
East Midlands	3,879	1,397,648	565,135	838,327	436,244
Yorks & Humberside	704,504	856,743	3,554,304	28,777,326	18,893,882
North West	294,463	5,118,714	2,799,348	13,612,014	13,911,808
North	291,969	945,913	1,901,698	2,426,046	5,080,129
Wales	45,875	51,682	970,626	407,845	2,941,003
Scotland	150,085	410,654	4,374,063	6,925,574	12,320,462

Appendix 5: UK Priority Areas Designated by the Commission

Counties (local authority areas): Central, Cheshire, Cleveland, Clwyd, Cornwall, Derbyshire, Dumfries and Galloway, Durham, Dyfed, Fife, Greater Manchester, Gwent, Gwynedd, Hereford and Worcester, Highlands & Islands, Humberside, Isle of Wight, Lancashire, Lincolnshire, Lothian, Merseyside, Mid Glamorgan, Northumberland, Nottinghamshire, Salop, South Glamorgan, South Yorkshire, Staffordshire, Strathclyde, Tayside, Tyne & Wear, West Glamorgan, West Midlands, West Yorkshire.

Travel to work areas: Workington (Cumbria), Coalville (Leicestershire), Corby (Northamptonshire).

Non-priority Areas Receiving Social Fund Money: Avon, Berkshire, Borders, Cambridgeshire, Devon, Dorset, East Sussex, Essex, Gloucestershire, Grampian, Greater London, Hampshire, Hertfordshire, Norfolk, North Yorkshire, Oxfordshire, Powys, Somerset, Suffolk, Surrey, West Sussex, Wiltshire, Warwickshire.

Appendix 6: Protocol Agreements (Thomson Grand Public)

Thomson Grand Public-European Metalworkers' Federation Liaison Committee

Taking into account the supranational character of the activities of the THOMSON GRAND PUBLIC Division, the signatories agree to set up a Liaison Committee, which will provide economic data on the industrial and trading situation with regard to THOMSON GRAND PUBLIC operations in Europe.

I – Composition

- The Managing Director of the firm THOMSON GRAND PUBLIC or his representative, together with the managers concerned.
- 15 representatives of trade unions organisations affiliated to the European Metalworkers' Federation (E.M.F.)

II – Allocation of Seats

- 1 seat is reserved for a representative of the European Metalworkers' Federation.
- 14 seats are attributed to the representatives of trade union organisations affiliated to the E.M.F., or represented by the E.M.F., appointed from among the employees of this Division.

They are allocated as follows:

- 6 seats for the French organisations
- 4 seats for the German organisations
- 2 seats for the Italian organisations
- 2 seats for the Spanish organisations

III – Procedure

The Committee will meet every six months on THOMSON GRAND PUBLIC or E.M.F. initiative, notice being given six weeks in advance.
The venue for the meeting will be chosen by THOMSON GRAND PUBLIC, which will meet all interpretation costs.
The travel and accommodation costs incurred by participants in these meetings will be met by the E.M.F.
All persons appointed who are employed in the THOMSON GRAND PUBLIC Division will be guaranteed payment of full wages during attendance of sessions of the European Committee.

Participants' names must be communicated to THOMSON GRAND PUBLIC at least two weeks before each meeting.
One of the two annual meetings must precede the annual session of the European Branch Committee.

IV – Competence

The Liaison Committee shall be informed of the economic, industrial and trading activities of THOMSON GRAND PUBLIC.
It will be informed, prior to the implementation, of major structural, industrial and trading modifications and changes in the economic and legal organisation of THOMSON GRAND PUBLIC.
It will be informed of measures taken and planned for adapting the organisation and workforce to technological change as well as adapting employees' skills in the light of employment problems.
The members of the Liaison Committee may express opinions, in the light of the information supplied, on all the areas defined above.

V – The E.M.F. is to have access to the documents transmitted to the European Branch Committee.
It undertakes to respect the confidential or secret nature of these documents, as the case may be, vis-à-vis third parties.

VI – This protocol is concluded, on an experimental basis, for a period of two years as from 1st January 1986. The parties shall meet in the three months preceding its expiration in order to decide whether or not to renew these provisions.

PARIS
7th October 1985

EUROPEAN METALWORKERS' FEDERATION	THOMSON GRAND PUBLIC
represented by Hubert THIERRON	represented by Jean-Jacques PEUCH-LESTRADE

F.U.L.C. I.G. METALL C.F.D.T. C.G.T.-F.O. U.G.T.

The European Branch Committee

Considering the European character of the activities of the THOMSON GRAND PUBLIC Division, the signatories agree to set up a European Branch Committee, which is a new institution that must not lead to a

diminution of the role of the French Branch Committee resulting from the agreement of 28th February 1984 signed with the representative French trade union organisations at THOMSON GRAND PUBLIC Division level.
This body must provide information for representatives of personnel employed in the THOMSON GRAND PUBLIC Division, at European level, on its economic, industrial and trading situation.

I – Composition

- The Managing Director of the firm THOMSON GRAND PUBLIC or his representative, together with the managers concerned.
- 26 employee representatives appointed by the representative trade union organisations in France, Italy and Spain, at the Division level, from among the elected members of the Works Committees or Councils of subsidiaries of THOMSON GRAND PUBLIC and, in the case of the Federal Republic of Germany, by the Central Works Councils or, failing this, by the Works Councils.

II – Allocation of seats

In order to counter any disparities that may result from strict application of the rule of proportional representation in relation to the number of employees, each country will be represented, a priori, by 2 employee representatives.

Allocation of the other seats will be in proportion to the number of employees in the Division in the four European countries concerned, i.e. currently France, Germany, Italy and Spain.

On the basis of the total workforce as at 30th June 1985, employees of subsidiaries are to be represented as follows:

- French subsidiaries are represented by 13 members
- German subsidiaries are represented by 8 members
- Italian subsidiaries are represented by 3 members
- Spanish subsidiaries are represented by 2 members

The employee representatives of each country will be appointed, as laid down in paragraph 1, in accordance with the number of elected council members, as per the tables annexed to this protocol.

III – Procedure

The Branch Committee will meet once per year and will be convened by the management of THOMSON GRAND PUBLIC.
An ad hoc Committee may be constituted in respect of each problem

liable to modify the industrial and trading position of the Division at European level. At its first meeting, the European Branch Committee will determine all details regarding the setting-up and operation of the ad hoc Committees.
The meeting costs (room and interpretation, as well as the accommodation and travel expenses incurred in respect of attendance of this meeting) will be met by THOMSON GRAND PUBLIC.
Employee representatives will be guaranteed payment of full wages for the duration of the meeting.
The names of the members of the European Branch Committee will be communicated to THOMSON GRAND PUBLIC by the appropriate bodies as per paragraph I before 31st December 1985.
The members of the European Branch Committee shall hold office for a period of two years.
During the two-year period of office, no other appointment may be made except in the following cases:

- Departure from the company or Division
- Change in trade union affiliation
- Loss of seat on a Works Committee or (Central) Works Council
- For the Federal Republic of Germany: Removal from appointed post by the Central Works Council or, failing this, the Works Council following the said Council's declared loss of confidence.

IV – Competence

The European Branch Committee will be informed of the Division's economic, industrial and trading activities in Europe and of the measures taken and planned for adapting personnel of subsidiaries in the countries concerned to technological change and adapting their skills in the light of employment problems.
The European Branch Committee will be informed, prior to implementation, of all major structural and industrial changes provided the decision is taken at Divisional level.
The European Branch Committee will be informed of economic and legal organisational changes in the Division (acquisition or transfer of subsidiaries).

V – Duration

The present protocol is concluded, on an experimental basis, for a period of two years as from 1st January 1986. The parties will meet in the three months preceding its expiration in order to decide whether or not to renew these provisions.

PARIS
7th October 1985

French trade union organisations
C.F.D.T.
C.G.C.
C.G.T.
C.G.T.-F.O.

German Works Council or Central Works Council members
GBR NEWEK
GBR DEWEK
GBR SABA
GBR TELEFUNKEN
GBR DAGFU
GBR NORDMENDE

Italian trade union organisations
F.U.L.C.

Spanish trade union organisations
U.G.T.
C.G.O.O.

European Metalworkers' Federation

For and on behalf of the firm
THOMSON GRAND PUBLIC
Jean-Jacques PEUCH-LESTRADE

Appendix 7: Joint Opinions of the Val Duchesse Working Parties

The New Technologies Working Party

The joint opinion adopted at the March 6 meeting of the working party on 'Social Dialogue and the New Technologies' (see *European Report* No. 1297), which was convened by the European Commission following the November 12, 1985 meeting at the Val Duchesse Chateau in Brussels between representatives of the Union of European Community Industries (UNICE), the European Centre of Public Enterprises (CEEP) and the European Trade Union Confederation (ETUC), has now been made available in English. The full text of the opinion is reproduced below:

A) Training and Motivation

The participants in this group issued the following joint opinion concerning the part of their work related to training and motivation:

1. They took the view that the process of introducing new technologies would be economically more viable and socially more acceptable if accompanied, amongst other things, by effective training and greater motivation for both workers and managerial staff, factors which, in their view, constitute a genuine investment.
   To this end, every member of the staff of the firm, at all levels of responsibility, should be encouraged to make the necessary efforts at adaptation and training, also through personal commitment.

2. They also stressed that vocational training – comprising basic training, in-service training and retraining – should be able to satisfy the demands of workers, firms, the economy in general and of the internal market in particular. From this point of view and in the spirit of this opinion, the work carried out by the Commission and by CEDEFOP on the development of training systems and their comparability needs the active support of both sides of industry and of the Governments. A system for the mutual recognition of qualifications should be rapidly introduced at European level.

3. They point out that responsibility for basic training, whether provided by the education systems or the basic training systems, lies with the public authorities.[1] However, in order to ensure greater consistency between training and the requirements of the economy

and of firms and workers, the authorities should consult and involve the social partners more than they do at present.

4. With a view to the adaptation of the training systems, they consider that the social partners must actively contribute towards the transition of young people from school to working life, more particularly by developing the Community programme of pilot projects. In this context, they stress the need to reorganise the education systems so as to make them more efficient – from basic training to training in advanced skills – and promote greater versatility and the acquisition of basic skills required for the transition of young people to adult working life. Priority should be attached to the development of a continuous process of guidance and counselling as well as to the training of trainers and to the methods of training needed in order to meet these requirements.

5. They also consider that in-service training should enable employees to adapt swiftly and continuously to structural changes in the firm, and that the costs of such training should be borne primarily by the firm itself. Information and consultation of the workforce or, depending on national practice, of its representatives, on training programmes carried out by the undertaking, would help to increase employees' motivation by also improving their understanding of the changes facing the firm.

6. They stress that retraining measures must enable employees to find work or another job – as set out in paragraph 2 above – either in the same firm or elsewhere. It will, in principle, be the firm within which the worker continues to be employed with different skills which will have to bear the cost of these measures. However, at the same time, they emphasised that the economic and social value of a retraining policy implies that public vocational training bodies should play a part so as to ensure a proper distribution of the costs, and a better utilization of resources. By contrast, the burden of retraining workers who no longer continue to be employed by the original firm will have to be borne by the public authorities or the firm which recruits them.

7. They also took the view that in-service training and retraining would be more effective if backed up by a policy designed to improve the forecasting of trends as regards skills and employment, particularly at regional and local level, so as to promote convergence between the respective aims of training and employment.

8. As regards the implementation of a vocational training policy for small and medium-sized enterprises, a more detailed study should be made of the ways and means by which the specific characteristics of these undertakings should be accommodated.

9. Special attention should be devoted to unskilled first job seekers, particularly as concerns people under 25 years of age and women.

(1) Unless provided by the firms themselves.

B) Information and Consultation

Acknowledging the need to master and manage the changes resulting from the process of industrial transformation now in progress, so as to make them effective and socially acceptable, the members of the working party issued the following joint opinion on that part of their work which relates to information and consultation in connection with the introduction of new technologies in firms.

1. To clarify what follows, 'Information and Consultation' must be understood as applying to workers and/or their representatives, in accordance with the laws, collective agreements and practices in force in the countries of the Community.

2. The participants recognized the need to make use of the economic and social potential offered by technological innovation in order to enhance the competitiveness of European firms and strengthen economic growth, thus creating one of the necessary conditions for better employment and, taking particular account of progress in the field of ergonomics, for improved working conditions.

3. The participants stress the need to motivate the staff at all levels of responsibility in firms and to develop their aptitude to change, amongst other ways by means of good information and consultation practices.
   They consider that such motivation will be all the higher if all the staff are in a position to understand the economic and social need for structural and technological change and the potential which such change offers to firms and to the workforce.

4. The participants note that, in most countries of the Community and also in many industrial sectors, there exist various forms of infor-

mation and consultation procedures and negotiating practices. Whilst accepting the diversity of the existing procedures, they consider that best use should be made of the existing procedures.

5. Both sides take the view that, when technological changes which imply major consequences for the workforce are introduced in the firm, workers and/or their representatives should be informed and consulted in accordance with the laws, agreements and practices in force in the Community countries. This information and consultation must be timely.

   In this context:

   - Information means the action of providing the workers and/or their representatives, at the level concerned, with relevant details of such changes, so as to enlighten them as to the firm's choices and the implications for the workforce;

   - consultation of the workers and/or their representatives, at the level concerned, means the action of gathering opinions and possible suggestions concerning the implications of such changes for the firm's workforce, more particularly as regards the effects on their employment and their working conditions.

6. Both sides consider that information and consultation may, in certain circumstances, require an obligation to observe secrecy or confidentiality in order to prevent any damage to the firm.
   The conditions relating to such confidentiality and the power to withold the secret or confidential information, as also the need to provide timely information concerning major changes in the terms of employment and working conditions of the staff concerned fall within the scope of the laws, agreements and practices in force in the countries of the Community.

7. Both sides state that information and consultation must facilitate and should not impede the introduction of new technology, the final decisions being exclusively the responsibility of the employer or of the decision-making bodies of the firm. It is understood that this prerogative does not exclude the possibility of negotiation where the parties take a decision to that effect.

8. In order to improve understanding of the new technologies, promote the acquisition of new skills and enhance adaptability, both sides express the wish that appropriate training for both employers

and workers be developed.
In this connection, both sides express the wish that the Commission develop ways and means of contributing to this process.

9. Despite their differences as to the appropriateness of resorting to Community legal instruments, both sides recognize that it is worthwhile encouraging the development of information and consultation practices in matters relating to the introduction of new technologies in the countries of the Community.

10. Furthermore, both sides note that, on the basis of a variety of practices, adaptability and flexibility are developing throughout the Community. To this end, the two sides confirm their readiness to continue the social dialogue on the implications of the introduction of the new technologies.

The Macro-economic Working Party on the Cooperative Growth Strategy for More Employment

An in-depth exchange of views on the economic situation and employment in the Community was held at the meetings of the Macroeconomics Working Group (set up after the meeting between UNICE, CEEP and ETUC with the Commission on 12 November 1985), and the Commission's 1986-7 Annual Economic Report was discussed.

UNICE, CEEP and ETUC confirm their agreement on the basic principles of the Community's cooperative growth strategy for more employment and support the general thrust of the economic policy by the Commission in its 1986-7 Annual Economic Report.

They call on the governments of the Member States to make a greater effort to ensure that the cooperative strategy is effectively implemented and declare their willingness to cooperate.

Full or broad agreement was reached on the following points:

1. In spite of the progress made on the employment front, unemployment is still too high. Unless additional efforts are made, it will not fall sufficiently in the medium term. The aim in implementing the cooperative growth strategy is to bring about a significant and lasting reduction in unemployment over a period of several years. In order to do this, more jobs must be created through increased investment based on improved business profitability and reinforcing the competitiveness of the European economy. Public invest-

ment also has an important role to play in this respect, without jeopardizing the medium-term consolidation of public finance.

2. The creation of durable jobs will be threatened if inflation rate are not kept low. A stable financial environment encourages the propensity to invest. Monetary and budgetary policies should be managed in such a way as to ensure that inflation rates remain low or continue to fall. The social partners also share some responsibility for containing inflation.

3. Real interest rates should fall further, with account being taken of the world economic situation and savings behaviour. The liberalization of capital movements should help direct savings towards productive investment.

4. The internal market must be completed rapidly. This will make it possible to release considerable growth potential which will reinforce the positive effects which the implementation of the cooperative strategy will have on investment and growth. Completion of the internal market should be accompanied by taking account of social policy and by the development of structural policies to strengthen the Community's economic and social cohesion as it is defined in the Single European Act.

5. Research and development must be promoted so that the Community maintains or regains its technological competitiveness, particularly in 'high-tech' sectors. The Community should also encourage the implementation of the major mobilizing programmes which are such as to promote growth and employment.

6. Improving the level of skills in the labour force and vocational retraining are important elements in developing employment and the competitiveness of the European economy. Training costs represent an investment. Employees at every level should be encouraged to take training courses.

7. The freedom of world trade should be maintained and developed within the framework of GATT. The Community has a special responsibility in this respect. Generally, an effort must be made to continue to combat protectionist trends, unfair practices and escalating subsidies, the effect of which is to distort the conditions of competition. In certain cases, temporary bilateral or multilateral agreements could help to overcome specific problems.

8. In the framework of the cooperative strategy, moderate growth of real per capita wage costs below productivity gains should be maintained for some time to come in the countries in which it is already practised, and it should be applied in the other countries. But the other elements of the strategy must be implemented simultaneously. This will make an important contribution to improving business profitability and competitiveness as well as speeding up the implementation of job-creating investment. It is important here to highlight the link that exists between the moderation of wage costs – a factor for increased profitability – and higher employment.

9. Appropriate tax measures, the development of new forms of financing, and easier access to risk capital can also strengthen investment and employment, notably in small and medium-sized firms.

10. Public investment and infrastructure investment have suffered under the process of budgetary consolidation, and there is at present some leeway to be made up here. Stronger expansion of such investment will make an important contribution, on both the supply and the demand sides, to achieving higher and sustained growth. Such investment should be regarded not as a way of compensating for the lack of private investment, but as a complementary investment undertaken in the general interest. Its financing could be achieved in the framework of a healthy budgetary policy through the restructuring of budgets and through the use of budgetary headroom that already exists or will be created by the growth process: furthermore, in a number of major instances, reliance on private financing seems possible and desirable. In this connection, the following distinctions were made:

    (a) public investment or infrastructure investment which is profitable in itself but which, without public initiatives, would not be carried out at the appropriate time because of its scale or because of its long pay-off period (for example, the Channel tunnel and the high-speed train link between Paris, Brussels and Cologne); in the case of this type of investment, private financing can most easily be envisaged;

    (b) public investment or infrastructure investment which is economically profitable in overall terms because it represents a precondition for private investment or for the development of certain countries or regions; in the case of this type of investment, on the basis of rigorous economic calculation, certain forms of cofinancing by the private sector can be examined;

(c) public investment intended to meet justified public or social needs; its profitability must not be seen solely in economic terms: deciding on the priority projects in this area is also a matter of political judgment; cofinancing by the private sector is more difficult to envisage, but not to be ruled out in all cases.

UNICE, CEEP and ETUC are convinced that dialogue is an important element in the effective implementation of the Community's cooperative growth strategy for more employment. They are prepared to continue the dialogue, especially on questions not yet resolved (e.g. reduction in government spending and in taxes and social security contributions, the adaptability of financial, commercial and labour markets, revision of certain regulations, more flexible wage formation, reorganization and duration of working time, etc.).

Brussels, 6 November 1986.

Appendix 8: Social Affairs and Employment

Background Documents

Treaty establishing the European Economic Community, Rome, March 25, 1957. Articles 100, 117-128

Resolution of the Council of January 21, 1974 concerning a Social Action Programme (EC Bulletin S. 2/74).
Commission Communication to the Council on Work-sharing of May 5, 1974.
Caborn Report on Enterprises and Governments in International Economic Activity (EP Doc. 66.923).
Report of the House of Lords Select Committee on the European Communities on the draft directive for informing and consulting the employees of undertakings with complex structures, in particular transnational undertakings. HLSC. HL.250 (1980–81).
Report of the House of Lords Select Committee on the European Communities on the Memorandum on Employee Participation in Asset Formation. HLSC. HL.249 (1980–81).
Council Resolution on the Promotion of Equal Opportunities for Women (03 1982 C22/7).
Report of the House of Lords Select Committee on the European Committee on the draft Directive on voluntary part-time work HLSC. HL216 (1981–82).
Report on the House of Lords Select Committee on the European Communities on the draft Directive on temporary work HLSC. HL65 (1982–83).
Department of Employment and Department of Trade and Industry Consultative Document on Draft European Communities Directive on Procedures for Informing and Consulting Employees and Draft European Communities Fifth Directive on the Harmonisation of Company Law (November 1983).

Commission reports

Report on the Systems creating Incentives towards the Acquisition of Capital Assets by Workers (Asset Formation) (COM.DOC.V./252/1/71).
Report on the Protection of Workers in the event of Individual Dismissals in the Member States of the European Communities. (DOC.V./812/75).
Report on the Stage reached on February 12, 1978 in the Application of Equal Pay (COM(78)711).
Report on the Contract of Employment in the Law of Member States of the European Communities: Denmark, the United Kingdom and Ireland.

(Labour Law Series, No. 11, May 1977.)
Comparative Study of Employees' Inventions Laws in the Member States of the European Communities (Labour Law Series, No. 2, July 1977).
Report on Employee Participation and Company Structure in the European Community (COM(75) 570, November 1975).
Report on Problems and Prospects of Collective Bargaining in the EEC Member States (DOC.V/394/78).
Memorandum on Asset Formation (COM(79) 190).
Report on Discrimination in Occupational Pension Schemes.
Commission Memorandum on the Reduction and Reorganisation of Working Time (COM/82/809, December 1982).
Commission Communication to the Council on Technological Change and Social Change (COM(84) 6).
The New Commission's Priorities in the Field of Social Affairs and Employment (Tuckman Report) (DOC.2-1753/84).

Case Law of the European Court of Justice

Case 80/70, *Defrenne* (retirement pensions).
Case 43/75 *Defrenne* (equal pay).
Case 149/77, *Defrenne* (retirement age).
Case 129/79, *McCarthy's Ltd.* v. *Smith* (equal pay).
Case 96/80, *Jenkins* v. *Kingsgate (Clothing Productions) Ltd* (equal pay).
Case 69/80, *Worringham & Humphreys* v. *Lloyds Bank Ltd* (equal pay).
Case 12/81, *Garland* v. *British Rail Engineering Ltd* (equal special benefits).
Case 19/81, *Burton* v. *British Railways Board* (equal treatment relating to voluntary redundancy).
Case 248/83, *Commission* v. *Federal Republic of Germany* (equal treatment for men and women).
Case 151/84 *Roberts* v. *Tate & Lyle Industries Ltd* (equal treatment of men and women in redundancy).
Case 152/84 *Marshall* v. *Southampton and South West Hampshire Area Health Authority (Teaching)* (unequal treatment concerning retirement age).
Case 262/84 *Beets-Proper* v. *van Lanschot* Bankiers NV (equal treatment in conditions covering dismissal).
Case 150/85 *Jacqueline Drake* v. *Chief Adjudication Officer* (equal treatment in matters of social security).
Case 237/85 *Gisela Rummier* v. *Dato-Druck GmbH* (equal pay-classification systems).

	Opinion of Economic and Social Committee	Opinion of European Parliament	Approval by Council of Ministers	Comments
DIRECTIVES AND RECOMMENDATIONS				
Directive 75/117 on the application of the principle of equal pay for men and women contained in Article 119 of the EEC Treaty Issued 19.11.73 OJ 1973 C114/46	28.3.74 OJ 1974 C88/6	25.4.74 OJ 1974 C55/45	10.2.75 OJ 1975 L45/19	The directive provides for equal pay – for the same work or for work to which equal value is attributed. Discrimination on grounds of sex is prohibited and job classification schemes must be based on the same criteria for both men and women. **UK implementation:** The directive has been implemented by the Equal Pay Act 1970, the Sex Discrimination Act 1975 and the Trade Union and Labour Relations Act 1974. The EEC Commission instituted infringement proceedings against the UK (among other Member States) on the grounds that it had failed to implement the directive properly. The European Court of Justice ruled that the Equal Pay Act is inconsistent with this directive (Case 61/81 Commission v. UK). The UK Government, therefore, amended the Act in 1983. It is now possible to claim equal pay for work of equal value where no job evaluation scheme exists, or where such a scheme discriminates by sex. However, it remains to be seen whether the changes are sufficient to bring the UK fully into line with Europe.
Directive 75/129 on Mass Dismissals Issued 1973	27.6.73 OJ 1973 C100/12	16.3.73 OJ 1973 C19/10	17.2.75 OJ 1975 L48/29	The object of the directive is to compel companies to notify the competent public authorities when large scale redundancies are considered, to give the authorities the right to intervene and to enable employees or their representatives to make representations in advance. The Commission services are currently drawing up a report on the state of implementation of the directive. **UK implementation:** The directive was implemented by Part IV of the Employment Protection Act 1975.

Council Recommendation 75/457 addressed to the Member States regarding the application of the 40 hour week and 4 weeks' annual paid holiday ——— Issued 27.11.73 OJ 1974 C8/27	30.5.74 OJ 1974 C109/50	25.4.74 OJ 1974 C55/49	22.7.75 OJ 1975 L199/32	This urges Member States to adopt a 40 hour week and a minimum of 4 calendar weeks' annual paid holiday. The deadline was December 31, 1978. **UK implementation:** Recommendations have no binding force (Article 189 of the EEC Treaty) but they do have strong persuasive authority. This recommendation was supported by the CBI and the TUC. (See page 341 for subsequent development.)
Directive 76/207 on equality of treatment of men and women as regards access to employment, vocational training, promotion and conditions ——— Issued 12.2.75 OJ 1975 C124/2	25.9.75 OJ 1975 C286/8	29.4.75 OJ 1975 C111/14	9.2.76 OJ 1976 L39/40	This complements the equal pay directive 75/117 by prohibiting all discrimination on grounds of sex in the conditions for access to all jobs and all types of vocational training. The directive does not prejudice the operation of pregnancy and maternity provisions. **UK implementation:** The directive has been implemented by the Sex Discrimination Act 1975 which makes it unlawful for an employer to discriminate on grounds of sex or against married persons in recruitment, opportunities for promotion, benefits arising from employment, or dismissal. The EEC Commission instituted infringement proceedings against the UK (among other Member States) on the grounds that the UK legislation does not comply with the directive in respect of small businesses, private households and the self-employed. In November 1983 the European Court ruled against the UK. The Government therefore introduced amendments in the Sex Discrimination Bill, published in February 1986. These are to be further amended as a result of the Marshall judgement (see page 333). It is also proposed to amend the Employment Protection (Consolidation) Act 1978. The Code of Practice put into effect by the Equal Opportunities Commission in April 1985 is not legally binding.

	Opinion of Economic and Social Committee	Opinion of European Parliament	Approval by Council of Ministers	Comments
Directive 77/187 on the safeguarding of employees' rights in the event of transfers of undertakings, businesses or parts of businesses Issued 21.6.74 OJ 1974 C104/1 Amended draft 25.7.75 COM(75) 429	24.4.75 OJ 1975 C255/25	8.4.75 OJ 1975 C95/17	14.2.77 OJ 1977 L61/26	The 'Acquired Rights' directive provides that employee rights will be preserved when a business or part of a business established in the EEC is transferred to, or merged with, another business. These rights will be protected in 3 ways: a) the new employer will assume the rights and obligations of the former employer; b) there will be a ban on dismissals in connection with a transfer, although dismissals will be allowed for economic, technical or organisational reasons; c) employee representatives must be informed and consulted about the transfer. The directive does not apply to mergers affected by the sale of shares but only to those mergers covered by Directive 78/855. Two years were allowed for implementation. **UK implementation:** The directive has been implemented by regulations under the European Communities Act – the Transfer of Undertakings (Protection of Employment) Regulations 1981. The main changes provide for rights of consultation for recognised trade unions (which came into operation on February 1, 1982) and the continuation of the contract of employment (which came into operation on May 1, 1982).
Directive 79/7 on the progressive implementation of equal treatment of men and women in matters of social security Issued 31.12.76 OJ 1977 C34/3	23.6.77 OJ 1977 C180/36	15.11.77 OJ 1977 C299/13	19.12.78 OJ 1979 L6/24	The directive seeks to abolish all sex discrimination in the conditions of entitlement for and the duration and amounts of benefits received in respect of social security benefits – unemployment, sickness, disablement and old age pensions. It excludes widows' pensions, family allowances and occupational schemes from its scope but states that the principle of equal treatment should be extended to occupational schemes as soon as possible. Implementation was required by December 1984. An interim report published by the Commission in January 1984 summarised the progress made by Member States and discussed problems of interpretation. This report suggested that the U.K.'s invalidity care allowance should come within the scope of the directive. **UK implementation:** The Social Security Act and the Social Security (No. 2) Act 1980 have implemented the directive.

the protection of employees in the event of the insolvency of their employer ——— Issued 13.4.78 OJ 1978 C135/2 ——— Amended draft 23.3.79 OJ 1979 C125/7	30.11.78 OJ 1979 C105/14	17.1.79 OJ 1979 C39/26	20.10.80 OJ 1980 L283/23	unsatisfied claims of employees in respect of wages, sickness, holiday or retirement benefits or any gratuities, bonuses or indemnities, provided that the claims are made before the insolvency. The guarantee institutions must be financed by the employers, but public authorities and employees may also contribute. Full implementation of the directive was required by October, 1983. **UK implementation:** No significant changes in the insolvency provisions of the Employment Protection (Consolidation) Act 1978 will be required, but the scope of the Act will have to be widened to include employees of UK subsidiaries in the EEC.
Directive 86/378 on equal treatment in occupational social security schemes ——— Issued 5.5.83 OJ 1983 C134/7	15.12.83 OJ 1984 C35/7	30.3.84 OJ 1984 C117/169	24.7.86 OJ 1986 L225/40	This directive aims to eliminate discrimination on the basis of sex or marital status in occupational social security schemes which provide protection against sickness, invalidity, old age, early retirement, accidents at work and occupational diseases as well as unemployment. In addition it requires equality of treatment in the case of benefits due to survivors. The principle of equal treatment is to be applied to the scope of the schemes, to the conditions for eligibility, to the obligations to contribute and the calculation of contributions, allowances and to the conditions governing the duration and rights to allowances. However, the mandatory use of unisex actuarial tables in the calculation of benefits has been dropped from the final text. The necessary laws and regulations are required to be introduced by July 30, 1989, although full implementation can be delayed until January 1st 1993. **UK implications:** Adoption of the directive will require changes to social security and pension schemes, although there will not be an immediate requirement to abolish differences in retirement ages for men and women until the state scheme introduces such equality. Nor, because of provisions for exceptions, will there be a requirement to provide the same benefit with respect to AVCs, communication or money purchase.

	Opinion of Economic and Social Committee	Opinion of European Parliament	Approval by Council of Ministers	Comments
Recommendation 82/857 on flexible retirement Issued 10.12.81	28.4.82 OJ 1982 C178/30	16.9.82 OJ 1982 C267/71	10.12.82 OJ 1982 L357/27	This recommendation seeks a commitment from Member States to the gradual implementation of a flexible retirement age. The recommendation also urges Member States to review their existing retirement pension schemes in the light of the overall objective and to examine the feasibility of introducing phased retirement to ease the passage from full time employment to retirement. In 1986 a report on the progress made in implementing the recommendations. **UK implications:** Recommendations have no binding force.
Recommendation on the promotion of positive action for women Issued 26.4.84 OJ 1984 C143/3	21.11.84 OJ 1985 C25/28	25.10.84 OJ 1984 C315/81	13.12.84 OJ 1984 C331/34	This recommendation is designed to eliminate inequalities affecting women in working life and encourages Member States to adopt a strategy on positive action. It aims to encourage the participation of women in all occupations where they are at present under represented and at all levels of responsibility. **UK implications:** Recommendations have no binding force.
Draft directive on procedures for informing and consulting the employees of undertakings with a complex structure Issued 2.10.80 OJ 1980 C297/3	27.1.82 OJ 1982 C77/10	Text: 12.10.82 OJ 1982 C202/33 Resolution: 14.12.82 OJ 1983 C13/25		This draft directive, known as the Vredeling proposal, has been amended by the Commission. In its revised form it gives the representatives of workers, employed by companies with 1,000 or more workers, the right to receive regular information and to be consulted about aspects of company policy. Information on such matters as company structure, its economic and financial situation and foreseeable trends in production, sales, employment and investment is to be provided annually. Such information would be amended when up-dated information was provided to shareholders or creditors. Employee representatives are to be consulted 'with a view to attempting to reach agreement' before a decision is taken on matters likely to have serious repercussions for the interests of workers. Secret information may be withheld by management but an appeal procedure is to be set up to settle disputes concerning secrecy.

OJ 1983 C217/3				the Department of Employment issued a consultative document, in which the U.K. preference for a voluntary approach was stated. A special working group was set up to examine the proposal at the initiative of the Irish Presidency at the end of 1984 and has suggested a new text which lays the emphasis on social policy rather than company legislation. However the Labour and Social Affairs Council concluded in June 1985 that certain fundamental problems had to be resolved before further progress could be made. In July 1986 that Council adopted a conclusion (OJ 1986 C203/1) which will result in the proposal not being considered again until the beginning of 1989. However, it leaves the door open for the Commission to take further initiatives in this area in the meantime. This it has already attempted to do with respect to the introduction of new technology. **UK implications:** If adopted this directive would involve substantial changes in legislation.
Draft directive on part-time work ——— Issued 4.1.82 OJ 1982 C62/7 ——— Amended draft 5.1.83 OJ 1983 C18/5	28.4.82 OJ 1982 C178/18	16.9.82 OJ 1982 C267/74		The draft provides for part-time workers to have proportional rights in respect of remuneration, holiday payments, redundancy and retirement payments, to be supplied with written contracts of employment, to have priority when wishing to transfer to full-time work in the same establishment, and to be counted as part of the workforce. The proposal appears to have drawn a wide divergence of views between Member States. **UK implications:** Part-time workers already enjoy many of the rights which the draft seeks to provide.
Draft directive on temporary work ——— Issued 7.5.82 OJ 1982 C128/2 ——— Amended draft 6.4.84 OJ 1984 C133/1	27.4.83 OJ 1983 C176/8	7.7.83 OJ 1983 C242/47		The draft seeks to regulate temporary work and ensure effective supervision, particularly in the case of the cross-frontier supply of temporary workers. It aims to protect temporary workers by ensuring that, in general, they enjoy the same rights as permanent employees. At the same time, it seeks to protect permanent employees by reducing the 'misuse' of temporary labour. The Commission has published an amended proposal which takes into account the opinions of the Economic and Social Committee and the European Parliament. This is now under consideration by the Council of Ministers. The UK opposes the proposal.

	Opinion of Economic and Social Committee	Opinion of European Parliament	Approval by Council of Ministers	Comments
				UK implications: While the control of temporary employment agencies is already established in the UK, these would have to be amended. If the restrictions proposed on the opportunities to use temporary labour were introduced, they would require further substantial changes in UK law. The most significant changes would be in the field of fixed term contracts, as the proposal also seeks to protect workers recruited on this basis.
Draft directive on parental leave Issued 19.10.83 OJ 1983 C333/6 Amended draft 15.11.84 OJ 1984 C316/7	24.5.84 OJ 1984 C206/47	30.3.84 OJ 1984 C117/176		This draft Directive formed part of the 1982–5 Community Action programme to promote equal opportunities for men and women. The proposal is designed to ensure equality between the sexes when family leave is granted to look after young children. Parents of either sex who are in full-time or part-time employment and have children under two years of age would be eligible for parental leave after the termination of the mother's maternity leave. Similar provisions would apply to adoptive parents. Leave would be available on request, provided the employer is given adequate notice. No upper time limit is specified in the proposal, although there would be a minimum guaranteed period of three months. The proposal provides for Member States to introduce parental leave allowances, payable from public funds. The proposal also makes allowance for limited periods of leave for pressing and important family reasons. Member States would specify the minimum entitlement. Both the European Parliament and the Economic and Social Committee have supported the proposal. A House of Lords Select Committee supported parental leave but not leave for family reasons. **UK implications:** If adopted, this Directive would involve substantial changes in UK legislation and have considerable cost implications.

Draft recommendation on the reduction and reorganisation of working time — Issued 23.9.83 OJ 1983 C290/4	24.11.83 OJ 1984 C23/54	19.12.83 OJ 1983 C342/147		The Commission's draft recommendation follows lengthy discussions with employers' and employees' representatives in the Community. The draft calls for a common approach towards the reduction and reorganisation of working time. This would consist of reductions in individual working time so as to allow positive employment development. It also calls for a stricter limitation of paid overtime hours. When discussed by the Council of Ministers in June 1984, the U.K. was alone in opposing the proposals. **UK implications:** The U.K. Government is opposed to this measure. Recommendations have no binding force.
Resolution on a second programme of action on safety and health at work — Issued 4.11.82 OJ 1982 C308/11	28.4.83 OJ 1983 C176/16	20.1.84 OJ 1984 C46/126	27.2.84 OJ 1984 C67/2	This resolution extends to the end of 1988 the provisions of the first action programme which expired in 1982. The main objective of the action programme is to increase the level of protection against occupational risks by increasing the efficiency of measures for preventing, monitoring and controlling these risks. The programme encourages the provision of suitable training information and relevant statistics.

Appendix 9: OECD Guidelines

The guidelines cover seven areas: general policies, disclosure of information, competition, financing, taxation, science and technology, employment and industrial relations. The latter section reads as follows:

Enterprises should, within the framework of the law, regulations and prevailing labour relations and employment practices, in each of the countries in which they operate:

i respect the right of their employees to be represented by trade unions and other *bona fide* organisations of employees, and engage in constructive negotiations, either individually or through employers' associations, with such employee organisations with a view to reaching agreements on employment conditions, which should include provisions for dealing with disputes arising over the interpretation of such agreements, and for ensuring mutually respected rights and responsibilities;

ii a) provide such facilities to representatives of the employees as may be necessary to assist in the development of effective collective agreements,

ii b) provide to representatives of employees information which is needed for meaningful negotiations on conditions of employment;

iii provide to representatives of employees where this accords with local law and practice, information which enables them to obtain a true and fair view of the performance of the entity or, where appropriate, the enterprise as a whole;

iv observe standards of employment and industrial relations not less favourable than those observed by comparable employers in the host country;

v in their operations, to the greatest extent practicable, utilise, train and prepare for upgrading members of the local labour force in co-operation with representatives of their employees and, where appropriate, the relevant governmental authorities;

vi in considering changes in their operations which would have major effects upon the livelihood of their employees, in particular in the case of the closure of an entity involving collective lay-offs or dismissals, provide reasonable notice of such changes to representatives of their employees, and where appropriate to the relevant governmental authorities, and co-operate with the employee representatives and appropriate governmental authorities so as to mitigate to the maximum extent practicable adverse effects;

vii implement their employment policies including hiring, discharge, pay, promotion and training without discrimination unless selectivity in respect of employee characteristics is in furtherance of established governmental policies which specifically promote greater equality of employment opportunity;

viii in the context of *bona fide* negotiations with representatives of employees on conditions of employment, or while employees are exercising a right to organise, not threaten to utilise a capacity to transfer the whole or part of an operating unit from the country concerned nor transfer employees from the enterprises' component entities in other countries in order to influence unfairly those negotiations or to hinder the exercise of a right to organise;

ix enable authorised representatives of their employees to conduct negotiations on collective bargaining or labour management relations issues with representatives of management who are authorised to take decisions on the matters under negotiation.

Bibliography

ABENDROTH, W, 'Histoire du Movement Ouvrier en Europe.' *Petite Collection*, Maspero, Paris 1967

ALLOT, P, 'Britain and Europe: A Political Analysis.' *Journal of Common Market Studies*, Vol XIII, No 3, March 1976 pp 203–23

ALTING VON GENSAU, F A M, 'European Political Integration'. *European Year Book* XI. 1963

ARBUTHNOT, H and EDWARDS, G, *A Common Man's Guide to the Common Market*. Macmillan, London 1979

AREN, R, 'The Crises of the European Idea'. *Government and Opposition*, Vol XI 1976, No 1, Winter 1976, pp 5-19

ARON, B and WEDDERBURN, K (eds), *Industrial Conflict; A Comparative Legal Survey*, Longmans, London 1972

Association of District Councils, *EEC Policies: Views on issues of concern to District Councils*, 1985

AUGER, J, *Syndicialisme des autres syndicats d'Europe les internationales syndicates* (Collection: Comprendre pour agir) Les éditions ouvriéres, 1980

BALASSA, B (ed), *European Economic Integration*. North Holland. New York and Amsterdam, 1975

BALDRY, C, *et al*, 'Multinational closure, and the case of Massey Ferguson Kilmarnock', *Industrial Relations Journal* Vol 15 No 4, 1984 pp 17–31

BALFOUR, C, *Industrial Relations in the Common Market*, Routledge and Kegan Paul, London 1972

BALL, G, 'The Promise of the MNC', *Fortune* 74, No 6 June 1967

BAMBER, G and LANSBURY, R, *International and Comparative Industrial Relations*, Allen and Unwin, London 1986

BARANOUIN, B, *The European Labour Movement and European Integration*, Frances Pinter, London 1986

BARBER, J and REED, B (eds), *European Community: Vision and Reality*. Croom Helm for the Open University, London 1973

BARJONET, A, 'Le Marché Commun, c'est l'Europe allemande', *Le Peuple* No 528, 1957

BARKER, E, *Britain in a Divided Europe 1940-70*. Weidenfeld, London 1971

BARRY-BRAUNTHAL, T, 'Will European Unions become inward-looking?' *European Community*, September 1972

BEBR, G, *Judicial Control of the European Communities*, Stevens, London 1962

BEEVER, C R, *European Unity and the Trade Union Movement* (European Aspects Series D: Social Science No 2) A W Sythoff, Leyden 1960

BEEVER, C R, 'Trade Unions and the Common Market', *Planning* 1, PEP, London May 1962

BEEVER, C R, *Trade Unions and Free Labour Movement in the EEC*, Chatham House/PEP, London 1969

BEHRMAN, J N, 'Industrial Integration and Multinational Enterprises', *The Annals of the American Academy of Political and Social Science*, September 1982

BEHRMAN, J N, *National Interests and the Multinational Enterprise: Tension among the North Atlantic Countries* Prentice Hall Inc, Englewood Ciffs, New Jersey 1970

BELOFF, M, *The United States and the Unity of Europe*. Faber, London, 1963

BERGMAN, L, *Multinational Corporations and Labour in the EEC: A Survey of Research and Developments*. Presented at the Meeting on Multinational Corporations and Labour, The International Institute for Labour Studies, Geneva, 5-7 December 1973

BERNSTEIN, M, 'Labour and the European Communities', *Law and Contemporary Problems* 26 No 3 Summer 1961 pp 572–88

BIEBER, R and PALMER, M, 'Power at the Top – EC Council in Theory and practice,' *The World Today*, Vol XXXI, No 8, 1975 pp 310–17

BJØL, E, *La France devant l'Europe*, Munkogaard, Copenhagen 1966

BLANPAIN, R, ETTY, T, GLADSTONE, A, GÜNTER, H, *Relations between management of transnational enterprises and employee representatives in certain countries of the European Communities* (a pilot study) Research Series No 51, International Institute for Labour Studies, 1980

BLANPAIN, R, *et al*, *Workers Participation in the European Community: The Fifth Directive*, Deventer, Netherlands 1984

BLANPAIN, R (ed), *Comparative Labour Law and Industrial Relations* Deventer, Netherlands 1985

BLANPAIN, R, 'The Impact of Recent Developments in the EEC on National Labour Law Systems', *Relations Industrielles* 31, No 4 1976 pp 509–21

BLANPAIN, R, *The Vredeling Proposal: information and consultation of employers in multinational enterprises*, Deventer, Netherlands 1983

BLANPAIN, R, *The OECD Guidelines*, Kluwer Deventer, Netherlands 1982

BOHNING, W R, *The Migration of Workers in the UK and the European Community* Oxford University Press, London 1972

BOURGUIGNON, R *et al*, 'Five years of the directly elected European Parliament', *Journal of Common Market Studies*, Vol. XXIV no. 1 September 1985 pp 39–60

BOUVARD, M, *Labour Movements in the Common Market Countries: The Growth of a European Pressure Group*, Praeger Special Studies in International Economics and Development, New York, Washington, London 1972

BOUVARD, M, *Labour Movements in Common Market Countries*, Praeger, London 1972

BROWN, W (ed), *Changing Contours of British Industrial Relations*, Basil Blackwell, Oxford 1981

BRUSCO, S, 'The Emilian Model: Productive Decentralisation and Social Integration', *Cambridge Journal of Economics* Vol. 6 no. 2 1982 pp 167–85

BULMER, S and WESSELS, W, *The European Council Decision Making in European Politics*, Macmillan, London 1987

BUSSEY, E M, 'Organised Labour and the EEC', *Industrial Relations* 7 No 2 February 1968 pp 160–70

BUTT PHILIPS, A, *Pressure Groups in the European Community*, University Association for Contemporary European Studies, London 1985

CAIRNCROSS, A, *et al, Economic Policy for the European Community: The Way Forward*, Macmillan, London 1974

CAMPS, M, *Britain and the European Economic Community*, Oxford University Press, London 1964

CAMPS, M, *European Unification in the Sixties: From the Veto to the Crisis*, Oxford University Press, London 1967

CAMPS, P, 'European Unification in the 1970s', *International Affairs*, Vol XLVII, No 4, October 1971 pp 671–8

CAPORASO, J A, *The Structure and Function of European Integration*, Goodyear, California 1974

CASTLES, S and KOSACK, G, *Immigrant Workers and Class Structure in Western Europe*, Oxford University Press, London 1973

CBI, *EC Employment Policy* Internal Paper, London 1987

CBI, *A Europe for Business*, London 1985

CBI, *The European Community and Social Engineering*, London 1986

CHAPMAN, D, *The Road to European Union*, Sussex European Papers, Brighton 1975

COATES, K, *Joint Action for Jobs*, Spokesman Books, Nottingham 1986

COLLINS, D, *The European Communities, The Social Policy of the First Phase*, Martin Robertson, London 1975

COLLINS, D, *The Operation of the European Social Fund*, Croom Helm, London 1983

COLLINS, D, The Impact of Social Policy in the United Kingdom, in EL-AGRAA (ed) *Britain within the European Community: The Way Forward*, Macmillan, London 1983

COLLINS, D, 'Towards a European Social Policy'. *Journal of Common Market Studies* Vol V No 1 September 1966 pp 26–48

COLLINS, D, *'Social Policy' in LODGE Institutions and Policies of the European Community*, Frances Pinter, London 1983

COLLINS, D, *The European Communities: The Social Policy of the First Phase*, Vol I: *The European Coal and Steel Community, 1951–70*, Vol II: *The*

European Economic Community, 1958–72. Martin Robertson, London 1975

Commission of the European Community, 'Single European Act', *European Community Bulletin*, Supplement 2/1986

Commission of the European Community, 'Report on the Development of the Social Situation in the Community in 1972', Brussels 1973

Commission of the European Community, 'Employment Problems: View of business men and the workforce', *European Economy*, No 27, March 1986

Commission of the European Community, 'The Draft Fifth Directive on the Structure of Public Limited Companies', *Bulletin of the European Community* Supplement 8/75 Brussels 1975

Commission of the European Community: 'Youth Training in the European Community', *Social Europe* Supplement No 3, 1987

Commission of the European Community; 'The Structure of Public Companies: Amended Proposal for a Fifth Directive', *Bulletin of the European Community* Supplement 6/83, 1983

Commission of the European Community, 'Employee Participation and Structure in the European Community', Com (75) 570 Final Brussels 1975

Commission of the European Community, 'Comparative Survey on the protection of employees in the event of the insolvency of their employer in the Member States of the European Community', Com (76) 305 Final Brussels 1976

Commission of the European Community, 'Proposal for a Council Directive on the Protection of Employees in the Event of Insolvency', Com (78) 141 Brussels 1978

Commission of the European Community, 'Draft Proposal for a Council Recommendation on Flexible Retirement', Com 81 Final Brussels 1981

Commission of the European Community, 'Part Time Working', 24th February 1982

Commission of the European Community, 'Employee Information and Consultation Procedures – Amended Proposal', *Bulletin of the European Community* Supplement 2/83 Brussels 1983

Commission of the European Community, 'Report from the Commission to the Council on the Application of the Council Recommendation of 20th December 1982 on the Principles of a Community Policy With Regard to Retirement Age', Com (82) 857 Final Brussels 1982

Commission of the European Community, 'Draft Council Recommendations on the Reduction and Reorganisation of Working time', Com (83) 543 Final Brussels 1983

Commission of the European Community, 'Amended Proposal for a Council Directive concerning the Supply of Workers by Temporary Employment Businesses and Fixed Duration Contracts', Com 84 (159) Final Brussels, 1984

Commission of the European Community, 'Proposal for a Council Decision adopting an action programme for the training and preparation of young people for adult and working life', Com (87) 40 Final Brussels 1987
Commission of the European Community, 'Problems of Social Security – Areas of Common Interest', Com (86) 410 Final Brussels, 1986
Commission of the European Community, 'Report of Social Developments 1986', Document Brussels, 1987
Commission of the European Community, 'The Implementation of the New Community Action Programme on the Promotion of Equal Opportunities for Women' Com (85) 64 Final Brussels, 1985
Commission of the European Community, 'Employment of Disabled People', Com (86) No 9 Final Brussels, 1986
Commission of the European Community, 'Third General Report 1969', Brussels 1970
Commission of the European Community, 'Community Policy on Migration', Com (85) 148 Final Brussels, 1985
Community Markets, 'US Firms oppose Vredeling', April 1983 Issue No 4, *Financial Times*, London
COOK, C and SKED, A, *Post War Britain – A political history*, Penguin, Harmondsworth 1983
COOMBES, D, *Towards a European Civil Service.* London, Chatham House/PEP London 1968
COOMBES, D, *Politics and Bureaucracy in the European Community.* Allen and Unwin, London 1976
CORBETT, R, 'The 1985 Intergovernmental Conference and the Single European Act', in PRYCE, R (ed) *The Dynamics of European Union*, Croom Helm, London 1987
CORDOZO, R and CORBETT, R, 'The Crocodile Group' in LODGE (ed) *European Union: the European Community in search of a future*, Macmillan, London 1987
COX, R, *Production, Power and World Order: Social Forces in the making of history*, Columbia University Press, New York 1987
CRIPPS, F, 'The British Crisis: Can the left win?' *New Left Review* July/August No 128 1984 pp 17–27
CRIPPS, L, 'The Social Policy of the European Community', *Social Europe*, January No 1 1987 Brussels pp 51–62
CROUCH, C, 'Future Prospects for the Trade Unions in Western Europe', *The Political Quarterly*, Vol 57 No 1 Jan–March 1986 p 5–18
CROUCH, C (ed), *State and Economy in Contemporary Capitalism*, Croom Helm, London 1979
CROUCH, C, *Trade Unions: The Logic of Collective Bargaining*, Fonanta Paperback, London 1983
CROUCH, C, *The Politics of Industrial Relations*, Manchester University Press, Manchester 1979

DAHLBERY, K, 'EEC Commission and the Politics of the Free Movement of Workers', *Journal of Common Market Studies*, Vol VI No 4, 1968, p 310–333

DAGTOGLOU, P D (ed), *Basic Problems of the European Community*, Basil Blackwell, Oxford 1975

DAVIDSON, J, 'Free Movement of Workers', in LODGE, J (ed), *Institutions and Policies of the European Community*, Francis Pinter, London 1983

de CELLO, M, 'European Community Factors of Disintegration: The Pressure of Economic Difficulties' *International Affairs*, Vol 4, No 3, July 1984 pp 67–93

de GRAVE, M, *Dimension européene du syndicalisme ouvrier*, Université Catholique, Louvain 1968

DENIAU, J, *The Common Market*, Barrie and Rockliffe, London 1968.

DENTON, G R (ed), *Economic Integration in Europe*, Weidenfeld and Nicolson, London 1969

DENTON, G R and COOPER, J J N (eds), *The European Economy beyond the Crisis: From Stabilisation to Structural Change*, Wilton House, London 1977

Department of Employment, *Employment: The Challenge to the Nation*, HMSO CM 49474, London 1985

DEUTSCH, K W, *Political Community at the International Level, Problems of Definition and Terms*, Random House, New York 1970

DORFMAN, G, 'From the Inside Looking Out: The Trade Union Congress in the EEC', *Journal of Common Market Studies* Vol XV No 4 June 1977 pp 248–271

DORFMAN, G, *Government versus trade union in British Politics since 1968* Macmillan, London 1979

DUNNING, J H, *Japanese Participation in British Industry*, Croom Helm, London 1987

EDWARDS, C, *The Fragmented World: Competing perspectives on trade, money and crisis*, Methuen, London 1985

EDWARDS, G and WALLACE, H, 'Note of the Month: EEC – the British Presidency in Retrospect', *The World Today*, Vol XXXIII, No 8, August 1977 pp 283–6

EDWARDS, G and WALLACE, H, *A Wider European Community? Issues and Problems of Further Enlargement*, Federal Trust, London 1976

EDWARDS, G and WALLACE, H, *The Council of Ministers of the European Community and its President in Office*, Federal Trust, London 1977

EMERSON, M, 'Regulation and deregulation of the labour market: policy regimes for the recruitment and dismissals of employees in industrial countries', Harvard University Mimeo, June 1986

ENDERWICK, P, *Multinational Business and Labour*, Croom Helm, London 1985

Engineering Employers' Federation, *Priorities for the European Com-*

munity, London 1985

ETUI, *Employment, Investment and the Public Sector*, Brussels 1982

ETUI, *Industrial Policy in Western Europe*, Brussels 1981

ETUI, *Public Investment and Job Creation*, Brussels 1984

ETUI, *The European Economy 1980-5: An Indicative Full Employment Plan*, Brussels 1980

ETUI, *The Reduction of Working Hours in Western Europe, Second Part: Analysis of the Social and Economic Consequences*, Brussels 1980

ETUI, *Trends in Collective Bargaining in Western Europe*, Brussels 1983

Europe Unites. The story of the campaign for European unity, including a full report of the Congress of Europe at the Hague, May 1948. Hollis and Carter, London 1948.

European Parliament (1969), *Resolution on the Position Taken by the European Parliament in Regard to the Fundamental Problems of European Community Policy*, 3rd November 1969

European Parliament (1986), *European Social Area*, Document A-2-137/86

EVANS, O, *Britain and the EEC*, Victor Gollancz, London 1974

FEATHER, V, 'Trade Unionism at the European Level', *Millenium* Vol 111 No 3 Winter 1974-5 pp 201-7

FELD, W, 'National Economic Interest Groups and Policy Formation in the EEC', *Political Science Quarterly*, Vol LXXXI, No 3, September 1966 pp 392–411

FELD, W, 'Political Aspects of Transnational Business Collaboration', *International Organisation*, Vol XXIV, No 2, Spring 1970

FILD, J, *The European Community in World Affairs: Economic Power and Political Influence*, Alfred Publishing Co, Washington 1976

FITZGERALD, MJ, *The Common Market's Labour Programs*, Notre Dame, London 1966

FITZMAURICE, J, *The European Parliament*, Saxon House, Farnborough 1978

FOGARTY, M P, *Work and Industrial Relations in the European Community*, PEP European Series No 24 London 1975

FOGGON, G, 'The Origin and Development of the ILO and International Labour Organisations', in TAYLOR and GROOM (eds) *International Institutions at Work*, Frances Pinter, London 1988

FONTAINE, P, *Le Comité d'action pour les États-Unis d'Europe de Jean Monnet*, Centre de Recherche Européennes, Lausanne 1974

FORSYTH, M, 'The Political Objectives of European Integration', *International Affairs*, Vol XLiii, No 3, July 1967

GALLOWAY, P, 'Multinational Enterprise as Worldwide Interest Groups' *Politics and Society* 2 No 1 1971

GENNARD, J, *The Multinationals: Industrial Relations and Labour: The Trade Union Response*, University of Nottingham, in association with the Institute of Personnel Management, London 1976

GENNARD, J, 'Job Security, Redundancy Arrangements, and Practices in selected OECD Countries', Paper prepared for OECD September 1985
GEORGE, S, *Politics and Policy in the European Communities.* Clarendon, London 1985
GLASSON, J and McGEE, T, *EEC Aid and Local Authorities: Some Research Findings – an Interim Report,* Oxford Polytechnic 1983
GOUREVITCH, P, *et al, Unions and Economic crisis: Britain, West Germany and Sweden,* Allen and Unwin, London 1984
GRAHL, J and TEAGUE, P, 'The British Labour Party and the European Community', *Political Quarterly,* Vol 59 No 1 Jan-March 1988 pp 72–85
GRAHL, J, 'L'evolution de la politique européenne des principales formalities politiques', *Revue Française de Civilisation Britannique,* 1987 pp 121–137
GRANT, W and MARSH, D, *The Confederation of British Industry, Hodder and Stoughton, London 1977*
GRANT, W and SARGANT, J, *Business and Politics,* Macmillan, Basingstoke 1987
GRANT, W, 'British Employers Associations and the Enlarged Community', *Journal of Common Market Studies* Vol XI No 4 1983 pp 226–293
GÜNTER, H, 'Labour and Multinational Corporations in Western Europe: Some Problems and Perspectives' in KUJAWA D (ed), *International Labour and the Multinational Enterprise* Praeger, New York 1975
GUNTER, K, 'Union Responses in Continental Europe', in FLANAGAN and WEBER (ed), *Bargaining without Boundaries,* University of Chicago Press, Chicago 1974
HAAS, E B, 'The Uniting of Europe and the Uniting of Latin America', *Journal of Common Market Studies,* Vol V, No 4, June 1967 pp 315–43
HAAS, E B, *The Uniting of Europe: Political, Social and Economic Forces,* Stanford University Press, Stanford 2nd edition 1968
HALLSTEIN, W, *United Europe,* Oxford University Press, London 1962
HALLSTEIN, W, *Europe in the Making,* Allen and Unwin, London 1973
HANSENNE, M, 'Is the EEC Afraid to Guarantee Fundamental Social Rights as Flexibility Takes Over?', *Social and Labour Bulletin,* International Labour Organisation, Geneva, No 3, 1987 pp 369–73
HARRIS, D, *The European Social Charter,* University Press of Virginia, Charlottesville 1982
HARRISON, R J, *Europe in Question,* Allen and Unwin, London 1974
HAYWARD, J, *Trade Unions and Politics in Western Europe,* Cass, London 1980
HAYWARD, J and WATSON, M (eds), *Planning, Politics and Public Policy: The British, French and Italian Experience,* Cambridge University Press, Cambridge 1975
HEATHCOTE, N, 'The Crisis of European Supranationality'. *Journal of Common Market Studies,* Vol V, No 2, December 1966 pp 140–1

HEILPEKIN, M, 'Freer Trade and Social Welfare: Some marginal comments on the Oslin Report' *International Labour Review* Vol No 3 1957, pp 173–193

HENIG, S, *Power and Delusion in Europe: the political institutions of the European Community*, Europotentials, London 1980

HEPPLE, B, 'The Crisis in European Labour Law', *Industrial Law Journal*, Vol 16 no. 2 1987, pp 77–87

HEPPLE, B, 'Community Measures for the Protection of Workers against Dismissals', *Common Market Law Review* No 14, 1977

HEPPLE, B, 'Harmonisation of Labour Law in the European Community', *Essays for Clive Schmitthoff* pp 14–29, 1982

HEPPLE, B and FREDMAN, S, *Labour Law and Industrial Relations in Great Britain*, Deventer, London 1981

HERMAN, V and LODGE, J, *The European Parliament and the European Community*, Macmillan, London 1978

HEWSTONE, M, 'Tapping the Eurobarometer', *Times Higher Education Supplement* 24th October p 14, 1986

HILL, C J (ed), *National Foreign Policies and European Political Cooperation*. Allen and Unwin, London 1983

HODGES, M (ed), *European Integration*, Penguin Books, London 1972

HODGES, M and WALLACE, W, *Economic Divergence in the European Communities*. Allen and Unwin, London 1981

HOFFMAN, S, 'Obstinate or Obsolete? The Fate of the Nation-State and the Case of Western Europe', *Daedulus*, Vol 95, Nos 3–4, Summer 1966 pp 862–915

HOLLAND, S, *Uncommon Market*, Papermac, London 1980

HOLT, S, *The Common Market: The Conflict of Theory and Practice*, Hamish Hamilton, London 1971

HONTHYS, S, 'Aspects Européens et Internationaux du Syndicalisme', *Chronique de Politique Etrangére* Vol 38 July 1974 pp 621–45

HOSKYNS, C, 'Women, European Law and Transnational Politics', *International Journal of the Sociology of Law*, Vol 14 no. 314 November 1986 pp 299–316

House of Commons Employment Committee, 'The European Community's Employment Initiatives' – Minutes of Evidence, Wednesday 22nd April 1987

House of Lords Sub-Committee on the European Communities, EC Regional Policy 13th Report Vol 2 1979

House of Lords Sub-Committee on the European Community, 37th Report Vol 2, 1980

IDS, *Transfer of Undertakings*, Employment Law Handbook, London 1984

ILO *Social Aspects of European Economic Cooperation*: Report by a Group of Experts, Studies and Reports, New Series No 46 ILO Geneva 1956

IONESCU, G (ed), *The New Politics of European Integration*, Allen and Unwin, London 1973

JACOBS, E, *European Trade Unionism*, Croom Helm, London 1973

JANSEN, M, *History of European Integration 1974-75*, Occasional Papers of the Europa Institut, Amsterdam 1975

JENKINS, P, *Mrs Thatcher's Revolution: the ending of a socialist era*, Cape, London 1987

JUNG, V, KOUBEK, N, PHIEL, E, SCHEIBELANGE, I, *Aspects of union policy in Western Europe: Economic concentration and political integration as a challenge for the trade unions* Translated from WWI-Mitteilunger, 10/1971

KAMIN, A, *West European Labour and the American Corporation*, Bureau of National Affairs, Washington 1970

KASSALOW, A, *In European Unionism: with some implications for American Unions* (The Frank McCallister Memorial Lecture) Roosevelt University, Chicago December 1971

KAHN-FREUND, O, 'Social Policy and the Common Market', *Political Quarterly* Vol 32 No 4 1961 pp 341–52

KATZ, H and SABLE, C, 'Industrial Relations and Industrial Adjustment in the Car Industry', *Industrial Relations Journal* Vol 24 Fall 1985, pp 295–315

KENDALL, W, *The Labour Movement in Europe*, Allen Lane, London 1975

KERR, J C, *The Common Market and How it Works*, Pergamon Press, London 1977

KINDELBERGER, C P, *Europe's Postwar Growth: The Role of Labour Supply*, Harvard University Press, Cambridge Mass 1967

KINDELBERGER, C P, *American Business Abroad*, Yale University Press, New Haven and London 1969

KINDELBERGER, C P (ed), 'European Integration and the International Corporation', in BROWN, C (ed), *World Business, Promise and Problems*, New York 1970

KINDELBERGER, C P, *Marshall Plan Days*, Allen and Unwin, London 1987

KIRCHNER, E J, *The Role of Interest Groups in the European Community* Saxon House, Farnborough 1983

KIRCHNER, E J, 'Interest Group Behaviour at the Community Level' in HURWITZ, L, *Contemporary Perspectives on European Integration*, Macmillan, London 1980

KIRCHNER, E J, 'International Trade Union Collaboration and the Prospects for European Industrial Relations', *West European Politics* Vol 3 No 1 January 1980 pp 129–138

KIRCHNER, E J, *Trade Unions as a Pressure Group in the European Communities*, Saxon House Press, Farnborough 1977

KIRCHNER, E J, *An Empirical Examination of the Functionalist Concept of*

Spillover, Case Western Reserve University, Cleveland 1976
KITZINGER, U, *The Challenge of the Common Market*, Basil Blackwell, Oxford 1961
KITZINGER, U, *The European Common Market and Community*, Routledge & Kegan Paul, London 1967
KITZINGER, V, *Diplomacy and Persuasion*, Thames and Hudson, London 1973
KLASSEN, L H and DREW, P, *Migration Policy in Europe*, Saxon House, Farnborough, Hants 1973
KOEPKE, G, 'Union Responses in Continental Europe' in FLANAGAN and WEBER (eds), *Bargaining without Boundaries*, University of Chicago Press, Chicago 1974
KRAUSE, L, *The International Economic System*, The Annals of the American Academy of Political and Social Science, September 1982
LACROIS, A, *La GGT et le Plan Marshall*, Cahiers de l'Institut Maurice Thorex 4/1974
LAMBERT, J, The Constitutional Crisis, 1965–66. *Journal of Common Market Studies*, Vol IV, No 3, May 1966 pp 195–228
LAMBERT, J and PALMER, M, *European Unity, A Survey of European Organisations*, Allen and Unwin, London 1968
LANDAU, E, 'The Rights of Working Women in the European Community', *European Perspectives*, Brussels 1985
LAVIEC, J P, *Syndicats et Sociètès Multinationales*, La Documentation Française, Paris 1975
LAWSON, R and REED, B, *Social Security in the European Communities*, Chatham House/PED, London 1975
LAYARD, R, *How to Beat Unemployment*, Oxford University Press, Oxford 1986
LECERF, J, *La Communautè en pèril: Histoire de l'unitè européenne*, Gallimard, Paris 1975
LEHMBRUCH, G and SCHMITTE, P C, *Patterns or Corporatist Policy Making*, Sage, London 1982
LERNER, D and AREN, R (eds), *France Repeats EDC*, Thames and Hudson, London 1957
Les premiéres élections européennes (juin 1979). Les institutions et le bilan de la CEE. *Le Monde*, Dossiers et Documents, Supplement, June 1979
LEVI, H, *Trade Unions and Technological Change: A Comparative Survey*, European Centre for the Improvement of Living and Working Conditions, Dublin 1985
LEVIN, K, 'The Free Movement of Workers', *Common Market Law Review*, Vol 2, No 3 1964, p 300-5
LEVI, C, *Crise de l'ètat national, firmes multinationales et mouvement ouvrier*, Fèdèrop, Lyons 1977

LEVINSON, C, *International Trade Unionism*, George Allen and Unwin, London 1972

LIEBER, R J, *British Politics and European Unity, Parties, Elites and Pressure Groups*, University of California Press, Berkeley 1971

LIEBHABERG, B, *Relations industrielles et entreprises multinationales en Europe*, Presse Universitaire de France, Paris 1980

LINDBERG, L and SCHEINGOLD, S A, *Europe's Would-be Policy: Patterns of Change in the European Community*, Prentice-Hall, New Jersey 1970

LINDBERG, L M, *The Political Dynamics of European Economic Integration*, Oxford University Press, London 1963

LINDBERG, L M, 'Decision Making and Integration in the European Community', *International Organisation*, Vol XIX, No 1, Winter 1965

LINDBERG, L M, 'Integration as a source of Stress in the European Community System', *International Organisation*, Vol XX, No 2, Spring 1966

LINDBERG, L M, 'The European Community as a Political System: Notes Toward the Construction of a Model', *Journal of Common Market Studies*, Vol V, No 4, June 1967 pp 344–87

LINDLEY, B, *New Forms and New Areas of Employment Growth: A Comparative Study*, Commission of the European Communities, Brussels 1987

LIPIETZ, A, *Mirages and Miracles: The Crisis of Global Fordism*, Verso, London 1987

LODGE, J, *European Union: The European Community in Search of a Future*, Macmillan, London 1986

LODGE, J (ed), *The European Community: bibliographical excursions*, Frances Pinter, London 1983

LODGE, J (ed), *The Institutions and Politics of the European Community*, Frances Pinter, London 1983

LODGE, J, 'The Single European Act': towards a new Euro Dynamism?' *Journal of Common Market Studies*, Vol XXIV no 3 March 1986 pp 203–24

LODGE, J, 'Towards a Human Union: EEC Social Policy and European Integration', *British Journal of International Studies*, Vol 4 no. 2 1978, pp 107–34

LONDAU, E, *The Rights of Working Women in the European Community*, European Prospectives, Brussels 1985

LORWIN, L, *The International Labour Movement: History, Politics, Outlook*, Harper and Brothers, New York 1953

LYON-CAEN, G, 'La constitution de syndicats européens est une nécessité inscrite dans les faites,' *Le Monde Diplomatique*, September 1972

MADELIN, A, 'Creating a Single European Market II: A French View', *World Today*, London Royal Institute of International Affairs, March 1988

MANDEL, E, *The Debate on Workers Control*, in HUNNIUS, GARSON, DAVID, CASE, (eds), *Workers' Control*, Vintage Books, New York 1973
MANDEL, E, *Europe vs America: Contradictions of Imperialism*, New Left Books, London and New York 1970
MANIGAT, M, *La Confédération européenne des syndicats et le syndicalisme mondiale* Publique Etrangére No 5 1973
MANN, C J, *The Function of Judicial Decision in European Economic Integration*, Martin Nyoff, The Hague 1977
MARTINET, G, *Sept syndicalismes* (L'Histoire Immèdiate), Editions de Seuil, Paris 1979
MARX, E and KENDALL, W, *Unions of Europe*, University of Sussex Centre for Contemporary European Studies, Brighton 1971
MASELET, J C, *L'Union politique de la Europe*, Presse Universitaire Française, Paris 1978
MEADE, J E, *et al*, *Case Studies in European Economic Union*, Oxford University Press, Oxford 1962
MEADE, J E, *The Theory of Custom Unions*, North Holland, Amsterdam 1955
MELLORS, C, 'Promoting Local Authorities in the European Community', European Information Service, Occasional Paper No 1, London
MENNS, B, SAUVANT, K P, *Multinational Corporations, Managers and Development of Regional Identification in Western Europe*, The Annals of the American Academy of Political and Social Science, September 1982
MÉNY, Y and WRIGHT, V (ed), *The Politics of Steel: Western Europe and the Steel Industry in the Crisis Years* (1974–1984) W de Gruyter, Berlin 1980
MERGAN, R, *West European Politics since 1945: The Shaping of the European Community*, Batsford, London 1972
MEYNAUD, J and SIDJANSKI, D, *Les Groupes de Pression dans la Communauté Européenne*, Editions de l'Institut de Sociologie de l'Université de Bruxelles, Brussels 1971,
MEYNAUD, J and SIDJANSKI, D, *Les Groupes de Pression dans la Communauté européene* Montreal University, Montreal 1969
MILLWARD, M and STEVENS, M, *British Workplace Industrial Relations 1980–1984*, Gower, London 1986
MILWARD, A, *The Reconstruction of Western European 1945–51*, Methuen, London 1984
MONNET, J, *Memoires*, Fayard, Paris 1976
MORSE, E I, 'Transnational Economic Processes' in KEOHANE and NYE (eds), *Transnational Relations and World Politics*, Harvard University Press, Cambridge Mass 1973
MOWER, A G Jr., 'Human Rights in Western Europe', *International Affairs* LII, 2, April 1976, pp 235–251
NAIRN, T, *Atlantic Europe?: The Radical View*, Transnational Institute, Amsterdam 1975

NAIRN, T, *The Left Against Europe*, Penguin, Middlesex 1973
National Academy of Engineering, *Technology and Global Industry*, National Academy Research, New York 1987
National Association of Pension Funds, *Submission to the House of Lords Select Committee on the European Communities on Social Security in the European Community*, Session 1987–88 3rd Report 1986 p 162
NOEL, E, *Memorandum de la Commission sur la Programme d'action pendant la deuxième stage*, European Commission, Brussels 1962, p 27
NOEL, E, 'Some Reflections on the Preparation, Development and Repercussions of the Meetings between Heads of Government', *Government and Opposition*, Vol XI, Vol 1, Winter 1976 pp 20–34
NORTHRUP, H R and ROWAN, R L, *Multinational Collective Bargaining Attempts*, University of Pennsylvania, Philadelphia 1979
NYE, J and KEOHANE, R (eds), *Transnational Relations and World Politics*, Harvard University Press, Cambridge Mass 1971
OFFE, C and WIESENTHAL, H, 'Two Logics of Collective Action – Theoretical Notes on Social Class and Organisational Form', in ZETLIN (ed), *Power, Politics and Social Theory*, Random House, New York 1983
O'GRADA, C, 'The Vocational Training Policy of the EEC and the Free Movement of Skilled Labour', *Journal of Common Market Studies* Vol III no. 2 1969 pp 11–109
O'HIGGINS, M, 'International Standards and British Labour Law', in LEWIS (ed), *Labour Law in Britain*, Basil Blackwell, Oxford 1986
OLLE, W and SCHOELLER, W, 'World Market Competition and Restrictions upon International Trade Union Policies' *Capital and Class* No 2 1977
O'NUALLAIN, C (ed), *The Presidency of the European Council of Ministers*, Croom Helm, London 1985
PADOA SCHIOPPA, T, *et al*, *Efficiency, Stability and Equality*, Oxford University Press, Oxford 1987
PALMER, M and LAMBERT, J, *European Unity: A Survey of European Organisations*, Allen and Unwin, London 1968
PANITCH, L, 'Trade Unions and the Capitalist State', *New Left Review* February 1981
PAULUS, D, *La Création de Comité permanent de l'emploi*, Brussels 1972
PEEL, J, *The real power game: a guide to European industrial relations* McGraw Hill, London 1979
PELKMAN, J and ROBSON, P (eds), 'Making the Common Market Work,' Special issue, *Journal of Common Market Studies*, Vol XXV no. 3 March 1987 pp 181–269
PELKMAN, J, 'Economic Theories of Integration Revisted', *Journal of Common Market Studies*, Vol XVIII, No 4, June 1980 pp 333–54
PEREZ-CALVO, A, *L'Organisation européene de la confédération mondiale du travail*, Imprimerie Christmann, Essey-les-Nancy 1976

PETTACIO, V, 'The European Social Fund, Phase I in Positive Retrospect', *Journal of Common Market Studies* Vol X No 3 March 1972, p 249-267

PHILIP, S, *Les Nouvelles Perspectives du Syndicalisme International face aux firmes Multinationales,* Thése pour le doctorat d'Etat en Science Politique soutenue à Grenoble, le 30 juin 1978 (miméographe)

PICCOTTO, S, 'The Limits and Prospects of Trade Union Internationalism', *International Journal of Sociology of Law* No 10 1982 pp 315-317

PICKLES, W, *How Much has Changed? Britain and Europe,* Basil Blackwell, Oxford 1967

PIEHL, E, 'Comparability of Vocational Training Qualifications in EC Member States', *Cedefop Flash* No 2 1987

PINDER, J, 'Positive Integration and Negative Integration: Some Problems of Economic Union in the EEC', *The World Today,* Vol XXIV, No 3, pp 88-110, March 1968

PIPKORN, J, 'The Draft Directive on Procedures for Informing and Consulting Employers', *Common Market Law Review* No 20 1983 pp 725-755

PIPKORN, J, 'Comparative Labour Law in the Harmonisation of Social Standards', in European Community *Comparative Labour Law* 1977

POULLET, E, and DEPREY, G, 'The Place of the Commission within the Institutional system', in SASSE (ed), *Decision making in the European Community,* Praegar, New York 1977

POWER, J, 'Europe's Army of Immigrants', *International Affairs,* LI, 3, July 1975, pp 372-386

PRAIS, S J, *Vocational qualifications of the labour force in Britain and Germany,* National Institute of Economic and Social Research, London 1981

PRYCE, R, *The Dynamics of European Union,* Croom Helm, London 1987

PRYCE, R, *The Politics of the European Community,* Butterworths, London 1973

PUCHALA, D, 'Of Blind Men, Elephants and International Integration', *Journal of Common Market Studies,* Vol X no. 1 1972 pp 267-84

REED, B, *Social Security and Health Care in the Context of the European Community,* Chatham House, London (PEP European series No 23) 1975

RICHTER, I, *Political Purpose in Trade Unions,* Allen and Unwin, London 1973

ROBBINS, B, 'The EEC's New Social Dimension', *Personnel Management,* November 1985 pp 40-44

ROBBINS, L J, *The Reluctant Party: Labour and the EEC, 1961-1975,* Ormskirk and Hesketh, London

ROBERTS, B C, 'Industrial Relations and the EEC', *Labour Law Journal* Vol 24 no. 8 August 1973 pp 484-90

ROBERTS, B C and LIEBHABERG, B, 'The European Trade Union Confederation: Influence of Regionalism Detente and Multinationals' *British Journal of Industrial Relations* Vol 14, No 3 November 1976 pp 261–274

ROBERTS, B C, 'Multinational Collective Bargaining – A European Prospect?' *British Journal of Industrial Relations* Vol 11, No 1, March 1973 pp 1–19

ROBERTSON, A H, *European Institutions*, 3rd edition, Stevens, London 1973

ROBINSON, A, *The European Parliament in the EC policy process*, Policy Studies Institute, London 1984

ROJOT, J, 'The 1984 Revision of the OECD Guidelines for Multinational Enterprises', *British Journal of Industrial Relations* Vol 23, no. 3 1985 pp 379–97

ROUX, R, 'The Position of Labour under the Schuman Plan', *International Labour Review* 76 1957 pp 61–72

ROWTHORN, B, 'The TUC's Programme for Recovery' *Comment Journal* March 1982

SAMUELSON, K, *Trade Unions and the Multinationals* Swedish Employers Confederation, Stockholm 1979

SARGENT, J, 'British Finance and Industrial Capital and the European Communities', *West European Politics*, Vol 6, No 2, April 1983 pp 14–36

SASSE, C (ed), *Decision making in the European Community*, Praeger, New York 1977

SASSON, D, 'Labour and Europe', *New Statesman*, 13th November 1987

SAUNDERS, C, *From Free Trade to Integration: Western Europe*, Chatham House/PEP, London 1975

SDP, *Industrial Relations: A Fresh Look*, Consultative Paper, London 1986

SELLIN, B, 'Comparability of Vocational Training Certificates in the Member States of the European Community', *Vocational Training Bulletin* No 18 1985

SHANKS, M, *European Social Policy Today and Tomorrow*, Pergamon Press, Oxford 1977

SILLETTI, D, 'European System for the International Clearing of Vacancies and Applications for Employment', *Social Europe* No 2 1987 pp 11–14

SPINELLI, A, *The Eurocrats*, John Hopkins, Baltimore 1966

STEWART, M, *Employment Conditions in Europe*, Gower Economic Publications, London 1972

STREECK, W and SCHMITTER, P L, 'Community, Market, State and Associations? The Prospective Contribution of Private Interests Government to Social Order', *European Sociological Review* No 1 1985 pp 119–389

SWANN, D, *The Economics of the Common Market*, Penguin, London 1970

TAYLOR, J, 'British membership of the European Communities: The

Question of Parliamentary Sovereignty', *Government and Opposition*, Vol X, No 3, Summer 1975

TAYLOR, P, *The Limits of European Integration*, Croom Helm, London 1983

TAYLOR, P and GROOM, A J R, *International Organisation*, Frances Pinter, London 1978

TAYLOR, P, 'The Concept of Community and the European Integration Process', *Journal of Common Market Studies*, Vol VII, No 2, December 1968 pp 83-101

TAYLOR, P, 'The Politics of the European Communities: the Confederal Phase', *World Politics*, Vol XXVII, No 3, April 1975 pp 336-60

TAYLOR, P, 'Interdependence and Autonomy in the European Community', *Journal of Common Market Studies*, Vol XVIII no. 4 June 1980 pp 370-87

TAYLOR, P, *International Cooperation Today: The Universal and the European Pattern*, Elek Books Ltd, London 1971

TAYLOR, P, 'The Obligation of Membership of the European Communities', *International Affairs*, April 1981

TEAGUE, P, 'The Alternative Economic Strategy: The Time to go European', *Capital and Class* No 29 Summer 1985 pp 43-72

TEAGUE, P, 'The British TUC and the European Community', *Millenium Journal of International Studies*, January 1989 forthcoming

TEAGUE, P, 'Labour and Europe, The Response of British Trade Unions to Membership of the Community' unpublished PhD thesis, University of London 1984

TUGENDHAT, C, *Making Sense of Europe*, Viking, London 1986

USHER, M, *European Court Practice*, Sweet and Maxwell, London 1983

VAN DEN BRULIKE, J, *Investment and disinvestment policies of multinational organisations in Europe*, Mantem and Klemmer, Boddeyn 1982

VAN MEERHAEGHE, M, *International Economic Institutions*, Martinus Nighoff, 4th revised edition The Hague 1986

VANDAMME, J (ed), *Pour une nouvelle politique sociale in Europe*, Economica, Paris 1984

VAUGHAN, R, *Post-war Integration in Europe*. Arnold, London 1976

VERNON, R, 'Multinational Business and National Economic Goals' in NYE and KEOHANE (eds), *Transnational Relations and World Politics*, Harvard University Press, Cambridge 1971

VERNON, R, *Sovereignty at Bay: The Multinational Spread of US Enterprise*, Basic Books, New York/London 1971

WALLACE, W and HODGES, M, *Economic Divergence in the European Community*, Macmillan, London 1983

WALLACE, H and EDWARDS, G, 'European Community: The Evolving role of the Presidency of the Council', *International Affairs*, Vol LII, No 4, October 1976

WALLACE, H and EDWARDS, G, *The Presidency of the European Communities*, 1979
WALLACE, H with RIDLEY, A, *Europe: The Challenge of Diversity*, Chatham House Papers, Routledge London 1985
WALLACE, H, *National Governments and the European Communities.* Chatham House/PEP, London 1973
WALLACE, H, 'Institutions in a Decentralised Community', *New Europe*, Vol V, No 3, Summer 1977 pp 21–34
WALLACE, H, WALLACE, W and WEBB, C (eds), *Policy-Making in the European Communities*, Wiley, London 1982
WALLACE, H, *The Budget of the European Communities*, UACES 1980
WALLACE, W and HILL, C, 'Diplomatic Trends in the European Community', *International Affairs*, January 1979
WALLACE, W, 'Wider but Weaker: The Continued Enlargement of the EEC', *The World Today*, Vol XXXII, No 3, March 1976
WALLACE, W, *Britain in Europe*, Heinemann, London 1980
WILLIS, F R, *European Integration: New Viewpoints*, OUP New York, 1975
WINDMÜLLER, J P (ed), 'European Labour and Politics: A Symposium (I) (II)' *Industrial and Labour Relations Review* 28 No 1 October 1974 pp 3–88
WINDMÜLLER, J P, 'European Regionalism: A New Factor in International Labour', *Industrial Relations Journal* Vol 7 no. 2 Summer 1976 pp 36–48
WINDMÜLLER, J P, *Labour Internationals: A Survey of Contemporary International Trade Union Organisations*, New York State School of Industrial and Labour Relations, Ithaca 1969
ZETLIN, M, *Power Politics and Social Theory*, VAI Press, San Francisco 1983
ZURCHER, A J, *The Struggle to Unite Europe, 1940–58*, New York University Press, New York, 1958

Index